OFF THE PAGE

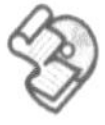

OFF THE PAGE

LITERARY AND CULTURAL CRITICISM AS MULTIMEDIA PERFORMANCE

Tom Lavazzi

Parlor Press
Anderson, South Carolina
www.parlorpress.com

Parlor Press LLC, Anderson, South Carolina, USA

Printed in the United States of America on acid-free paper.
S A N: 2 5 4 - 8 8 7 9

Library of Congress Cataloging-in-Publication Data

Names: Lavazzi, Tom, 1955- author. | TEZ (Theater group)
Title: Off the page : literary and cultural criticism as multimedia performance : texts and scripts / Tom Lavazzi.
Description: Anderson, South Carolina : Parlor Press, [2020] | Series: Aesthetic critical inquiry | Includes bibliographical references. | Summary: "Off the Page offers a series of critical "scripts" exploring various cultural texts, and a working definition of performative criticism grounded in poststructuralist literary, cultural, and performance theory. TOM LAVAZZI is Professor of English at CUNY-Kingsborough and directs the critical performance group TEZ: http://www.tezperformance.org"-- Provided by publisher.
Identifiers: LCCN 2020008340 (print) | LCCN 2020008341 (ebook) | ISBN 9781602352469 (paperback) | ISBN 9781602352476 (hardcover) | ISBN 9781602352483 (pdf) | ISBN 9781602352490 (epub)
Subjects: LCSH: American literature--History and criticism.
Classification: LCC PS121 .L29 2020 (print) | LCC PS121 (ebook) | DDC 810.9--dc23
LC record available at https://lccn.loc.gov/2020008340
LC ebook record available at https://lccn.loc.gov/2020008341

978-1-60235-246-9 (paperback)
978-1-60235-247-6 (hardcover)
978-1-60235-248-3 (pdf)
978-1-60235-249-0 (ePub)

3 4 5

Aesthetic Critical Inquiry
Series Editor: Andrea Feeser

Book Design: David Blakesley
Image manipulations, Ellen La Forge, *TEZ*

Parlor Press, LLC is an independent publisher of scholarly and trade titles in print and multimedia formats. This book is available in paper, cloth and eBook formats from Parlor Press on the World Wide Web at http://www.parlorpress.com or through online and brick-and-mortar bookstores. For submission information or to find out about Parlor Press publications, write to Parlor Press, 3015 Brackenberry Drive, Anderson, South Carolina, 29621, or email editor@parlorpress.com.

In memory of Armand Schwerner

and for Zoe, now and always

Contents

Acknowledgments

Sections of the introduction, on Armand Schwerner's work, have appeared in *Text 8*, 1995; *Talisman*, 19 and 21/21, 1998-99 and 2001, respectively, and *Poetry Criticisms 42* (Gale), 2003.

"Niagara on the Rocks: Featuring Margaret Fuller, Henry James, and a Strata of Other Voices...": Performed at the International Conference on Narrative Literature (Simon Frazer U., Canada), Performance Studies International (Northwestern U) and City Lights Theatre Co., Savannah, GA (full-stage production).

"Legal Discourse v Poetic Discourse: The Case of Charles Reznikoff": Performed at the Poets of the 30's (National Poetry Foundation); published in *Sagetrieb*, 13.1-2, 1992.

"The Monroe Project": Performed at the International Conference on Despair and Desire, Performance Studies International [excerpt] (Wales, UK); published in *Post-Identity*, 3.2, 2002 (http://quod.lib.umich.edu/cgi/t/text/text-idx?c=postid;idno=pid9999.0003.2*).

"Monroe/Me (auto)bio," by Zoe Randall [included in the "Monroe Project"], published in *Performance Practice*, 1997.

"The Beat Poetry Games": Performed at Poets of the 50's (National Poetry Foundation) and Performance Studies International [excerpt] (Wales, UK); excerpts published in *Mantis: Journal of Poetry, Criticism, and Translation*, 3, 2002 (http://www.stanford.edu/dept/DLCL/mantis/M3/ContributorsM3.html).

"Poetics of Protest: A Fluxed History of the 1968 DNC": Performed at the Poets of the 1960s [excerpt] (National Poetry Foundation) and Performance Studies International [excerpt] (Brown University). "Punching the Line: Yippie, Fluxus, and the 1968 DNC," precursor to "Poetics of Protest," published *Rhizomes: Cultural Studies in Emerging Knowledge*, 9, 2004 (http://www.rhizomes.net/issue9/index.html), and *English Studies Forum* (http://publish.bsu.edu/esf/ppp.htm /).

Stirr'd Up Everywhere: first performed as "A Whitman Collage," Whitman Centennial Celebration, CUNY; SKEP Performance Gallery, NY; Space 2B, NY; published *as Stirr'd Up Everywhere*, an artist's book by A Musty Bone Press, 1995; e-version, *The Little Magazine*, 22.2, 2001(http://13th-moon.net/html/litmag.html); collected by MOMA/Franklin Furnace artists' books archive, the Brooklyn museum (featured in recent group show, "Working in Brooklyn," 2/3-4/16, 2000), the Cleveland Art Institute, Banff Art Centre, and others.

"Eat, Drink, Be Merry, for the Food of the Performance Is Inedible" ["Monroe Project" (self)commentary], published in *Performance Practice*, 1997.

"Avatars and Acting Bodies: Notes Toward an Aesthetics of Liminality, or, Where Have All the Subjects Gone?" Published in *Women in Performance*, 14.2, 2005 (http://www.womenandperformance.org/issue28.html).

Pieces Referred to but not Included in This Collection

"Contents: One Other" (performance script + installation video), based on "Strategies of Othering in Aphra Behn's Oroonoko" (source article/textual performance): FSU Conference on Film and Literature, City Market Artists' Center (Savannah, GA), Performance Studies International (Arizona SU), Digital Arts and Culture (Georgia Institute of Technology); published, respectively, in *Utah Foreign Language Review*, '98 and *Journal of Research*, 1998.

"Fantasy.com" (Žižek and pornography): presented at MLA, 2001; published in *Rhizomes: Cultural Studies in Emerging Knowledge*, 5, 2002-2003 (http://www.rhizomes.net/issue5/index.html).

Special thanks to Cafe Lalo, 83nd between Broadway and Amsterdam, NYC, where I spent many hours with a coffee, plate of steamed eggs and herbs, tiramisu, scripts('s) spicing...

Thanks to Jerome Rothenberg for including me in the starting lineup, Binghamton University, 1989.

Zoe especially, Kate

Those who clap, frown, scratch their heads...

OFF THE PAGE

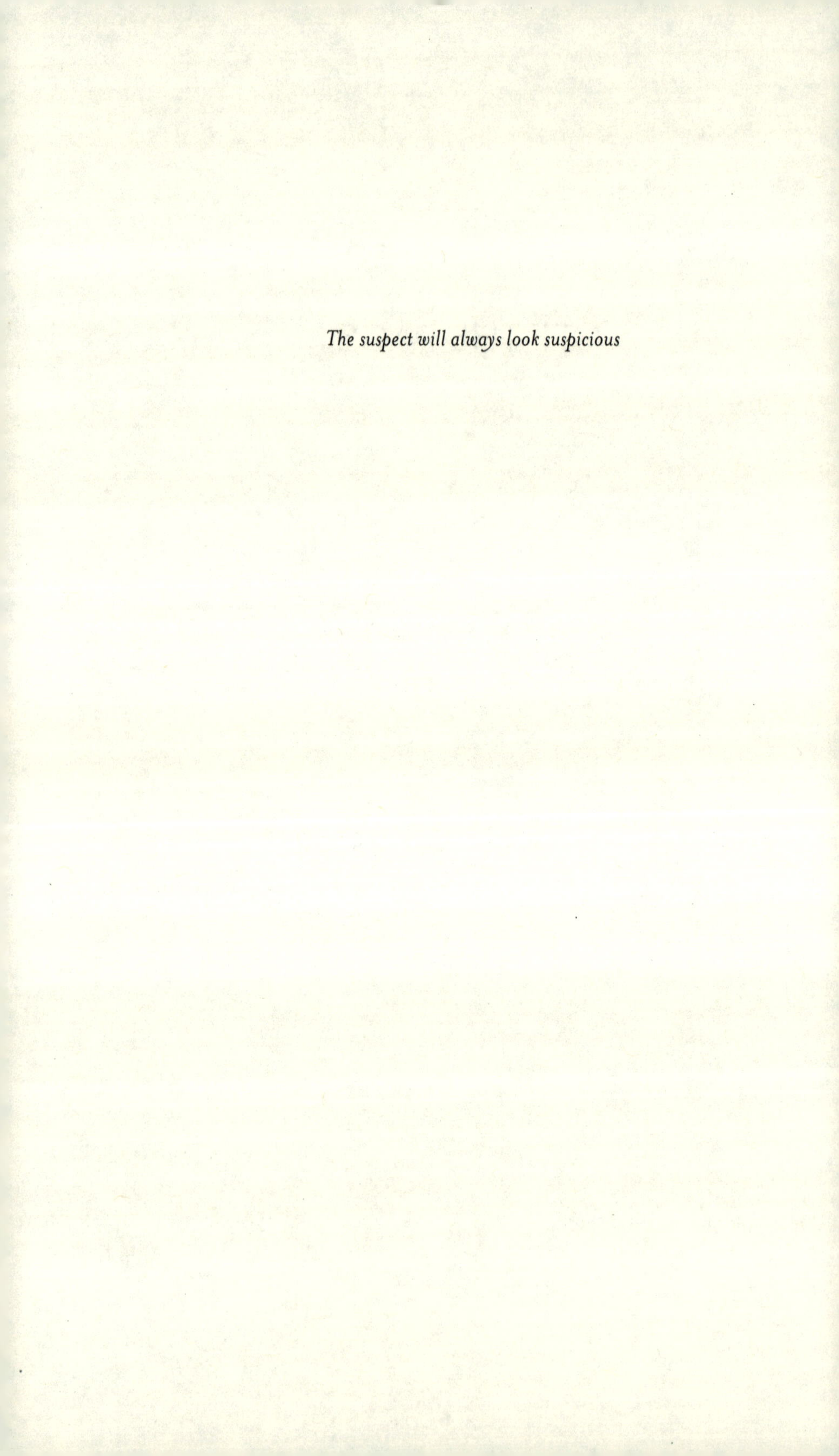

The suspect will always look suspicious

In(troductory mani)festo

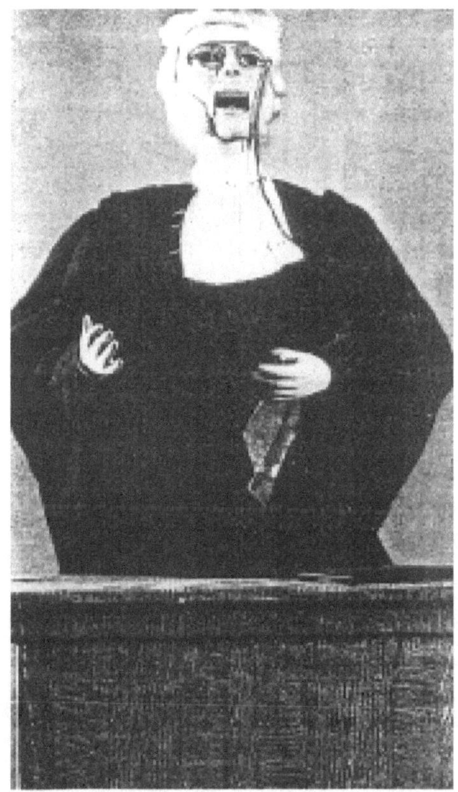

Fig. 1: Mechanical talking professor; New York Public Library. Public domain,

Please repeat the question?

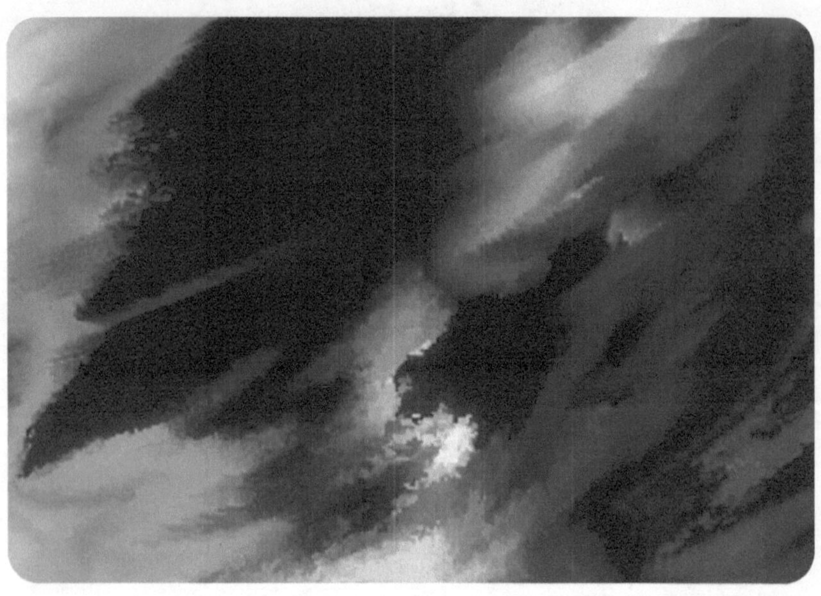

MM image manipulation, Ellen La Forge, *TEZ*

1 In Search of the Critical Grail: Performative Sub(di)versions

Well, let him ride, but where shall he go?

—Parzival

We have begun.[1] Walt Whitman, in *Specimen Days*, as he images himself pitting pages against wind, surf, street life, seasons or reasons, leaf for spinning leaf (turning, now, in my image, as his reader calls to him)... In the Renaissance, Foucault theorizes (*The Order of Things*) language was understood not as an artificial human construct, but a phenomenon among other phenomena in nature; or, rather, words, embedded in things—divinely implanted—were the signatures of their force. Yet my quest—my search for the critical grail—is through a wilderness of verbal and visual signs as figured by postmodern literary and cultural theory, a wilderness of codes and names trembling with an Otherness just missed, a legend always pursued.

Listen... the (X) voices... Yes, we have, so...

*

I must begin again with a denial. This is not a book of interpretation, if interpretation means tracking explications, solutions, or covering one's tracks, but of possibilities: experiments, inventions, and dis-coverings. This book provides a theoretical framework for the phenomenon of performative criticism, and presents a collection of scripts based on close readings of/encounters with American literary and cultural texts—ranging from a 19th-century nature journal/Civil War diary (Whitman's *Specimen Days*) to a 20th-century political "happening" (or series of happenings—the 1968 Democratic National Convention). The methodos practiced in these writings ("actscriptions," for this moment) draws from a bricolage of poststructuralist literary, semiotic, and cultural theory (including some tendencies in postmodern ethnographic and performance theory, as well as trends in modern and contemporary poetics). I will use the jargon of the academy, but not always in acceptable ways; the approach is not historical, nor am I interested in charting influences. It is the paying

1. The proceeding, here foregoing, speculations are unrveriviable; any resemblance to accepted theories or criticism is delusive, not coincidental.

of a particular kind of attention, a dialogic stance, and the ensuing performance that bring these various works together.

*

What I mean by performing criticism, from one (obtuse) angle, might occur like this:

Start with a discursive bit at the top left or center of the "page"/work space—a quote (or part of a quote) from a critical or theoretical work; drop bottom right—a quote from a Poe story and/or a related work of fiction; move slightly above this narrative position and to the left—partially superimposing (over the fictional narrative) a bit of autobiographical narrative associated with this; shoot halfway up the page on the diagonal—a single word, a name, a pictograph derived from a printer's symbol; then down and flush left—number play, printer's jargon, cabalistic equations; then perhaps an up and down (or back and forth) movement, starting from top and bottom and side margins and working in, or vice versa (inside out), shuttling between quotes from the initiating text(s) and commentary (mine, someone else's), often substituting lines of one for lines of the other ("primary source" quote suddenly changing to commentary and vice versa), collapsing distinctions between "primary" and "secondary" inscriptions. Then I must consider print size, font, and other visual effects (such as broad, translucent ink-wash swipes top to bottom, overlaying the interacting text fragments). Then it begins to cohere; a "dramatic" shape, or better, a pattern of energies is traceable: these diagonals or partial X's, this top-bottom opposition: these are the rhythms of Poe's "Xing a Paragrab," the story I have chosen to "analyze." The collage raises several issues, not just discursively but actively in the very rhythm of its structure: What goes on behind (beneath, around) the printed page; the printer as *bricoleur*, substituting "x"s for stolen "o"s (as does the protagonist in Poe's tale); the multiplicity of authorship—what escapes authorial control; the resulting "cabalistic" message that no one authored (i.e., arrived at procedurally, rather than personally), producing, ironically, the various (psychological) reader effects (suspicion, outrage, fear, delight) registered both within Poe's story and in "reader"/viewer response to the critical collage. By demanding a nonlinear, vexing reading process, the collage communicates these themes intellectually and viscerally, giving the reader an experience of the levels of discourse (from printer's slang to mysticism) and interpretation and reception operating simultaneously in (and upon) the text. That is, it enacts a field of inquiry. And, just as, in this situation, the "critic" becomes "artist," so the reader becomes a performer *in* the visual/language collage, invited to reenact the ordeal of its textual torsions, the visual/textual rhythm of the collage forming a variation on the conflictual nature of the host text.

A multimedia work in its own right, the collage can then function both as partial *mise en scene* (as backdrop, prop) and "dramaturge" for a live, staged performance, giving an embodied presence to the voices and other performance objects suggested by the collage-cum-script. A reconfiguration, or "further textualization" (George Quasha's term) and reframing of these performance elements can take the form of an artist's book, which then becomes a meta-script for successive performances. (see Script 6, *Stirr'd Up Everywhere*, a collage poem based on Walt Whitman's *Specimen Days*, for an example of a counter-flow to this movement—visual collage as textual reenactment-cum-(rein) scripting of initial/initiating multimedia performance).

This movement, or drift, from textual performance to performed text begins by charting the discourse territories of a text, then etching them into greater definition, not along the authorial narrative or characterological lines, but along the fault lines, following a disruptive logic that roughens the surface, cracks open a space for dialogic (often conflictual) encounters among the discourses floating the surface voices; stirs into dramatic confrontation (disturbs) discourse borders normally kept in check by the surface narrative. This can also result in a distorted, fragmented phenomenon, a babble overwhelming and misrecognizing the once clear and coherent structure.

Such performative detourings, critical sub(di)version, from more straight-forward paths of literary analysis can lead a reader in a flash to insights only partially, or much more cumbersomely, reconstitutable in discursive prose—as Parzival, wandering in the woods, found most when *not* looking *for*, attentively...

*

A constant shifting in position; my mission—to turn the question to face not an answer but a further question, and to question all answers...

*

To catch the text in the act of a Deleuzian becoming (something Other...)

*

At the risk of romanticizing this practice, I will put it this way: Just as there is an Other, *differance* ("O" here In the sense of Lacan's "R," not "*A*" as "symbolic order," superego injunction) that eludes ethnographic cognizance (i.e., an ur-Other that churns below/through individual others/otherness), so there is an ur-Text, or virtual Text, that we can glimpse, but not completely grasp (as William James says of being). There are many interpretatively generated versions of a work, but there is only one ongoing ur-Text, which is only secondarily accessible. To immerse ourselves within Ur-Text, to "see" it from the "inside," would be to lose (critical) consciousness, to enter a trance-like or deeply meditative state. However, although we cannot capture, contain, or effectively detain the flow of Ur-Text within the straps of semantico-referential discourse, we can detect it. We can trace it at the subdiscourse level as it resonates through and around authored text (small t) in homophones, puns, metonymic clusterings, cross-textual doublings, and sound associations—Roland Barthes' "third language" (*The Pleasure of the Text*), which "releases the prisoners, scatters the signifieds," shatters discourses; a space of "pulsion forces" and "musicality" (Julia Kristeva, *Revolution in Poetic Language*) heard under, over, and through words, disrupting from within the smooth, logical flow of sense (which Gilles Deleuze figures as a body without organs).[2] Performative criticism can operate at the rhetorical level, as well, tracing echoes and patternings of various ideologically motivated discourses and counter discourses, exposing thetic oppositions and confluences that constitute the authorial voice, dis-posing/decentering the coherent text.[3] (Listen to the voices splitting the seams of subjectivity, the disintegration of authorial self-presence...). Responsive to—and in an attempt to comprehend, or, more accurately, re-present—ur-Text,

2. Musicality, for Kristeva, is a de-articulating force that fractures the illusion of coherent, authorial self-presence projected by syntactic/semantic units, and redistributes language particles in unexpected, unintended patterns.

3. for Julia Kristeva (Desire in Language), the "thetic" = any positional, i.e. articulated, moment.

performative criticism releases text into a field of shifting discourse positionality, a self-annihilating and self-dispersing Textuality that melts down hermeneutical shields, revealing (allowing us to see and hear) a text as if for the first time, as its repressed Other(ness) breaks through, as text is disturbed by ur-Text.

Criticism that recognizes such a Text (or such a relation between text and Text) must also question and transform itself. Criticism becomes an *act*, a practice, a praxis. Interpretation = (ritual) performance. It involves a challenge to, if not the temporary abandonment of, the hermeneutical ego; a striking through the dominance of ~~alphanumeric~~ articulation and the production of "meaning" through semantic chains. It involves an unself-conscious giving over to that which it "criticizes," a temporary withdrawal from the role of objective observer, displacing ~~hermeneutics~~ with acute attention to the wilderness that is T murmuring through text, and return to an always-on-the-alert academic platform that acknowledges the effect of T on text.[4] Proof of the critic's involvement with the works at hand; evidence that the critic has intimately experienced its rhythms and torsions, its structuring forces, should be apparent, not just in *what* is said, but in the style and mode of presentation, allowing language (i.e., conceived here as multiple/interwoven sign systems) to "dis-possess us," call us "away from ourselves" (Diane Davis, *Breaking Up (at) Totality*..., 118, commenting specifically on Eduardo Cadava's notions of semiotic drift). A work of criticism that performs its knowledge allows the reader to re-experience the joy and/or angst of the critic's coming to knowledge, to reenact the intercourse between reader and t(T)ext

While empowering exploded texts (whether they are critically or self-detonated), the performative critical t_f(T)ext can self-reflexively include the narrative of its own annihilation. Now, this is to allow the text (the one analyzed, the one analyzing—there is always only one text, the present one) to always be/know/include its other; to be simultaneously (and in turn) self, not self, and not not self—to be always on the move and under erasure. Text (big T) is the movement between texts (the inbetweenness within and among texts). The aca-

4. Another way to express the relationship between Text and text is t_f(T): "t function of T," where T is the domain, the set of all possible discourses (including counterdiscourses, both authorial and extra-authorial), of semiotic, and subsemiotic activity—a process of endless semiosis (Barthes' term)—out of which authored texts (t) are generated as tentative resistances.

demic or manufacturing voice is just one among many in the interplay between reader and work (one which can be played on/through, as in the *Monroe Project*, Script 3); knowing this it must check itself—its urge to command. It may, for instance, enter the voice mix of the complexly alive text via the margins (*Stirr'd Up Everywhere*, and the Poe collage sketched above), letting the otherness of the Text flood over it. Listening for the polyvocality of texts, (re)sounding texts, performative critics may freefall, in more radical mutterings, through their structuring discourses and enter a highly charged, prediscursive space whose semic/seismic events demolish language as we know it (*Stirr'd Up...* moves in this direction, as do, to varying degrees, most of the performances in this collection), redistributing its particles through endless permutations and recombinations. Highly radicalized performative criticism defamiliarizes (itself and the text/other), cuts the air lines connecting critical practice to surface institutions (replete with rhetorical pump stations); it by turns submerges, loses itself in the Other, and returns for air; strips off its ideological wet suit, writes in fragments and dispersions (like breaking bubbles) to get at and get out, the authoritative voice asserting and losing itself, asserting and losing itself; my voice, as reader/interpreter, becomes one current in a sea in which, as in the quantum world or the field of poststructuralist ethnography (see below), the observer becomes part of the observed. We witness/reenact the drama of the hermeneutic voice entering the flux of discourse, its assertions piling through the pre-thetic, semic flow in order to anchor and still discourse at the rhetorical level above; we see it in the act of structuring meaning (as the Scholar-Translator figure in poet Armand Schwerner's *The Tablets*, who dramatizes a situation that occurs in the act of reading) inflating "Truth" to create bubble economies of doxa. As performative critics, we must act as Melville's Confidence Man, circulating among a matrix or nexus of masks and voices in a citational shell game, no one of which is the "real," "true," "authentic," "original" voice. In the reader's psyche, as in the fully exploded/expanded/heteroglossic Text, voices are always meeting, contending, paralleling, merging, mimicking, echoing, and, as it takes place there, so can it be reenacted on the page, and off, in a drama of form.

It is we, the readers, the writers of performative criticism who must release the suppressed voices, the counter discourses, the disruptions and ugliness—blemishes and aharmonic eruptions—that are the actual beautiful face of the Other. It is we who have beaten the voices down; will we now allow ourselves—our authoritative, truth-claiming selves—to be breached, to allow the reemergence of an Otherness not located in (or just in) the text *per se*, but between our reading activity and its texture? Actually there is the one Texture that includes us both, text(s) and reader, language and unconscious; there is no subject-object division at the subauthorial level. As in the world of high-energy physics figured through S-matrices, there are no distinct "particles," just "processes," so at the pre-thetic level of textual analysis, the Text sounds in reader and reader in the text. There are no readers and texts, but a flow of energy, inarticulate, producing the need for articulation, spinning the shell of a word around its absence; an endless flow, unarrestable or only tentatively so, coalescing now as the semiotic complex of voices and discourses known as the reader—which you would call your"self," I would call my"self"—and now as the matrix of discourses and rhetorical positions known as a "text." It is an otherness always everywhere present, flowing through author, text, you, me—all readers. As I concentrate on Text (ur-Text), whatever I can consciously say about it, short of a glossolaliac babble, will always only be partial, even as I push myself to the realization that I always "say more than I know" (Lacan) (Am I, without knowing it, reading *you*, other readers at this moment and the next century, though I can't locate you in the present text? No matter how many voices I dis-cover, there will always be those missing, a not yet riddling through the yet again, though putting pen to paper in a macro, and not a quantum world, I can not "yet," never "will" be in the full presence/possession of Text.) The Text, as a gathering of discourses/voices resonant with surplus meanings and interpretive contexts (or reading encounters); as wild, semic flow glimpsed in *aporias* within voices as well as breaches between voices, can never be grasped, will always outrun our claims. Text, or ur-Text = open discourse formation X endless semic drift.

And this, I acknowledge, is to indulge in the outrageously romantic.

Yet language is slippery. "Sip" may see itself in "slip," but if we sip at language, we taste only a fraction of what it has to offer. Slipping and sliding over the entire surface of a text, of language, plunging (not merely dipping) into the mess of molten mass of language—again there, we sense a tectonic shifting, as of laden plates, where the signified, to paraphrase Lacan, slips away from the signifier, or vice versa, and "sip" finds itself again in "Slip." Language is sipslippery...

***

Performative criticism, then, does not mean simply hermeneutic self-reflexiveness or readerly self-assertiveness, but the critics hearing their voices in dialogue with other critics' voices, with the discourse provinces brought into play by the text under scrutiny. Rather than defensively trying to silence, subordinate, dominate, and generally colonize those other voices/discourse-territories, or disavow them through the *doxa* (AAAAcademically-rated) of exegetic ponzi schemes, they must be ready to give way to them, to put their own voices in jeopardy, to risk losing themselves in the polyvoiced uprising that is the Text wrested from authorial control, both from the author of the text and from the authorizers of the text. Hence, by restaging the interpretative drama around a Brechtian "alienation-effect" that puts our own commentary in quotes, so to speak, by placing it in dialogue with other voices/discourses, we put our position as textual police on trial/under erasure. Reaching (or breaching) a limit point, the critical text can become a heteroglossic, multimedia(ted), dialogic performance: attending to intertextual plottings and doublings, whether or not an author "intended" them; practicing digression and indirection, hermeneutical indiscretion, excessive distorting repetitiveness. It becomes a conduit for the conflict or the chorus of voices, inviting reader/listener participation and reenactment. Critical writing becomes the creation of a collage of found or documentary material, incorporating quotes from various sources, as the Whitman collage (Script 6),"Legal Discourse vs. Poetic Discourse" (Script 2), and "The Poetics of Protest" (Script 5); of discourse-impersonations spinning off a base text (whether a Poe short story, a contemporary poem, or a pop-culture icon, human or otherwise—"Niagara on the Rocks..." and the "Monroe Project," Scripts 1 and 3, respectively), of moments of personal lyricism, confession, and discursive commentary (most of the scripts incorporate these gestures); it is a text, too, that coexists with itself as somatic performance, theoretical clearing house, and critical analysis (again, the "play" based on Reznikoff's *Testimony*, "Niagara on the Rocks...," the "Monroe Project"). I am interested, that is, not in writing *about* texts, but in writing *through* them, as John Cage writes through *The Cantos, Finnegans Wake* (*X*), and Thoreau's notebooks. I want to play along with a text, rather than reduce its play, to feel along a line of discourse for the soft spots, or for the hum of the dialogic—a host text's urge toward performance—and to consume the text by reinscribing its energies, re(con)figuring it as a work of desire. The interpretative act, with its cast of thousands, must be practiced to the point of exhaustion. An "interpretation," from this perspective, is a multi-voiced/multi-media-amplified trace of, or script for, a dramatic encounter among reader, text/Text, and author. The scene of criticism becomes a "happening."

&

(On the train. A rectangular table. Father on one side, daughter on the other. Turning over cards. As we slow to a stop, rows of frame houses; roofs of snow, yards of snow; each separate, individual, the same.)

My quest ... a wilderness of verbal and visual signs ... legend always pursued. Theory of strange faces... echoes and uncanny recognitions ...

&

The Text as Other: Reading in the Field

"This," the present inscription, as a book of performances—of textual performances and of scripts for performing texts—may be momentarily focused through a metaphor of postmodern ethno-graphic procedure—a record of a reader/interpreter/fieldworker entering the terrain of the Text/Other and re-presenting what is encountered there within the deconstructive, epistemo-ontological discourse of the open work. The point is to locate multiple points of entry into texts that appear closed—or, rather, to dislocate our standard points if entry—and to allow ourselves to be seduced by Texts that already offer themselves openly to us. Just as, ethnographically, we can never know another "as it is" in itself; just as the quest for complete self-presence and objectivity is fallacious from the outset—the quest itself the self-verification of an ideological stance—so we can never know Text completely. The "fact" of the text as a bibliographic identity or printed entity is no more assuring of closure or complete comprehension then is the fact of the existence of a village constructed on a particular site at a particular latitude and longitude with (at any one time) a certain number of inhabitants. Is the village today the same as last year? ten years from now? Or even at the same moment perceived by different inhabitants (Cf. .Žižek's take on "parallax")? Similarly, Is the text now, as perceived and consumed by one reader, the same as that consumed by another? Or ten years from now by the same reader? Or when our own revisionary voices reopen a text (tomorrow, next year, 20 years from now) to revise our own previous commentary? Is it (text or village), even in the same moment as we look at it, only what it seems to say to us— what we believe it to be saying? Or is it *only* what we believe it to be? Can it not not be other except as we other it? Are Texts, as Others, inherently unknowable? In Saussurian semiotics, an element defines itself by what it isn't (i.e., by binary opposition), which logically requires definite identity on either side of a difference. But textual villages, like human villages, are subject to change. What are "villages" but agglomerations of inherently unstable sign systems, *mise en abime*, produced by human thought? Texts and cultures (including "sub" or "counter" cultures) are networks—gatherings and intersections—of discourses.[5] The text wants to be the consciousness of a culture, its self-verification of its own (*propre*) existence, its belief in itself, its inn, its in-itself (God=Word).

A delimiting, specular hermeneutics forces Texts to speak our way, much like early modern anthropological accounts of others reinscribe them in our voice.[6] Yet the other as(in)itself—Text or culture—exists in a plurality, a heteroglossia of its "own"; its field is the field of "paralogy" (as Lyotard defines it), which opposes the discourse of experts. Paralogy is adaptive, chameleonic, appropriative; paralogists carve their own space within the space of dominant institutions and discourses. Paralogic discourse may be parodic, oppositional, or simply self-assertive and/or self-indulgent. Such discourses are resistant in that they strike off their own identity or sense of independence from an empowered, dominant discourse; they may also traffic, undetected, beneath it—as in the singing voices passed among field hands in the African-American discourse of slavery. Therefore, in the early stages of ethnographic investigation, when other cultures did not see them-

5. From the point of view of Actor-Network Theory (see Bruno Latour, especially *Aramis, or, The Love of Technology* and *We Have Never Been Modern*), there are no self-substantial identities or subjects—whether objects or persons—only nodes, crossing points or stations of networks and processes.

6. See Minh-Ha on Malinowski, in *Woman, Native, Other.*

selves in competition with their Western-authored representations, they could not be said to have been paralogists (except perhaps within their own internal rhetorical/structural dynamics). Today, however, when others write about themselves (appropriating the Western academic discourses and formats), and when they cannot not be aware of what has been/is being written about them (Kevin Dwyers, for example, in *Moroccan Dialogues,* presents his material to his "subjects" for approval)-when one, that is, understands her/himself as subject of, subjected to—this is less so, and current ethnographical writings often bear the traces, or openly acknowledge, the competition of discourses. Yet the classical, authorial text (literary or anthropological) has always ghosted its own o(O)therness, and therefore has always been in a state of internal conflict and disavowal, though to readers siding with authorial imperialism its surface may appear smooth and secure.[7]

An ethnographer, like any observer (literary critic or experimental physicist), can self-reflexively admit his/her own role in the drama—hence moving from the position of politician or hegemonist to paralogist—or self deludingly maintain the persona of an objective, authoritative/authorial, single-voiced, disinvolved presenter. Several recent ethnographic performances are provocative in this regard, attempting to establish themselves, at the outset, as multivoiced texts contextualizing (placing diacritical marks around) the ethnographer's voice. Barbara Babcock's documentary texts, James Clifford's emphasis on ethnographic surrealism (particularly in the texts of Michael Lerris), and Michael Taussig's relocation of the ethnographer/writer within the ethnographic field (a voice among others) are familiar examples. Trinh Minh-Ha's paralogical restaging of the ethnographer-other dialogue by functioning as the other writing about herself repositions the dialogue. In Minh-ha's meditation on the phenomenon of ethnography, *Woman, Native, Other*, the western-trained ethnographer and non-western other meet in the same person, showing that the other—that anyone—is always already a matrix of (often conflictual or contradictory) discourses. Overlaying the non-articulability of a pure "Otherness," as non-articulable, as noted above, the other's self-image is influenced by what has been written about him/her by

7. Jayne Tompkins notes such a reader-effect in pre-modern exploration narratives, which appear objective but are really rhetorical maneuvers in—and traversings through—ideological fields ("'Indians': Textualism, Morality, and the Problem of History," in Gates, 59-77).

western anthropologists; the others will always present themselves, to some extent, according to what they think the observer wants to hear, and of course they can always withhold information—they package themselves, so to speak, for foreign consumption. We can never free ourselves, as observers, from a certain way of seeing, as Jane Tompkins has noted in her studies of Native Americans ("'Indians': Textualism, Morality, and the Problem of History," in Gates, *Race, Writing and Difference*). Gloria Anzaldua's *Borderlands*, like Min-Ha's text, dramatizes how the other, when writing about herself, slips through our ideological fingers; she only partially translates herself for the Anglo-American reader—much of the text remains in a mixture of Spanish, North Mexican dialect, and Tex-Mex, uninterpretable/impenetrable—*uninhabitable*—to the reader who can only read generally. Anzaldua confronts us with her otherness; she resists easy definition and remains linguistically complex. She makes us realize how little the term "Mexican-American" means when applied to a culturally and linguistically diverse group—like a rubber glove on the end of a stick that flaps against objects but grasps nothing, the label prevents us from sensing the distinctions among Mestizos, Chicanos, Raza, and Tejanos. But Anzaldua does not advocate giving up her Americanness for her Mexicanness; when she writes in English, she is not writing in translation, but in one of the many dialects that are part of her linguistic and cultural identity. To live in the borderlands (as irreducible other, as positionally conscious ethnographer, as performative critic, as quantum wave) means to straddle many cultures (worlds, dimensions, sign systems), to be a semiotic acrobat versatile in several tongues. One living on the margins between cultures/sign systems (Tejano or performative critic) must be able to code switch according the needs of the situation: standard English in the office and Tex Mex at lunch hour; analytic discourse at the "office"—the business, for example, of writing *DLB* entries—and experimental blocking (out) of a cultural dialogos *between* office hours (when, say, image can rub up against text, tracing a more expansive network of relationships). One must become adroit in the art of *metissage*, as Francoise Lionnet terms this multivoiced, mobile sense of self (*Autobiographical Voices*).

In her analysis of Abla Farhoud's play *When I was Grown*, Jill MacDougall claims that "ethnographic description and interpretation of culture is a scriptual activity" ("Growing, Growing, Growing, Grown," in Slyomovics, *Feminist Ethnography and Performance*). Reversing this formulation, we can think of inscription as an ethnographic activity. As critics, we often treat Texts with a myopia similar to that with which anthropologists once treated (and some still treat) their subjects/informants. Like old, emasculated authors code armed, we become textual authorizers, if not textual racists, excluding, devaluing, repressing certain aspects of a text's being —especially its pre-thetic, and extra-textual *jouissance*—while valorizing others. The thing to look at again in a reader's reading and an ethnographer's study is not so much the point made as the act and manner of making the point and the ideology that tutors (or "internally persuades," to use Bakhtin's phrase) the act. As James Boone (*Other Tribes, Other Scribes*) has astutely observed, it's not just that the anthropologist/critic intervenes in the culture/Text in order to reinscribe it, but that we code others as they code themselves as they code us as we code ourselves. Our thinking always already occurs within a frame—C-O-D-E—and nothing but specular activity passes between each point on the "subject-object" continuum. To break out of the specular appropriation of Text/Other, however temporarily, we must step back and become spectators of our own scriptive maneuvers, jostling among othernesses; we become (self)parologists. We must not only be able to lose our places in texts, but to catch ourselves in the act of seeing—enacting a way of seeing. We must, with a degree of humility, acknowledge our function as *bricoleurs*, making do with the "givens" of we know not what, creating assemblages, cutting versions of texts and/or others that cannot even be self-possessed, that we come to know, as we fabricate them, less and less, knowing only the jostling. Though this does not guarantee that we can see something else (or Other), it enables us to let go; it prepares us for the "real work" (Gary Snyder's phrase) of self-deconstruction by creating an opening (a mind space) for affective, transformative interactions (what performance theorist Richard Schechner calls "efficacy rituals").

As discourse constructs composed of multiple voices (including the critic's), Texts are part of an ongoing construction without clear boundaries that extends over the entire psycho-social field. Michael Taussig (*Shamanism, Colonialism, and The Wild Man*) has noted that Shamanistic healing rituals in South America function within a vast and complex net of familial, tribal, political, and religious relationships; the Shaman is not just an herb doctor and divine, but a psycho-therapist, social worker, and political analyst as well. To heal patients means to examine their functions in the entire social structure—enquiring into their family lives, who their friends and enemies are, and their positions in the community—as well as their spiritual states, physical conditions and the immediate physical causes of the illness. The healing event itself is like a Schechner-directed performance: the Shaman often lives with her/his patient and the patient's, family during the curing period; their lives intertwine. There are breaks in the ritual: a Shaman may interrupt his/her chanting to comment on her/his experience as a healer or to critique her/his chanting, to share a joke with the patient and /or neighbors who drop in to check on the patient, to have a chat with the patient, or simply to step outside and urinate. The "doctor's house call" is a social event. The healing ceremony is not unlike a postmodern production of Brecht.

The Shaman and the postmodern critic arrive at the same point, though miles/cultures apart: the point of staying off or deferring the point: nomadism. Nomadism means having no place of permanent abode; an endless passing through, mouthing and interlacing of discourses/materials. The meeting/crossing place of these discourses is carnival, dramatic tension, performance. Nomadism: no closure or rest in any one ideological position, rhetorical stance, medium, image, gesture, rhythm, phoneme, grapheme, identity, or life; only a momentary, "rested totality" as poet Louis Zukofsky phrases it—a few lines, a poem, a half life—all are moments. Sometimes, overcome by our own time, time sense, or sense of timing, the cadence eludes us. Jacques Derrida, Gilles Deleuze, Bruno Latour, Julia Kristeva, Gloria Anzaldua, Roland Barthes, Mikhail Bakhtin, Armand Schwerner—all nomads. Few voices registered in these pages who aren't.

Figured ethno-pathologically, performative criticism stages itself on the site of the Other, on a body of language. At first, a "primary" text becomes a host upon which the interpretive text feeds, but a symbiotic transformation soon takes place, a mutual infestation, and both become something other in the exchange. In fact, criticism can be said to exist only in this dynamic and by no means "objective" interrelation. The self-preserving critical text strengthens itself axiomatically on a hierarchic relationship between "self" and "other," which are constructed/fictional/functional forms, but the performative critical text acts as a pathogenic carrier or agent that weakens the defenses of text against Text, self against not-self. It does not improve academic appetites, for which a healthy, specular text in which interpreters find what they want is the best stimulant. The function of performative criticism is to inject a dis-ease into ideologically generated, procedural, semiotically stabilized textual productions in order to effect a transformation. This praxis necessitates juxtaposing variant readings of texts by the critic so that claim meets counter claim, demonstrating how any thetic position is tentative and subject to change, and requires opening the text to contamination, to a disintegrative microsemiosis from within and a disjunctive macrosemiosis from without.[8] An important function of performative criticism, then, is to open a space that can accommodate explorative anti-surgery, a surgery concerned not with extracting and suturing; not with reducing complications, but increasing them, healing by making (un)whole(+some), opening the text inside (self-same) out (cultural field/other), like Fluxus artist Wolf Vostell's detoured ("prepared") TV sets, deprogrammed to unchannelable, indecipherable receptibility (see John Hanhardt, "De-Collage and Television: Wolf Vostell in New York, 1963-64," in Milman, *Fluxus*).

*

From a tamer perspective, Social Text Theory conceives of texts as processes, always in action (in the act of...). This is especially true of play texts, as Philip Gaskell has discussed them ("Night and Day: Development of a Play Text," in McGann, *Textual Criticism*):[9] Each reading/performance of a work is a further production of it, live enactment producing several (more or less specular) versions of the text/other, so the Text/work is always in the making and, to trope consumer economics, is never a completely consumable product, can never be (adequately) packaged (of course, even in supermarket economics there are always more donuts than are in the box, but they are not more identical

8. As above, t is affected by T. The critical text (c) is in turn influenced or distorted by contact with the complex function $t_f(T)$. T, then, is the driving force behind all textual functions—those that are authored and those that escape authorial control—whether generated in opposition to it or in celebration of it. A pseudo-matematical expression of this relationship: the performative critical text (P) = $c_f[t(T)]$. There are no constants in this equation.

9. See Jerome McGann's *Textual Criticism and Literary Interpretation* and David Greetham's *Theories of Text* for the ideological groundwork of Social Text Theory.

donuts, despite the simulations of mass production).[10] The effect of such a gaze (or glaze) is to emphasize the Text as a multivalent (if not militant), dynamic phenomenon extant beyond the printed page, elusive to the point where immediate experience of particular versions "in the field" displaces total comprehension; closure and definition are indefinitely deferred.

George Quasha, writing about the dialogue (or "dialogos," as he terms it) between written and oral versions of texts, refers to this phenomenon as a "further textualization." When we consider texts in the hands, ears, and minds of readers, we are always already beyond (between, through) the printed page.[11] As Valentin Volosinov has theorized ("Discourse in Life and Discourse in Art," in *Freudianism: A Marxist Critique*), the reader is present, is already in the text even before the act of inscription. From this perspective, authors who "intend" meanings for their readers disavow that their works are always already pre-intended by these readers, who are (co)authors of what is produced in the name of another. Moreover, reader involvement is often concretely apparent in the composition process; many pre- (and some post-) publication manuscripts are manifestly indeterminate, heteroglossic constructs, physically written (and overwritten) in several hands, as authors revise in response to readers' and editors' comments (Pound's revisions of Eliot's *Waste Land,* as evidenced in Valerie Eliot's edition of the poem including facsimiles of original drafts, is an extreme example). The concept of univocal, original authorship is a dissimulation at every stage of the creative process (so long as there are living authors or scholars to bring out new editions, or so long as there are readers/audiences), and even in the early, formative phases of a composition, where we would expect it to operate most, it operates least. As the reader is, then, always an author (whether in the position of author or reader), and as readers are always already writers, whether they know it or not, so authors both read and rewrite (as they are read and rewritten by) their readers. Original authorship? The medieval concept of *Jeux* is closer to the mark. Medieval poets conceived of themselves not as unique authors, the "owners" of a particular voice or style—most early lyrics were anon-

10. For an application of Social Text theory to the study of contemporary poetry, see my "Editing Schwerner: Versions of Armand Schwerner's 'design tablet'" in *Text 8,* Ed. Jerome McGann

11. Differentially, computer-based "interactive" texts are simulations of this process.

ymous—but as adaptors or rearrangers. Today, we still create original concoctions (whether we admit it or not) of what is more or less consciously available. Originality does not arrive *ex nihilo*. A *tabula rasa* can only be that which has never entered social, semiotic consciousness, that which has no cultural being (like Lacan's Real—perturbing, but itself an unreachable, unknowable, theoretic space)—i.e., that which is nonextant—and so can only be a rhetorical fiction. "Nothing will come of nothing" is a call for more language—always more language—not to disguise the breach, but to keep it open (that Lear figures the "heath" as "barren"—as perhaps he must—is the "real" tragic fiction).

Actor-Network Theory (ANT) provides a further paradigm, via sociological theory, for expanded textuality—for perceiving texts, or in fact any cultural object, as nodes in networks rather than closed constructs. In a recent article in *Symploke* ("Re(X)locating the Critical Self: the Global Subject in an Electronic Age"), I point out that ANT (Bruno Latour, *We Have Never Been Modern*; John Law, *Actor-Network Theory and After*) supports expanded self-awareness and critical consciousness by encouraging us to view society as "fibrous" everyday "collectives," metonymic networks of "self-evolving systems" openly structured around particular economic/commercial, political, educational, interpersonal, pragmatic, and psychological dimensions in temporary, productive configurations, rather than as fixed hierarchical and taxonomic orders (Gearoid O Tuathail, "Postmodern Geopolitics? The Modern Geopolitical Imagination and Beyond"). In ANT, the human actor conceives him/herself as occupying a particular position (or set of positions) in a (de-personified) "materially heterogeneous" (Law and Kevin Hetherington, "Materialities, Spatialities, Globalities," par. 9) network that consists of objects and concepts as well as animate beings, rather than as a smooth, self-coherent—dissimulating, sutured (Žižek)—(touring) subject; from the point of view of ANT (and its sister discipline, STS—Science and Technology Studies), subjectivity, along with other materialities (objects, technologies, bodies, texts) are "relational effects or emergent phenomena" (Law and Hetherington, par. 10).[12] ANT, like Marxian

12. Such mobilizations of critical thought away from closure can contribute to what David Gruber theorizes as "deontological," expanded subjectivity, or a dispersed sense of self in which "subjectivity that knows itself as bounded…, will be compromised in favour of understandings of integrated cross-platform architectures" (par. 9); the "skin ego" (Didier Anzieu's phrase) is

economic theory, gives the cultural critic a methodos to (re)view the "hidden" relations in the processes of cultural (re)production, to (re) move "lived" experience back from the commodity/spectacle[13] to the realm of material (inter)relations, offsetting (to the extent it is possible) ideological violation in order to realize (as clearly and completely as possible) the networks that articulate global flows for all manner of productions/products, from tennis shoes to political slogans to books and works of art. ANT informs Craig Saper's theory of "Networked Art." Tracking social theory into aesthetic praxis, Saper proposes experimental artistic collectives, or oxymoronically "intimate bureaucracies," that deploy "social networks" to create a kind of "social sculpture"; this is achieved partly by troping depersonalized systems of mass production and distribution, detouring the "trappings and systems of bureaucracies" to establish "intimate connections among participants." These small groups of artist-participants, or co-creators in an ongoing artistic event, can participate either face-to-face, through mailings and assemblings (as in Richard Kostelanetz's various Assembling Press anthologies in the 1970s and '80s—see below),[14]

---

just one phenomenon among others. But even that may be only a temporary holding pattern. Extrapolating from the AI work of techo-theorists such as Darko Stefanovic, Jian-Qin Liu, Andy Clark and Victor Vitanza, Grubar predicts that, at the cell level, bio/biomolecular computing technologies will produce the "Whatever child" who, from birth, is interconnected with "Whatever anywhere at all time," affectively eliminating the apprehension of inside v. outside; though hard to frame in conventional syntax, this "self"distuptive/redistributive "laugher-in-*techné*," as Diane Davis terms it (*Breaking Up (at) Totality*..., 118) suggests not *thinking* of "ourselves" differently, but *experiencing* the "self" as "Whatever" (maybe not possible to say "there is") everywhere at—with developing nano technologies, what may eventually be— no-time.

13. cf, Guy Debord, *Society of the Spectacle*: "all that was once directly lived has moved away into a representation" (61)

14. A delightfully perplexing, if not mildy mind-boggling example of proto-"networked art" from the '60s: Daniel Spoerri's (with Robert Filliou and Emmett Wiliams) collaborative collage text *An Anecdoted Topography of Chance* (Something Else Press, 1966), in which the object/leftovers on the artist's (Speorri's) dinner/worktable become the (dis)ordering principle for a series of descriptions and brief personal narratives related to the history and current context of each object (annotated initially by Spoerri, subsequently by Filliou and later by Williams as he translated the book from French to

and/or through the Internet. Of particular interest for the current collection, is the emphasis of these collectives on process rather than product, or on an anti-productive (in the commercial sense), a-teleological process bringing to the cultural field not completed works, but "instructions and scores for performance and poetic situations," or further production, making use of raw, mass-cultural materials ("found objects, texts and images"—post marks and postage stamps, for example) rather than individualized expressions (Saper, *Networked Art*, 149-52).

Just as Social Text Theory and Actor-Network Theory (re) conceive texts as something more than the present array of words on a page, probing beyond authorial control to interpersonal (and global, in the case of the latter) networks—networks that, in ANT (as in recent techno-theory—n. 12. above), articulate human-non-human/other assemblages—so too, recent performance theory sees performance "texts" as a complex social-historical-cultural phenomenon, not just as actors on a stage. Victor Turner (*On the Edge of the Bush*) sees staged drama as a reenactment of social dramas, which he conceptualizes in a four-phase process—breach, crisis, redress, and reintegration or permanent schism. Performance becomes, from this perspective, in theorist Jon McKenzie's words, a "living reactualization of socially symbolic systems," or, more broadly, "embodied enactment of cultural forces" (8). Richard Schechner pushes the roots of theater as "restorative behavior" (Schechner's phrase) deeper, to nomadic hunting cycles; his tripartite mapping of seasonal hunting movements encompasses Turner's scheme. He describes, for example, how, during their hunting circuits, nomadic tribes would occasionally meet; the place of meeting becomes, temporarily, the site of performance (as a place of citation), marked by human use as a "theater" only for the duration of

English), each of which is cross-referenced, cross-textually, via a system of note markers, with drawings of the objects accompanying the entries. Readers are invited to contribute their own "annotations and comments," related especially to the *arrondissement* of Spoerri's Paris apartment, to appear in "supplements" to be published at "irregular intervals" (Xiii). A map, or "snare picture," of the table, as it appeared on 10/17/61 at 3:47 PM, is sketched on the inside dust jacket of the book, the numbered outline of each object corresponding to a numbered section in the book; the numbering is semi-arbitrary—higher numbers clustered mostly to the right and lower to the left—so that the reading path is non-linear, roundabout, grasped at once as a randomized image, rather than a syntactical and semantic order.

the festivities. Thus Schechner sees drama as originally rising out of a social-cultural-seasonal complex. He defines a three-phase rhythm—gathering, performance, and dispersal—as the base beat of all performance ("From Ritual to Theatre and Back," *Performance Theory*); Turner's four-part scheme occurs in the second stage of this broader pattern (i.e., the breach, crisis, redress, reintegration formula requires a society already gathered around and "witnessing" the breach and the ensuing social drama). Schechner's sense of cadence can be seen in his work with The Performance Group in the 60s and 70s (since 1980, the Wooster Group, artistic director Elisabeth LeCompte). He pushed the boundaries of theater further and further out, eliminating not only the fourth wall but all the walls, putting into question/ripping apart the partition (here a virgule) between theater and not-theater. Pre-performance activities—rehearsal, warm up, and gathering of the audience (Schechner would often greet audience members personally and seat them himself)—the performance itself, cool down and post-performance discussions (among members of the cast and the audience, as actors and spectators mingle) were part of this broader rhythm of performance. Even street activity became part of the show. During rehearsals of *Mother Courage* in the late 60s, Schechner kept the garage door open—passersby could "happen" (more or less) unexpectedly onto a performance, and whatever was happening outside could, potentially, enter into the rehearsal space ("Toward a Poetics of Performance," *Performance Theory*) (think of microphones turned toward the street in a John Cage "concert"). Finally, a TPG production included not only a text (or texts), but material from the actors' personal lives and a rich texture of inter-cultural (as well as intertextual) references (today, the Wooster Group supplements this with live and prerecorded video feeds and computer-generated sounds, creating a more high-tech mediated, *mise en scene*); folding this in with the social dynamics noted above creates an expansive, indeterminate (undecidable), highly energized work vectoring through a complex network of socio-cultural, technological, and formal interrelations.

Performance theory, social text Theory and postmodern anthropological theory point us to a Text dispersed out(without)side; poststructuralist semiotic theory, literary theory and cultural theory may point us that way and/or the other direction, toward imploding text. Either way we come, antiperspectivally, to the no-place of Text. If reading is performative (through selection, repetition, reenactment), whether a specular confrontation or an exercise in "negative capability" (to the extent that is possible); if texts can be (re)perceived/conceived as voice zones/territories in dramatic conflict; if criticism can become a creative act, then why reinstitutionalize it, subordinate it to the police action of hierarchic essay structure and a detached, disembodied, impersonal tone? To ignore or consciously suppress the ubiquitous Otherness that is always already breaking through the solid-seeming, representational (if we're talking about, say, a conventional novel) or discursive surface of a text is simply to miss, or under read, the event of the Text. Performative criticism should be sensitive to the quantum disobedience of Texts (activity at the sub-word and sub semantic level) as well as to the interplay of voices and more or less conscious strategies that structure a text; it should register, as fully as possible, the life of Text, re-presenting (reenacting) it in a form that opens it (out of itself), rather than packaging it for easy intellectual consumption. This is a matter not only of responsiveness, but responsibility. For Diane Davis, conscientiousness in a "postfoundational world" requires a "posthuman ethics" that should "not be about shutting down the flow, but opening it up"—listening for the "noise" and "excess" in language, the "laughter-in- language" so that we may announce/pronounce it, as voices in the breach that "laugh with the laughter that is laughing language" (*Breaking (Up) at Totality...*, 113-114)—to whatever takes us beyond/through our (Humanist-centered) selves to/into posthumanist Otherness...

&

Performative Criticism as Multimedia Bricolage Practice[15]

In the mid-50s, poets in America and Europe began to popularize public readings in nontraditional spaces—bars and coffee houses—and began experimenting with multi-media presentation of their works—reading with musical accompaniment, for example. In the 60s and 70s, inspired partly by experiments with intermedia art (especially performances/happenings staged by Fluxus, the international al-

15. I detour this sign from Levi-Strauss' *The Savage Mind*, in which he deploys "bricolage" to describe the process, in "primitive" societies, through which a limited store of everyday materials, not "sacred" in themselves, are adapted to a variety of ritual contexts.

liance of composers and visual artists) and the advent in America of ethnopoetics (investigations into the artistic and/or ritual practices of non-mainstream ethnic cultures—especially Native American—within Western culture), an emphasis on text as performance emerged (as, for example, Jerome Rothenberg's controversial translations and adaptations of Native American oral poetries in influential anthologies like *Shaking the Pumpkin* and *America A Prophecy*). However, while the avant-garde of American poetics in the post WWII era has been concerned with performing texts, many postmodern American and European anthropological, literary, cultural, and performance theorists have concentrated on experimentation with textual performance—performative writing. This is not to say that these are mutually exclusive camps. Certainly many of Rothenberg's and Allen Ginsberg's poems and those of many members of the Black Mountain School, most notably John Cage, Charles Olson and Paul Blackburn, as well as the work of performance poets like Jackson Mac Low and Armand Schwerner, hold their own as textual performances. Groups like the Language Poets also work in both territories (Charles Bernstein sometimes stages minimalist performances of his work). The multimedia practices of performance art collaboratives also blur the distinctions between critical and creative, intermedia and (print) text-based performance: Historically, Fluxus, as noted above, founded in 1962 by George Maciunas, specialized in minimalist, anti-art performances incorporating text, objects and live action, often in the form of a "Happening."[16] More recently, the Critical Art Ensemble, for example, juxtaposes current social-political-cultural theory with popular imagery; Delhi-based Raqs Media Collective's culturally critical activities take the form of multimedia installations, a web and print based journal, urban interrogations, software design, discussion lists and workshops conducted at the Centre for the Study of Developing Societies in Delhi; the V-Girls stage mock academic panels at conferences, the Guerrilla Girls trope—detour—mass marketing techniques by promoting feminist critical consciousness on T-shirts and posters and, pseudonymed as dead female artists and suited in gorilla masks, perform public critical-consciousness-raising actions; Mabou Mines overlays an evocative and playful imagism with slapstick,

16. According to Alan Kaprow, the site-specific, open form nature of Happenings involved language play, (re)deployment of found materials, and the collapsing of boundaries between audience and actors (*Essays on the Blurring of Art and Life*, 16-20).

wordplay and high theory, suggesting a critical mind gone awry, losing its way/place within its own structuring discourses. From the other(another) side, a theorist like Lacan, many of whose "texts" originate in lectures, can be seen both as theoretician and performer. Richard Schechner and Richard Foreman are both performance theorists and performers. Though Schechner does not perform his theoretical texts, Foreman does, and the experience of either a Schechner or a Foreman production is, in a sense, a *being in* (rather than speaking about) epistemology. It could also be argued that Artaud's "theory," only partially available in his texts, can be grasped only in an Artaudian production.

However, for the most part, critics and theorists who present their work "performatively" tend to concentrate on textual, or "writerly," performance.[17] Susan Howe is a critic as well as a poet whose texts cross critical and poetic discourse, and whose writings are stylistically performative. Literary critic Sherman Paul's diaristic hermeneutical style tropes critical "objectivity" and raises questions about the location of voice in generalized, uninflected, institutional discourses; his writing practice confuses (or fuses) supposedly opposed genres such as the scholarly essay and the memoir (see, for example, *In Love with the Gratuitous: Rereading Armand Schwerner*).[18] Going a bit further afield, Richard Kostelanetz's Assembling Press compilations are book-length collages with as many authors and voices as pages; *A Critical (Ninth) Assembling (Precisely: 6789)* (1979), for example, presents one-two page critical "commentaries" on experimental writing, many of which are themselves formally experimental, layering and juxtaposing text and imagery, recycling words and letters as elements in an overall design *a al lettrisme* (the French art-text movement that plays on intensities of language at the graphemic level, in the shape, density and motility of letters).[19]

---

17. A term coined by Barthes to distinguish between texts that play (self-reflexively) with language or otherwise ac(act)knowledge (partly surrender to) their polysemous (and polyphonous) texture and those that those that simply accept language as a means to a representational end ("readerly" texts).

18. Beyond registering the personal (with)in academic discourse, the Internet offers opportunities to extend textual performance into extra-literary, non-RL venues (see the Flash version of my article, "Fantasy .Com: Zizek and Internet Pornography, Game One" produced independently by *Rhizomes*' web designer, www.rhizomes.net, Issue # 5).

19. Tom Conley traces the roots of letterism to the Rennaissance, when the "graphic display of writing" gave letters a life of their own, enabling

Gloria Anzaldua, Norman O. Brown, Edmond Jabes (*The Book of Questions*), Derek Pell (*Assassination Rhapsody*), Jalal Toufic (*Over-sensitivity*), Ihab Hassan (especially in *Paracriticisms*), Michael Benamou (in *Performance and Postmodern Culture*), Herbet Blau, Henry Sayre (in *The Object of Performance*), Julia Kristeva ("Sabat Mater"), Jacques Derrida (in *Glas, Spurs, Limited Inc.*, and *The Post Card*), Jacques Lacan (in *Ecrits*), Roland Barthes, Georges Bataille, James Clifford, Greg Ulmer, Daniel White (*The City of Disney*), bell hooks, Eve Sedgwick (*A Dialogue on Love; Fat Art, Thin Art*), Barbara Babcock, Robert B. Ray ("The ABC of Visual Theory") (*Visible Language* 22.4), Avital Ronell (*The Telephone Book; Crack Wars: Literature, Addiction, Mania*) and Diane Davis (*Breaking Up (at) Totality..*) also immediately come to mind as writers whose work blends lyric, theoretic/philosophic, autobiographical, and documentary forms of writing, and plays on these various types of writing and on the arrangement, structure, and visual appearance of the text. Clifford mimes a postcard format in the disruptive center of the *Predicament of Culture*; Hassan's *Paracriticisms* and Michael Benamou's *Performance and Postmodern Culture* present intriguing

---

them to "produce other meanings [other than through their detonative, or transcriptive, function] in physical shapes and in their movement across the page"; through this "dialogue of form and substance," artists' works may "take control of themselves," riding on the shape of a grapheme to "generate numerous figures and [extra] dimensions of meaning," but also risk disintegrating into "ribaldry" (as in Rabelais' *Gargantua*) (*The Graphic Unconscious in Early Modern French Writing*, 2-4). The postmodern French movement develops this cross-textual graphemic resonance into a form of critical consciouisness and a methodos of creative resistance in its own right. Founded in the 1940's by Rumanian emigre artist Isodore Isou, *Lettrisme* exploited the visual and aural properties of letters as a way of short-circuiting over(ideologically)determined modes of artistic production. This led, in the 50's, to Hypergraphics, based on the fragmentation, decontextualization/defamiliarization, and visual (re) arrangement of graphemes from a wide range of writing systems, including invented ones; in the 60's and 70's, Isou conceived "Meca-art, using the material world as medium, and "Supertemporal" art, ongoing, open-frame events in which the audience/participants create the "work." Letterism crisscrosses several aesthetic territories of the 60's and 70's, including (most immediately) Situationism (the French art/critical culture movement founded by Guy Debord in the late 50's), concrete poetry, assemblage, happenings, minimalism, and concept art. Current letterist practices deploy sound poetry, mixed media works, and films to present a poly-semiotic approach to cultural communication based in intense, almost meditative attention to the depths and resonances within the material surfaces of (visual and verbal) "language."

examples of alternative formatting, such as "shaped" and collage texts; Derek Pell's *Assassination Rhapsody*, a meditation on/deconstruction of the *Warren Report*, deploys collage and found/documentary graphics along with verbal elements to disturb its host text; in Ronell's texts, font, layout, and page space, rather than serving silently as background format, shift to a frontal semantic function; Davis breaks up page space with, for example, biographical inserts/asides about her "subjects," as well as common dictionary definitions of key terms encountered in the main text, that run parallel to her (main stage) theorizations based on those writers' works; Jalal Toufic's scriptive musings on cinema, *Over-sensitivity*, and Herbert Blau's on theater, *The Audience*, verge on meditative practice; Robert Ray plays against abstract systems of order by alphabetically arranging, in a typographically and spatially playful format, associatively and cross-textually connected concepts and figures in modern and postmodern culture, hermeneutics and textual theory, from Apollinaire, Barthes and cinema, to collage, concrete poetry, constructivism, dandyism, the epigraph, footnoting, and glossing; to indexing, Oulipo, William Carlos Williams, Poe ("X-ing a Paragrab") and Arno Schmidt's tome *Zettels' Traum*, itself a dense parody of textual paraphernalia, all the entries touching, in one way or another, on the visual structures and surfaces of language as, quoting Oulipoean Raymond Queneau, "props for inspiration" (438), or as means of short-circuiting syntactic/semantic chains dependent on the assumption of signifier as shell for the—and any particular—signified. These are writers who *write* performatively.[20]

As examples of textual performances, Derrida's *Glas*, Kristeva's "Sabat Mater," and Babcock's "Arrange Me into Disorder" are especially worth noting. All use columnar or patchwork page layout, so that the discursive text itself appears to be in dialogue with itself; the univocal illusion is broken by the fragmentation of the page, which no longer has the look of unified prose (the business suit of page formats; we can imagine a similar deconstruction in fashion design—layers, eclectic accouterment, clashes in style, texture, and color, *trompe l'oeil* prints, etc.). However, though the material in the columns or patch-ins may not be directly or logically related, there are metonymic, cross-column plays, which deter the separatist integrity or self-integral identity of any

20. See Jerome McGann's "Deformance and Interpretation" (*Radiant Textuality*) for a fascinating study of the revelatory potential of writerly critical performance.

single block. Puns, homophones, repetitions, and sound doublings enable a reader to pass sub- (or hyper-) textually among the various blocks and patches, regardless of linear placement of a block or syntactic/semantic sequence within a block (in *Glas*, for example, Hegel's speculations on the Immaculate Conception, abbreviated by Derrida as the IC, are picked up by the sound of Genet's "*Jm'ec*" in the opposing column). So the text functions as a plurilogue: there are the voices in the columns/blocks, and another/other voice(s) released by readers' performances as they move among blocks more or less enigmatically, more or less consciously, with more or less understanding about what's going on among the several blocks, enacting a dialogue that may, ultimately, be uninterpretable, or endlessly interpretable, which amounts to the same thing. These columns can (as in Derrida's "Sollers" in *Writing & Difference*, and in Babcock's collage text) include or consist entirely of large blocks of quoted material imported into the host text, thus parodying the principle of textual citation, which subordinates interpolated material to authorial intentions; in Derrida's and Babcock's texts, quotes and docu-blocks are allowed free play, like a Poundian collage, and each piece interacts with every other piece in a more or less democratic manner—including the (author's?) own words, which have no more or less weight than other, nonauthorial inscriptions. In Babcock's text, the dialogue enacted by the quotes can vary from reader to reader; Babcock does not "integrate" the quotes into a controlled, self-contained, unified discussion, though her introduction to this textual activity does act as a thematic overseer for the activity itself. (In an extreme instance of this sort, the question arises—who is the author? When the author function is displaced by that of arranger or designer, can we still speak of "authored" texts? In the current collection, "*Stirr'd Up Everywhere*" and "Poetic Discourse v. Legal discourse" are performative responses to the question). Kristeva's "Sabat Mater" also "cross-dresses," playing on discursive and poetic forms of writing. As the right column (left brain?) analyzes and historicizes the myth of the Immaculate Conception and the Virgin Mary, the left (right brain) side is a rhythmic and imagistic evocation of the pains and confusion of childbirth (is Kristeva right-handed, when writing cursive?). The column arrangement of the distinct, though by no means completely separate voices creates a Brechtian alienation effect—they are allowed to coexist and flow in their own way, coinciding in unexpected, unexplained ways.

In *The Tablets*, an excellent example of poetry as textual performance, contemporary poet Armand Schwerner demonstrates the exegetical (surplus) value of work that strains against containment in a lyric framework, playing against/through post WWII prosodic conventions as well as scholarly reconnaissance, and encourages a similar *detournement* among his readers.

The poem series begins with a "Key" to its own translation/ interpretation:

KEY:
.... untranslatable;
+ + + + + + missing;
(?) variant reading;
[] supplied by the scholar translator.

from "Tablet I"

all that's left is pattern* (shoes?).

*doubtful reconstruction

I rooted about...like a.......sow* for her pleasure

*atavism: a hieroglyph; perhaps 'a fetal pig,' 'a small pig,' 'goddess'

the (power)* for all of [us]!

*perhaps 'damage,' if a borrowing; cf. cognate in N. Akkadian: 'skin-burn'

....

The Tablets is a poetic sequence (begun in the mid '60s and left incomplete at the poet's death) inspired by Sumero-Akkadian cuneiform writing. Most of the tablets are introduced by prose headnotes, the voice of which is ambivalent: sometimes they seem to be written in Schwerner's voice, as metacommentator; other times they appear to be written by the "Scholar-Translator," who presents and (often disruptively) comments on the tablets (see asterisks in excerpts above), talking about himself in the third person; more often than not, both these voices merge with Schwerner's as it occurs in his own notes ("Tablets Journals/Divagations"), a further textualization appended to the tablets. Since Schwerner works fictionally with (rather than within) a paradigm of "primitive" poetries transmitted down through the millennia via scholarly editions (so that the question of an "original" voice/poem reverberates back through itself, in a hermeneutical feedback loop), his project is postmodernist and revisionary, not nostalgic or revivalist. In the trans-candescent afterglow of the Emerson of "Circles," a tireless experimenter, "an endless seeker with no Past at [his] back," Schwerner imaginatively, persistently tunnels through historical and archaeological knowledge of man; he hopes to uncover a "new [/old] language" and uncodified modes of being/otherness beneath our already written, ready-made "Pasts," a process that exposes his own language to the risk of disintegration in roped off *aporias*, the black holes in our civilized self-consciousness. But Schwerner also recognizes the ludic potential of such a stance, as he pursues his self-annihilating objective with an intensity that often breaks into self-laughter: Mocking the poem's obsessive archaeological scavenging, "Tablet XXVI" promises to push back 16,000 years "to reveal an articulation" (*Tablets* 74); as the quote from "Tablet I" above shows, the poem perceptively parodies over-zealous scholarship that often reinters what it brings to light under ponderous mounds of emendations and annotations.

The Tablets is a texture of verbal and nonverbal/visual signs, including, in "XXVI," rebus poems (a gesture toward both ancient pictographic writing and American "concrete" poetry of the 1960s and 70s); a patchwork of sound and silence; of statement and drift from statement; of (self)parodic presentations of various, often unassignable critical/literary/fictionalized "selves" (is the speaker in the headnotes Schwerner as Ur-editor, or the Scholar-Translator? and to what extent are the "archaic," fragmented, often lyrical voices specular projections of the previous two?). Tutored by the fragmentary emergence of ancient poetries into the present, as well as by Ezra Pound's theories of the vortex and "luminous detail" and Charles Olson's concept of composition by field, the poem functions as a timeless (though time-conscious) bricolage of voices and images, rather than as a lyric centered in the monody of a single author/persona.

Postmodern American poetry must attempt to "restate man," as Charles Olson says in "Human Universe," "to repossess him of his dynamic" (167) (though such a "dynamic" can dispossess "him" as it restates being across/through discourse and subject/object barriers as a Whatever being-present—see n. 11, above). *The Tablets* challenges the reader/listener's role as passive receptor; by making poetry a "playful and difficult activity" composed of "disparate and disjunctive modes and voices" ("Journals," SRN 117)— "voices" animate and inanimate, sometimes sounding through a "subject" (as the S-T), more often than not fragmentary, part-object.... Hence Schwerner incites the reader/ hearer to participate in the text's creation, and suspend (if not disband) a stable sense of self/identity. As printed text and as performance (score to be performed), *The Tablets* counters what Victor Turner calls, in *From Ritual To Theatre*, our "voyeuristic" relationship to the world, "which we rationalize as 'objectivity'" (100). "No more spectatorism!" Olson shouts up at the bleachers.

One of the writing-effects of my own work on *The Tablets* is to extend this play by further commenting on an already over(self)determined text. Cued by the host text, my essay ("Textual Performance / Performing the Text," excerpted in *Talisman*) is self-consciously performative, often digressing, disrupting its discursive progress with "poem-commercials"—mini collages deploying bold type, parentheses, and upper-case letters to trace a counter or supplemental message through consumer discourse, diverting it to metaphysical purpose[21]. In addition to these brief textual station breaks, the essay assembles self-consciously tentative interpretations based on imagistic and metonymic patterns subject to change at the turn of a page or even within or between lines. An intensive though necessarily open-ended reading of the poem is carried out through a heteroglossic mixture of discursive, autobiographical, narrative, and poetic forms of writing; no single discourse is adequate to re-present, to reenact, the complex play of mind traced by the language of Schwerner's poems.

TH E

T AB

---

21. Along the lines I'm suggesting here, the "poemmercials" become participatory discourses, no matter how uncomfortable the collaboration my at first feel.

L E T S

"Don't **LET** another second **GO** by..."

...a real-life answer..."

"It pays to (D)**IS**cover."

TH E
T AB

L E T S

***

As evidenced by encounters with a poem like *The Tablets*, opening such *aporias* or fissures in scholarly, academic writing creates fields of free play that allow the interpreter and the interpreted, the writer and the written-about, the reader and the read to be inter-engendering, and to strengthen the possibilities of communal bonding. Pound-wise, modernist poetics also foregrounds the collaborative textscape of performative criticism. Though many have rightly criticized Pound's totalitarian politics, the conceptual turbulence created by his works (not just *The Cantos*, of course, but the influential essays collected in *The Spirit of Romance*, *Make It New*, *The ABC's of Reading*, and *Guide to Kulchur*, as well as his translations from the Chinese and of Fenollosa, among others) and words about his works continue today. What concerns me here is the essentially collaborative nature of *The Cantos*, and the movement of mind in *The Cantos* and *Kulchur*, a rhythm Pound theorized in his concepts of the vortex and the ideographic method of composition (see Laszlo Gefin, *Ideogram, History of a Poetic Method*, for a thorough discussion of Pound's theory and practice of the ideographic method). An ideogram is a cadence produced by the interaction of a poem's parts; hence sometimes whole poems, and even pairs and groups of poems can constitute a single ideogram (and, by extension, a cultural era). These ideograms then act as vortexes (or "paideums," when speaking of cultures) "into which, through which, and out of which ideas are constantly rushing." Individual ideograms/poems in *The Cantos* are made up not only of images and statements in the speaker's voice (a rough & ready, often abrupt and hurried voice, at pains to find a language that can keep pace with the rapidity of thought and experience), but also documentary material—bits of quoted language, stories, chunks of history and economic theory—and "luminous details" (images, stories, ideas, and quoted material that capture the essence or flavor of a person or period). These poem/ideograms are multi-voiced, linguistic collages. Hence Ezra Pound does not simply "write" poems, but engages intensely, collaboratively with his "subject." Quoted material imported into a single poem may come together at points, but also veer away, retaining an identity that shares in but is independent of the poem; the meaning of a documentary fragment is not exhausted by its context. Much like Armand Schwerner's *The Tablets*, *The Cantos* run in an open field, and resist closure, despite their Roman numerals. Such writings suggest we all live within an atemporal abundance that can only with great allowances be kept in linear order. All order, no matter how diverse, is exclusive; Pound's *Cantos* push for maximum complexity and as comprehensive an order as possible by evading reduction to (an easy) thematic consistency. They escape complete interpretation and cognizance at any one time or from any single point of view. Ezra Pound, i.e. the set of discourses that converge in the name, the inscription labeled "Ezra Pound" that we read in the writings, is itself a vortex.[22]

22. This is not to say that Pound aims at Zen "no style," which would be pure collage. The voice(s) in *The Cantos* oscillates between local and global detail, present and past; lives a rhythm of withdrawal and return, escape from and reentry into the personal, much like the elusive "I" in Whitman's *Specimen Days*. Pound taught us to think in tangentials and radial arcs, vectors and energy graphs rather than straight and logical lines. Pound's workings have many significant ramifications for modern and contemporary prosody To name just a few: Buckminster Fuller's phenomenology of the knot as a "patterned integrity"; Gary Snyder's spiral image motifs—Milky Way, conch shell, vulva—and his concept of the poem as dynamic energy construct; Joseph Riddel's theory of the poem as a function of—as the trace of—energy exchanges; Hugh Kenner's emphasis, in *The Pound Era*, on the poem as an energy network. That Pound could achieve this, at the time that he did, when so much was against it; that he could let his own poems escape him, at a time when authorial control dominated the scene of criticism and other master ideologies were about to commit atrocities beyond human imagination ...what better proof of his anti-totalitarian turn of mind, in the face of his fascism.

However, though Pound looms large in the canon, much of the contemporary poetry scene frames him out, or comprehends him only as a statue passed on the way into the hall of the Modernist Lyric. We have lost (or covered) his tracks. For example, Jerome Rothenberg's remarkable anthology *America a Prophecy* (Random House, 1973) opened up the field of American

Challenging, elusive, and brilliant as such modernist and postmodernist (re)creative inscriptive actions are, however, the majority of them are textual interventions that stage themselves on the printed page—the Amphitheatre of performative criticism, rather than cross-semiotic, multi-media enactment (though *The Cantos* and *The Tablets* push the envelope); moreover, in terms of critical practice, a dominate tendency of many such "writerly" explorations—with the exception of Ulmer's work on Lacan and Derrida (*Applied Grammatology*), and the work generally of Clifford, Taussig, Teresa de Lauretis, Hassan and a few others—is, as suggested above, an obsession with the personal, or "personalization" (i.e., autobiographical retouching) of otherwise conventional academic discourse that respects semiotic boundaries, resulting in the neglect of other performance territories (in *The Object of Performance*, for example, Sayre pushes beyond the personal gesture when he describes his response to a Carolee Schneemann performance as a dialogic event—as he concentrates on the performance, concepts/key words from other discourses are called to mind and imaginatively "collaged" with Schneemann's action, words, and images—the inter-

---

poetry to a range of sources and influences including pre-Columbian art, Native American ritual, blues lyrics, Shaker ritual, and Eastern religion; the anthology itself is structured like a collage, juxtaposing, for example, in a typical multi-page sequence, a Mayan myth, a modern blues lyric, Native American pictographs, and contemporary poems. Yet, Rothenberg's anthology was out of print until recently, while the *Norton Anthology of American Poetry* is readily available (even Donald Allan's *The Postmoderns*—now in its second edition—which attempts to offer alternate American poetries, is, by comparison, limited and conservative in its selections; not to denigrate Allan's anthology, but it doesn't open out onto a heteroglossic plentitude as Prophecy does). The fact that, in the early '80s, I could go through two years at one of the country's leading writing workshops and not hear *Prophecy* mentioned, and that I could obtain a copy only through extra effort and expense (burrowing a copy from the library and Xeroxing it) while almost every college sophomore had one or more *Nortons* on his/her bookshelf; the fact that even when initially editing this note, nostalgia waking to an Internet search, I could only find one, used, "acceptable" copy of *America* on *Amazon* (thankfully not the case today, at least for the time being...) tells me something about our culture's anxieties, its paranoid sense of self, and the great disappearing act that its identity is based on. Alternative gatherings of texts, like marginaliced voices, often founder into silence, into the vague sea of the unauthorized, of what doesn't compete because it isn't allowed into play. And such silences delimit an image of who we are(n't).

personal giving way to the intertextual; in his assessment of Barthes' critical prose, however, in the book's penultimate chapter, Sayre retrenches in the autobiographical, noting chiefly how an idealizing lyric voice rubs against more formal, academic discourse, leaving us with a sense that performance = (primarily) personal response). However, an autobiographically grounded, writerly style is only one of many possible positions in an improvisational dialogue of form and language experiments catalyzed in the confrontation of reader and text.[23] (Ask Melville's Confidence Man, or a Zen master—alert, mobile, processual, responsive reading/performance includes a lot of discourse shifting—and each media presents its own set of discourses—and positional leap-frogging). As demonstrated by the "actscriptions" gathered here, criticism restaged as $c_f[t(T)]$ operates on a somewhat broader formal arena to realize the full potential of *mise en scene*, or multimedia critical "happenings" (interpretive audio-visual environments integrating image, gesture, sound, music, lighting, voice and objects as well as the spoken and written word), as a strategy for a literary and cultural hermeneutics (we were already on the way: Artaud downplays the sacrosanct treatment of text, as referential, syntactic/semantic units, in conventional theatrical production). As experimental praxis, performative criticism is a de-centered, mobile, nomadic, ecological, collage approach that does not so much recontextualize text as trace its confluence with/within a fluid cultural body in a state of "mixed semiosis" (Gilles Deleuze). Avoiding the privileging of any single form of discourse or sign system, performative criticism acknowledges that printed text is important—may even often be dominant—but also recognizes that, in the wilds of Text, the next thing "said" may often be or, following Artaud, Zen masters, and The Three Stooges—a slap of the hand across the face (of a text).

&

But what are the motives and consequences of multimedia criticism, from a semiotic point of view? To answer this question, it may be helpful to review Derrida's theory of Grammatology *vis a vis* Saussurian linguistics.

Let me see. Oh!

---

23. See Marianna Torgovnick's "Experimental critical Writing" (*Profession 90*) for an insightful discussion of the dialogue between the personal and the academic.

Confronted by such speech acts, represented here in words alone (i.e., solely as textual phenomena) the Saussurian system is tongue-tied. In performance, we see that the exclamations are not part of a single semantic chain, but rather two discontinuous ones brought together by chance: not a command followed by realization (though it could also be that), not "let me see...oh, now I see," but "let me see that," or, reaching out to grasp some thing, or idea, absent mindedly—oops! I've spilled my coffee! —another circumstance intervenes. True, the experience can be linguistically represented—though not re-presented—but it first has to be translated into a form that Saussurian linguistics can understand: i.e., it must be explained, described, transcribed (as in brackets above, stage directions); hence the source of narrative, a story (in this case about words) that can seem to be told in words alone (in a conventional novel, for example, the narrator can translate for us; in a play, the explanation can be "naturally" worked into the dialogue itself). But given the two simple, direct speech acts recorded above, it's hard to tell, going just by their linguistic traces, what story/stories are being told. This demonstrates the circumstantial lack or loss, the something missing or left behind in the direct transcription from experiential semiotic field to graphic-linguistic field, if access to the former is cut off, ignored, or overlooked by the latter. If we want to reenact, re-experience the situation as it happened above, the secondary verbalization required by "writing" (in the conventional sense) generates a further distance, sustains an absence, an abeyance.

But, it could be argued, we can have an experience of language itself—or an equivalent experience in language. True. But then we are talking about nonrepresentational language, and again Saussure can be of little help (Saussurian linguistics is, after all, concerned with meaning, and not abstract language painting; his system depends on the signifier-signified-referent triad, no matter that the sign is arbitrary or motivated). The point here is that no single sign system—verbal, gestural, phonic, pictographic, etc.—is fully adequate or self-substantial; there's always something happening at the margins of any sign system, as at the margins of any particular discourse; all are only moments, thetic moments, in the heteroglossic, collage-like flux that is Writing in a larger semiotic sense.

Let Me See. Oh!

Something suddenly done and the consequence of that, though as printed statements there is uncertainty. Binary analysis is short circuited and the Saussurian doxa faces, if not imminent collapse, at least a moment of self-doubt, a question (?) that corkscrews through its structural integrity. One thing Saussurian linguistics overlooks is the intonation of the words, which can be gotten only in performance and which, of course, can send the meaning in several directions—Let me see. Oh! What a wonderful surprise! Oh! I'm shocked! —shocked! (Oh! I'm [really] shocked!) Oh! Such a disheartening disappointment... (shavizzz!). So there are no fixed signifier-signified-referent relationships. The signifiers above can have quite different meanings and referents, depending on the situation, and while they must always appear the same in print and in a system of fixed binary oppositions that determines their meanings by mutual difference, yet a collocation of various performances of these "same" utterances will reveal their different and even contradictory senses. A particular "sense" may of course be limned by context, but the context itself, if set in alphanumeric code, is deferential, mumming a *mise en scene* that escapes full articulation, a photo illusion fading without a chemical "fix." A moment's insecurity means that we're aware of a something else/other, a something (and to say "thing" is still misleading) missing/we're not getting; my words are not full presences but traces, but of what?

Derrida's concept of writing (like Barthian semiotics), and his theory of Grammatology take into account such surplus, or excess meaning produced by extra-verbal environments (visual, phonic as well as phonemic, performative). This is all part of the expanded semiosis—Writing—of Grammatology. The Saussurian team fumbles its plays in this larger field, not just because it is "language" centered (in a narrow sense), but due to the strategies of its structural analysis. Saussurian linguistics fixes on the difference between self-coherent written signs, rather than on embedded *differance* (often traced, in Derridian analysis, by a homophone or pun). Saussurian linguistics not only depends on (bad) faith in the entitative identity of signs on either side of a binary opposition, but ignores (or evades, detours) extra-literal (or at least extra-graphemic) phenomena as well. Derrida both sees and hears language (and not as a fixed phonemic-signifier-signified construct). Take the classic detouring—deferring, differing—from *difference* to *differance* (which, in French, sound the same, though they are graphemically dissimilar); if we just see or just hear the words (i.e., take them as either written or verbal), then we miss something either way (as Heisenberg discovered earlier in the previous century, if we try to fix the position of an electron, we sacrifice the measure of its momentum); only the spoken and written forms taken together can give us an experience approaching the sense of play that *differance* "means," which suggests the insufficiency of any one approach. Or take the play among "site," "cite," "sight." Any one of the written signifiers, when sounded (off page, or out of sight) can lead by homophone to the other two; a string of ghosted associations and identifications are on the loose. Semantic context may determine selection, but it does not stop (though it impedes) semic (and metonymic) drift. The word in itself is undecidable and indeterminate; signifier-signified relationships that seem fixed at one level dissolve at another: when we see "site," we may imagine a building site, but sounding it we may also be building on quotations. This gratuitous and highly productive play is Grammatology. As Derrida demonstrates, writing occurs within and before speech (i.e., "always already" occurs). Even a grunt is an act of language in the Jakobsonian sense (or stretching the Jakobsonian sense) that involves selection (of certain sounds) along with combination (not necessarily with—or just with—other sound units, but with intonation, facial expression, and gestures). An utterance occurs within a matrix of sign systems; it is, in fact, a crossing and simultaneous overlaying of self-coherent systems—a theory of the sign acknowledged by semiotics in its broadest sense.

The sounded deconstructs the written and vice versa, but the whole field of play is Writing. Just as Derrida deconstructs the hierarchy of speech over writing (in which speech is essentialized as the original and writing as the copy), so he prevents the construction of a counter hierarchy that would subordinate speech to graphic writing. He shows that one inhabits the other from the outset—in fact it is no longer a matter of one or the other, since both are part of the larger phenomenon, Writing. He turns Saussure's "difference" into *differance*, which Saussure was saying all along without knowing/admitting—without *hearing*—it ("I say more than I know," Lacan), just as "*Parole*" (lived language) is a synchronic distortion of "*La Langue*" (a language system, as transmitted diachronically)[24]—one is always already heard through the other, into the future, where what we now speak will also mean

24. See Saussure's *Writings in General Linguistics*, especially parts 1-3.

something other, or yet another. So we should keep on our toes, and off our point. From the point of view of performative criticism, a Text can be seen to exist as a semiotic complex of overlapping sign systems figured forth from an unlimited, multidimensional and multimedia semiosis ("phono-picto-graphic" is Ulmer's hybrid adjective for this breed of textualization); to keep off the point is to remain in circulation among/between these sign systems. The goal of Grammatology, as of Artaudian theater, Ecoian semiotics, and Zen kōan instruction, is not to create a more comprehensive system, but to place all systems on trial by pushing them to their limits, exposing their *aporias*, pushing them till they fall, playing them to exhaustion or, as Kristeva says, seriously, intensely reading them till they break into laughter.

&

We could have come to this point—the value of multimedia presentation of critical works—via another route (or subroute, one of the echoes we've heard, out here, in the rattle of keys). In the *Anti-Oedipus*, Deleuze deconstructs Freudian psychoanalysis with its dependency on the family triangle. Conceiving of the psyche as a desiring machine, he claims that the libido directly invests the social field; in the early stages of psychic development (what would be for Lacan and Freud the pre-Oedipal or pre-genital stages), the child is just as attracted, for example, to an electric wall outlet as to its father's penis. Seeing around and through the massive Oedipal myth, Deleuze reinscribes it as a story told about the field of desiring-production; 19th century psychology is another character in a bourgeois moral tale of the family (along with the division of labor and the concern for provenance and hierarchic structure in language analysis and later, with Saussaure, dualistic semiotics), a repressive conservatism that keeps humanity harnessed to the yoke of "mummy/daddy," as Artaud puts it.

Deleuze's intriguing deconstruction of Freudian psychoanalysis reveals the central role Freud played in the construction of the ideological novel we came to know as 19th century culture and society. The implications for psychoanalysis and, by extension, performative criticism, are tremendous, since, like the open, dialogic text, Deleuze demonstrates how the psyche works itself out over a vast, multimedia (and multidimensional) terrain, of which the nuclear family is only a part.[25]

Despite Freud's narrativization of the unconscious, his psychoanalytic practice, and more significantly his reflections on this practice, foreground key concepts of bricolage criticism. Freud was

---

25. However, this does not alter the significance of certain Freudian concepts and practices to poststructuralist thought, such dream analysis and its obsession with the instability of signs. The case histories became the source and testing ground for the categories Freud developed for dream interpretation, and have since become important to both psychoanalytic criticism and deconstruction. In "Analysis of a Fragment of a Case of Hysteria," for example, opposition (a particular sign "meaning," alluding to, or including its opposite) occurs in the interpretation fire = wetness. Condensation is demonstrated in Dora's first dream of the jewel box, associated with both male and female genitalia and specific events in Dora's past—i.e., a gift from HK; the pearls given by HK to FK are a nexus of similar meanings—drops of sperm, a homosexual desire for FK represented by the drops/pearls that Dora desires but in her dream are given instead to FK. Displacement surfaces in the substitution jewel box-genital above, but also of Freud for HK and both for the father, redirecting and defusing an incestuous desire. Overdetermination occurs in Dora's second dream, where she takes a male role, wandering alone through an uncannily familiar city; many factors determine this scene—photos from a family album, postcards from a potential suitor, her having earlier shown visiting relatives around her own town, etc. Transference passes through the metonymy of cigar smoke (Dora's father, HK, Freud); also, through his role as alter ego, Freud becomes a substitute for Dora's father and plays a complex part in the psychic drama in which she transfers certain behaviors to him, altering the terms of the analyst-analysand relationship and undermining, or at least challenging, the supposedly objective role of the analyst/observer; things Freud says, unconscious behaviors, his very presence partially determine, or interfere with, the progress of the analysis. Ambiguity, or the multilayered polysemy of signs, is also apparent. In Freud's analysis of Dora's dreams, certain signs function as "switch words," allowing one to jump tracks, or travel along different or opposite rails simultaneously, as in the fire-bedwetting equation above. There is actually a more complex matrix in play here: fire relates to passion but also to water, not only to put out the fire but, paradoxically, to feed it—i.e., sexual wetness; so we may trace "fire" along two different paths, one via its apparent opposite, to come to the same point, love. Also, in general, the emphasis on the relationship between language and sexuality, and on signs as displacements for desire are important concepts in poststructuralist thought.

the first to read the unconscious (this is turned about later, of course, by Lacan's theory of language as structured like the unconscious) not by editing it to fit a template of predetermined and fixed symbolic patterns (though he tended to focus on recurring motifs which by now have become Freudian hallmarks, logos of psychoanalysis), but in a case-specific manner. So, for example, in recounting his analytical sessions with the hysteric Dora, he notes how specific daily events—observations, experiences, bits of language—including events in her childhood and the present (the "exciting causes") were translated, by her unconscious, into the symbolic vocabulary from which her dreamwork was composed. Her equation of fire with bedwetting, for example (see n. 25), is not a general "rule" of the unconscious, but a function of Dora's personal history and present circumstances.

Freud, then, especially via Lacan, Deleuze and Slavoj Žižek, has been an important influence on the poststructuralist sense of language as performance—mobile, processual, dynamic, self-interactive, and polysemous. His work is also important from the point of view of the specular reinscription of the other. In reading Freud, our approach to the case histories should be marked by uncertainty and suspicion. Applying his own technique of reading through a negative assertion to its repressed double, when he says we "shouldn't" read the histories as a "*roman a clef*," then of course we should. Freud tells us that the analytical situation made it impossible to take notes, so his reports were written after the fact, from memory. What we get, in the case of a description of a dream, for example, is a double coded inscription—a recollection of a recollection—Freud's memory of a patient's memory of her/his dream; the dream in itself is unknowable, seen only through screens and filters. Also, Freud confesses that where his memory failed him, either losing the thread of an analytical session and/or his initial conclusions, or omitting a specific exchange of dialogue, he filled the lacunaes with materials and deductions from similar cases, creating a kind of patchwork from different times, circumstances, and voices; the seams, though they can be traced, are by no means clearly marked. Where is Freud inventing, where inserting from earlier or later findings? how much of the dialogue is as it occurred? how much is Freud the novelist, building toward suspenseful conclusions, and how much is reportage (itself a dissembling concept)? We cannot not approach the text without a degree of suspicion, some slight dis-ease, knowing we can't really know what it is we are reading. Also, Freud admits that in transcribing Dora's second dream he put things down not as they "happened," but as they came to mind during his "rewriting" which, for us, is the only place they can happen. We are encouraged to reenact the analytical experience in reading Freud's text—i.e., we approach the text with the same sense of doubt and ambiguity he shows when interpreting dreams, suspecting that for whatever is said, there is a surplus or excess, a ghosted other, something not said or something in addition. Performative criticism, as well as other reader-performative theories of textual interpretation/intervention (such as psychofeminism, dialogism and discourse analysis, reader response theory, and poststructuralist ethnographic theory) have had their sessions with Freud.

&

*

Recall (re-envision) the Poe "canvas" imaged toward the beginning of this introduction. And/or imagine this: a pure tone, a sign wave, in sight and sound; a man alone mumbling, his mumblings merging with other mumblings, in other registers. There is no off-stage, as we see preparations being made for the next "event" (but what was the previous one? we are always already ahappenin'). Now, an ordinary story is being told, riddled by beams of light (streaming not from lasers, of course, but household, hand-held flashlights...).

*

When one starts challenging limits, as Derrida did generally; when one starts playing with language (moving nonlogically through puns and homophones, or indiscreetly crossing the bar that separates one linguistic identity from another, as Barthes' *S/Z*), then one becomes performative as a writer and reader, willfully recreating texts or, in the case of a Text that encourages reader intervention/participation, co-creating them. In romantic prosody—especially *via* Coleridge and Wordsworth—the author figured himself as a co-creator with nature; in the postmodern era, since we can view "nature" as inscription rather than a stand in for the Lacanian Real, the term has shifted from co-creator to reinscriber, collaborator, or, perhaps, co-director, indicating the potentially endless plurilogue among reader-writers, readings and the written, for we are all both readers and writers, rewriting the written, rewriting "nature," if not the Real. An interpreter, then, is also an "original author" (in the same capacity that any author can be "original" who works from within his/her own, or that of his/her social group's, ideology), creating her/his own analytical fictions. The bar between critic and ("primary") author has always been an imaginary and convenient one, stemming from an era in love with taxonomies and subjectivities; now, in an age of simulacra and metafictions, we can see ourselves equally all as co-creators of each other's textual selves. And, as discussed above, our field of play has (if we attend to it) broadened to include extra-verbal materials. There is no reason to frame a self-coherent text of printed words out of the multifarious semiosis of which it is a part; all (the whole set of interrelations, to paraphrase Dilthey), as Derrida has demonstrated, is writing, and when as writers (interpreters/original authors, the distinctions collapse) we allow the nonverbal into our "texts," we cross the boundary between written and gestural enactment, between silent reading performance and sounding of the Text. We see Texts not as end results, as completed works, but as open works; not as fully present entities at the final stage of a teleological process (as long as there is yet another reader, yet another performance), but as way stations, networks and gathering points of discourses, nodes of energy exchange, vortexes—like primitive theaters, where discourses meet (readers', authors', texts'), affectively interact, and disperse, reconfiguring and permuting indefinitely as discourse contexts change. This does not mean that there are no distinctions, no differences among interpreter's text(s) and interpreted text(s), between writerly performance and gestural enactment, between one discourse and another or among several discourses and rhetorical positionings, but that these phenomena are continually in dialogue with each other and themselves, and that they are not self-coherent entities but always already undermined (indeterminable) from within. Such loss of permanence, of clear-cut identity and stable definitions need not cause anxiety, however, if we have learned to let go—let it "drop," as poet Michael McClure says—if we accept and practice semiotic non-attachment.

&

C(s)i(gh)ting the Grail

Performing criticism, in a writerly or somatic format, means putting our(scriptive)selves in a field where borders are always subject to change and never exclusively or clearly defined, where local strategies, if not the "rules" of play, are situational, generated by bricolage method. In an interview with Burton Hatlen, Carl Rakosi describes late poet Robert Duncan's eye disorder: while speaking, he would fix you with one eye as the other wandered freely (Hatlen, "Interview with Carl Rakosi"); as critics and readers, we must be imaginatively strabismic, fixing on textual structures, however temporary, while moving freely around, through, between, and behind various textual positions, following word sounds, associations, puns, resemblances, dissemblances, divergences; we must explore uncharted territory, follow cross-textual leads and clues that may lead nowhere, if hermeneutical closure is the goal, or that may reveal breaches (*briseur*) opening into Text. With the text flat open on the desk, the blocks of print are undeniable, self-present facts. The page is silent and white, selfless, a prop and background, the virgin mother to the babes of articulation, absorbing light. Yet, as we turn the page (still bound at the spine with all others—the *charniere*, hinge, turning point) it becomes translucent, as the text on the other side bleeds through (now the *charniere* sans *gond*-without its pin, hinge unhinged). There is the Other present in the one, the not-I in the I, the shadow of not-self in the self (and *charniere* is just a grapheme away from *charnier*—the "mass grave" of epistemological solvency). There is no more recto v. verso, as they "vecto" into each other. *Legends*, a collaborative book by several of the Language poets, plays on this effect by printing the "image" of a poem—front and back of a typescript—recto and verso on a single leaf. Should we ignore such textual phenomena? Turn the page quickly don't look get on with it—" produce" the reading; we have a product to put out, our attainment of understanding, consumption of knowledge, don't look *now*.... We seek some *thing*—resolution, goal, end to effort, realized structure dissolving into a reality-effect, a moment of achieved being, a "home," an evocation of Truth produced by the diligent pursuit, if we are readers, or angst-ridden erection, if we are "writers," of syntactic and semantic neighborhoods—yet we may overlook (over read) the infinite play of Text. Like the narrators in Alain Robbe-Grillet's *The Erasers* and in Poe's "The Man in the Crowd," we cruise the impenetrable surface of the hermeneutical narrative, never any closer to finding what we seek only *because* we seek it, while this wandering, uncharted flow, this potentially endless cross-textual, intertextual and un-author-ized circulation of language and imagery is always already our (anti)destination. Such digressive, wasteful activity, such exegetical detritus produced in the wake of interpretative closure—such gratuitousness is *most* productive.

Essentially, performing criticism means attentive, self-reflexive practice, a working with text, rather than pre-scriptive or automatic coding of textual activity. Performative critics refuse to claim total comprehension of Texts; they are willing to sacrifice structure, clearly defined or unidirectional focus, and even alphanumeric catwalks to allow themselves now and again to wander freely and at large—" go native"—within and around texts. In *Drifting on a Read*, Michael Jarrett offers jazz improvisation as a paradigm for postmodern critical writing, in as much as improvisation signifies on, or interprets, a host melody; Jarrett observes that in musical notation, the *obbligato* is an ornamentation or supplement to the printed score, whereas in jazz improvisation, the supplement is required—"excess becomes essence" (64). I am willing and thrilling to let my writing be affected by my reading, to riff on my readings—analytic excessiveness, lyric generality, and ribald conceit are sometimes the result[26]—to give up the life raft of an authoritative stance

26. Experimental filmmaker Pete Rose's *The Pressure of the Text* (1983, 17mins.; www.peterrosepicture.com), a witty parody of crit-speak (a kind of "Ph.D vaudeville," as a *Boston Globe* reviewer phrased it) demonstrates how critical discourse, if left to its own rhythms and devices—rereading itself, so to speak—can generate (or degenerate into) a glossolalic, self-deconstructive self-performance. At the beginning of the film, Rose, as a be-spectacled academic, promising to be "concrete" and "avoid generalizations," pedantically announces the basic premise of his lecture—to discuss "issues we've all been thinking about... the whole idea of language, and in particular its relation to a kind of 'body-tongue'." The lecture quickly becomes incomprehensibly abstract, to the point of devolving, ironically, as promised, into its opposite: As the pace of the "lecture" speeds up, it becomes inceresingly less intelligible, yet phonically and viscerally more concrete as the lecturer, excited and agitated by turns (perhaps frustrated by his own self-incomprehensibility) spews a string of heavily consonantal vocables, derived from a remix of critical terminlogy and fragments of critical terms, permuting eventually into the passionate jabber of an invented language; the recombinant academic remix streams as pure jargon (i.e., nonsense)that seems to restructure itself into an untranslatable language. The mashup of critical discourse eventually chrystalizes in a quote from

and flow with the text, rather than dress the Text to suit the hermeneutical party ("flow" in Schechner's sense: dramatic flow involves the loss of the (ego of the) actor in her/his enactment, which is not to say in a representational illusion of character—Brechtian performances can have flow). To achieve flow in critical writing requires a sacrifice of the authorial/authoritative identity of the hermeneut/interpreter; it may also lead (as it has in the current collection) to a letting go our obsession with words (even though at one extreme this fetishization frees words from semantic chains to become self-sufficient art objects, as in *Lettrisme*—see above, n. 19) and opening the critical field to a condition of mixed semiosis. When criticism becomes meditative, multimedia practice, it achieves flow, and perhaps is no longer "criticism." This is the risk.

As poststructuralist ethnographers and/or literary critics, we can learn from the Jewish Midrashic and Zen tiesho traditions: we can gain most satisfaction not from a delimiting self-validation, but from disintegrative euphoria, by opening ourselves and our texts to as much as possible of what there is to be discovered in the life of the Other, of the Text (including its life as, in Jerome McGann's words, a "social text"). We must become "feminine," in Lacan's, sense, in our encounters with texts (woman = "not all"). We must initiate the critical act with an attitude of mind-opening self-doubt, an awareness that we never have it *all*, a potentially productive sense of inadequacy. Are we ready to acknowledge our involvement with the text/other, our willingness to offer "partial" readings of the Other, to lose ourselves in the text and live with the loss, to let it always go beyond us (as the found material in Ezra Pound's *Cantos*)?

There is a Grail; it has always been where Parzival left it—in a state of mind and contour of experience. Parzival, like a wandering hermeneut, obsessed with finding the meaning of the Grail, gives up his narrative quest—paradoxically ceases following the tracks in the story and loses track of the story—so that the narrative can reach its goal—the dis-covering of the Grail. The oppositional rhythms of

---

Wittgenstein, appearing as a subtitle on an imageless (black) background, as the soundtrack falls silent: "Whereof one cannot speak, thereof one must be silent." By bearing down on—signifying on—its signifying practices, the text undermines its identity as a detached, authoritative account of (textual and/or other) phenomena, and becomes itself an irreducible, intractable, unaccountable and un-re-presentable phenomenon.

Text must yet remain active beyond the frame of the epic and beyond containment in any one semiotic system if the whole t_f(T)text is to be found. Similarly, to disinterpret is to disenchant critical stories told about texts, to break the spell of hermeneutic orthodoxy and to re-enchant the critical enterprise with a vision of multimedia heteroglossia. This collection presents a theory of critical performance, a justification of a writing practice, and a practice of that theory—an anti-narrative of what we do when we do interpreting. Others may find a direct path more appealing; it may lead them to the Grail. Yet we are all implicated by the search: all of us, as our paths parallel, intersect, contradict, are at once and interminably here, in these letters — s e a a r c h r e a c h — in the endless variations of this search that is the Grail. Text = Grail.

*****

In the foregoing, I have attempted to lay out the theoretical groundwork for a multimedia(ted) approach to semiotic analysis, distinguishing between "writerly" and more fully performative critical projects. Following this introduction are six examples of performative criticism, each focusing on a specific American literary and/or cultural site/cite: Niagara Falls (i.e., the history of representations and simulations, from the 16th century to the present, that *are* the "Falls," from the point of view of cultural semiotics, focusing especially on Margaret Fuller's and Henry James' travel writings), Objectivist poet Charles Reznikoff's *Testimony: The United States 1890-1915* (a poetic portrait of America based on trial transcripts), the 1955 Six Gallery reading in San Francisco (headlined by Allen Ginsberg, Gary Snyder, Michael McClure, Philip Whalen, and Philip Lamantia) that awoke America to Beat-bop rhythms, Marilyn Monroe as produced in the 1953 film *Niagara*, and the 1968 Democratic National Convention in Chicago (the resulting piece re-visions Yippie antics leading up to and during the 1968 DNC as Fluxus performances, casting Abbie Hoffman as Yip-Zen clown). This section of the book concludes (circling back to, or re-cycling, the 19th-century) with a reproduction of my performance collage/artist's book, *Stirr'd Up Everywhere*, a textual reenactment of a multimedia critical performance based on Walt Whitman's Civil War/nature diary *Specimen Days* (the typescript is cacographically overwritten with translucent colored markers). Preceding the "Postface" (a self-effacing head borrowed from Jerome Rothenberg), which returns, in tone and spirit, to the more broadly-based theorizations of the "Introductory manifesto," two "Closing Gestures," spinning off the Monroe Project (Chapter 5), offer some final considerations of the role of performative criticism—as realized by TEZ productions in particular (see below)—within a hybrid RL/VR cultural condition.

Since the book's chapters, straddling personal, historical, and cultural contexts, are formatted to be read as multi-discourse critical texts and scripts for multimedia (re)enactment, a brief head-note, including a description of the *mise en scene* of the text as previously staged, a discussion of performance variants of the piece (where applicable), and a brief comment on the critical/theoretical goals of the piece, introduces each script. In addition to sharing an agenda—to deploy cultural "texts" as vehicles for performative critical (self) intervention, i.e., critical (s)mashups—these chapters are linked by shared thematic concerns and by partial material recyclings—imagistic and theoretical refrains—creating patterns of unity and transformation through diverse semiotic territories. As indicated above, the pieces play on a wide range of current theoretical concerns and cultural issues, including the construction of gender, the role of the critic in constructing the literary or cultural text she/he analyzes, the influence of dominant discourses (such as academic and legal discourse and product design ideology) on the creation and evaluation of cultural objects, and the role of the consumer/audience in cultural (re)production. While each performance script has its own list of works cited, I also include, in the end, a select bibliography of theoretical sources and other performance-oriented work relevant to the current project.

TEZ Bit

In 1995, I founded the critical performan 1ce group TEZ (Techno-Eschatological Zippers, Telos-Entropy Zoomers, Theo-Epistemological Zappers, go on...), which has presented versions of the pieces at literature and performance studies conferences in the US, Canada, and the UK. Founding member Ellen La Forge created digital imagery for the "Monroe Project" and the "Beat Poetry Games" and had a hand in designing elements of the sets for the "Monroe Project," "Niagara on the Rocks," and "Poetics of Protest." In addition to this word and image collaboration, the texts of the scripts incorporate bits of dialogue and arguments that took place during the drafting process ("Niagara on the Rocks"), as well as whole chunks of material in voices other than my own (founding member Zoe Randall's "Monroe-Me" (auto)bio, for example, included in the "Monroe Project"); bits of "field" data—recorded, first-hand interviews ("Niagara on the Rocks"); quoted blocks of Critical Legal Studies theory ("Legal Discourse v. Poetic Discourse"); advertising and other consumer—newspaper and magazine—text ("The Beat Poetry Games"); transcripts from the Chicago Seven Trials, quotes from other period documents and a "current events" fact sheet ("Poetics of Protest"); material from Whitman's *Specimen Days*—including quotes from Civil War soldiers—and critical commentary on Whitman's work (*Stirr'd Up Everywhere*).

As the above instances of collaboration indicate, the scripts gathered in *Off the Page* are broadly in dialogue with their cultural *milieu* (from the immediate and personal to the most distant commercial discourses). The *mise en scenes* of TEZ performances, built around a variety (store) of techno-props, interrogate and (critically) exploit the possibilities of a wide range of pop technologies, from the silly (such as computerized audio toys and helicopter-launching pens) to the sophisticated ("live" digital painting), in a context of Fluxus-oriented, though textually rich, performance art. However, while the TEZ aesthetic is kaleidoscopic, deriving from the perception of a semiotically multifaceted postmodern condition of competing discourses, every gesture in a TEZ performance is sourced in the host text(s); there is quite a bit of gratuitousness, but nothing arbitrary. TEZ deploys performance, in Jon McKenzie's definition, as a "mode of experimental resistance" attempting to conduct "mutational forces across the entire performance stratum, releasing desires and intensities from the contexts that constrain them"; often contained within academic conference settings, they work especially at the "interstices of institutions...temporarily subverting [or at least calling Into question] their normative functions" (McKenzie, 235, 8). For more about the group, or to contact us, please visit the TEZ web (www.tezperformance.org) (in an off moment, or at work when no one's looking...).

***

A note on indexes. The book does not have one. If included, I left the page blank for the reader to chart her/his own correspondences. An index can be, in the vein of Daniel Spoerri's *An Anecdoted Topography of*

Chance (see n. 14, above), not only a concordance of cited terms and authors, but also a tracking of cross-textual associations/connections among (dis)similar terms/concepts. Such an "Index" would self-subvert its function as a GPS for specific references by offering an alternative *methodos* for reading—or performing a reading of—the subject/text: whereas some terms could chart the same through a sequence of pages (albeit a sameness with a difference—in context), others could divine a *difference*, veering away (from the self-same) based on sound, image, and/or concept resonances. In the event of this collection, "Whirlpool" could "index" "dynamos" and, alliteratively, "swirling" (as well as other whirlpools), while "whirlwind" corresponds with "spin," "spiraling," "twisters" ...

&

Let the voice of the mani(in)festo have the last word. Not only by an extravagant style, as Geoffrey Hartman describes it (*Criticism in the Wilderness*), but by an answerable style, can we give the reader an experience of a text, and not just words about it. As critics, we can choose either to respond creatively to texts, or to keep our distance from them. A creative response does not mean simply losing oneself in a text, or only becoming self-reflexively aware of the ideologies, theories, and expectations one brings to a text, but also following a text's leads, wherever (through whatever semiotic wilderness) they may take us, being able to "shape shift," like the Hindu goddess Dolma who exists in twenty-one forms—now playing the authoritative critic, now the intimately involved reader, now the investigative, scholarly editor; by turns performer *and* director, (co)creator and commentator, but never resting in any one position or claiming to have possession, or total knowledge, of the text. We must be ready, as the chapters of this book demonstrate, to write performance—works that have their fullest effect in live, multimedia presentation. The cup, be it goblet or chalice, always becoming something other, always in (re:)search, is unfathomable, immeasurable. In the game of performative criticism, there can be no hermeneutic (or formal) closure; no static, readerly reflection but, to (re)cite Zukofsky, only a "rested totality." $c_f[t(T)] = (P)$.

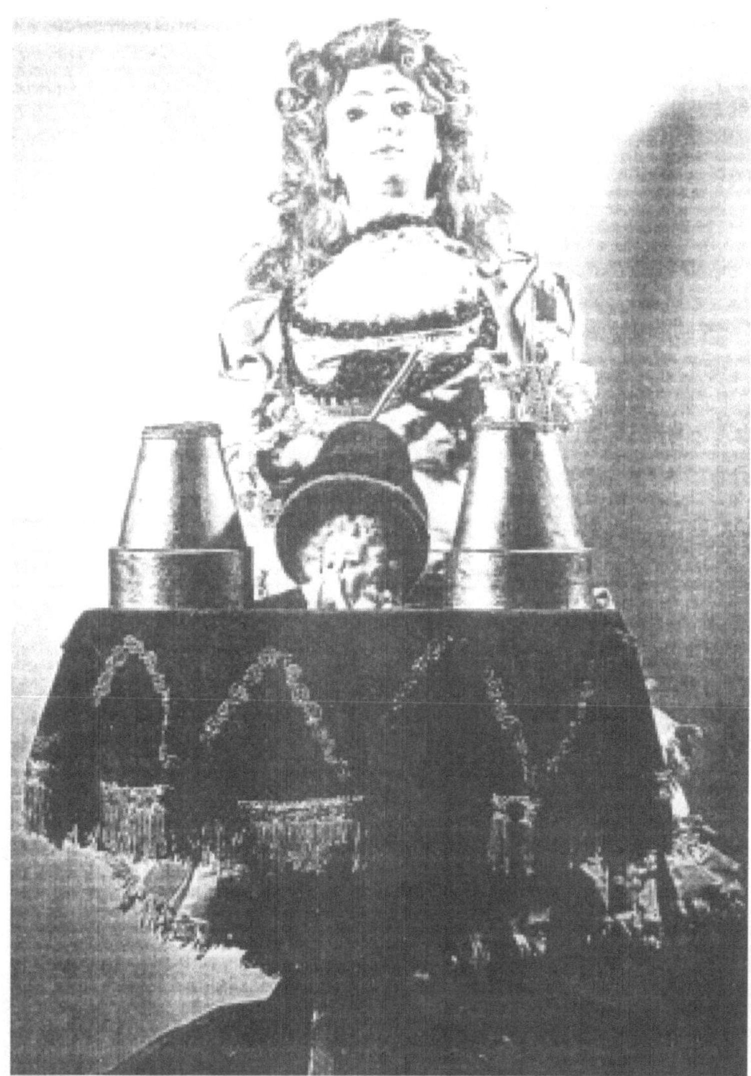

Fig. 2: The magician's double. New York Public Library. Public domain.

Let's Go Textualizing

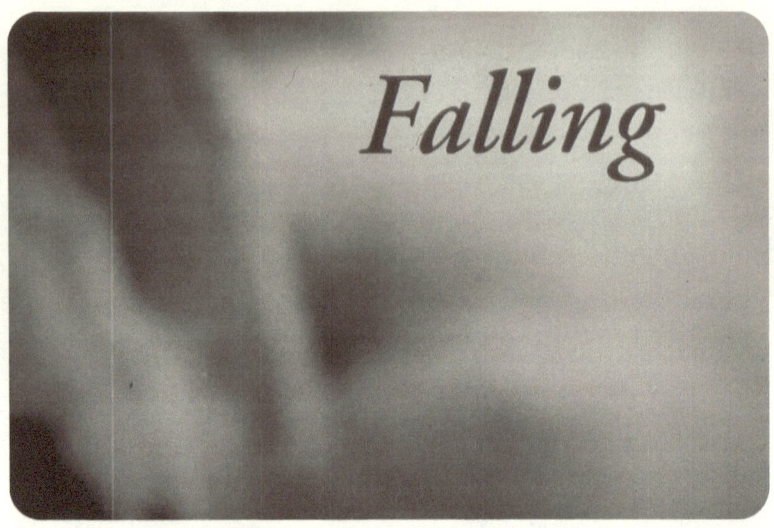

Fig. 3: Writing the falls . . .

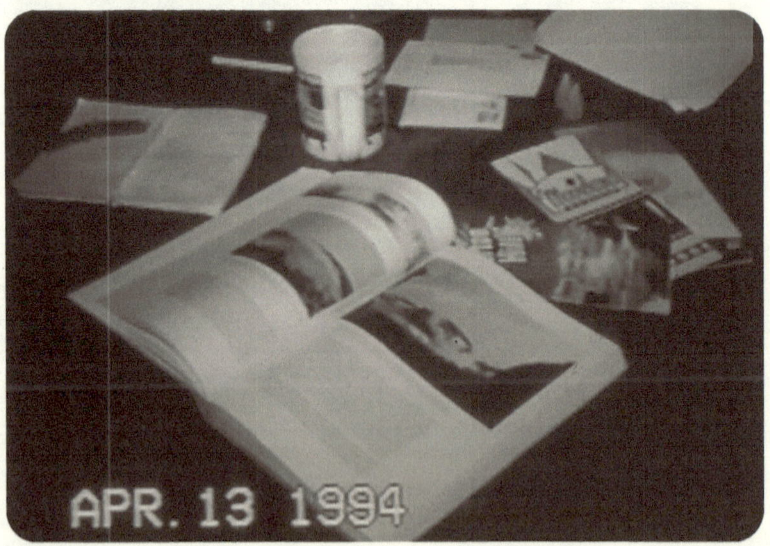

Fig 3a: The Falls being written . . .

2 Script 1: Niagara on the Rocks: Fissuring Margaret Fuller, Henry James and a Strata of Other Voices (with Zoe Randall, TEZ)

Performers: T, E, Z

The setup. A large strip of newsprint attached to a wall or sandwich board, sequencing (not necessarily in order of occurrence) the thirteen segments (or modules, or "scenes") of the performance; when a segment is performed, it is crossed off or checked for possible reperformance. Two long conference tables, at the center and margins of the performance space, containing an array of props, including "actual" Falls souvenirs. Two large roll-out movie screens, toward the rear on each side, for slide projections. Two music black stands down front containing small sound-effects devices and other props. Three video monitors: one on a mobile cart, in the main performance area; another deep center, outside the boundaries of action; the third monitor up front, off to the side—it will become a video window, featuring "live" computer manipulations of the Falls, and a "personalized" souvenir tour, in later scenes. Front and center are a small table and two chairs, to be used in the "Falls Fashions" and "Modern Housekeeping Cabins" segments. Large, 3-D numbers, which illuminate on cue, are placed on the floor, screens, and prop tables: tour stops, action-by-number.

On the first video monitor (mounted on the mobile cart) appears a "home movie" fetishization of the Falls, manipulated and overwritten with a character generator (see Video Appendix); the tape is manipulated at various points during performance (paused—" frozen"—rewound, rerun, fast forwarded, stopped, started). The second monitor (rear center) presents a spot lit souvenir hunt through the dark of our Manhattan apartment, intercut with a night walk along the Niagara River to the verge of the Falls; this tape runs continuously, "offstage," in the dark gap between slide projections, its slow-motion expressionistic eeriness further distorted by manipulating color and contrast controls on the monitor...

During the piece's single intermission, a little mechanical fountain dribbles muckish water over a strata-gram of the Falls; the fountain is banked with jelly candies in the shape of "American Indian" heads and animals; orange candy circus peanuts are distributed in small brown paper bags labeled generically: "one edible property"

****

As the audience enters, a simulated trill sounds over and over; the source is a mechanical bird hung upside down mid stage. T walks about the stage, scattering colorful miniature marshmallows, and eventually sticks one over the bird's beak, at the same time as he clamps its feet together, causing the song to abruptly stop.

He exits. E releases a mechanical weasel chasing a ball; it tumbles about the stage until T reappears, rushes for the toy and pounces on it, pulling the ball apart to expose the mechanism.

T [*To himself, amplified*]: "So that's how it works!" [*exits quickly...*]

[Tape 1—"Rose, Rose..."
Joseph Cotton, soundtrack from *Niagara*.
Generally, audiotape effects consist of sound clips
from *Niagara* collaged with documentary material,
including shopping mall interviews;
see "**Audio List**" for a more complete
description of individual cuts]

[slides: abstract color washes
derived from "night walk" vid. (see above);
title fragments]

[*voice "offstage"*]

THERE IS A LINE TO FOLLOW—A BRAID OF MANY STRANDS,
SUSPENDED BETWEEN ANY TWO POINTS. KEEPING YOUR BALANCE
IS THE TRICK—LEANING AGAINST THE SHIFTING WINDS
OF DISCOURSE, WHITE NOISE BELOW. YOU'VE GOT TO LISTEN
WITH THE WHOLE BODY...

[*Z & T cross and re-cross the performance space, "throwing" their voices into the surrounding darkness via telescoping plastic baffles of MegaMouth*™ *portable sound effects devices (courtesy Toys 'R Us)*]

Niagara on the Rocks:

Fissuring Margaret Fuller, Henry James,

and a Strata of Other Voices.

A **Complete Scenario,**

including Appendices, Bibliography,

and **Precise Stage Directions**

for Performance, along with

Descriptions of Properties, Interlinear Commentaries,

and inscription of the

Original Scene of Performance

in *Vancouver, British Columbia,*

on the

________ *day of April, nineteen hundred* ______

[*Z & T exit*]

(*unless otherwise noted, E's is an "offstage" voice, spoken softly, but amplified—a voiceover, disembodied presence—from the "tech booth"—itself a component of the* mise en scene)

[slides A, B: blank]

E: "Ah we ke yat."

T [*entering*]: Repeat…

Z [*offstage*]: Tears.

E: It could be raining.

Z [*crossing stage in yellow poncho, exiting*]: "I want to walk."

T: "what's wrong?"

E: It is raining…

T: Say something.

E, Z: "Ahwekeyat":

E: "end of the water."

[Tape 2: "Look, honey, you can
see it from here…"]

T: It's ok. We can do it again… at least it's all here… or most of it… [*exit*]

E: Vancouver: "Niagara" neon streams ghost light down brick wall, mirages pools in darkened grimy windows…

Z [*entering*]: "You can stay there, but it's…uh… not a very nice place":

T [*entering*]: Call girls? low down striptease…

E: Perhaps table dancing?

Z: Room 1250, Simon Fraser University. Several long conference tables… One has become a prop table…

T: like a shelf in a variety store…

Z: another will itself become a prop for certain scenes. A video monitor on a wheeled cart big enough to ride in;

E: perhaps to go over in…

Z: the monitor also plays a choreographed part.

T [*as Z fans out tourist brochures*]: when it enters this space within… the space enclosed by… that space where the performance will be served, space which will become a semiotic field of play, which, up to now, has been traversed by the discourse of presenter and respondent… questions…? We will take fifteen minutes for…)
[Tape 3: foghorn]

E: [*Z & T begin to distribute brochures*] **Pas de Trois with Video or, Electronic Media and the Dialectics of Desire** [*when a section is completed, it is crossed off the "Big List" with a giant Niagara pencil.*]

E: Distribute tourist brochures [*pause as T & Z distribute*] …

T [*examining props, picks up a black plastic top hat, revealing*]: a white unicorn in a glass filled globe! [*Nothing! Z examines T*]

[Tape 4: "Oh!"]

E: Put on the hat and hold the paperweight in both hands [*T does one, not the other*], close in to your body, at genital level... Roll in Falls [*Z rolls in the Falls*].

T: Snow drifts through water; a depthless Maid of the Mist slides jerkily past a 2 D Falls... [*moves toward TV*]

Z [*finding unicorn*]: (I am several feet away.)

[slide C: shadow wash and text;
cut to black]

E [*as Z picks up the unicorn*]: falling... [*appears briefly on screen, superimposed over fall of color or shadow*]

*

Z: Question: do ladies ever go under the falls?

E: (*Every Man His Own Guide...*, 1852, page 45. See bib.)
[*the answer: Z winds or pretends to wind the unicorn music box, offering it to T; it is beyond his reach; E simultaneously winds another music box—a second unicorn, with broken leg, its globe lost; she amplifies the irritable, cranking sound as T bows jerkily to*]: the lightless screen—a mirage self, a hand reaching out... [*T tips hat, extends hand with imaginary paperweight toward screen*] stationary camera, from a distance; white noise—falling water...
Z: speaker static?

E: Slight alterations in the texture... it's not a still image... [*T straightens*]

[slides A, B: series of 3-4
colorized stills from Falls video;
cut to black]

Z: Coming attractions: light effects electronically produced in the camera while recording, pulsing through the image a spasmodic bio-code, echoed by a leitmotif of freeze frames created impromptu during studio editing sessions.

E: Various inscriptions, also generated during these sessions (see "The Falls: The Movie" appendix) will overwrite* the "blank page" of...

[Tape 5: "Rose...Rose..."]

T: overdetermine the video representation of...

E [*T dances jerkily to music box rhythm*]: one note at a time [*as T turns, Z turns—two close, disconnected figures on a music box*]

[slide B: color wash and text,
falling, cut to black]

[Tape 6, MM Sings "Kiss"
from soundtrack of *Niagara*]

E [*overlapping tape*]: a confluence of...

Z: shall we dance? [*T, getting the swing of it, and the unicorn, begins to dance around the video monitor*]

E: music-box groom—unpinned!

Z: video-box bride, unmoved...

E [*after MM's "per fec tionnnn..." Z screeches in with a New Year's Eve noise maker; T stumbles back into productive motion—see below*]: Various sonic devices are used to interrupt and mark scenes... Mall tape!

[Tape 7: shopping mall interviews]

Pause Falls, Roll back. [*T has placed the hat and paperweight back on the table, and crosses off* **Pas de Trois** *Z performs as instructed, rolls Falls back and to one side of the performance space.*]

T: rock... falling rock...

***

Z: Question: should we preserve it as it is now, as it was, or as it will be at some future point when it reaches optimum quality?

[slides B: 3 in quick succession,
dissolving into each other:
human form silhouetted against the Falls,
backing into it,
diminishing...]

T [*bringing Falls forward, releasing it; handing Z an envelope*]: This just came for you.

Z [*reading title on envelope*]: "natural forces at work on the falls" [*hold on action*]

[slide A, B: parallel frozen Falls]

E: American Falls International Board, *Preservation and Enhancement...* (also opening question, above; see bibliography: This is a report made by a joint team of Canadian and U.S. engineers and presented to the Secretary of State, Washington, D.C., and the Secretary of State for External Affairs, Ottawa, Canada:

[slide A, B: cut to black]

T: The answer is... [*T freezes Falls; Z opens envelope, remains in tableau*]

E [*mysteriously*]:

12 May, 1953

Sir,

I have the honour to transmit a copy of the Report of the International Joint Commission to the Governments of Canada and the United States of America on remedial works necessary to preserve and enhance the scenic beauty of the Niagara Falls and River... [*Z lets bits of torn paper fall*] in accordance with...

[Tape 8: eerie music, swash]

T: The Reference of October 10, 1950, reads: "Recommendations concerning the nature and design of the remedial works necessary to enhance the beauty of the Falls in the Niagara River *by distributing the waters so as to produce an unbroken crestline on the Falls* [italics mine], in accordance with..."

E: the objectives of the ... bearing in mind the provisions of the... recommendations concerning the allocation of the task of construction of...
T:

Niagara on the Rocks:
Fissuring...

[slides A, B: sudden bright images—
colorful drawings and maps of Falls,
seen from above; cut A to black]

[*to audience*] (There are actually two reports, one presented on 12 May, 1953—including the above "Letter of Transmittal"—and the other on 6 June, 1974; the previous citations are from the latter.)

[slide B: Tommy Trent's
cartoon "going over"; cut to black]

E [*low, intense*]: *The envelope is empty* [*Falls off. Z crumples envelope; E crumples scrap of paper, amplified. Both toss*]

E: "Tehatkahtous..."

T: "I have the honour to be, Sir,"

[slides A & B: black]

Z: "looking all over..."

[*T distributes cue cards to Z & E*]

*

***

*

E: **Your Tour Guides**

[*E, Z & T prompt each other during the following scene with cue cards*]

T: (Z begins, I think… "Ladies and gentlemen…") …

[slides A, B: flash, hold, black:
two stunters, one waving from a barrel,
the other with head bandaged]

Z [*blows whistle; E cues*]: Hi! Welcome to Negative Ion Tours

T [*Z cues*]: Those happy little genital ticklers…

E [*T cues*]: (see Donaldson, *Niagara, the Eternal Circus*, 228).

Z [*E cues*]: I'm Jan

T [*Z cues*]: changed to Halley, for the H

E [*T cues*]: and I'm Jimmy

Z [*E cues*]: changed to Mike, for M

T & Z [*Z cues*]: And we're your tour guides today! [*T cues: "chummy laughter"*]

T: Well, where should we begin, Halley?

E: Janly

Z: Well, Mikey…

E: Jimmmm

E: M, my name is Margaret, my husband's name is…

Z: you know everyone begins at the falls [*Falls on*], so let's start there

T: (*Donaldson, Niagara, the Eternal circus, p. 230. Jimmy/Mike's tone is artificial enough; quotation marks are unnecessary*) In addition to first hand on the spot eyewitness accounts, you will hear accurate and authentic reproductions of historical voices, visitors of previous centuries...

[slide B, flash & fade:
neon musketeer]

Z: In comfortable ideomobiles, or all-rhetoric vehicles, you will trace various discourse paths over about and through the falls [*T displays comic book-like, illustrated map of Niagara Falls*], "a pleasant way to get an overview"

[slide A, flash and fade: night highway
from T's video trip to Niagara]

T: (*phrase compliments of Favorite Short Trips in New York State.*) a journey through representations...through representations of representations*

E: F for...

*[slide A, flash & fade:
man in souvenir shop, seated next to tripod
that later disappeared]

Z: a five-minute spin over the falls in a... what looks like a

T: (fragments from Webster, Harriet. *Favorite Short Trips in New York State*) ... natural wonder, source of power, climax of the Great Lakes system, tourist attraction, great lyric poetic experience

[slide B: rack of *Niagara Mystery* comic books]

Z: (see section 7, Preservation and Enhancement...) a plastic bubble with a propeller on top!

E: H, for Harriet

T: See a multitude of re(pro)ductions of the* Falls...

*[slide B, flash and fade: fountain spray CU]

Z: from naive renditions to sophisticated diagrammatic analyses...

T: Hear excerpts from the U.S. Congress, Senate,* Committee on Public Works... *Hearings*: actual dialogues! —plans to litigate the flow, to "restore the scenic beauty" and for "Power and other purposes and other purposes..."

*[slide A: *Hearings*, title page; the
effect is as of a play bill]

Z: of the most accessible and famous... (*Fodor's Vacations in New York*)

T: See how Niagara's crestline has altered

[slide A: poster from *Niagara*
starring Marilyn Monroe and Joseph Cotton;
an enlarged M M, accentuated curve of hip, reclining at the lip of the
horseshoe
—its concave echoing (with a roar?) her convex]

E: Mmmmm for

Z: Follow the scripts of Niagara's—" Niagara, The Tour's"—earliest authors [*T "tours" space*] to create a dramatic viewing experience...

[slide B: Johnson's *Everyman's Guide...*,
title page; playbill effect; cut to black]

T: Or be your own director [*Z displays Fodor's* Vacations in New York]: choose among the numbered sites: rearrange citations from a contemporary guide; block out a personal path within the prefabricated cultural space...

Z [*coming forward*]: But no Niagara "happening" is complete without...

T [*running upstage*]: don't be afraid to reenact the...

Z [*legs spread, head back*]: "ludic explosion..."

T [*thrusting head between Z's legs*]: (Rob Shields):

Z: choose among various props [*point out props, like game show prizes*]—"

commodified embodiments of North American sexual fantasies"

T: (Shields *Places on the Margin* 153—see bib!).

Z & T: Niagara—The Fetish:

Z: do it yourself!

[slide A—Z caressing her naked back
with a two-handed plastic backscratcher;
cut to black]

T: The praxinet parallel portal is the primary point of entry to the Niagara semiotics area, from above...

E: syntax courtesy Fodor's *Vacations in New York State*

Z: This is Niagara, the Hyperreal...

[slide B: cover of *Tommy Trent's Niagara Falls Mystery!*
a comic book history of the Falls]

T: You may shop at the House of Simulations

Z: we also have mimes, magic tricks, a striptease, diorama, and stunts... [*T mimes: closes a curtain, spins around, curtain "rods" becoming gestures to audience, directing them into image*]
T: Niagara—a vector through cyberspace: HTTP:\\www.fall.gathering and dispersal of * discourses!

*[slide A: empty film can
in the "can" (airport men's room)]

E: "Have you been...?"

T: "It's got to be on the tour..."

Z: "you've got to see..."

E: "we'll meet you at..."

Z: "want your picture with...?"

T [*dropping to knees, crooner style*]: arrangements from available facsimiles in the Americana bargain bins!

Z: Yes, they do take plastic...

E: (Fodor's *Vacations in New York State*).
Z: (Holograph signatures only, please!)

T: A 20-minute minitour of the pop culture phenomenon includes a glimpse into the making of "Niagara—Bottoms Up" plus a ride in the "subliminator" for a highly elevated view of this technologically sophisticated "earth work" (not recommended for the literal minded) ...

[slide B: Ride Niagara brochure, fade;
cut A, B to black]

Z: (rhetorical outline supplied by Fodor's *Vacations*) an information booth, displays, automated vending, and daily screenings of *Naturally Niagara*, which captures the falls from every possible position in 70mm and six-channel sound

T: (adapted from Fodor's *Vacations*) you will definitely "get wet"

[slide A, flash and fade:
"Indian maiden" going over]

Z: (*Vacations*); of course, it's all perfectly safe

T: (ditto). But any tour of Niagara Falls begins with the falls themselves...

E: (Fodor, Donaldson—public domain)

[slides A, B: title screen from *Niagara*,
the film; cut to black]

[Tape 9: theme music from *Niagara*]

[T luunches a toy helicopter as Z distributes a xeroxed sketch of the Falls with cursive commentary; E gives a squeeze to the penguin honker, bringing the scene to an ear-piercing close]

***

E:

Doing the Falls, Part I

[slides C (hand-held projector):
images begin to drift]

[don't forget to cross off "Your Tour Guides"]

Z [*handing T, at podium, a stack of cards*]: Following the described points in order will take you from the present Niagara Falls to its point of origin at... [*T veers away from rostrum*]

[slide C—center: book as Falls,
pages flipping]

T [*electronic gameshow gong. T selects a large index card*]: Albany, New York: SUNY Press, 1981. *Colossal Cataract: A Geological History of...* [*puts card in clip board*]

Z: Follow the road off the island via the bridge. At the end of the bridge make a left (downstream) turn... [*T* may *be facing image*]

[slide C—low left: research area
for the 1974 *Report*,
looking down from above;
key sites are labeled]

1 [*first* official *tour stop. When a stop is reached, the electronic buzzer sounds and the number lights* up]

T [*card on wall*]: New Brunswick: Rutgers University Press, 1992. June 10, 1843. "Since you are to share with me such footnotes as may be made on the pages of my life during this summer's wanderings... this magnificent prologue... [*gesturing to Falls video and slide*] Yet I... have little to say, where the spectacle is for once great enough to fill the whole life and supersede thought, giving us only its own presence." [*attempts to reattach card to an image; it falls*]

E [*muttering, as "absent anonymous relative"—see below, page... —crosses stage, wrapped in yellow poncho*]: ("this yet unknown drama")

Z: (But where is she exactly, Margaret Fuller, as she begins the process of self-textualization... [*T may read some of the site annotations on the slide*]

E: remedial works necessary to enhance the beauty of the Falls in the Niagara River *by distributing the waters...*

Z: (in the pagescape of her summer's journey, the Falls occupies the locale of the prologue, graphed in a texture of chain lines, a subtle grid that channels the flow of ink)

T [*E prompts*]: *so as to produce an unbroken crestline...*?

Z: Loop over, under, [*T crosses under and over his own motion*] rise to [*pause Falls*]

[slides C—high: graphically analyzed—
pix[i]elated—rainbow over fake postcard shot
of Falls from above illuminated; cut to black]

2

T [stop two; *bending to read card on floor*]: New York: Routledge, 1991: a traveler, following a prescribed itinerary... spatial movement symbolizes movement towards an encounter with the sacred and momentary distancing from the social order and space of daily life...

Z: (see Shields, 120-21):

T [*squatting*]: Fuller at Table Rock, on the verge of the Falls: "There all power of observing details, all separate consciousness, was quite lost." [*to Z*]: Look, it doesn't matter... so long as the work gets done. We can...

Z [*cutting T short*]: and falling...

[slide C—starts high, then drops:
a tiny Bellini, 1873,
dangling at the end
of a single line, plumb on the Falls;
cf. Adamson, *Two Centuries of Changing Attitudes...*]

T: (Bellini!)
Z: Pause. [*release Falls*] At this point (station C6), the vertical distance to the Maid-of-Mist pool is 51 m (167 feet). Read the plaque or not. Turn left (downstream). [*watching T closely*] Turn right at the stop sign... Turn left at the second signal... the *second* signal... [*T struggles to keep up with the projected images: following directions does not always lead him in the right direction*]

[four slides, B, A, B,
one for each syntactical beat of the text:
tour brochure—" Mysteries of the Mist,";
Niagara Museum "set"—daredevil barrel;
a souvenir in domestic context]

3

T [*finding card at stop 3*]: Boston: Houghton, Mifflin, & Company, 1884; 1871. "Lake Ontario, seemed to me, as regards a certain dull vacuity in this episode of travel, a kind of calculated preparation for the uproar of Niagara—a pause on the threshold of a great impression." [*holding card to forehead*]

Z [*aside to "T" as T, sternly*]: in your window, angled south and west, with a view of the water, lost in plurtexities... listen to your clothes tumbling in the dryer!

T [*podium attitude, with script*]: A different beginning. Henry James and Fuller only seem to be heading...

E: reading...

[slide A: array of images—
the prop table]

[Tape 10: comical music]

T: in the same direction. He really tropes her. Notice the difference: a "spectacle" that gives "us only its own presence" v a "calculated preparation." What is "its *own* presence" if it is a "spectacle"? Fuller adapts rhetoric of the grand illusionist: this consciousness that has been "superseded," this submersion of self into the other, is itself a rhetorical gesture. James acknowledges from the first—the falls is nothing else but its inscription; James "shops" the falls as compositional material...

Z: Debit: one lover, one voice, more or less?

E: H and M had a race
up and down the pillow case...

Z: Double back and intersect...

T: "giving us only its own presence...

Z: (careful, the Falls has retreated 11.4 km—7.1 miles—during the last 12, 300 years):

T: making us content with itself and with what is less than itself."

[slides B: previous two in "reverse"
daredevil barrel, "Mysteries..."]

E: falling water...

[slide A: section of a tour map—
the Whirlpool, Whirlpool
Rapids, and viewing stations,
colorized; see Tesmer, *Colossal Cataract*...]

T: Less than—which self?

[slide B: brief superimposition
of James and Fuller over whirlpool image]

E: (Enter absent "anonymous relative," sheathed in a plastic hooded rain poncho; * walks about, not all together aimlessly, exits)

*[slide B, hold and fade:
anthropomorphic shadow in revolving doors]

[*video: inscription appears over Falls: "signal… sending"; see Video Appendix*]

Z [*almost a whisper*]: "There is no escape, still this rushing round you and through you. It is in this way I have most felt the grandeur—somewhat eternal, if not infinite."

E [*like a carnie barker*]:

"Enjoy your own 'personal journey' over Niagara Falls in a computer-controlled motion simulator…"

[slide B: neon sign "Circus Whorl" (the "d" framed out) briefly superimposed over postcard whirlpool image]

[Tape 11: "What's all this…?"]

T [*podium*]: One inscription must overpower another, others… if she is to believe her experience—that is, her text… It is the sound of her "own" words she feels rushing through her… [*trades in script for cards*]

E: recommendations concerning the allocation of the task of construction…

Z: Have you packed all you need? Follow the parkway as it crests and flows, * hugging the shoulders of the gorge; turn right, keep right, make the second right [*T begins a slow turn which becomes continuous*], pass through the revolving doors toward the check in station:

*[slide B: 2-3 quick cuts: revolving doors superimposed over whirlpool image]

4

T [*turning, returning, as if passing through, back through, revolving doors; stop four*]: 8/21, 22; 1951. United States. Congress. Senate. Committee on Public Works. *Niagara Falls and Niagara River, NY. Hearings before a subcommittee of the Committee on Public Works…* [*spin, vertigo*] to authorize the construction of certain public works on that river for power and other purposes, and for other purposes: enhance the scenic beauty…provide the most beneficial use...considering that the quantity... recognizing that the supply... desiring to avoid a continuing waste... have agreed upon the following articles... [*hands card to Z*]

Z: "other purposes" and "other purposes"?

T [*reading from clipboard*]: By legislating the Falls, we dislocate its power to our systems of (rhetorical and political) power: channel its flow, like stops on a tour map...

[slide B: illustrations of an
18th century contraption designed
to convey boats over the Falls
superimposed over cartoon of Falls or Whirlpool]

E:

like any inscription of the "other."
the Falls and Congress have a race...

Z: Exit. Immediately get into the left-hand lane. Go through the turn-around and take the Parkway north (downstream) [*T shoots, spins, shoots. His interpretation of Z's choreography has been a confusion of turns and counter turns, often working against his own motion and momentum*]

[slides A, B, A: three quick beats—
reconstruction and erosion of Falls,
then B black]

5

T [*reading from cards*]: The direction of the whirlpool can be reversed by decreasing the flow over the... [*look up from card*]

[slide A: bridge collapse]

Z: fall of texts. Albany, New York: SUNY Press, 1981: The Honeymoon (Falls View) Bridge collapsed into the Niagara Gorge on January 26, 1938.

T: Bridges pass over, also connect [*bridging card in hand*].

Z: The prospect Point rockfall occurred in 1954.

T [*reading from script*]: This rock had been legislated in '51.

Z: The Schoellkopf Power Plant collapsed into the Gorge in 1956.

T: And so the referent cannot be trusted. Does the signified still stand?

Z: Circle back around the wax works, arrive at a doubling:

[slide A: date & time documented
chance superimposition of color bars
displacing rainbow over a dewatered Falls]

6

T [*Z hands card*]:
(Call 905-374-RIDE...?) [*pockets card; Z & T arc away from each other*]

E: (pause Falls, roll back) [*Z performs*] Senator Cain. I think that you mentioned presumably an international body which had in hand now the preparation of a report and recommendations, and I did not quite understand that reference....

[slide B, two flash and fades: 3-D model
of a rope walker, front of Tussauds Wax Museum;
Blondin with manager on back]

T [*read from clipboard*]:

1,100' OF 3" THICK HEMP ROPE @ $2.25 PER FT.,
RISING FROM 162' ON THE AMERICAN SIDE TO 170' ON THE
CANADIAN.
A 40 LBS., 38' POLE: GRASP IT FIRMLY, BUT NOT TOO TIGHTLY—

E: LIKE A PEN... NO

T: DIVINING ROD

Z: NO—BAR OF MUSIC...

T:

THUMBS OUT ALONG THE BAR
TRAVELING LIGHT
EITHER WAY AT ONCE,
NEITHER THE WAY I WANT..

[Tape 12: "...if you step this way,
I'll show you a little better where it happened":
tour guide, *Niagara*]

Z:

NOW, IMAGINE RIDING ON HIS BACK:
IN THE CENTER, FOR 40 FT., NO GUYS... DIPS AND SWAYS...
"UNTIL I CLEAR THIS PLACE, BE A PART OF ME, MIND, BODY, AND SOUL;
IF I SWAY, SWAY WITH ME. YOU ARE NO LONGER , YOU ARE..."

E: Release Falls. [*Z enters, releases*] (absent relative: one foot before the other in a wide arc and pause, midway, stylized sway, exit) [*masked T as relative, performs in reverse, not exactly as directed*]

[slide B, flash and fade: anthropomorphic shadow w/video camera, tracing footprints]

T: B for...

* * *
* *

E:

Virtually Yours, or Table Dating

[slides A, B: Slide images include Niagara souvenirs in Z's apartment: a refrigerator magnet depicting the "Falls Illuminated," laminated; a velveteen wall hanging iced with

various tourist sites, a photograph
of us in a magnetic Niagara frame, etc.]

[*Niagara shopping bags in hand, Z & T browse the props; an object is "bought" with theoretical currency—quotes from Barthes'* Mythologies *and Baudrillard's* Selected Writings). *Quotes are written on index cards; after reading a quote, we exchange it for an object of equal value by putting the selected object in the shopping bag, folding the quote in half and putting it in the object's place on the table.*]

Z: Honey, can I have some Barthes coinage?...

T: The less ya have da more Dalose.

E: (Be Gilles...see *Capitalism and Schizophrenia*, page...)

T [*placing script on table; getting an overview*]: "This transformation of shopping into an experience can occur in any setting...."

[slide B]

E: "The World in a Shopping Mall, Margaret Crawford. (*In Sorkin,* Variations on a Theme Park, *28.*) ...

Z [*considering a Niagara placemat, turning it over like the page of a book: winter, verso; summer, recto; images laminated in plastic*]: "The quick-change artistry of plastic is absolute. It is less a thing than the trace of a movement. It is a spectacle to be deciphered: the very spectacle of its end products."

[slide A]

E: (Barthes, "Plastic," 97). Buy. (she also takes a fat plastic pen that looks like a red missile; very phallic, with a multicolored flow, too.)

[*T examines a breast-shaped ceramic mug, with a protruding nipple spout—" From Niagara Falls, with Love"—as if it were an archaeological artifact*]

E [*a real find!*]: It's a tit mug!

[slide B]

T: "In order to become object of consumption, the object must become sign; that is, in some way it must become external to a relation it now only signifies.... This is no longer a lived relation: it is abstracted and annulled in an object-sign where it is consumed."

E [*rushing*]: Baudrillard, "The System of Objects," 22 [*T forms lips around nipple of mug*]. Buy!

Z [*selects a tiny camera, puts it to her eye, aims at the audience...click*]: "The mirage of the referent..." [*doesn't buy*]

[slide A: blank]

E: (Marriage? with what?... Baudrillard, "The Political Economy of the Sign," 92.) [*With each click a postcard scene of Niagara Falls wheels into place; T may describe some of these to the audience, but decides not to buy*].

T [*picking up a small TV key ring and peeking into a hole in back, so that the blank screen faces audience*]: "Various animated, singing characters suspended in balloons above the aquarium!"

[slide B: black]

E:? Fodor's *Toronto*!

T [*replaces TV on table, pushes objects about, fidgety; finds a postcard*]: "The spectacle itself, as the concrete inversion of life, is the autonomous movement of the non-living."

E: (Debord, *The Society of the Spectacle and Other...*, 63).

Z: Let me see if I can make you feel better [*E projects souvenir on T's chest—their picture framed in a magnet*]

[slide C]

T: Ah... Thanks... Objects brought back into relation with the self, the body...

[*remote cordless electronic doorbell*]

E:

Oceanside
Apartment
Hotel

By The Sea 1847 Pendrell St.
On English Bay Vancouver, B. C.
Near Stanley Park Canada V6G 1T3
Close to Downtown (604)682-5641

T: Want to see who that is? I'm in the...

[slides C: cut to black; A: anthropomorphic shadow filed w/tropical plants]

Z: It's in *you*... [*as T remains in tableau with image, Z looks under the table*]: "Ideology only corresponds to a betrayal of reality by signs; simulation corresponds to a short-circuit and its reduplication..."

[slide A & B: hotel brochures; parallel projections of stylized synthetic "fun"]

E: It *is* you. (Baudrillard, "Simulacra and Simulations," 182.)

Z [*from under table*]: This was cut from the original production. Now he's got me on all fours at the sound of a bell. Unilateral decision. Ideological betrayal of the collaborative process He quotes, adapts, collages, orchestrates, directs... Give some up...

T [*spinning back into action, reading from postcard*]: How about this: one sample from each discourse sealed in an envelope. "The nominees are... the winner is..."?

[Tape 13: tense music, breathless scream]

Z [*simultaneous with tape*]: Umm... Let's try... [*coming at T from below behind with tiny "screaming" hatchet; E sounds alarm*]

[slide B: black, followed
by A, below]

***

E: **Popular Fall Lines**

[E prompts the following scene with cue cards; Z & T, in turn, cue E]

[slides A: Niagara Falls in prints,
painting, and photography,
1678-1969; photographed from reproductions
in Adamson and other secondary sources]

[T performs as puppet]

T: Falls Fashions

Z: (Fall Falls?)

[message on video: the falls see

Falls-C
falsies

false ease

see falls

(false, see?)]

T: All seasons... If you're historically conscious...

E: (Falls off.)

T: and like a rudimentary version, with a postmodern taste of premodern naivete—the "freshness of native feeling," as Hawthorne would say

[slide]

Z: this Hennepin 1678 print should suit. Notice the extended arm of the onlooker on the right, the exaggerated signing of awe in contrast to the depthless space and marshalled lines of the falling (pouring?) water.

T: Very carefully graphed...

Z: like those nylon cord waterfalls in shopping malls...

T: Uhuh... Now, Margot...

E: from Rhonda, for M

T: I'm sure we've all heard of the "Illuminated Falls": every night the falls is awash in colored light, perhaps in homage to that famous rainbow—or "Iris"—so often captured by pen and brush.

Z: Ah, that's a beautiful sight, isn't it, Herb?

E: from Bob, H.

T: Yes. And this next piece, a color sensation, a painterly "illumination," should be an inspiration to any decorator.

[slide]

This 1894 impressionist rendering by John H. Twachtman should go nicely with your summer sunroom suite

Z: A cool one-piece. Absolutely delicious. It could also help brighten up a darker room.

T: True...

Z: By the way, did you know that the Falls was first illuminated in 1860, using 200 Bengal lanterns? 50-60 were placed behind the Falls, making it appear, according to reports of the time, like a "cascade of diamonds."

T: Umm. That show was for the benefit of the Prince of Wales, wasn't it?

Z: He was the center of attention, all right: at once spectator—the highest ranking one, to be sure—and spectacle, though Blondin, the "Prince of Manila," performing the same evening, did him one better—walking the high wire on stilts.

T [*chuckle*]: Now how about this next ensemble: John Vanderlyn's

[slide]

General view of the Falls and Rapids of Niagara (1840-41).

Z: Reserved and dignified... Though usually I don't go for black and white reproductions, this one seems to work well.

T: Ah, yes, living room or den I'd say.

Z: Right, and how about for the office or board room? This next piece comes with a touch of primitive vitality; This is Thomas

[slide]

Davies' *Niagara Falls from Above* (1762-68); neither too much detail nor too varied a palate, but cool, colorful, and lively

T: and did you notice the Indian potentate in the corner? the sense both of authenticity and an authoritative presence...

Z: Yes. A view fit for a CEO. And how about this comfortable-

[slide]

looking two-piece *en cadre*. One of the more conservative lines of N F Cropsey (1860, framed).

T: Ah, sweet—boudoir or library

Z: and a restrained elegance: we look out on the bright scene—the couple, at ease in a benevolent landscape—from behind a dark, cool archway, as if contemplating the tableau from a cloistered courtyard.

T: Yes, nature and the human seem to have found their proper relations.

Z: (in the mind of the perceiver.)

T: But compare with this next piece, a much bolder design. From

[slide]

John Vanderlyn (1832) again, but along much different lines.

Z: Yes. *The Horseshoe Fall from Below Table Rock*. Strong lines and deep shadows. A really stunning outfit. Definitely a mantel piece—fire blazing underneath

T: Yes—fire and water—raging fire, roaring falls (a bit of Freud, Eh? bedwetting to extinguish the tabooed desire?)

Z: Urrr... But here comes the one that puts the others to shame.

[slide]

Church's 1857 *Niagara*. A real museum piece. Let us read you some reviewers' comments: Church's canvass shows that "Even this awful reality [i.e., Niagara Falls] is not beyond the range of human imitation";

T: "Water surges over several rocks and a snagged branch, as it runs toward the drop; some of it white and foamy, some of it dark and glassy, some green with shallow speed. The whole painting is masterly."

Z [*to T*, "unnaturally"] I won't do this; it goes on too long.

T [*as T*]: Ok, but the citations. The first, I think, is Ruskin. The second is from the *New Yorker*, "The Talk of the Town": "The Lip" 3/3/86.

E [*prompting, cued by T*]: "Looks like..."

T: Looks like the real thing, all right.

E: as rain...

T [*recalling*]: (Raintree Grill! Rainy day Vancouver. Grilled Romaine. Can't remember the train...

Z: Church's palette is carefully tuned to nature!

E: ...of thought?

T: it was about the previous line—you balked at "the real thing."

Z [*prompting/commanding*]: "It demonstrates..."

T: It demonstrates Henry James' idea perfectly: that the imagination, especially the moral imagination, is a balloon always in danger of drifting off, if not tethered to reality...

Z: (Emotional or literal?) ...

T: Needs a large room, but not too close to drapery or other fixtures.

Z: This next piece is ideal for the study, the office, or even

[slide]

a child's room: wherever civilized values and strength of mind—with a twist of imagination—are to be kept before us. John James Barralet's allegorical canvass, *Science unveiling the Beauties of Nature to the Genius of America* (1814), is unique in the Falls lines due to its somewhat "offbeat" iconography (the multibreasted Science, for e.g.).

T [*aside*]: ok, you can cut this one down too, if you want, awright?

E [*prompting*]: "Good for..."

[Tape 14: "I'd rather walk"]

T: Good for theme suites, too. Sensual detail in the service of enlightenment...

Z: Played off against curtains, it strikes one of those clever design poses that produces a sense of sophisticated haute couture in any setting.

T: And what's this? A rather bold ending to the show. Anonymous,

[slide: American Falls Dewatered]

as these designers often are; probably pirated from The American Falls International Board's "American Falls Dewatered" collection. The latest deployment of "Fashion X," or "De-fashion"—recycling of anti-art images to make a deconstructive fashion statement…

Z: notice the décolletage…

T: and a strong accent of neo-Marxist Sub-Couture—exposing underlying strata.
[*E makes noise; squeezes her honker; Z & T break, stand*]

***

Z [*out of character*]: We've got to stop. In less than 24 hours…

[slide B, flash & fade: excessively tattooed lady
pivoting before mirrors; cut to black]

T:

Less than a turn, *
before the music stops—
and the bride and groom?
you and me?

Z: You're compulsive… [*hands T a letter from clipboard*]

E: (T, staring across performance space, stands, as If to approach… the absent relative? — turns sharply stage center to face…)

[slide B, flash, hold, fade:
superimposition over dewatered Falls:
anthropomorphic shadow reflected in
museum glass zoomorphic display;
or,

two anthropomorphic shadows superimposed—
home video reflection of video maker and Cotton from *Niagara*]

T [*abruptly facing audience*]: "Please arrive early so that arrangements can be made with other panelists"?

E: You're doing just fine. "Ska-nah-wah-ti"

T & Z: *"over the water"*

[slides A, B: black]

*
* *
* * *

[*Optional Interlude: "T's Recital." See* ***Tom's Appendix***]

E:

Enhancement and Preservation

[slides A: geological charts,
maps, and graphs]

[*move Falls to side and back*]

T:

and rock...

[*As Z begins the lecture, using a jumbo Niagara pencil as a pointer, skims through Tommy Trent's comic book history of the Falls*]

Z: The earth...

T: "wearing half glasses, halfway down her..."

Z [*aside*]: Yes. I'd forgotten that...

Z: "Z [*half glasses half way down her nose*]:" The Earth was formed 4,600 million years ago; if we compare the geologic history of the earth with a 12-month calendar year, the earth was born on January 1, Midnight,

New Year's Eve... [*remembering*] 4 a.m. Oceanside Apartments, #103. He comes to bed. I wake, put on my red robe, boot up, and take my turn...

[slide B, hold and fade:
dated Falls winter scene]

T [*cautioning*]:

falling...

[slide A: chart—earth's formation
compared to a 12-month calendar year]

Z: Note that 1 second in calendar time = 150 years in geologic time, 1 minute = 9,000 years, 1 hour = 540,000 years, and so forth. Given this analogy, we see that two minutes before midnight, also on New Year's, yet only 12,000 years ago, Niagara Falls began.

[slide B, hold and fade:
dated tropical foliage—
ten minutes after B, above]

Z [*drifting back, accusingly*]: next night I sleep straight through; by the morning, my words have changed.

T: "I didn't... I don't remember doing it... well, it was 3 a.m.—what could I...?"

E [*interrupting, prompts*]: "And considering..."

Z: And considering that in a relatively short period of geologic time—from that night to the present—the Falls has eroded a gorge 7 miles long, we wonder what the geologic future of this New Year's baby will be....

E: (you know he's waiting his chance)

T: [*interrupting*] This is about Niagara Falls, isn't it? Well, according to Tommy Trent [*shows audience a phallic-looking illustration of Goat Island from*

Tommy's Niagara Falls Mystery!] the goats ate it!

E: Go ahead—just try 'n' eat me.

Z [*read quickly, monotone, Brecht; T blocks her face with comic book image as she reads*]: "Excuse me, excuse me, professor..." You read Tommy Trent's history of Goat Island, your face in my face, the obnoxious schoolboy, spitting out your words, pointing at the phallic illustration: 'and what do you think this looks like? Huh? Huh?

[slide B (optional), flash, hold:
phallic island; cut to black]

E [*prompts*]: "the exposed..."

Z: Please check your sources... stratigraphicologically speaking...
E: Uhhh

Z: the exposed walls of the gorge are comprised of Devonian sedimentary rocks: [T] Lockport Dolostone, Rochester Shale, and

T [*simultaneous*]: "as time passes, a legacy of discourses about a given site becomes sedimented in popular imagination and memory..."

E [*following T's quote above*]: Shields, *Places on Margin*, 27

Z: Irondequoit Limestone—each of these rocks varying in degree of erosional resistance

T: (emotional?)

Z: due to their physical and chemical composition, and the thickness of the beds [*T is disruptive*]—each sharing a common denominator of stress... [*to T, or the moment*] just stop!

E [*prompting*]: "just stop!" ... "imposed by...

Z: imposed by the surface flow of the Niagara River and the uplift and weight of glaciation.

Additionally, due to glaciation, the shale beds, and to an even greater extent the Lockport Dolostone, have developed an extensive system of[T] fractures and fissures. Note the horizontal

[slide A: mechanics of erosion; squiggly arrows show paths of ground water seepage]

T [*simultaneous*]: Textual sapping: the flow of non-sense, of sound, metonymy, and pun; [E] of resemblance and opposition in nondualistic continuity; fissuring and undermining of coherent structure from within; a semiostatic pressure fragmenting the rock-text; a destabilizing drift of signifiers away from a fixed signified...

[slide B, flash & fade:
museum cartoon—man struck by lightning]

E [*over T*]:

That's 905-374-R-I-D-E—
the "ultimate thrill"

Z [*continuing, simultaneous w/T, struggling to sustain the rhythm of logic*]: and vertical joints in the dolostone caprock. These joints allow ground water to infiltrate the rock, exerting hydrostatic pressure upon the bed, thus forcing the rock apart. As a result, the undermined dolostone caprock, hanging in brief dramatic suspension, eventually collapses under the pressure of the surface flow into the basin of the gorge below.

T: Tips its hat, so to speak...

E: signed in Washington on February 27, approved by the Canadian Parliament on June 14, consented to by the United States Senate on August 9...

Z: The erosional effects on the Falls are twofold: The

[slide A: map showing various stages of crestline erosion]

crestline of the Falls is steadily retreating—note the extent of...

T [*interrupting, responding more to the graphics then the text*]: Will the real Falls please...

Z: retreat in just 300 years; [*pauses, points to slide*]

E: In Iroquois legend, the lip of the Horseshoe was formed by a dying serpent: grimace of its final contortions, continuous chant of its plunge...

Z [*overlapping*]: and since the force of the American Falls is only 1/10 the force of the Horseshoe Falls...

E: "force of the falling..."?

Z: it cannot erode the Talus mounding in its basin...

E: "flow of the rhetoric over..."?

Z: implicating the eventual disappearance of the American Falls into nothing more than cascading...

E: table talk

Z: rapids.

E: Happy New Year... Just a kiss to say goobye, M. M., mmmm?

[slide B, flash & fade: Z looking through a view scope at the Falls]

Z [*"putting her foot down"*]: These concerns led to the establishment of the International Joint Commission in order to determine whether or not erosion of the Falls could be controlled, and whether Talus removal from the American Falls would prove beneficial—all in an effort to preserve the beauty of the Falls and render it a safe object of contemplation.

E: Don't look now...

Z: Many of the commission's findings were based on simulations made on a

[slide A: giant of the Falls:
a female scientist—no Marilyn Monroe—
in knee boots working up the model]

1/50 scale model (22' X 4'). From June to November 1969, the American Rapids Channel and the American Falls were dewatered and found unstable; the United States Army Corp of Engineers anchored huge blocks of

[slide A: labeled display of rock bolts]

dolostone with rock bolts; [T] they stabilized rock cliffs at Luna...

T [*simultaneous, walking to prop table, selects a plastic water pitcher; begins experiment/ magic trick*]: production of the Falls as cultural artifact, an "earth work..."

Z: Island and Bridal Veil Falls with cable tendons; drainage holes

[slide A: model showing cable tendons]

were drilled to relieve hydrostatic pressure. The talus at the base of the Falls was measured and mapped, the contours of the underlying bedrock charted, and the model constructed. Though...

E: P. T. Barnum built an elaborate model of Niagara, complete with running water, and added it to his American Museum in 1843... Harris, *Humbug! the Art of P. T. Barnum*, chs. 2 & 3

Z [*simultaneous*]: various talus arrangements were demonstrated and photo documented on the scale model... [*hesitant pause*]

T: "illusion is no longer possible because the real is no longer possible" ... [*As Z lectures, T pours from the pitcher of cloudy water into red, blue, and green plastic glasses; though no liquid falls from the lip of the pitcher, and the glasses remain dry, the level of the water in the pitcher apparently decreases*]

E: Baudrillard, "Simulacra and Simulations,"177

[slide A: versions of model Falls; eventually A goes blank]

Z [*simultaneous with T*]: removal of talus was determined to be too...

T: "There will therefore be in striptease a whole series of coverings placed upon the body of the woman in proportion as she pretends to strip it bare..." [*adds drops of red, blue, yellow color to the water in the pitcher staining it reblulow: a muck of the primary*]

E: Barthes, "Striptease," 84.

T: "these classic props... make the unveiled body more remote..."

Z [*simultaneous with T*]: expensive. Diverting more water to the American Falls, in order to check the much more rapid crestline erosion of the Horseshoe...

E [*simultaneous with T*]: just slip a little this way, dear... let it go... a free fall, into my arms. There's so little time...

T [*Removing a submersible penlight from his pocket and shining it around inside the empty glasses*]: "Molten silver..." "sheet of crystal glass..." "cascade of diamonds..." [*plunges penlight into the pitcher*]. River of phosphates.

Z [*simultaneous with T*]: was not aesthetically desirable for the Canadian side. However...

E [*simultaneous with T*]: See "Aesthetic Appendix" for photos of variations simulated on the model...

Z [*simultaneous, fretfully*]: The Corps of Engineers optimistically noted that...

T: The "classic props" of science— taxonomies and statistics; geological analyses and measurements; the stratigraphy and speed of flow (5720 m^3/sec (202,000 cfs))— all that which claims to expose and explain the falls, to dis-cover it, to tell the story of its orogeny and evolution...

Z [*has been gradually losing the sense of what she's saying*]: due to the diversion of water to power plants, the erosional process has decreased since prepower-project days....

T: does best what it intends to eliminate—further complicates and "muddies" what must remain semiotically irreducible.

Z [*grasping at a ledge of statistics*]: This is partly because the flow of surface water is limited to 100,000 cubic feet per second from April 1-September 15, 8 a.m. to 10 p.m., and from September 16-October 31, 8 a.m. to 8 p.m. (prime tourist times), and...

T: But this ruse of an exhibitionist discourse[E] is so thoroughly persuaded by its own reifications[Z] that it has become naively self-reverential, believing itself to be the "true" reflection of the world it simulates.

E [*simultaneous with T*]: He-no has returned, creating power and light without clouds.

Z [*simultaneous with T*]: further cut to 50,000 cubic feet per second all other times. In any case, the final decision was not to detract from the present scenic value of the Gorge, but to allow the "forces of nature to...

T: It answers to no other discourse—the striptease of the real, the most convincing act in the music-hall of cultural (re)productions. [*By the time T finishes his minilecture, with its accompanying visual demonstration, Z has also finished, but she has not so much ended her lecture as given it up, the pauses between her words having gotten longer*]

Z: continue as they are," except in situations where the safety of the spectator...

[*T demonstrates "old Joe," a wooden doll in a barrel: lift the barrel and a spring-mounted erection flips out; he turns the doll on its side, like the comic book illustration of Goat Island*]

E: (You listen, knowing the timing must be right......)

[slide A: dry bob: American Falls dewatered;
cut to blank]

T [*continuing; Z is silent, staring beyond the performance space*]: "This mirage of the referent, which is nothing but the phantasm of what the sign itself represses during its operation, the sign attempts to mislead: it permits itself to appear as totality, to efface the traces of its abstract transcendence, and parades itself as the reality principle of meaning...

E: (Baudrillard 92?).

Z [*picking up the tail of the quote while, in a moment of inspired ludicrousness, stripping off her shirt, revealing various anatomical features re-covered with name cards, some mislabeled as geological features and processes—" sapping, "striating" ...*]: But latent discourse diverts manifest discourse not from its truth but towards it and makes it say what it did not wish to say..." Baudrillard 149! [*T—honks, alarms, sirens*]

E: deterred, detoured...

[Tape 15: "Occupational therapy!";
a table kicked over]

T: Yes, that's it! I have a photograph... [*affixing a xerox of a stratagraphical analysis of Niagara Gorge to Z's bosom*]: "This is a self-liquidating project."

E: United States Congress, Senate, Committee on Public works; 20, paragraphs 6 & 7 [*T Explodes a champagne popper, immediately falls to his knees and extends his arm in exaggerated imitation of early caricatures of Falls admirers, as colored paper streams down over her.*]

E: Depending on how long the performance has taken up to this point, we may put fake ice cubes in the glasses and "serve" the audience with tidbits such as "sorry we've run out of..." "may we suggest..." beautiful, eh?" "'couple o' colors I never heard of before...'" (Ray, Fr. *Niagara*—the film)

T: "No. No substitutions."

Z falling, falling…

[slides A, B: black]

***

E: Falls on, forward.

[*Falls on; Z & T both escort it to the middle of the performance space*]

Z [*singing as she wheels in Falls*]: D, my name is double-sided, my other name is…

T:

"Tahtootahoo." Repeat.

**

Z [*quoting herself*]: "I'm drained. I can't think…"?

T: Aaa… [*domineering, self-mocking*] "We have to do it again. We'll be up before…"

E: tongue tied theorists

Z [*taking over T's lines*]: "We can't look like complete fools."

T [*reconsidering Z's lines*]: "What's it matter, if I have a two-sentence concentration span…"

E: in a universe of simple predicates…

T: "Awright. But not from the beginning; from 'Virtually Yours.'"

Z [*caustic*]: "Ok. ok. Here, you just buy the placements and the…"

E [*read rather rapidly*]: "'where is it? —pen. Don't forget to fold your card No, wait, that's my quote, isn't it? Where's your card? You've got to be more careful Write it out again Here, I'll do it No, your handwriting is better What does this say? I can't read my own…'"

T: "That's pretty much it, all right, that sounds like me. I see your point—what I put you through…"

E: Colonel Schull. That's a lot of water under the bridge, Sir, but to try to clarify the previous reference: There is a parallel action which is going on at the present time, this design of the necessary structures here, and, on the other side…

*

E:

Doing the Falls, Part II

7
T [*handing Z a notebook*]: Your turn. Proceed on either side of the gorge, are in parallel… [*Z hesitates*] At this point, the width of the Niagara River is about 2580 km (8500 feet). Open the notebook, pass the leaves back over the spiral binding, stop at page 14:

[slide A: fossil snail, a type indigenous
to Niagara Gorge sedimentary deposits]

Z [stop 7. *Reading from notebook, attempting to figure this out by acting it out*]: "I turn the corner of the long desk, step up, open dark, leather bound volumes, one after another…" Can't make out… "Leaving this room, I pass into another. Unreadable frescoes on the ceiling; one like clouds of grey mist, where patches of paint have fallen away—an opening, gap in the image, echo of footsteps, key turning in a lock, 1/4 turn of the handle, turning a corner—a long table, low bar of light—opening a book, turning leaves…" [*T, as absent relative: a brief pas de deux, pantomiming Z's movements from across the performance space as she moves through these lines*)

[slides B: three quick dissolves:
directional signs/commands to the "Tunnels,"
accordion elevator door,
cityscape in winter, fade to black]

[slide A: reflection of a gloved hand reaching toward reflection of a stone nude winter window Niagara Park greenhouse]

Z [*from script*]: But on this side there is still Fuller: "here there is no escape from the weight of a perpetual creation."

T [*gesturing to imaginary library stacks*]: Sedimentary layers of meaning…

E: Those leather-bound volumes containing lists of signifiers designating still more signifiers, inscribing directions, the spatial coordinates of that "more" —dark volumes like dams holding back the flood of representations—of creations…

[Tape 16: "The key's in the door."]

Z: "At times a secondary music rises; the cataract seems to seize its own rhythm and sing it over again, so that the ear and soul are roused by a double vibration."

T: So, one may arrive by a parallel service road at:

American Falls International Board, *Preservation and Enhancement of the American Falls at Niagara. Final report to the International Joint Commission*, 6/1974: "with regard to talus removal, a policy of enhancement was followed. Talus reduces the symmetry of the American falls with the horseshoe and diminishes the simple grander of the two together." How does that change her tune?

[slides A & B: three parallel dissolves: winter and mist LS of the Falls]

Z [*wandering, thoughtful*]: How sensitive is the human ear? Eras of compacted voices. What did you hear, opening or closing a book? "the echoes of…"

T: The "simple grandeur of the two together"? A dedoubling vibration…

Z: the listening mind…

T: mind of the mist.

Z: I recognize the style.

E: This play of discourses, deferring, referring to, pursuing an object that they locate outside themselves, which is figured as their consummation, their end, destination...

[Tape 17: Cotton: "That's some confession..."]

T "Tahtootahoo"—" Entangled."

Z: (If there is *an* object, referent, is there then *a* discourse?)

[Tape 18: The Shredded Wheat king: "toodaloo"]

[slides A, B: blank, black]

E:

TENSION AND SUSPENSION. VIBRATION.
YOU CAN FEEL THE VOICE IN THE WIRE.
AVOID THE SILENCES, THE GAPS BETWEEN UTTERANCES—
COME DOWN SURE ON THE PULSE OF THE SYLLABLES...

* * *

T: Carefully maneuver around the junked barrels and cable spools...

Z: "splendid MOVING DIORAMA of NIAGARA FALLS" (cf. 1840)?!

[slide A: black]

T: Revise it.

* * *

* *

**** *

*

E:

The Diorama

or nonchromatic synchronization and collocation of diachronic views and discourse positionalities of…

[slide A blank, B black]

E: Falls off!

[*Falls—roll forward and to one side; off*]

[*T as Vanna White attaches one end of a large roll of white paper to monitor, slowly unrolling it over the blank screen and continuing on across the room, gesturing illustratively as blank slides flash vividly on the "screen"; perhaps some fireworks-like pulsing color fields, too; see "The Diorama" appendix for optional text to appear on roll, and "Zoe's Appendix" for optional "Zoe's Song" following optional text; as Z unrolls, T follows, after bit, rolling back up and placing roll on prop table or atop monitor*]

* *******

E: **Absent Relations**

[slides A, B: "Rainbow Cabins,"
red-lit tunnels]

[*T pushes Falls off to one side;*
most of the video messages appear during this and two
later scenes: "Modern Housekeeping Cabins" &
"Wish You Were Here." See "Video Appendix."]

[*T & Z loop Burroughs adding-machine tape around their heads (like a mini Diorama), at once binding them together and masking—censoring—their eyes. E sets up a computer window at their table, and, through live manipulations, produces changing scenes of the Falls. As theme music from* Niagara *plays, Z shuffles postcards and deals out two hands*]

[Tape 19: *Niagara* theme]

T: Try some fancy Dans!...

E: Don't forget the pulsing red thing.

T: Uh... right. [*T presses the smoke stack on the little train again and sets up a flashing red beacon, like a warning signal at a crossing.*] What a view!

Z: Is that Windows?

[*When the theme music stops, they begin to play the cards, reading from their hands and discarding into a mail bag; these discards will be delivered in a later scene. The quotes on the cards are read in dialogue with the silent text overwriting the video Falls. They play until one of them goes out. Constrained by the paper bond, they play this scene with self-conscious poise, holding the cards up before their eyes like blindfolded psychics... Messages on the postcards include theoretical quotes, bits of narrative, and personal notes*]

E: *see* the "Postcards" appendix...

[slide A: a rebus code,
from Tommy Trent's Niagara Falls Mystery!
"tent," "tree," "scroll," "funnel," "pulley," "bat,"
+ or - various numbers & letters =*]

E: * answer: "to enter the secret tunnel pull third bar."

T [*as Z @ T play, the electronic cordless digital doorbell beeps*]: Want to get that? [*continue playing.*]

E: I'll get it. [*doorbell beeps again*]

[Tape 20: "Bring the missing persons file!"]

*

E: **Doing the Falls, Part III**

[*pull Falls to center of performance space, switch on*]

T [*wheeling in Falls, hands Z card*]: Take some time out... Somewhere above

A6. "Tour of the shopping mall." Read the plaques:

[slide A: plaque:
"We have visited..."]

Z [*reading from a card, looking about*]: New York, Routledge, 1992. "Dramatic atriums create huge floating spaces for contemplation, multiple levels provide infinite vistas from a variety of vantage points, and reflective surfaces near and far" (Margaret... Crawford! "The World in a Shopping Mall" [*flips card*]

T: (Sorkin, *Variations of a Theme Park...* ,14).

[slides A, B: Niagara sites:
Minolta Tower brochure, postcard
aerial view of Falls, a string of Postcards]

E: "just looking": "cognitive acquisition" (Crawford, Sorkin, *Variations*, 13).

[slides A, B: scenes from a shopping mall—
Niagara props, LS of mall with escalators]

T: What level did you read that on? Take the moving walkway—an escalator, if it inclines—and make another selection:

[slides A, B: commodities,
a rack of *Niagara Falls Mystery* as B slide,
racks of cards like image steps]

8

Z [*sit on prop table; stop 8*]: *Journal of Historical Geography*, 1991: "spatially itinerant but values and attitudes susceptible to change with distance from the strictures and discourses of everyday life" (Rpt. in Shields, 122). [*slips card in bra*]

T: Both good getaway values... Turn right from Power Vista (thanks to the subcommittee of the committee), and left (downstream):

[slide A: photo representation of chocolate swirl cake, Falls View restaurant]

9

Z [*heads upstage; stop 9*]: 1884; 1871. "The great spectacle may be called complete only when you have gone down the river some four miles, on the American side, to the so-called rapids of the Whirlpool..." Just browsing... [*place card on table*]

[slide A: CU of cake]

E: "even to look is to be immersed" (James, 373).

T: go on...

Z [*returning to script, podium; as Z lectures, T wraps himself with the diorama roll*]: James eases us down to the whirlpool itself, as his journey is always through a set of simultaneous, complementary representations. First inscribing the cliffs above the Whirlpool in a gallery tour—a "specimen of the noblest cliff scenery.... As it stands, Gustave Dore might have drawn it"— he arrives at the whirlpool itself, best seen from above:

[slide A, B: museum model or comic drawing of whirlpool, and photo aerial view]

"From this point of view, it seems to me by all odds the finest of the secondary episodes of the drama of Niagara, and one on which a scribbling tourist, ineffectively playing at showman, may be content to ring down his curtain."

T: Just writing?

[Tape 21: falling body]

Z: James' narration is nothing less than a perfectly executed stunt [*by now, T has completely mummified himself in white paper, and begins to unravel*], a trick with lines and mirrors, as his language holds us in a text, where Gustave Dore, James (as author), and Niagara are equivalent signifiers; what we read *is* the event (or, our *reading* is the event, its reenactment), costumed as autobiographical reportage. And so the Falls becomes a portable object of aesthetic consumption.

[slides A, B: souvenir shop tour]

E: "Recommendations concerning the nature and design of the remedial works..."

T [*giving Z a hand down from the podium*]: Let's continue. [*directing*]: (Pass through "9" en route to "10"): From this vantage point, we can now perceive the Whirlpool, as though we might not be in it... And look what else pops up in the eddies [*T directs Z's gaze downward; at the sound of the bell, injects a card*]:

[*rewind Falls a few seconds*]

[slide A: whirlpool collage]

10

Z [*reading from a card; stop 10*]: "The slight circles that mark the hidden vortex seem to whisper mysteries the thundering voice above could not proclaim... it is fearful, too, to know as you look that whatever has been swallowed by the cataract is like to rise suddenly to light here": Fuller! [*drop card into "whirlpool." Z continues to stare at the floor; T tries to peer over into the pool, but all he can see is script*]

[slide B: CU: spiraling through
the rib cage of dinosaur, Niagara Museum]

E: Such as: a leather-bound volume; a tiny daredevil, suspended from 100 feet of India rubber; "classic props of science"; "a shiny, black top hat"; a fragment of discourse; "identical letters dated October 10, 1950"; a statistic: "Maximum depth at the Whirlpool is 38 m (126 feet)."

[slide A, B: —anthropomorphic shadow, foliated;
Jean Peters and Cotton as shadows]

T: (this is also a good spot to see excellent rock exposures of the Upper Great Gorge—Lockport-Grimsby):

E: Henry and Margaret leave a trace
up and down the discourse space

T: Maximum depth at the Whirlpool is 38 m (126 feet).

*

[slide A, B: a mummy behind the Falls,
a CU of H. James in a red tunnel;
cut B to black]

E: Work in progress... [*Z & T circle about each other*]:

T: Ok, right, anyway it begins something like that, with some editing, some rewording and clarifying or further complication... [*Z fast forwards Falls a few seconds*] and it ends with a guy going over Niagara Falls in a Grand Am! * Goddamn, can't you see it? here's this guy who just broke up with his girlfriend; the relationship was brief but intense and, like everything else in his life, had the trance-like texture of a reality that never becomes quite real.

[slide A: MM behind the Falls
screen of water]

[Tape 22: "Where's he trying to go?"]

Z [*spinning a little friction whirl toy that emits sparks*]: this is not so much a strata as swirl of discourses, whether they break, give themselves over to that about which...

[slide A: gypsy fortune teller
mechanical doll]

or claim to master and contain, they are always fugitive from their own power, endlessly pursuing their own self-averted faces...

T: What level did you buy that on?... [*Z & T: a regimented swing dance*] Left, *Niagara: Voices on the Brink*, center, open, take notes, push forward; right, *Places on the Margin: Alternative Geographies of Modernity*, center, notes, push forward, stack; left, forward, center, stack; right, forward, center stack; return stack to shelf 180. Next stack. Whole stack...

[slide B: "circus whorl..."]

[*Z & T spin each other; whenever E speaks, they dip*]

Z: "*The Falls*, Written and Directed By...."

E: *Stereographic Views of...*

T: *Niagara: A Novel*

Z: *Niagara Falls: 100 Years of Souvenirs*

E: *Niagara Falls and Niagara River: Hearings before a subcommittee of the Committee...*

T: *Preservation and Enhancement...*

Z: *The Society of the Spectacle and Other Films*

E: and other...

T: *Niagara Falls: The Eternal Circus...*

E:

"Open every day, all year round."
$1.00 off with this coupon.

[slide A: Niagara Museum sign
rushing toward a vanishing point]

Z [*spinning free*]: Coherence is obtained through the formation of a combinational matrix or a repertoire: hence a functional language is established, but one that is symbolically and structurally impoverished (Baudrillard, "The System of Objects," 20).

T: ... to drive the goddamn maroon Grand Am he's rented—color of the lover's bedroom walls! —over the Falls like a barrel—right into that vacant anti-center, that blanked-out sector [*dipping no one*]

[slide B: Wheel of love]

no one's ever seen...

Z: in an elbow of spinning currents that give the rapids its name (?)

E: James?

II

T: Turn toward...

[slide A: anthropomorphic shadow:
Joseph Cotton emerging from a stairwell]

Z [*turn toward..., away from...stop 11*]: The world's largest steel roller coaster... 1,000 feet of tunnels, double spirals, giant loops...!

[Tape 23: Polly screams]

E: Fodor's *Toronto*! (absent relative reenters, wrapped in white paper, with book)

[slide B: abstract color wash
derived from night scenes of the Falls]

[slide A: broken Oliver Hardy doll
(arm missing, hand stuck to face)
and roses]

T: Now we're on a track. Left, down three flights, through the revolving doors... turn toward... [*Z turns toward T*]

E: (*absent relative continues on*)

[slide A: Z walking away]

T [*swinging out of Z's way*]: Pass through the double doors, right down the corridor, left down the escalator, come around left up the escalator, right down the hall, through the double doors... take a lunch with you... [*Z acts this out, trying to keep up and on course; she barely has time to realize, in her confusion, that she's back where she started, before reading the next line*]

[slides A & B parallel, B reverse: six shots in rapid succession, narrating a dead-end sequence —following signs "To Tunnels," "Do Not Enter," "Exit." End with parallel shots of MM, walking away]

00:00. Now:

12

Z [*reads, stop 12*]: Senator McClellan: Senator Lehman, that is a very thorough and well-presented statement, I may say. But I am going to have to be instructed...

T: Senator Lehman: I would, if I may...

Z: Senator McClellan: I am trying to get a general idea...

T: Senator Lehman: It is, I believe, tunneled; but with regard to the technical aspects...

Z: Senator McClellan: General Chorpening, will you make a brief statement?

T: General Chorpening: Mr. Chairman, we have here Colonel Schull, district Engineer at Buffalo...

[slides A, B: black]

Z: Senator McClellan: Colonel Schull...?

[*buzzer*]

* * *

* *

E: Roll back Falls. Pause [*Z moves Falls back toward prop table*]. Let it roll! [*standing next to the Falls, Z quickly rolls up unraveled diorama, lets it unroll to her feet. She pauses the Falls.*

E: **Writing the Falls**

[Tape 24: *Joseph Cotton*]:

"Let me tell you something... You're young, you're in love—well I'll give you a warning. Don't let it get out of hand like those falls out there. Up above... did you ever see the river up above the Falls? It's calm, and easy; when you throw in a log it just floats around. Let it move a little further down it gets going faster, hits some rocks and in a minute it's in the lower rapids and... nothing in the world including even God himself I suppose can keep it from going over the edge. It just goes." [*While tape plays, T brings in a tv tray with colored markers, drapes diorama over sandwich cue board, the Falls video, and begins to draw symbols on the paper—a rebus Falls.]*

[slide B: anthropomorphic shadow: Joseph Cotton in Polly's (formerly Rose's) room at Rainbow Cabins]

E:

reduced xerox facsimile of
Ride Niagara coupon
should appear here

* * *

[slides A, B: photos of various props at their consumer distribution sites]

[Tape 25: Mall interviews]

[*As T draws, the shopping mall interviews are heard on tape. When he finishes, he stands back to appraise his work; Z releases the video Falls*]

T: Ok, Z, lets imagine it cinematically—luminous screen in the dark, that sort of magic, though we're not aiming at mass consumption here, but we might as well think about putting it together this way. Opening sequence: study of the Falls; a montage—from above, below, behind (in the cave), etc. These are not all humanly probable perspectives... soundtrack: silence, or the white voice of the Falls that says everything and nothing. Attitude: ambivalence, mystery, fear; questioning without knowing what the question is, as the camera draws closer and jumps back, moves in again and leaps back; what does it mean, this immense destructive force, anti-center of self-annihilation that is also the "honeymoon capital of..."?

Z [*interrupting*]: when do I rattle? I forget...

E: "You forget, you forget. Try to stay with the flow...

E & T: now!" [*Z impatient, frustrated, rattles the paper, while T makes exaggerated gestures, imitating 17th & 18th century illustrations of Falls tourists; he may go down on his knees. E buzzes and T collapses tray. Z lets diorama fall*]

E [*Z faces audience*]: "Yes, I interrupt him—mid-fragment, mid-backspace, shift(ing), rubbing the side of his nose with his little finger, eyebrows knitted, exasperated sigh—his mother in St. Louis doing crossword puzzles—four letter word..." [*Z turns to T, hard stare*]

[*T turns to audience*] "But the other thing was, I originally conceived this section as a mime, with the Falls interviews, then decided to add the directorial bit; you opposed it—too talky (a snag in the "flow"?) [*T turns away, toward Z thoughtfully*] ... or was it your way of rebelling against being an accessory, a prop, holding up the paper for me to write on...?" [*Z rips the "illuminated" Falls from the roll and tucks one end under the monitor, so that it drapes over the cart.*]

[*Z pauses Falls*]

**

Z: "He has disappeared:"

T:"Ho no we a to"

E: **See You at the Bottom**

[Tape 26: Cotton; roar of the Falls sound under]

"Why should the Falls drag me down here at five o'clock in the morning—to show me how big they are and how small I am? to remind me that they can get along without any help? All right, so they've proved it, but why not? They've had ten thousand years to get independent—what's so wonderful about that? I suppose I could too only it might take a little more time..." [*Roar of Falls. While tape plays, Z escorts Falls up front, Vanna White style, releases them... roar of TV Falls picks up from Niagara soundtrack*].

[*Falls sound up*]

[slides A, B: various 19th- and 20th-century stunters]

[*T puts on Speedo goggles, tests the air with a finger, and gestures like a high wire performer*]

E: He-no lived under the Falls.

Z [*just as T is about to go over*]: *People Weekly*. 25 June, 1990: 89-92. "The secret of her obsessive dream now lies with her, somewhere under the roiling waters at the foot of Niagara Falls."

T [*lifting goggles, simultaneously, reading from a magazine*]: "The Falls Guy." *Saturday Night* 108.3 (April, 1993): 46-48. "A red-and-white sphere, about four feet in diameter, made of steel with a hatch on top, sits in his shed near his village. Sometime this year he intends to climb inside that ball, curl into a fetal position, and, with the help of a dozen strong-armed and strong-willed friends, send himself hurling over the most powerful waterfall in the world, the Horseshoe at Niagara..."

Z: "She was confident enough to leave her car downstream and make dinner plans."

T [*simultaneously*]: "At the edge of the Falls the voice in the darkness said..."

Z: "'Make sure people understand this was not a stunt; this was a quest.'"

T: "'okay, you're going over. Good luck.'"

Z: Isn't it relevant that he's Canadian—Why cut that? And how about the photo of him with his barrel—it looks like the New Year's Eve ball they drop on Times Square.

[slide A: final stunter; B black]

T [*adjusting goggles*]: "He just replied..." [*Z pauses Falls and displays it, turning it around, mimicking a magician's assistant "proving" that the trick box is not rigged; T about to jump...fogged goggles!*]: fogged window of the Grand Am? No. From the roar and mist of the falls, and that gesture like a kiss, cut to steam rising from a bath in the lover's apartment; thrust of water from the spigot—just being turned off. Intimate. Naked bodies. The rough scrubbing sponge on the back (that sound, just a whisper of the Falls). Then the sudden, passionate moment of love making. At orgasm, accidentally, the faucet gets turned back on—which one? (*Z releases Falls, stares at T*) "see you at the bottom."

[tape 27: Falls, loud; car horn]

Z: "see you at Howard Johnson's." [*volume up on video Falls, supplemented by audio tape**]

T: More vider, please! AHH HA HA HAAA! [*Falls sounds are by now quite loud. T "goes over," stumblesaulting through the video cart, breaking through the rebus Falls; Z as absent relative, first signs melodramatic awe, then, swept up in the momentum of the leap, desperately tries to learn the steps. The audio tape stops abruptly stops; Z & T dance "offstage"—i.e., toward the prop table—in mock triumph.*]

[slide A, B sequence—T going over:
sliding board at a motel pool;
B is reverse sequence]

E: (the absent relative...)

[slide A: reflection— stone nude
in tropical window]

[*volume down on Falls*]

*

**

Z: The Niagara you won't see: Lights out. [*pause Falls*]

[slides A, B: black]

E: The great serpent had no respect for the dead or living: eating corpses, spreading pestilence. He-no killed him with a flash of lightning, and went west.

We take a tour with a flashlight and camcorder. Falls of Falls post cards tumbling down bathroom wall. Cartoon map of Niagara Falls tacked to foyer wall, over bicycles. Velveteen scroll hung over the sofa. Brochures spread out on the coffee table and bed. Dark rooms filled with "representations of representations."

*

[*Falls on*]

E: **Modern Housekeeping Cabins**

[Tape 28: "excuse me... your shadow"]

Z [*handing me a postcard from TV*]: Something for you.

[slides A, B, flash & fade:
"Video Vacations"]

T: It's from Polly: "Don't worry, I'm just one of those logs that hang around in the calm."

[*Falls: roll back; in these last two scenes, the
Falls is a rush of printed messages
and codes in pulses of light*]

[slides A, B: black]

[Tape 29: MM]:

[*finishing the song begun in scene one*]: "Take me. Darling don't forsake me. Kiss me hold me tight..." [*As Monroe sings, we sheath ourselves in hooded rain ponchos; something begins to protrude from underneath...a backscratcher, from mine, and from hers a big pencil! We mechanically caress each other...moan, swoon... Monroe stops singing, but the record continues)*]: "love me love me tonight..." [*As the last word is sung, sound of a needle ripping across plastic as Cotton breaks the disk to pieces. We quickly throw off the ponchos*]

E: He has returned...

T: "We can cut this scene if we have to."

Z: "No—the postcards!"

*****

E: **Wish You Were Here**

[*Falls: center*]

[*we put on official hats, and deliver the postcards discarded during a previous scene ("Absent Relations"). T carries a plastic airplane on a nylon string (the propeller actually spins!); I take the train. We circulate through the audience.*]

[slides A, B: A: image of the Falls, black;
image of Monroe and Cotton on
the set of *Niagara*, black;
souvenir "Indian" dolls, black;
B: three images of the Falls,
schematized and dewatered deterred detoured;
washed-out postcard, color bars]

E: Here's one for you, and for you, and for you. Wish you were...

[*Falls: rewind past the beginning, to the color bars, and run.*]

[*After we distribute mail, we remove hats. T puts on a plastic top hat; I find and wind the music box, but do not release it*]

E: **"That Most Wonderful Iris."**

[*I take off my hat to the color bars, like a mechanical doll, then turn it over, empty.*]

Z [*facing audience, gesturing in a slow arc*]: Ahhh…

[*The video image goes black, leaving only the sound of the Falls…*]

[slide B, black]

[Optional Tape 30: Falls]

E: (absent relative: upstage, partially obscured by shadow, if a shadow is available, turned out as an American "Indian" souvenir, body painted "I 'fell' for you at 'Ni ha ga rah,' re-presents Z's gesture, though differently)
E: Listen. "Ga wen ne sen ton." Repeat.

[Tape 31: three voices:
"don't cross us off your list…"
"let me stay dead…"
"toodaloo…."*]

*E [simultaneous]: *tout* à *l'heure*

All: "Ga wen ne sen ton"

Z: Those tears… [*walking offstage*]

T: "It's ok. We can still *do* it…" [*bowler hat back on, offering the heart weight*]

E: The serpent writhes, her lip twitches, Monroe shifts a hip, and they follow the flow…

Z [*offstage*]: "bottom lip quivering. Couldn't stop it…"

E: hitting the rapids, and *Niagara* is…

[*T turns, haltingly, in various directions—facing an absent me, E, and ultimately the audience, looking desperately for a dancing partner*]

All:

"Gawennesenton..."

T: "her voice scattered..."
[*turning away, I stare into the liquid heart—an answer, or yet another question?*]

[Tape 32: "Rose... Rose...?"]

[*slides dark, VCR off, TV on; video snow transposed by game show, the TV "itself." Z, T, & TV take their bows... TEZ announcements: "We're available for Tupperware parties, graduations, showers, and briss..."*]

Audio List

1. George [*eerie* Niagara *theme music fading to background as Loomis, slipping quietly into bed after his dawn walk to the base of the Falls, whispers to the dissembling sleeper*]: "Rose?... [*slightly louder*] Rose?"
2. Ray [*Ray and Polly have just arrived at Rainbow Cabins; Ray notes the Shredded Wheat factory in the distance*]: "Honey, you can see it from here!" [*laughter*]. Cabin manager: "The Falls are that way..."
3. [*Maid of the Mist fog horn*]
4. Polly [*in George's room just after dark, gets her first glimpse of the "illuminated Falls" through "Venetian" blinds*]: "OH!"
5. George [*as 1. above*]: "Rose [*quietly*]... Rose..."
6. [*Rose sings "Kiss" on the patio of Rainbow Cabins; Ray drinks a Coke*]
7. [*Interviews conducted at South Street Seaport, NYC.*]
8. [*eerie echoey music, creepy base. The camera picks up an uncanny silhouette in the bushes out back of cabin 2. Inside, in bed, Polly has displaced Rose (hospitalized after the shock of seeing the "wrong" man—her lover—on the morgue slab); George, returned from the "dead" is unaware...*]
9. [Niagara *theme music*]
10. [*Parody of* Niagara *theme music, as Ray observes Rose's walk*]
11. Chief Inspector Starkey [*visiting the recently hospitalized Rose*]: "What's all this?... I wanna talk to 'er." Doctor: "Come around in the evening, she'll be out till then."
12. Falls tour guide: "Now right over there on June 30 1859 Blondin a French tightrope walker made his famous walk right over the

Falls… if you follow me I'll show you a little better where it happened." [*tense creeping background music*]

13. [*tense music, breathless scream, as George strangles Rose in the bell tower*]
14. Rose [*bells, echoey: "Kiss"; Rose having just learned that George is "missing," turns down Ray's offer of a ride*]: "I'd rather walk." [*bells continue, sound of footsteps*]
15. George: "occupational therapy!" [*smashing his model car against the wall, kicking over a coffee table*]
16. Manager, Rainbow cabins: "The key's in the door."
17. George [*to Polly, in his room*]: "that's some confession to make, in' it…"
18. The Shredded Wheat CEO [too all others]: "toodaloo"
19. [Niagara *theme music*]
20. Chief Inspector Starkey [*after discovering an identified body in Niagara Gorge*]: "bring in the missing persons file!"
21. [*sound of a body falling to the floor*]
22. Ray [*riding in police car, tracking George in the stolen cruiser; sirens*]: "Well… where's he trying to go?"
23. [*As 8., above. When the shadowy figure enters her room…*]
24. [*George delivers this monologue from the dark interior of cabin 2, as he and Polly gaze through Venetian blinds at the illuminated Falls*]
25. [*continuation of 7., above*]
26. [*"stuck" car horn; George has jammed the horn with a stick to decoy the marina watchman*]
27. Ray [*posing Polly on the chaise lounge for a typical "cheesecake" snapshot; Rose's presence briefly darkens over her body*]: "wha… oh [*nervous laugh*] oh, just a minute please, wou..would ya mind—your shadow…"
28. [*Rose continues song begun in 6., above*]
29. [*taped from opening sequence of* Niagara, *looped*]
30. [Optional: sound of Falls]
31. Chief Inspector Starkey: "I know you've seen enough of the Falls for one trip, but… don't cross us off your list."

George [*forcing Polly into a narrow hollow, Cave of Winds catwalk*]: "Let me stay dead." Polly: "Take your hands off me."

The Shredded Wheat King: "Well, toodaloo for now [*laughter*]. Pip pip, c'mon mamma" [*more laughter*].

32. George [*as 1. & 5., above*]: "Rose… Rose…"

The Diorama

[*quotes read by Z and E, unless otherwise indicated*]

"Reader! Have you ever been to the Falls of Niagara?"

E: (Joseph Ingraham, *A Manual For the Use of Visitors...*, 1834).

"...words cannot describe it, nor can any imagination, I think suggest even an approximate idea of its terrible loveliness. I feel half-crazy whenever I think of it"

E: (Frances Anne Kemble, 1833).

"When one stands near the Fall, and looks down into this most dreadful Gulph, one is seized with the Horror, and the Head turns round, so that one cannot look long or steadfastly upon it"

E: (Louis Hennepin 1698).

167' X 2500'

"... water piled on water, pinned on water, hinging and hanging on water, breaking, crashing, whitening in shocks altogether watery"

E: (Henry James, 1871).

"This is a self-liquidating project"

E: (U. S. Congress, Senate, Committee..., 1951)

T, E [*prompting*]: Cut it, cut it, cut it more...

Z: But should we bring in a Canadian voice:

> An alien song. Though day by day I listen...
> Is there no meaning in your ceaseless song...?

E: (Bates, Katherine Lee. "The Song of Niagara."
Canadian Magazine 35 (May, 1910): 58)?]

"Foam can even be the sign of a certain spirituality, inasmuch as the spirit has the reputation of being able to make something out of nothing"

E: (Barthes, "Soap-powders and Detergents," 1957; 1996—The froth of pollution?).

T: It might be interesting to project postcard images onto the blank paper…

"What has come over my soul and senses? —I am no longer Anna—I am metamorphosed—I am translated—I am an ass's head, a clod, a stone, a petrification—for have I not seen Niagara, the wonder of wonders, and felt—no words can tell what disappointment!

E: (Mrs. A.B.M. Jameson, 1836).

"Topological, hydrological, geological, flora, and fauna interlock with human agriculture, industry, power, navigation, and tourism"

E: (*Enhancement and Preservation…*, 1974).

A compendium of Niagara's features in all seasons and conditions, day and night. Accompanied by music and commentary, unrolling the grand canvas took an hour and a half
E: (Elizabeth McKinsey, 1985).

"…everything from schlock to quality"

E: (Fodor's *Vacations in New York*, 1991).

"The voluptuous curve of her hip rhymes with the curving lip of the Horseshoe Falls"

E: (Tom Marshall, *Niagara: Voices on the Brink*, 1991).

"This paper will be great for the kids…for birthday parties…rolled across the floor…everybody drawing on it at once."

T: In the final shot of this sequence—slow pan, from above—we glimpse a man in a yellow rain coat, leaning way out over the railing, the roar is deafening… a kiss… and then?

"Happy were the first discovers of Niagara, those who could come unawares upon this view and upon that, whose feelings were entirely their own"

E: (Margaret Fuller, 1835).

T: (*a keychain train; press its smoke stack and it sounds like a departure.*)

***

[*see* ***Zoe's Appendix*** *for song she would rather not have sung*]

Postcards

(*The following quotes are "played" during "Absent Relations" and delivered in "Wish You Were Here."*)

1. "The effect of this mighty cataract upon the mind, might perhaps be worthy of the attention of a metaphysician" (Captain Basil Hall, 1827).
2. 2 tent tree scroll/ funnel pulley 30 bat/ to enter the secret tunnel pull 3rd bar
3. Dearest Mother, / The Falls are lovely; M. loves the shopping—so much money. I miss you. / H.
4. "The Falls themselves mean and symbolize nothing, which makes them available for anything" (Rob Shields).
5. I haven't seen the Falls yet. We arrived late last night, and I didn't want my first sight of them to be in artificial light.
6. "I have seen the Falls, and am all rapture and amazement" (Thomas Moore).
7. Everybody's a comedian around here. You can't imagine how many times we've heard, "Slowly I turn…."
8. "Water, water everywhere. After Niagara one would like a dry strip of existence" (Margaret Fuller).

9. You should hear the roar! Tom's snoring is merely a whisper in comparison. Love.
10. Not a bad idea for a screenplay—But do you think it will float? The Grand-Am, I mean.
11. "The depth of the River at the plunge pool below the Horseshoe Falls is 46m (150 ft), at the Whirlpool it is 38m (126 feet), and at Lewiston-Queenston it is 30m (100 ft)" (Jerold C. Bastedo).
12. They're something of a wholly different order, a reality that doesn't belong in our world.
13. There are advantages and disadvantages in collaborating with your lover.
14. "It neither falters, nor breaks nor stiffens, but maintains from wing to wing the lightness of its semi-circle" (Henry James).
15. He felt the heat around his wrist as he fastened the plastic band of the Armitron around it. It had been lying in the sun and had stopped ticking. He kept it on, thinking about how long it had been, and was aware that he had become erect.
16. The Falls...the shopping...and H. all to myself! Love, M.
17. Happy New Year! Love.
18. The average flow of the Niagara River is 5720 m^3/sec (202,000 cubic feet per second).
19. It's the American sublime! And to think that one day these cascades will no longer fall—I could cry.
20. "In order to become object of consumption, the object must first become sign; that is, in some way it must become external to a relation it now signifies...This is no longer a lived relation: it is abstracted and annulled in an object-sign where it is consumed" (Baudrillard).

falling
rock

falling

water
and rock

falling

Tom's Appendix

E:

T's Recital

[slide: blank]

[*Falls on, forward*]

T: I'd like to recite a bit of a favorite poem of mine...

The Spirit of the Falls... [*Z honks*]
The Spirit of the Falls
by Buckley, C H A

what towering form erects its figure here;
he checks the footsteps of inquiring man
as if it were a sentry at his post
to guard with faithfulness the narrow pass?
[*honk!*]
It is the rock of monitou, the pinnacle
on which the gloomy spirit of the gale
sits brooding... [*honks, beeps, siren*
—a messy barrage of sounds]

T: It's quite a good bit, really [*Z has begun to rewind Falls*]. In addition to "towering forms," it has tortured depths, "jagged summits," and even "masses dashed" by "inverted cones"! (if you want to hear the rest, perhaps after the show...) [*Z pauses image; after E's note, the video shuts itself off*]

E: The rest of the poem is:

sits brooding o'er the tide below that shows
his fearful frown reflected in the wave
or feels the movements of his busy hand
searching its depths and torturing its course
setting its full currents red in continuous pain!

How high the water—God his altar rears
with jagged summits from a liquid base

How green the moss that decks its time-worn crown
Like youthful forms that cluster round old age!
From yonder cliff, impending o'er the stream
with shadowy fringes of the evergreen
this massive pile, like an inverted cone
seems hurled in other years with giant hand
upon the kindred masses dashed below!

T, Maybe we could replace Buckley, C H A with Logan, John D. "Over-song of Niagara." *Canada Magazine* 29 Sept. 1907): 440. As follows:

Why stand ye, nurslings of Earth, before my gates,
mouthing aloud my glory and my thrall?...

[xxxxxx!]

One way to get in a Canadian voice, though.

"As the Worst; so the Best—
All haste to their rest
In the void of the primal Unknown."

The Falls: The Movie

(*Winter. Steady LS of Falls, American side, from above. River frozen over, distant white fall of water and thick undulating column of mist: this could be mistaken for a still image—no boats in the water, nothing going* over... *Sound: white noise. Several minutes pass, then...*)

(*still, upper left*):
Natural forces at work on the Falls

(*a few more minutes, then, center rolling*):

signal
sending

(*Light variations. Cut to CU. More light changes, apparently intentional—mixture of long and short flashes, or pulses. The screen a blur of mist and spray. Pull back to LS.*)

(center, still):

The general view lends
itself to horizontal
formats—postcards, paperweights…

(after a minute or so):

Is the present configuration… so
desirable that it
should be frozen for
all time?

(a little more time passes):

"Ni ha ga rah"

(perhaps 30 sec.):

Sapping:
the hidden Falls

(following after brief pause):

I really think I
should see it,
if I'm going to collaborate

(more light flashes, more urgent)

(rolling):

the thing in itself

(slow roll up & freeze):

An act of language
and imagination

(image remains frozen a few seconds, thaws, the camera is jolted, and the image is quickly caught and refrozen, before it has time to settle; brief sound cutout):

artificial stabilization

(slight pause):

the Falls is nothing less than…

(*more code flashes*)

Have you seen...?

(*flashes*)

is never all.

(*pause*)

"Ne au garah"

(*pause; these next few lines follow closely, rolling up left*):
Falls—C
falsies

false ease
false—see Falls

(*light flashes, then center still*):

blind mist color bars

(*the pace has begun to pick up; only seconds between some lines*)

(*still, lower left*):
Do you want your
picture with...?

(*still, upper left; the Falls measured up, down, and across in various formats*):
8 1/2 X 11, 3 X 5,
167, 167 X 2700,
3 1/2 X 5 1/2,
16, 16 X 22

(*still, upper center*):

A still picture,
a tableau...

(*still, center*):

...something of an image problem...

(*still, upper left*):
priced according to
stamps, cancellation
dates, images...

(*still, upper center*):

The actual volume of
water, mist, aeration
and turbulence could
not be simulated.

* * *

(*Point of view shift. The previous sequence of shots has been from above; we are now at the foot of the Falls, at the end of the Scenic Tunnel on the Canadian side, and much closer—MS to MLS—though the zoom lens is still our main tool of immersion*)

(*center, rolling*):

Something of a wholly
different order...

a reality that doesn't belong
in our world...

(*pause, then a rapid roll, center*):

"Ni a ga ra"

(*center, still, appearing together on screen*):

At 150th scale,
4 X 22

Do you want your
picture with...?

(*still center*):

It is no longer clear
what Niagara refers to...

(camera jolt, Falls lurches, caught and frozen at a 45°+ angle.
Scene shift: through a side window of the Scenic Tunnel, MS of Falls framed in huge ice formations; also shots of an "ice cave" formed from layering of snow and ice over rocks):

(upper center still):

Dramatic interplay of
water, rock, and
spray

(light flashes, becoming frantic; cut to blurred CU of spray and mist)
(rolling center):

utility and variety,
rhythm and balance
scale and proportion

(an impromptu, mildly irregular dialogue of freeze frames and motion, in response to the crazed light code; the camera begins to drift in arabesques, direction uncertain)

(upper center still):

A blind man selling views

(quick roll center):

"Niagara"

(lower left, still):
Kitsch souvenir
and personal documentation

(freeze/flashes—aharmonic jam; camera rocks & rolls, swerves, rises & falls; cut to black, white noise continues one-minute, silent shot of Falls (approximately 15 secs.), white noise continues 4 minutes, imageless.)

Z: Skanahwahti

E: "over the water."

Z: Splendid!

Zoe's Appendix

E:

Zoe's Song

[slides: blank]

[*As I roll up the Diorama, Z brings Falls forward, turns it on; recites...*]

Z [*tentative*]: I introduce myself talent-show style...

Oh the lovers come a thousand miles,
They leave their home and mother;
Yet when they reach Niagara Falls
They only see each other.

[*beep*]

To see the Falls they took a ride
On the steamship "Maid O'the Mist";
She forgot the Falls she was so busy
Being hugged and kissed.

[*noisemaker*]

[*Video Falls message: "A blind man selling views..."*]

He said, "Is oo my darling?"
He said "Whose darling is oo?"
He said, "Is oo my baby?"
And she always answered, "Goo-goo-goo."

E: honker!... [*T honks*]

T: (*"Niagara Falls," 1841.*) See Luther, Frank. *Americans and Their Songs.* New York: Harper, 1942. 108.

Bibliography (Select)

Adamson, Jeremy. Niagara: *Two Centuries of Changing Attitudes, 1697-1901*. Washington, D.C.: Corcoran Gallery of Art, 1985.

American Falls International Board. *Preservation and Enhancement of the American Falls at Niagara: Final Report to the International Joint Commission*. Niagara Falls, New York: np., 1974.

Baird, Hiram K. *The "Niagara": A Dramatic Narrative*. New York: New Voices, 1972.

Barthes, Roland. *Mythologies*. New York: Hill and Wang, 1972.

Bartram, John. *A Journey from Pennsylvania to Onondaga in 1743*. Barre, Massachusetts: Imprint Society, 1973.

Baudrillard, Jean. *Selected Writings*. Stanford: Stanford University Press, 1988.

905-374-RIDE (7433)–
call now!

Berton, Pierre. *Niagara: A History of the Falls*. Toronto: McClelland & Stewart, 1992.

Braider, Donald. *The Niagara*. New York: Holt, Rinehart & Winston, 1972.

Bristow, George Frederick. Niagara: *Symphony for Grand Orchestra and Chorus* [arranged for four hands by author]. New York: Lincoln Library for the Performing Arts, 1890.

Butor, Michel. *Niagara*. Trans. Elinor S. Miller. Chicago: Henry Regnery Company, 1969.

Canfield, William W. *The Legends of the Iroquois Told by "The Cornplanter."* New York: Wessels, 1902.

Cometti, Elizabeth, ed. *The American Journals of Lt. John Enys*. Syracuse: Syracuse University Press, 1976.

Cooper, William. *A Guide in the Wilderness, Or the History of the First Settlements in the Western Countries of New York, with Useful Instructions to Future Settlers*. Dublin: np., 1810.

Davison, Gideon Minor. *The Fashionable Tour*. Saratoga Springs: np., 1825 [citation fr. McKinsey, 301).

DeBord, Guy. *The Society of the Spectacle and Other Films*. Rebel Press, 1992.

Donaldson, Gordon. *Niagara! The Eternal Circus*. 1st. ed. Toronto: Doubleday Canada Ltd., 1979.

Douglas, Ann. *The Feminization of American Culture*. New York: Knoph, 1977.

Dow, Charles Mason. *Anthology and Bibliography of Niagara Falls. Vols. 1 & 2.* Albany: State University of New York, 1921.

Dubinsky, Karen. "Vacations in the 'Contact Zone': Race, Gender, and the Traveler at Niagara Falls." In Pierson, 251-69.

Dunlap, William. *A Trip to Niagara, or Travelers in America (a farce).* Richard Moody, ed. Dramas from the American Theater, 1762-1909. Cleveland: Cleveland World, 1966 [citation fr. McKinsey, 303).

Evans, Gail E. H. "Storm Over Niagara: A Catalyst in Reshaping Government in the United States and Canada During the Progressive Era." *Natural Resources Journal* 32.1 (Winter, 1992): 27-54.

"The Falls." Written and Directed by Revin McMahon." Rev. Variety 343.8 (3 June, 1991): 51.

Fuller, Margaret. *Summer on the Lakes. The Writings of Margaret Fuller.* New York: Viking, 1941. Rpt. *The Essential Margaret Fuller.* Ed. Jeffrey Steele. New Brunswick: Rutgers University Press, 1992.

Greenhill, Ralph, and Thomas D. Mahoney. *Niagara.* Toronto: University of Toronto Press, 1969.

Greenaway, Peter, Dir. *The Falls.* Motion Picture.[27] Script by Greenaway. Color, 185 mins. BFI, 1980.

Harris, Neil. *Humbug! The Art of P T Barnum.* Boston: Little, Brown, 1973.

Hawthorne, Nathaniel. "My Visit to Niagara." *The Snow-Image and Uncollected Tales. Works.* Centenary Edition. Columbus: Ohio State University Press, 1974.

Hennepin, Louis. *A New Discovery of a Vast Country in America. London, 1698*; Rpt. New York: Kraus, 1972 [citation fr. McKinsey, 284).

Herndon, G. Melvin. "A Grandiose Scheme to Navigate and Harness Niagara Falls" [on engineer and inventor William Tatham's "inclined plane" for the transporting of ships over Niagara Falls, as described in Tatham's Political Economy of Inland Navigation, 1799]. *New York Historical Society Quarterly* 58.1 (1974): 7-17.

Howells, W. D., et al. *The Niagara Book.* New York: Doubleday, 1901.

—. *Their Wedding Journey, With an Additional Chapter on Niagara Revisited.* Boston: Houghton, Mifflin, and Company, 1899.

Ingraham, Joseph *Wentworth. Manual for the Use of Visitors to the Falls of Niagara Intended as an Epitome of, and Temporary Substitute for, a Larger and More*

27. Though this film is not cited above and not directly related to "Niagara on the Rocks…", it now occurs to me that a view of the Falls (Niagara) might affect one in a similar way (vue)—see PostFace below, []—consider Cotton…

Extended Work, Relative to the Most Stupendous Wonder of the World. Buffalo: Charles Faxon, 1834.

International Niagara Falls Engineering Board and the International Joint Commission United States and Canada. *Report on the Preservation and Enhancement of Niagara Falls*. Washington & Ottawa: N.P., 1953.

Izard, Ralph. *An Account of a Journey to Niagara, Montreal, and Quebec, in 1765*. New York: np., 1846 [citation fr. McKinsey, 186).

James, Henry. "Niagara." *Portraits of Places*. Boston: Houghton, Mifflin, and Company, 1884.

Jameson. Anna. *The Falls of Niagara Being a Complete Guide to...the Great Cataract*. London: Nelson, 1858 [citation fr. McKinsey, 314; ellipses are hers).

Jameson, A. B. M. *Winter Studies and Summer Rambles in Canada*. London, n.p., 1838; New York, n.p., 1839; also in Dow, I, p. 210 [citation fr. McKinsey, 308).

Jasen, Patricia. "Romanticism, Modernity, and the Evolution of Tourism on the Niagara Frontier, 1790-1850." *Canadian Historical Review* 72.3 (September, 1991): 283-318.

Johnson, F. H. (Practical Surveyor, Resident at Niagara, and Author of Maps and Statistics of the Falls). *Every Man His Own Guide at Niagara Falls Without the Necessity of Inquiry or Possible Mistake; Including the Sources of the Niagara and all Places of Interest, Both on the American and Canadian Side, Embellished with Views of the Falls and Suspension Bridge, by the Best Artists, and a Large Map of Niagara River, by the Author, Also, a Full Description of the Several Routes from the Falls to Montreal, Boston, Saratoga Springs, Via Lake Ontario, Lake Champlain, Albany, New York, Etc*. Rochester: D. M. Dewey, 1852.

Kadlecek, Mary. "Love Canal—Ten Years Later." *Conservationist* 43.3 (November, 1988): 40-43.

"The Lip." *New Yorker* 62.2 (3 March, 1986): 28-9.

Madoff, Mark. "Niagara: Voices on the Brink." *Rev. Canadian Literature* (Spring 1991): 196-7.

McKinsey, Elizabeth. *Niagara Falls: Icon of the American Sublime*. Cambridge: Cambridge University Press,

Mortier, Willy. *Niagara: Jazz Suite for Clarinet Quartet. Bruxelles: Editions* J. Maurer, 1983.

Neill, Michael. "Tennessee Outdoorsman Jessie Sharp Challenged Niagara's Mighty Falls in a Tiny Canoe—and Lost." *People Weekly* 33.25 (25 June, 1990): 89-92.

Niagara [film]. Dir. Henry Hathaway. Starring Marilyn Monroe, Joseph Cotton, and Jean Peters. 20th Century Fox Corporation, 1953.

The Niagara Falls Electrical Handbook. Niagara Falls, New York: The American Institute of Electrical Engineers, 1904.

"Niagara Share Fund Will Liquidate." *Barron's* 22 July, 1991: 40-5.

Ogborn, Miles. "Other Studies: Places on the Margin: Alternative Geographies of Modernity." *Rev. Journal of Historical Geography* 17.4 (October, 1991):495-497.

Peacock, Shane. "The Falls Guy." *Saturday Night* 108.3 (April, 1993): 46-8.

Petrie, Francis J. *Roll Out the Barrel: The Story of Niagara's Daredevils*. Erin, Ontario: Boston Mills Press, 1985.

Pierson, Ruth Roach, et al., eds. *Nation, Empire, Colony: Historicizing Gender and Race*. Bloomington: Indiana UP, 1998.

Poe, Edgar Allan. *The Narrative of Arthur Gordon Pym of Nantucket*. New York: Viking, 1975 [rpt. 1986].

Roudolph, Jack. "Niagara." *American Heritage* 39.2 (March, 1988): 91-2.

Seibell, George A. *300 Years Since Father Hennepin: Niagara Falls in Art, 1678-1978*. Niagara Falls, Ontario: Niagara Falls Heritage Foundation, 1978.

Shields, Rob. *Places on the Margin: Alternative Geographies of Modernity*. New York: Routledge, 1991.

"Stereoscopic Views of Niagara Falls." Miriam & Ira D. Walach Division of Art, Photography Collection. Robert Dennis Collection of Stereoscopic Views. New York: New York Public Library—Research Library, 1860-1885.

Sorkin, Michael, ed. *Variations on a Theme Park: The New American City and the End of Public Space*. New York: Hill and Wang, 1992.

Tesmer, Irving H., ed. *Colossal Cataract: A Geological history of Niagara Falls*. Albany: State University of New York Press, 1981.

Trent, Tommy. *Niagara Falls Mystery [the comic book history of Niagara Falls]*. Balloonsville: 2-D, is happening…

Twain, Mark. "Niagara." "1601"; or, Conversation as It Was at the Fireside in the Time of the Tudors and Sketches New and Old. New York: The Golden Hind Press, 1933.

United States, Congress, Senate, Committee on Public Works. Niagara Falls and Niagara River, New York. Hearings Before a Subcommittee of the Committee on Public Works, United States

Senate, Eighty-second Congress, First Session, on S. 517, S. 1963, and S. 2021, Bills to preserve the Scenic Beauty of the Niagara Falls and River and to Authorize the Construction of Certain Public Works on that River for Power and Other Purposes and for Other Purposes, August 21 and 22, 1951. Washington: U. S. Government Printing Office, 1951.

Vidler, Virginia. *Niagara Falls: One Hundred Years of Souvenirs*. 1st. ed. Utica, New York: North County Books, 1985.

Watson, Richard. *Niagara: A Novel*. Minneapolis: Coffee House Press, 1993.

Welty, Eudora. "The Key." *The Collected Stories of Eudora Welty*. New York: Harcourt Brace Jovanovich, 1980.

I'M STILL OUT HERE. I'LL SHOW THEM... BUT WHO?
6/30/1859: 25,000 PEOPLE WATCHED
AS I CARRIED MY MANAGER ON MY BACK
—ALL THE WAY—
AND RETURNED, BACKWARDS, TURNING SOMERSAULTS
NEAR THE END.
AND NOW...
A ROPE'S
NEVER SILENT.
OR IS THERE JUST TOO MUCH TO HEAR?

WHAT SAY, FEET?

WELL, GO ON...

Dialogizing Jurisprudence

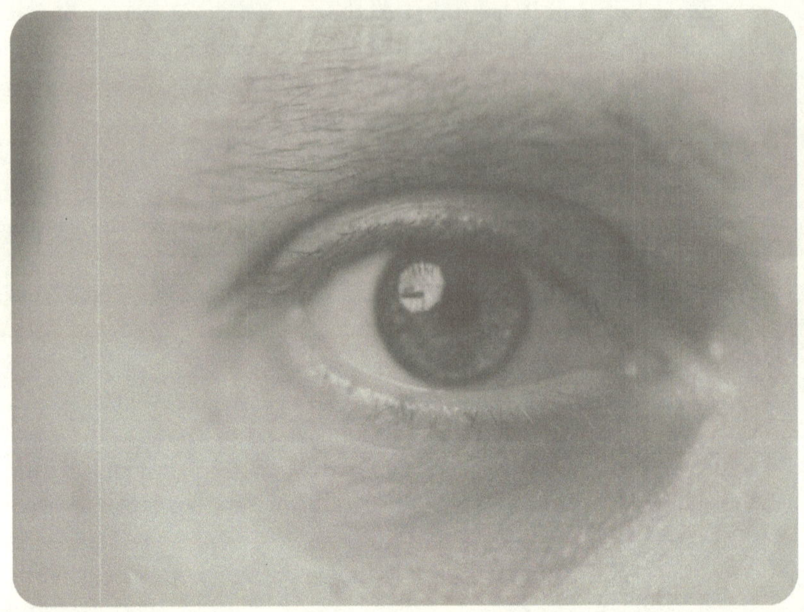

Fig. 4: Eye, witness.

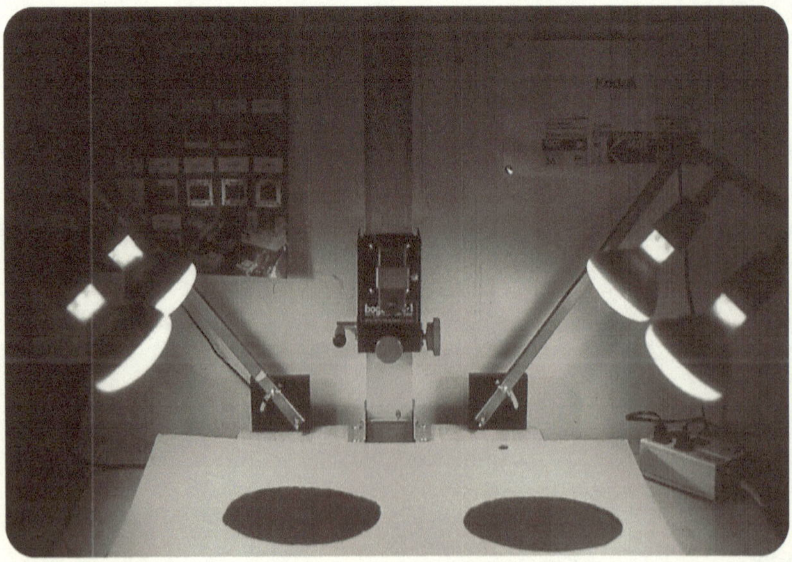

Fig. 5: 68 S. W. 989. Exhibit 2: photo op/set up for the "two-hole" experiment. Reproduction of projected images from "Poetic Discourse...".

3 Script 2: Poetic Discourse v Legal Discourse: The Case of Charles Reznikoff

Poetic Discourse v Legal Discourse: The Case of Charles Reznikoff is a performative interpretation of Charles Reznikoff's *Testimony: The United States 1890-1915*. Reznikoff's two-volume book of poems is based on law cases summarized in the National Reporter System (NRS). The courtroom trial (including the "setting" of the courtroom) becomes a structuring metaphor for the Fluxus-inspired performance piece whose *mise en scene* blends props and live action with video, slide projections, and verbal collage.[28] Discourses brought into play include the legal language of the National Reporter System (including adulterated quotes of witnesses), Reznikoff's poetic "refinement" of case summaries in the NRS, quotes from various works on legal discourse and critical legal studies, and my own commentary on the poems and the process of their creation. Just as Reznikoff "cuts up" his sources to create the poems in *Testimony*, I disrupt the lyric and narrative flow of Reznikoff's poems by putting them back into dialogue with their sources; throughout, the slides tell a story of parallel processes—Reznikoff's journey through the 1000s of pages of the NRS to arrive at a relatively small group of poems reenacted and parodied by my own journey through his sources and drafts, retracing the processes that produced *Testimony* to arrive at expanded performances of often quite short poems. Work produces more work. Reznikoff's obsessive cutting and editing inspires my verbal excesses and slapstick buffoonery; it is low comedy *vis a vis* high criticism. Two issues I'm concerned with are (1) the impossibility of litigating the irrational: how Reznikoff reclaims —through the "sincerity" of an "objectivist" discourse— the deconstructive potency of the criminal moment that the language and procedures of jurisprudence attempt to contain and control, defuse and repress; (2) how Reznikoff, as a poet working for a law book publisher, discovers his relation to/finds his way through the not-self (the thousands of pages of case histories) while I, troping my persona as his reader/interpreter, comprehend this performatively, finding my relation to/way through the mass of material by and about him, retracing and partially reinventing his own path through the not-self. We are both bricoleurs constructing tentative worlds.

28. The font deployed in the current transcription Mrs. Eaves OT.

Judge (J)
Prosecution (P)
Defense(D)
Bailiff (B)

To one side of the performance area, a prop table. Most props are visible; a toy train and a small black box are hidden. A sturdy table or desk marks the center of the space. At the other end of the performance field, a video monitor and a small, portable table, perhaps with wheels. Ideally, the Judge's podium is placed to one side of the performance arena, slightly elevated, equidistant from both performers and audience, and at a right angle to the latter. The audience becomes the fifth performer—part "jury," part impromptu and unpredictable chorus, silent and reflective, or contributing its voices to the plurilogue; its position partially determines the configuration of the performance space, the field within which what happens happens. The audience is that multiple consciousness (or nexus of consciousnesses) toward which all is directed.... The judge's voice is amplified, yet displaced from its source, coming from behind the audience, from above...

After the "lights out" command, the performance space remains suffused with ambient light from the dual projected images. This is the main light source for the piece; certain events are highlighted by a spot-flashlight operated by B.

* * *

[*P leafs through script, adjusts props; Bailiff runs in, looks up at Judge anxiously, intensely. P observes him in a handheld mirror—one of the props he happens to be examining at the time*]

J: Bailiff?

B: Ready for the jury, your honor?

[*silence; B keeps staring, at uneasy attention, at J; P smiles, broadly, sarcastically*]

J: [*condescendingly*] Bailiff...

[*B slowly looks round, chagrined, and runs back out; P switches on TV, sits*]

* * *

[***The "Deposition" is read by J while P watches a silent chase scene, an excerpt from the "real-life" crime show*** Cops. ***"Q" and "A" are read as "Question" and "Answer"; lights low...***]

J: Deposition

"Q."

[slide A1 B1[29]

"A. How to begin. With which Voice?"

"Q. Did you start out with the intention of scripting the poems as dialogues?"
"A. I started with the question of the criminal; how many of the poems didn't concern themselves with jurisprudence, with holdings, but took us to the point of a breach and left us there..."

"...Go on."

[slide A_2

"But the longer I looked at the poems and their sources—case summaries in the National Reporter System—I began to see there was something else going on—a kind of debate, a..."

J & P [***simultaneously**, **though differently***]: "conflictual dynamic."

J [***continuing***]: "What was most intriguing was the way in which this "debate" influenced the shape—the rhythm, tone, and structure—of the poem finally presented to the reader."

[***P rises, pauses video (B switches it off later), crosses to center table***]

Q. Do you find it better to ask and answer your own questions? Do you find your answers clearer, less hesitant, more to the point?

[slide A_3 B_2

---

29. For descriptions of slides, see the "Slide List."

P [***overlapping the second question***]: Who can tell if a question originates with the questioner, an answer with the answerer.

*

P: I see you trying to find your place in a discourse. Every morning, on the subway, leaving your wife at 14th street, continuing on across the bridge to your tryst with Corpus Juris

J & P [***differently***]: —the body of law.

P: Surrounded by the thousands of pages of the National Reporter System, painstakingly summarizing cases—a way to enter this discourse

J P: the body of law, law's body—

P: searching for an opening, even a crack, to "read it." Body law.

J: To make it speak.

P: And so you enter into a conversation with it, follow its leads but alter its course, reopen what it attempts to close over—

B: wiping away all that was held,

J: all the judicial opinions turning on a jurisprudential technicality...

D: "What I wanted to do was to create by selection, arrangement, and the rhythm of the words used as a mood or feeling."

P: I ride with you across the bridge in the morning, walk back with you in the evening...

J: back over Brooklyn Bridge,

B: across to the West Side...

D: up Riverside Drive toward Riverdale, as far as we can... walking, talking...

*

P: This fragmentary text: patchwork of poems, sources, comments; murderings and mutilations of discourse… [***looking at projected image of Reznikoff***] do I follow you in this? Your papers are open to public view, but do I have the right? Do I go too far?

J: The poem as evidence.

D: "I wasn't interested in what the jury held."

J: This is the evidence.

P: These are the facts.

J [***to jury/audience***]: It is for you…

P [***overlap, to audience***]: Corpus…?

J: to decide.

P: I'll cast out some speculations,

J: theoretical dots and dashes—

P: beams of light shot at random through the debris, the field of shattered codes…

J: a tenuous structure of articulations always on the verge of being swallowed by its *aporias*.

P: *Mise en abime* [***lights out***].

B: Take aim [***spot/flashlight on P***].

[slide B_3

*

[***opening statement, read by P***]

P: that poetic discourse that does not fully reveal its methods of production, its internal polemics, risks a subsequent loss of perspective on the part of the reader…

J: The opening statement is not to be taken as evidence.

P: that since the voices of witnesses presenting testimony are always already reinscribed, appropriated by the legal system, it should be emphasized that a poetry based on such testimony is a further appropriation, or reappropriation, of those voices, a further deposition in a train of depositions in a case that is undecidable; that just as Reznikoff recovers the criminal moment, so the dialogue that produces—that is the poems—should be represented; that it is both poetic and legal discourses that are put into quotes, in process/on trial through this dialogue; [***walking toward audience***] that the dialogue should be sustained, that it is our duty to expand texts in this way, that it is a service to you, the reader, an empowerment of your relationship to the discourses involved…

J: Step back! There are rules of decorum, counsel, and I am a proceduralist, today.

P that Reznikoff's poems not only demonstrate the impossibility of litigating the irrational, but that by cutting the "fact" out of the hermeneutical schema, the epistemological and rhetorical system that produces its meaning, Reznikoff's poetry becomes a hole—an ***aporia***—in legal discourse, its negative other; that Reznikoff uses the court's own language to trope its performance; that rhythmically, also, legal discourse forms a counter music to poetic discourse, or vice versa; that in all these ways Reznikoff's poetry is in contention with legal discourse, and that it is one of our tasks here today to reconstruct a portion of this dialogue.... that my position is somewhat false, since both plaintiff and defense are what I make them; in representing the plaintiff I am the plaintiff, but I am also the other… And I'm not sure who my client is… since it may be me—that is, the nexus of theories and ideologies I stand for—then I must be representing myself...

D: Objection! Self-reflexive.

J: Sustained! It does not behoove counsel to jeopardize the authority displayed in courtroom proceedings by carrying on in this way...please edit your commentary more carefully...

D: Edit it, at least.

[***Flashlight off. Except for the "hearing on evidence," the remainder of the performance takes place in semi-darkness; a faint, undersea luminosity...***]

*

J [***to audience***]: Anyone who is unhappy with what happens here today, if you disagree, certainly it doesn't have to stop here, there are ways that you can appeal...

***

D: *Testimony...*: "The Noise of Civilization"

J: I recognize—I do not call—witnesses

D: "The hum of machinery, the noise of wagons on the public
highways—
and the crowd watching a baseball game on a Sunday afternoon,
perhaps as many as two or three thousand,
shouting and stamping on the steps of the grandstand,
cheering and shouting
and heard half a mile and more away."

[slide A_4

[***J, D and B's lines are heard simultaneously, a murmur of voices not altogether sorted out, as if privately consulting about the evidence, under P's discourse***]

P: Floating up from the world of legal documents—53 A 289—no "evidence" of a legal issue, here. What kind of testimony is this?

D: This is an application for an injunction to restrain the making of noise, which, it is alleged…

P: from behind the bar-like crossovers of the early draft, the voice, perhaps once a personal voice, the evidential testimony of a particular speaker—

B: "From the appearance of the crowd, I imagined that either a prize fight or a horse race was about to take place."

P: recorded, relevant to certain holdings of the court, perhaps serving an appeal, affirmed or reversed—

J: Whenever a private right is invaded, and this court is called upon to protect it, and a proper case is made out…

P: here generalized to a condition…

J: this court is bound to give the remedy.

P: slips through, dressed as a modern lyric, an imagist poem (in whose voice?). Poetic discourse rewriting legal discourse rewriting witness account rewriting event…

B: "apparently caused by the yelling, cheering, and shouting… the stamping of feet… prevent my family and many of my boarders from the quiet enjoyment…"

P: an event cut out of a social-cultural flow to serve as evidence—for what crime? —in a courtroom collage. (Sitting in Part 30, King's County Supreme Court, I, too, could hear the traffic outside…

D: the noise of vehicles propelled along the public highways, and the like… a noise which, made to answer some useful purpose…

P: as the prosecution introduces a case of fraud). The lyric voice slips through—

B: "shouts, cheers, and stamping of feet... destroy the comfort of myself and my family..."

P: gets around the bars, while the commentary, initially central to the poem, is barred from the poem itself to a position of authority over it: "The noise of civilization." The poem a celebration of this noise, human and nonhuman.

J: one of the necessary accompaniments of modern civilization... will, if used for an unlawful purpose...

P: "Perhaps as many as two or three thousand." The poem ***is*** evidence; the comment sits in judgment.

[***P tapes a bar-like pattern on video monitor***]:

J: I will advise an order that the defendant, pending the suit and until the further order of the court, be restrained...

P: ("Perhaps," the rhetorical mediator, measures our distance from the realities it contemplates, acknowledges the "facts" as signs, marks on paper.)

J: Question for the jury: Can this filtering from the legal discourse a poetic discourse with a "theme"—the nondualistic confluence of oppositions that is the "voice" of civilization—

P [***simultaneously***]: "A careful reading of the affidavits leads me to the conclusion that the noise in this case does appreciably disturb..."

J: be considered a survival, even where the materials—the language—used to articulate this theme formerly occurred in a context to which such theme is clearly irrelevant?

[slide B_4

[***using black tape, D and B begin to "map" a dialogue between the projected images***]

P: the bar is surveillance... surveillance is a crossing... the crossing locates but does not recognize...

D:

To a discursive act, a discourse in act,
profoundly committed to the rules of popular knowledge
there was applied a question derived elsewhere
and administered by others.[30]

P: I tell you now, the case is not decidable.

[***B plays*** Cops ***through monitor tape grid: one minute; continues chase scene***]

[***P & D continue mapping (P taking B's place) to create lines of connection between source and poem—like word matching; they may also deploy arms, fists, or other parts of their bodies to "bar," or cross out, parts of source. They do this silently, or reading fragments of each, in turn and/or in conflict.***]

***

[slide A_5

D: *Testimony*, II, 122, X: "Episode in the Life of a Schoolteacher"

[***P removes suit jacket and sits attentively, facing D, as at a poetry reading; as D reads, P loosens and takes off his tie***]

"The Negro schoolmistress gave birth to a child—
her parents did not know and she did not want them to—
gave birth in the school's water-closet
and left the child under the water-closet on the ground.
Three Negro girls who went to the school
at recess saw the baby under a hole in the seat.
One of the girls had jumped up and said,
"Oh, there is a baby!"
It was raising its hands and kicking its feet
but its eyes were shut..."

P [***as D closes book and passing to B, who passes to audience***]: 68 S. W. 989

30. The voices of Legal Studies and Critical Legal Studies (see bibliography), centered on the page, are usually presented by J, and occasionally be P, D, and B.

J [correcting, or supplementing]: Exhibit 1

D: "and its mouth full of sand."

P [***simultaneously***]: sand...

J [***interrupting***]: Infanticide—Evidence—Sufficiency

P: hand... moving eye, blood on a hand a mouth full of sand what sort of cry...? a privy for a crib...what blocks the light? Silenced voices, buried voices.

[***during the following dialogue, J, P, D, & B interact with each other and the audience***]

D: The Negro schoolmistress gave birth to a child—

P [***to audience, standing***]: "When I left the house, I did not know that I was going to give birth to a child."

D: her parents did not know and she did not want them to—

P: "They do not know it now."

B: "We did not tell anyone about seeing the baby that day. I don't know why we did not."

J: Appellant testified that she left the house, feeling that she would have "an ordinary action," but about the time she reached the closet, felt an unusual pain, sat down upon the closet, and gave birth.

D: gave birth in the school's water-closet

B: "I got up and looked at it..."

J: "Defendant...

P [***simultaneous***]: (did they take her name away for you, Lula?)

D: "went out during 'books,' and went into the privy."

P: "I did not see her go in...

J: everything witnesses say is [*must* be] framed...

P: she did not tell me that she went in...

J: by the lawyers' questions.

P: but I know she did. I know that as well as I know anything else I have sworn to in this case."

D: and left the child under the water-closet on the ground

P [***to J, indirectly, with self-conscious rhetorical force***]: "and leaving it naked and exposed to the weather, without covering, food, and drink, and without nursing and suckling the infant as its age demanded..."

[slide B_5

D [***reading from the projected source, as edited by Reznikoff***]: was... charged... with killing her... child by... abandoning it [right] after birth and leaving it naked... to the weather... without... suckling...

B: "I was young and inexperienced,"

P: were these your words, Eula?

B: "and did not know what to do..."

P: so what did you do?

B: "so I left it..."

P: and then what? Why?

B: "and went back to the house, believing it was dead."

D: "'It did not cry or move, and I thought it was dead.'"

P: "It did not move nor cry, and, of course, I thought..."

J: The state relied upon the testimony of

D: Three Negro girls who went to the school

J: of which appellant was school mistress: Rachel Stribbling, Edna Stribbling, and Luala Kinchlow, 12-14 years of age

[***The testimony of the three girls, the defendant, and the poem itself often overlap, disorienting the latter***]

D: at recess saw the baby under a hole in the seat

P: The water-closet was about 100 yards from the school house, sets east and west, and has two holes in the seat.

D: The baby was under the east hole

B: "The baby was under the west hole."

J: are you sure?

D: "I am sure of this."

P: "We did not look through a hole in the seat, but saw the body through a hole in the floor..."

D: "We saw the baby from in front of the closet, where some of the planks failed to reach the ground. We did not see the baby through a hole in the floor, because there is none."

J: not characterized by the certainty which should justify...

P: "I am 12 years old."

B: "We saw the baby from behind the privy. It was between the two holes in the seat under the floor. We could not see it from in front of the privy..."

D: One of the girls…

P: Lula

D: had jumped up and said,

J: All three utterly fail to mention the fact until…

P: "We all saw it about the same time."

B: "I saw the baby at 12 o'clock… I saw it at 3 o'clock. I did not see it but once. I do not know why I told him that."

D: "Oh, there is a baby!"

P: "We never said anything else; just stood there a bit."

J: too uncertain and speculative.

P: "I saw some blood…"

B: "I never told a soul about this until the baby was found the next day."

D: It was raising its hands and kicking its feet

P: on Tuesday of Christmas week

D: about 12 o'clock

B: "It was crying, and moving its hands and feet."

P: "It cried, and raised its hands and kicked its feet."

D: "I heard something crying, and ran back to the house. I saw blood…"

B: blood on the floor…

P: "It did not cry or move, and I thought… of course, I thought…

B: I did not touch it at any time."

D: but its eyes were shut

P: and its mouth?

B: "I don't know whether it was shut or not, but do know that its eyes were shut. I could see its eyeballs. They were black. Yes, I just said its eyes were shut. I don't know what eyeballs are.

D: and its mouth full…

P: "it was about this long."

B: "It had some sand sprinkled over it."

D: "The baby's mouth was full of…

B: "I did not touch it, but did cover it up with leaves and dirt.

J: blood was observed…

D: "It was her right hand that was bloody."

P: "I don't know whether the baby was black or white."

D: "It was brown."

J: not being satisfied with the contradictory statements…

D: "It don't make much difference with me how I swear."

P:

The purported voice of legal authority
is in fact the voice of social power.

J: hmmm.

P [***simultaneously***]: Its mouth was full of sand.

D: "Have never talked about this case to anyone."

J: Eula Nobles was convicted of murder in the second degree, and appeals. Reversed.

[slide A_6

P: all this happening between the lines of Reznikoff's poem, which is another "version," based not on "eye" witnesses, but on a further edition (a recomposition) of the already prompted, tutored, and edited voices of the three witnesses and the defendant.

J [***interrupting***]: You bring back my—no, not my law school days…

…the problem of missing voices
in the official discourse of the law…

P: But in mixing down these voices to the "voice" of the poem, which we now see cannot be claimed by a single speaker, must be seen as rhetorical, the voice perhaps of a discourse with its "rules" (its "Methods" of composition and "Revision"); cannot be claimed, least of all by Reznikoff—a voice always already

D [***interrupt; light stick***[31]]: Objection—Jargon.

P: split (fissured)

J [***interrupt***]: Sustained

P [***becoming fainter and fainter, fading under the succeeding fragment of legal discourse read by J***]: whose tensions resonate through at least nine registers—the three girls, the defendant, the scripting

31. A six inch emergency light source, Cyalume[tm], "snap and shake" to activate; every time there is an objection, one is hurled in the direction of the object of the objection or objector. Light sticks have many practical uses, such as marking the scene of an accident, signaling, reading maps, etc.

and controlling voices of the lawyers (voices themselves tutored by the legal system they work within), the unidentified voice of the writer of the case summary, based on the anonymous notes of the court reporter; there are many lost words—fragments of testimony, what may have been discussed behind closed doors between lawyer and witness—that we will never hear.

J: [***read over P***]:

At its most fundamental level, the voices of litigants
are expressed and presumably heard, but, through a process
that is remarkable as well as largely unremarked upon, the law
selects among these voices, silencing some and transforming
others to conform to legal categories and conventions...

P: All this always already going on—rehearsals, decisions, exclusions, reinscriptions—by the time the poem arrives on the scene to (re)compose its "voice" out of these.

J:

most voices are silenced;
Those that survive do so in a barely recognizable form.

[***B prepares two (—) hole experiment. Placing a white glove on right hand, picks up a board with three holes in it: one large enough to fit head through, the other slightly smaller (these two are parallel); another, very small hole, barely noticeable except when light shines through it, is above the other two and off to one side. Holding board so that larger holes are horizontal, with his free hand B selects a red Cyalume, snaps, aims through one of two holes...***]

P: But the poem does not escape this murmur of voices by avoiding the legal discourse per se—what the court held, the jurisprudential points, the citation of precedence. Ironically, in evading certain aspects of legal discourse, the poem preserves its heartbeat by smoothing out and highlighting evidentiary language; yet syncopates its beat, too: in representing what the girls saw, in its linguistic reenactment of the moment of sight and recognition, the poem rides in on a point of view that can't be said with certainty to belong to any one of the witnesses; it invents a fifth point of view.

[***B shoots red light stick; P deflects shot; B notes exact time of occurrence***]

J [***as B shoots***]: Exhibit 2

P: The poem says (claims to know): There was a negro schoolmistress, she gave birth in a water-closet, she left the baby in the water closet, three negro girls—pupils at the school—saw it—but how? through which hole or holes? From above, through one or between two holes; from beneath from in front or behind, seeing the baby-object through one or more holes "under" one or more holes. The play on (through) holes is a visual restaging of the conflict of voices. But the poem keeps mum about the perspectival confusion, as well as the disagreements among the voices.

[***B shoots white light stick; as before***]

J:

This increased attention to voices
that...have been suppressed or ignored
has created a new, practical problem: that of
finding and hearing them.

[slide A_7

P: [***Taking holes from B***] How many holes are there? [***looking through holes***] The poem "decides" on a point of view, for one of the girls then "jumped up and said"—and so we are above, looking down through a hole, the only hole, though we can't say which witness, or perhaps the mother herself, might have looked through a hole or holes—i.e., the point of view originates in the poem's restaging of the moment; both poem and legal discourse rely, in the one case, for narrative impact, and in the other, to attain remedies, on a contour of suppressions and representations, imposed limitations on interpretations of the "evidence."

J: By hearing better we understand more.

P [***holes mask projected images of poem and source as P walks back and forth in front of them, holding board above head***]:

The girls sat on one of two or two of two holes, momentarily blocking the passage of light to the object beneath (forcing choice, as in the two-slit experiment in physics, or no choice); standing, however, their seats give them each two choices (or three, if inbetweenness is a choice): the possible combinations are 2-1, 1-1, 2-2, 1-2, 1-1, 3...

D [***interrupt; light stick***]: Objection! Obfuscation. Interference...

P: the poem gives us one...

J [***interrupt***]: Overruled

P: through which we see and "hear" the struggling inarticulate force beneath, under, through (struggling to be heard, be freed, be alive, be dead...) Yet,

[slide B_6

while jurisprudence must silence crisis—" It occurs to us that their testimony is too unreliable"—the poem redirects it, holding open still another hole that the court can't seal over... here a... there a... everywhere a... Odd or even, the texts are full of holes... ()

J:

The discourse which is the raw material of the case
is treated as if transparent, transformed in to a window
through which the law views the set of constructed meanings
it calls "facts."

P: What we see through the hole is an "objectivist" inaccuracy; an illusion of the dead brought to life? Inarticulate gesturings. It is not clear what is to be said, or what predication could clarify without creating a further self-deception; language, master of illusions; for even when it can speak, its mouth is—" always already"—" full of sand."

D: Objection—speculation, troping, repetition, structuration...

J: Sustained

[***B brings a napkin or rag to P, who flaps it open, with preemptory etiquette***]

J: There is a remote possibility that the child was born alive. But under the charge in the indictment the evidence must show: 1. That the child was born alive; and 2. that the mother (appellant) abandoned it with the intent that it should die.

P [***stuffing rag in mouth, in defiance; overlap***]:
At its most fundamental level, the voices of litigants are expressed
and presumably heard, but, through a process that is remarkable
as well as largely unremarked upon, the law selects among these voices,
silencing some and transforming others
to conform to legal categories and conventions.
[***P spits out rag***]

B [***overlap***]: Exhibit 3?

J: We do not believe the testimony sufficiently shows the truth of either of these propositions. The judgment is reversed and the cause remanded.

* * *

[slides A, B: blank]

P: Your honor, I request a hearing for inclusion of evidence.

J: Very well. [***to audience***] We will take a short recess. Bailiff, please conduct the jury out of hearing.

[***B leaves room***]

P: Your honor, I wish to begin my presentations of the poems with references to particular cases...

D: Your honor, I think the poems better without them, and that their inclusion would only bias the jury.

P: Reznikoff himself includes references to the National Reporter System in many of his drafts, but eliminates them from the published versions. Why eliminate this trace of another voice or voices? I submit that this decision may be partially influenced by the publication process itself, that the poems "look" more like lyric poems, look "cleaner" without the such references. Also, rather than biasing the jury, inclusion of such "leads" would broaden the field of inquiry.

D: This is speculation. Besides, elimination of the references has nothing to do with the "look" of the poem: we simply don't need such references. The poems stand on their own and, indeed, resonate on a more general level—the level of the human condition—without them. Pinning a poem to a particular source does not necessarily locate its "voice" (as you've noted yourself, the source is already a composite of translated voices), and attempts to limit the scope of the poem.

P: True, the poem stands on its own, but it also stands in relation to those other discourses—however altered they may be...

D: But he focuses on the criminal moment, not the legal discourse...

P: But we also lose the evidence of, the trace of a process, an interaction, an encounter or conflict among discourses, which is part of the history of production of the poem and puts both legal discourse and poetic discourse in process/on trial... far from limiting the scope of the poem, this perspective expands it; we can still see how the poem applies "generally," as you put it, to the "human condition," but we also gain insight into the specific discursive encounters out of which it arises—which also tells us something about the "human condition," the way work gets done, what commotion underlies the apparently stable surface of the "finished product..."

D: So why not present this hearing to the jury as well? Really, prosecutor, there are certain procedures that make a system work...

J: All right, counsels, please don't turn the courtroom into a stage for socio-political, ideological debates...

P: (what else is it.)

J: The evidence may be admitted, but not in a manner so as to bias the jury, or prejudice any of the litigants.

P: Your honor, I'd also like to include the court's holdings…

D: The prosecutor seems determined to beat the rabbits out of the bush… chopping the poems up the way he does is disenchanting enough…

P: It may be one of the unhappy tasks of critical investigation…

J: Counsel, you must give your audience—that is, the jury—more space for contemplation. You may start off the poem/collages with references to the NRS, but I will state the holdings myself at the end of individual presentations, if I judge such inclusions to be relevant.

D: and my evidence—my witness, my defense— will continue to be, as has been, the testimony of the poems themselves

***

J: 74 S.E. 138

[slide A_8 B_7

[poem read by D; as P & J interrupt, D keeps reading]

D: *Testimony…*: "Dangers at a Crossing"

"Driving his buggy along the highway
he came to a railroad crossing:
a freight car was blocking…"

P [***light stick; interrupt***]: Objection. Participle…

J: Overruled.

"…it

and had been left there for days.
A showman had left it,
and the stench of the wild animals in it
startled the horse."

[***B, standing at the portable table, opens a deck of cards***]

"As the driver of the buggy tried to go around the car,
the noise of rabbits jumping...

P [***light stick; interrupt***]: Objection. Rhythmic manipulation. Syntactic repetition...

J [***overlap***]: Overruled.

"...about
in a wire cage left on the station platform
added to the fright of the horse;
and the buggy crashed against the embankment of the railroad
just above the crossing,
flinging the driver out."

P [***picking up a rod with a Cyalume at each end, one red and one white, activates the red end. The succeeding text should be performed in the voice of an MC for a small road circus that fancies itself a big top, or in the voice of the announcer on People's Court; as P reads, he gestures to his own script and to B, D, and J, including them all in the show; B contorts himself, performs as a circus pony and is led around by P with rod and ridden by P. D blows whistle, performs circus antics***]:

> Ladies and Gentlemen...It thus appears that there was evidence of *two* causes which frightened the horse and made him run away, *2 causes—*

B [***contorting***]: Exhibit 4

P: the foul odor from the car, *and* noise made by rabbits. The *complaint* contains *no* allegation of negligence against the *defendant* with respect to the noise made by the ***rabbits***, and, if the *evidence* had shown that the horse was frightened by that alone, the case would have *failed*. But, while it is necessary to *recovery* to show that an act of *negligence* alleged in the complaint was one of the *proximate causes*, it is not essential to show that it was the *sole proximate cause*. There may be a recovery upon evidence tending to show that an injury was received by reason of the negligence alleged in the complaint operating as a proximate cause in conjunction with *another independent proximate cause*.

***B returns to his station at the portable table and begins to build house of cards, occasionally and absent-mindedly reading some of the evidence*]**

*

D: "Dangers at a Crossing"

J: the allegations of negligence and injury resulting therefrom

D: "Driving his buggy along the highway..."

J "that on or about the 9th day of July, 1909, while driving along the public highway leading from Cherokee Falls to his home at Gaffney, in said state and county, and while attempting to cross the tracks of the defendant at a regular crossing"

P: it is the accent and inflection of evidentiary discourse that takes the breath away...

D: "he came to a railroad crossing:
A freight car..."

P: "being used by the defendant"

B: "was blocking it"

P: "the public road or highway"

D: "and had been left there for days."

B: "negligently and carelessly"

D: "A showman had left it"

P [***to D***]: (the voice of a master of ceremonies is also stylized, rehearsed—a public voice, a rhetoric of cheap thrills riveting desire to its referent...)

D: "And the stench of the wild animals in it..."

J & P [***P parodically, as a Master of Ceremonies***]: That the freight car which was willfully and negligently left standing...

J: across said public crossing by the defendant, its lessee, agent, servant...

J & P [***P parodically, as above***]: and representatives, was very offensive, in that it smelled very foully, and gave forth a great stench

D: "startled the horse."

[***P the "contortionist," with script. Throughout this section, until J delivers his opinion, P attempts to make reading difficult. Passes script between legs, behind back, etc., while twisting about, trying to find the most uncomfortable reading position possible.***]

J: that plaintiff's horse was made afraid and became very much frightened by
reason of the foul smell and great stench arising from said car...
his horse was frightened and excited by the noisome odors emitted from the car

D: As the driver of the buggy tried to go around the car...

J: by reason of the willful and negligent blocking of said public road, or crossing

B: "the noise of rabbits jumping about
in a wire cage left on the station platform
added to the fright of the horse;"

J: ...became unmanageable, and in...

J & P [***P parodically, as MC***]: a surging and violent effort to get away from the foul-smelling car, which had been left standing across the public crossing...

J: as aforesaid—and in violation of the statute laws of this state, and a willful disregard of the rights of the plaintiff and the public—

[***D prods P with a stick***]

P: One discourse represents evidence. An event dismantled, coded, applied...

J: ran violently against the bank of the cut of the railroad, which came down even with the public road on the opposite side of the railroad, and just above the public crossing, and by reason of which the plaintiff was thrown violently...

P: The other represents an event that finally eludes it, the narrative letting go:

[***P flings himself about on floor, a combination of circus stunts and pratfalls***]

B [***Irritably, since the antics the jeopardize the stability of his construction***]:
"the buggy crashed against the embankment of the railroad
just above the crossing,
flinging the driver out."

P: and was greatly hurt and painfully injured.

J:

...essentially a visual language,
meant to be scrutinized in silence: it is,
in fact, largely unspeakable at first sight...

D [***pointing to poem***]: "a freight car...was across the public... highway, and had... been left standing there for days"

.....

P: one appropriates to control, to remedy contingency, the other reappropriates to release. Both are tough contestants. Real showmen.

J: On this vital point, the plaintiff testified, in substance, that a car in which wild animals were kept by a showman...

P [***performing various contortions with and upon the center table; D prods***]: and where are the wild animals in this discourse, rhetoric circling like the grand parade around a point of negligence, negligence..."operating as a proximate cause in conjunction with another independent proximate cause..." Legal discourse, the contortionist: "But, while it is necessary to recovery to show that an act of negligence alleged in the complaint was one of the proximate causes, it is not essential to show that it was the sole proximate cause... syntax doubling back on itself, obsessed with its own repetitions, structures stressed to the breaking point, a semantic pretzel man, deferring comprehension through a series of gaudy verbal twists, an obfuscating "accuracy." But this is a trop(e)-(t) ical...

D [***interrupt***]: Objection. Diversionary figuration, awkward...

J: Sustained.

D: delivery.

P: illusion— [***flinging self off table***] there is no adequate language, no answering discourse, no way to contain... [***enacts a preposition, bodily spanning the gap between chair and center table***] always a difference, a deferral, escape through an ambiguity, whole books written on prepositions—" through," "between," "beyond" ...

J: A preposition shows relationship, but the relationship is not clearly defined. Therefore the words, though small in size, give a great deal of trouble.

P: while animals left in a car on the track and in a cage on the platform reek audibly—" noisome odors"—through it all.

[slide B_8

P [***standing on head***]:

A show that's not kidding. You see what happens to the urge to distort, disrupt. The unruly not merely kept at bay, but channeled through a formidable rhetoric. Tongue tied. [***Now upright, gradually bends over, looking at audience between legs***] The contortionist watches you watching him. A "That" and six clauses; a second "That…a third, and we arrive at the animal… under heavy syntactic surveillance.

J: There's always a gun at your head

P: Impossible to speak without being incarcerated.

J: Action by W. L. Settlemeyer against the Southern Railway Company, Carolina Division. From a judgment for defendant, plaintiff appeals…

B: [***overlap; slides in a small, black box, hitting P***]: Exhibit 5

J: reversed.

*

J: (60 A 396)

[slide A_9

[***As following poem is read, P cautiously circles box***]

D: *Testimony…:* "They were sitting on their cots
and one of the two went towards the other
with [italics yours] a scissors blade;
the other was about to stand up *with* a razor in his hand.

The man *with* the razor
cried to the third man
"He is cutting me!"
The man *with* the scissors blade had stabbed him in the neck.
and the third man began pounding on the door of their cell for the guards."

[***P examines box fr. four sides***]

J:

The word "with" is defined according to:
(1) Literal interpretation;
(2) Interpretation based on intent;
(3) Common meaning;
(4) Etymology;
(5) Context

[***on "5," P looks inside, then quickly shuts box, tapping the bottom***]

P: Those on the ridge should look in both directions. Camouflage—"
law": "wall."

D: Your Honor, excuse, if I may…I've been a bit uncomfortable… to be admissible as evidence we must cite…

B: Objection! …

J: To what? You cannot! [***to D***] Don't worry, there's a list at the end; besides, we don't mean it as evidence, but to bring a theoretical tone, a scholarly decorum…

P [***walking to portable table, where B, to kill time, has been building the house of cards***]: The gun at your head is your head… How many clowns come out of a Volkswagen? Really a great trick.

[***B's flashlight illuminates the following scene. P collapses house by "jumping" hand over cards and striking table. Gesturing broadly, like a Reno magician, P then pulls out a "hand": "C-A-U-S-E" (spelled out on card backs, one letter per card); face value is a royal flush. While this is going on, J, B, & D continue with the next section.***]

*

J: 57 A 534:

[slide $A1_0$ B_9

D: *Testimony...*: "As they came near several freight cars,
the man who had been robbed cried out, "There he is!"
and a man ran out from behind one of the cars."

B: "Oh, it's a..."

D: "They shouted at him to stop
but he kept running
and they fired four or five shots:
one hit him in the back and another in the forearm..."

J: four or five, and two points of entry—this is certain.

D: "but he kept running until he fell.
When they came to him,
the man who had been robbed said
it was not him, after all."

P: Yet, "There he is." A sign that has the power to annihilate its referent, even when it's the "wrong" one. Is such a death, then, "rhetorical"?

***

J: 81 P 792 Delaney v State (Supreme Court of Wyoming, Aug. 1, 1905)

[slide A11 (B is black)

D: *Testimony...*: "The hunter..."

J: Stark: Plaintiff

D: "jerked the bundle free..."

B: freeing himself...fled from the house

D: "and started on a run to the buckboard where his horse and rifle were

and the rancher rushed back into the house
and came out with a loaded rifle,"

J: Defendant rushed into an adjoining room, procured his loaded
rifle, and came to the door,

D: "looking about for the hunter."

B: the latter at that time having...

D: "He had dropped his bundle and was crouching behind the front
wheel of the buckboard for shelter. The rancher saw him and fired:"

J: Defendant immediately raised his rifle, and, aiming at plaintiff...

D: "the bullet passed between the spokes of the wheel
and hit the hunter in a fleshy part of his..."

P: right

D: "hip."

B: entering Stark's ***right*** hip, and passing through the fleshy part from
right to left.

D: "He got up..."

P: arose

D: "with his gun
and walking backwards,"

P: sideways and backwards

D: "facing the rancher,"

P: facing the house, his rifle not raised or aimed, but with the muzzle
in the direction of the house endeavored

[slide B1$_o$

D: "tried to get in back of a shed nearby;"

P: and while doing so mistook witness Hamp, who had left the house to get out of the possible range of any shots that Stark might return, for the defendant, and fired at him…

D: "but the rancher…"

J: defendant

D: "after the first shot kept firing…"

P: fired the succeeding shots

D: "from a window—"

P: retired from his doorway to a less exposed place…

D: "until he hit the hunter again."

P: one of the bullets striking Stark at the inner part of the left eye, ranging downward and passing out of the right side of the neck.

J: There is some conflict as to the number of shots fired by defendant, but that question is immaterial. There were certainly a sufficient number. The physician who attended Stark testifies that there were eight bullet holes, counting the various points of entrance and exit…

P: In the poem, the whole event happens more cleanly, the

[slide $A1_2$

lines of motion are more direct—a less complicated dance. No moments of mistaken identity, no awkward movements (sideways and backwards), and only two implied points of entry. No witness Hamp running through the poem, through the space of contention, breaking the momentum of the narrative, splitting its force along two lines of development:

the conflict between Stark and the defendant slightly displaced, repeated slightly out of phase, reenacted as a struggle between Stark and the witness Hamp, who becomes the object of a dangerous transference—dangerous crossing—passing through the scene at just the wrong (or right) instant, becoming, in the urgency of the moment, the antagonist in someone else's fiction. Witness Hamp is a significant character in Stark's psychodrama, and though excluded from the poem's story, he crosses it like a shadow, disturbing its clean action, its driving rhythm.

J:

The construction... does not amount to the reconstruction
of a case history, but determines a matrix which operates
by a selection among the whole body of facts...
reported by witnesses,
and sets up a coding system for their interpretation.

* * *

P: And what's in the bundle? A violin. Stilled music in the cross fire. And the exact path of the bullets, the points of entry and exit—forensic choreography...

[slide B11

[***the following cross-examination is read as a deposition by J; at a certain point, P takes the role of the answerer. As it is read, B & D act out the crime as a dance, while P looks on. Light batons (dowel poles with Cyalumes attached to the ends?) are passed between dancers to simulate directions of fire as well as the entry and exit points of bullets; word strings are "fired" verbally as the light batons are thrown***]

J [***"Q" & "A" are read as "Question" & "Answer"***]: Q. The first thing that attracted your attention in connection with this difficulty was loud voices? [***B & D rush toward each other as P throws in bundle; they embrace, catching the bundle between them, spin & "quarrel"***] A. Yes, men apparently quarreling. Q. And then you saw Stark coming from the house? Did you see what he carried if anything? A. A bundle, with a blanket around it, tied up with a rope. Q. What did he do? Describe his movements. [***B & D break free; B goes down on his side ("takes cover")***] A. He was running, and he threw his bundle right upon or near the buckboard tongue,

D [***drags in B, pushes him to the floor, backs off, comes a bit forward, fires light baton at B***]:

Homicide—Felonious Assault—Questions for Jury

[***retreats***]

J: and I noticed him grab a hold of the buckboard tongue, and swing behind it. Q. Around the front of the buckboard?

B: [***rising, moving awkwardly away, returns fire***]:

Same—Assault Committed in House—Justification

P [***intercepting, relaying baton back to D***]: Yes, sir.

J: What did he do next?

D [***fires at B***]:

Same—Instructions—Duty to Retreat [***B backs off, turns***]

P: He stood there for a fraction of a second, looked back toward the house, crouched behind the buckboard, and reached over and grabbed his rifle, and drew it toward him.

D [***"solos" with baton—ballistic vectors of trajectory, points of entry***]:

Same—Duty to Escape

Same—Intent

P: It was right by the buckboard, and he drew it close to him.

J: And at this time there had been no shot fired?

D [***falling***]:
Appeal—Questions Reviewable—Errors Not Presented

P: No, the shot was fired next.

J: What was the next thing you heard?

P: I heard a shot.

J:

Some litigants limit their accounts in court
to issues that fit well within the framework of the law
while others do not choose or manage to do so.

P: The sound of a violin, its strings struck all at once.

J: William J. Delaney was convicted of assault with intent to kill, and brings error. Affirmed.

***

[***B gathers up the still glowing light sticks, builds warning line, a rope of light over floor & tables, marking the space of performance as the scene of an accident/crime/" happening"***]

[slide $A1_3$ $B1_2$

J:
Railroad Companies—" Accident at Crossing"—Evidence

P: [***as if introducing a play***]: Lortz v New York Cent. & H. R. R. Co.

J [***quickly slipping it in***]: (25 NY Sup. Ct. 252)

P: Plaintiff: Mary Lortz, administratrix of Frederick Lortz, deceased

Defendant: New York Central & Hudson River Railroad

Supreme Court Appellate Division, 4th Department; June 17, 1896…

J: Held, question for jury: was intestate able to distinguish the smoke from the mist and overhanging clouds?

P: evidence…clouds…heavy…clouds…

D: *Testimony…*: "A man… "

J: Frederick Lortz, the deceased. Place of residence: East side of Cedar Street, in the village of Batavia. Occupation: woodworker

D: "in his sixties and so near-sighted…"

J: several witnesses testified…and it appeared from their testimony, or that of some of them…that his eyes had been affected for a long time;

D: "the neighbors would see him in his garden
hoeing up and pulling out vegetables
instead of the weeds…"

J: he was intending to remove…

P: that, in order to see

D: "he had to hold objects four or five inches from his eyes…"

P: within four or five inches of his face

D: "to read the face of a clock, for example…"

P: to distinguish such objects as… or to read

D: "at all;"

B: that…he would feel around with his hands…to find what was plainly visible to others

D: "and in driving nails..."

J: in driving upon the highways,

D: "with a hammer..."

P: he had difficulty in distinguishing people and vehicles

D: "he would put on spectacles and bend close to..."

P: get very close to his nearest acquaintances

D: "the nails."

J and other circumstances were detailed pointing to a very serious difficulty in the eyes of the deceased, and great impairment of his vision.

D: "He had to cross the four tracks of a railroad..."

B: Nos. 1, 2, 3, and 4.

D: "to go to and from his job."
"That evening..."

J: the evening of April 16, 1889

D: "between six and seven o'clock
as he was walking home from work
an express train going west crossed
the street along which he was walking..."

J: along the side of Cedar Street, which street is nearly at right angles with the defendant's tracks. The deceased approached from the south, to within a few feet of track no. 1

D: "and he waited until the train passed."

P: Cedar Street is in the outskirts of the village...

D: "The sky was dark with clouds
and the train left a heavy cloud of smoke a few feet from the ground."

P: the wind prevailing blew the smoke in the direction where the
deceased stood, and seemed to be near him.

D: "When he started to cross..."
another train, ten of fifteen minutes late,
came from the west;"

P: along track...

D: "it made no signal when about to cross the street he was on,"

P: several witnesses who were observing...testified positively

D: "neither by bell nor whistle..."

J: Beisiegel v Railroad Co., 34 N. Y. 632: "the omission of the
customary signals was an assurance by the company to the
plaintiff that...

P: it was for the jury to determine whether, under the circumstances...

D: "and the noise of its coming..."

J: the noise of the west-bound passenger train may well have obscured
the sound of the approach of the train from the west, so that

D: "might well have been
taken as the noise of the train that had just passed."

J: This is an important circumstance in considering whether the
deceased was guilty of contributory negligence. Ingersoll v
Railroad Co., 6 Thomp. & C. 419; Powell v Railroad Co.,
22 Hun. 59; Leonard v Railroad Co., 42 N. Y. Super. Ct.
225. In Greany v Railroad Co., 101 N. Y. 425, 5 N. E. 425.
Danforth, J., quotes with an approval Shaw v Jewett, 86 N. Y.
616 in which it is said...

D: "He started to cross the tracks..."

B: Nos. 1, 2, 3, and...

[slide $B1_3$

P: A sudden death out of nowhere... obliterated text... The specificity of time and direction: the train was "10 of 15 minutes late," the deceased "approached from the south," the road ran at "nearly at right angles" to the defendant's tracks," the approximate speed of the train and deliberateness of the walk—he was "just stepping": these measurements like an awkward mechanism replicating the dead man's movements [***P mimes***]... two trains, one approaching and one leaving a crossing, heading in opposite directions (the one slightly off-schedule) such that, in the world of this nearsighted man, they were collapsed through routine into one. No vector can chart this journey...

Two trains, a single train, moving simultaneously in opposite directions—impossible, this side of the atom—one light bar scanning a page (at a speed = ...) makes all that follows possible... what follows?

[***P activates white end of light rod as pointer***]

[***B puts on a pair of oversized glasses with a roll of adding machine paper attached to one end; begins to unroll paper through lenses. After a strip of blankness, the following sequence appears: "1...2...3... evidence... cloud...heavy cloud... bound to see... provide against... question for jury..."***]

J: Exhibit 6

P [***pointing to projected image and to B; part of the text of B_{13} has been lost—washed out—in the xerox process***]:

A breakdown in mimesis. We, too, are unable to see—the train of syntax lost in the lacunae of the source—literal holes, the words that wouldn't copy, since their clarity would only be a ghostly presence... Reznikoff's reinscriptions only serve to make the omissions more quizzical: "the evidence tending to show / track one...was between daylight and the clouds.

[slide A1$_4$

even the court's own wordings can't avoid teetering back over this *aporia*,

D [***light stick; interrupt***]: again? Objection.

J: Sustained.

P: the spots where the diachronic link with

D [***light stick; interrupt***]: Objection.

J [***simultaneous***]: Sustained.

P: precedence, the synchronic chain

D [***light stick; interrupt***]: Objection.

J [***simultaneous***]: Sustained.

P: of syntax, the narr

D [***light stick; interrupt***]: Objection.

J [***simultaneous, a bit before D***]: Sustained.

P: ative chain of evidence slip into the undecidable...

B [***putting on moose ears and sticking head through one of three holes of the "privy" (see 68 S. W. 989, above***]: Moose on a beam...

D, J, & P [***all hurling light sticks***]: Objection!

P: The mimetic function of the copier slips up, true, but the representational function of language, claiming to tell what "happens," cannot "tell" (recognize) what happens, as the directions seem, at a quick reading (at what speed?) to double(over) themselves (as if struck) [***pointing to source***]: "the roar of the approaching train, as the noise of the west-bound passenger train may well have obscured the sound of the approach of the train from the west, so that"-"so that" this wording perhaps unintentionally reenacts the confusion of the deceased, as both directions are given from the point of view of the west.

J:

But, secure holders of power as they were,

[slide $A1_5$

could they really make us believe that they did not tremble
when they discovered every time that the aggressive monstrosity
of the "other" fell back on them...

P: The compass spins back on itself as opposite directions collapse into one, a particle "e" exchanged for a particle "w"—and who can "tell"?

J: "Railroad Companies—Accident at Crossing—Evidence."
Plaintiff intestate was killed... while he was attempting to cross..."

P: We do not normally anticipate what our world cannot rationally allow. The evidence was there? Perhaps if he had listened more carefully, he could have distinguished? Perhaps if we look more closely... [***begins to take small portable tv apart and, with an extendable "grabber," extracts the picture tube***] if we could get behind these images, through them... reimagings of what we put before them in a circus of our own specular simulacra... electron etchings. What if we let them put on their own show? Ask Lortz.

[slide $B1_4$

J:

The repetition or representation of something
is different from that something,
which becomes its other...

D: “evidence…cloud…heavy cloud….”

P: An accident at an unclear crossing; the defined self, on its way home, crossing the undecipherable, address of no one…

J: Question for the jury: was intestate able to distinguish…

[***P hands picture tube to B; B passes it on to audience/jury…***]

D:

but since the repetition or representation is all
one can have, it will always be “other”
than itself.

B: Exhibit 7

P: Sure, a failure of the copier, mistransmission of a signal…we’re mistaken—we’re always mistaken… (Reznikoff, too, is momentarily confused, thrown off track, as, in a draft of the poem, the east bound train is heading west, and must be “corrected”). [***P demonstrates on blackboard for jury***]

J:

The garrulous machinery
of the law… trying to contain
the question
that comes to [it]
and smother it in a fog of words.

P: “While he was bound to use his eyes, we cannot say that he was bound to use them in any particular manner, or at any particular instant in time.”

[***B brings colorful plastic train toy to center table: pump the handle and it spins through a little scene…***]

P: Who are we kidding?

J:

To some extent,
we are the victims of our own reification.

P: What is glimpsed between holes? The "wrong man" shot to death between freight cars (they don't have to be moving for the gap to open) ...

D: "and was struck..."

P: dancing around a silent fatal music... who are we...?

D: "by the [(w)] eastbound train, going thirty-five or forty..."

P: what we see is what? "Cloud," definite...a shadow knows—we have always (already) been "bound."

[***B spins train, which rings a tiny bell each time it passes a "crossing"; D blows the circus whistle—an airy, plaintive sound—without fluttering the ball; J tosses a penultimate light stick—slight arc, like a lonely firework—at the echo of "already"***]

* * *

[***P switches on*** Cops ***tape, watches briefly in silence, then pauses image and begins to put away props—making sure the Cyalume warning line is still in place and perhaps adding to it, rolling adding machine tape back onto glasses, repacking tv, etc.***]

[slide $A1_{6...}$ $B1_{5...}$
[advance slides to black]

J [***to all performers***]: Okay, tell me what happened. [***to audience***] The jury may offer comments.

*

B [***double voicing—audience/jury, witnesses?***]: "He was jumbling things for me so that I didn't understand it. And he was expecting me to understand what was going on there like I am a lawyer. I am not a lawyer. He failed to listen to what I had to say."

D [***picking up the context***]: Carrington: "By listening to what you had to say, do you mean the context and the, uh..."

B: "my presentation. And there's a reason why I spent that kind of time putting it together."

[***short pause; J looks at audience***]

*

J [***to P***]: O'Barr and Conley: "failure to construct meaning in a way that would have articulated with the court's agenda..."

*

D [***to self***]: "We have learned new ways to listen and have heard a great deal..."

*

J [***to jury***]: Goodrich: "What is needed...is an account of the appropriation of meaning and its restriction to specific institutional and discursive sites and modalities."

*

B [***to P***]: He can't be captured by any discourse, and makes a patchwork—a burlesque—of them; his testimony is complete sentences, yet the logic, if any exists, is fractured... and the surplus, doing too much—the surplus that carries him beyond motive and reason...

J [***to self, B***]: "The very idea of the objectivity and specialization of legal language functions consciously or unconsciously to exclude participation in the legal process."

*

P [***as if to himself***]: Answer. My own walk began before I knew I was walking, and will probably continue beyond what I perceive as its end... as I follow you across the East River, up the West Side to the Bronx... there are two bridges, spanning a river never identical with itself, never the self-same... always at least two, not running parallel, exactly, but never meeting, either...

*

D [***to all, or no one in particular, while lighting a final light stick and placing it in row***]: Foucault:" It was by doing a little more, by doing too much, that he could exchange the alienating labor of reason for the liberating work of desire" ...

[***B & D exit. P spins train, bell rings several times—a small, lonely sound—the rings growing farther apart, more distant, as train slows; P exits.***]

Slide List

A Series

1 early typescript of "Poetic Discourse v Legal Discourse"; pages irregularly fanned out—a layered, or sedimentary effect, like fragments of mica.

2 typescript of prop list for "Poetic Discourse v Legal discourse."

3 texts cited in "Poetic Discourse v Legal Discourse"; these, too, are stacked, or layered, on their sides, so that bindings with titles face camera.

4 Reznikoff's typescript draft of "The Noise of Civilization," written above an earlier holograph draft, which has been crossed out.

5 Reznikoff's xerox of 68 S.W. 989 (1902).

6 from Reznikoff's papers: holograph introductory note to Testimony.

7 from "Poetic Discourse v Legal Discourse": typescript draft of "Episode in the Life of a Schoolteacher."

8 Reznikoff's xerox of 74 S.E. 138.

9 typescript draft of Reznikoff's poem based on 60 A. 396.

10 Reznikoff's xerox of 57 A. 534.

11 Reznikoff's xerox of 81 P. 792.

12 from Evidence: dancing corpse.

13 CU of Reznikoff's typescript of "A man in his sixties and so near-sighted" showing revision—cross-outs, "x" s.

14 title page of Luc Sante's *Evidence*: outline of revolver with title printed on barrel.

15 from Evidence: an empty hallway; eye follows lines toward a vanishing point, truncated by a blank, closed door.

16 holograph ms: list of cases to be used in Testimony.
17 typescript draft of slide list for "Poetic Discourse v Legal discourse."
18 dark doorway of George's Camera, San Diego, CA, where I rented equipment to photograph Reznikoff's sources and drafts.
19 from "Poetic Discourse v Legal Discourse": holograph draft of script for "A man in his sixties and so nearsighted."
20 from Reznikoff's papers: holograph ms: outline of Testimony with list of subheads.
21 typical workstation: Toshiba laptop on desk; a script page visible on screen; next to computer, Xerox of typescript draft of a poem from Testimony; between computer and Xerox an assortment of pens and pencils.
22 copy stand used for photo-documentation; its four 3,200-degree flood lights bear down on a prop: the board with two (three?) holes used in 68 S.W. 989.
23 medium shot of Reznikoff, looking up, mouth open, background vague....

B Series

1 holograph ms: list of cases in NRS (National Reporter System) to be used in Testimony.
2 MS of Reznikoff before a stone veneer wall, in the act of speaking.
3 holograph draft of "The Method of Revision (Appendix II, 3, 4).
4 xerox of 53 A. 289 (the pencil markings are mine).
5 closeup of Reznikoff's xerox of 68 S.W. 989 (1902) showing revisions made directly on source.
6 from Evidence: dead children in a bead.
7 closeup of Reznikoff's xerox of 74 S.E. 138.
8 program for American Poets of the 1930s conference, adrift in black space.
9 Reznikoff's xerox of 57 A. 534.
10 closeup of Reznikoff's typescript of "Fight for a Violin," showing crossed out lines—"X" s.
11 from Evidence: dancing corpse.
12 collage: Reznikoff's marked xerox of 25 N.Y. Supp. Supreme Ct. 292 + typescript of poem
with revisions.
13 closeup of Reznikoff's xerox of 25 N.Y. Supp. Supreme Ct. 292 focusing on his reinscriptions of words lost in copying.

14 closeup of an eye—mine?
15 from Reznikoff's papers: calendar note: "re-examine for possible use."
16 collage from Reznikoff's papers: small spiral notebook with possible references to *Testimony* + epigraph (dropped from later editions).
17 typescript draft of final page of "Poetic Discourse v Legal Discourse" (a collage of quotes/comments that refer to Reznikoff, to the author of the critical performance, to poetic and legal discourses, as well as to whatever context the quotes were extracted from).
18 from Evidence: a man standing in the entranceway to a rooftop; this looks like the *end* of a journey, a door opening onto an outland above, beyond...; the lighting gives an unearthly luminosity to the figure in the doorway—a ghost effect?
19 from Reznikoff's papers: holograph note specifying projected dates of completion for various stages in the production of Testimony.
20 from Reznikoff's papers: holograph ms: page number references to cases in the NRS.
21 from Reznikoff's papers: holograph ms: breakdown of pages per section of *Testimony*—in inches.
22 self-portrait, reflected in corner window of George's Camera; camera taking photo displaces face; a red neon sign in opposite window is also reflected (I reverse the image so that it reads "correctly"— "OPEN).

Bibliography, Voices

Balkin, J. M. *Cultural Software: A Theory of Ideology.* New Haven, CT: Yale UP, 1998.

Binder, Guyora and Robert Weisberg. *Literary Criticisms of Law.* Princeton, NJ: Princeton UP, 2000.

Briggs, Robert. *Disorderly Discourse: Narrative, Conflict, and Inequality*. New York: Oxford University Press, 1996.

—. "Just Traditions? Deconstruction, Critical Legal Studies, and Analytic Jurisprudence." *Social Semiotics*, 11:3 (2001 Dec): 257-74.

Burke, Peter. *Eyewitnessing: The Uses of Images as Historical Evidence*. Ithaca, NY: Cornell UP, 2001.

Bryant, Margaret M. *English in the Law Courts: The Part That Articles, Prepositions and Conjunctions Play in Legal Decisions*. New York: Columbia University Press, 1930.

Campos, Paul F., Pierre Schlag, and Steven D. Smith. *Against the Law. Constitutional Conflicts*. Durham: Duke University Press, 1996.

Carrington, Paul D. *Empirical Studies of Civil Procedure*, Part 2. Duke University Law School, 1988

Cohen-Cheminet, Genevieve. "Charles Reznikoff: New World Poetics." In Lagayette, 122-45.

Conley, John M., and William M. O'Barr. *Rules versus Relationships: The Ethnography of Legal Discourse*. Chicago: The University of Chicago Press, 1990.

Crystal, D. and D. Davy. *Investigating English Style*. London: Longman, 1969

DuPlessis, Rachel Blau and Peter Quartermain, eds. *The Objectivist Nexus: Essays in Cultural Poetics*. Tuscaloosa, AL: U of Alabama P, 1999.

Fine, Richard. "Authorship Cross-Examined by Critical Legal Studies." *Revue Française d'Etudes Américaines*, 78\(1998Oct):60-72.

Fineman, Martha Albertson, and Nancy Sweet Thomadsen. *At the Boundaries of Law: Feminism and Legal Theory*. New York: Routledge, 1991.

Finkelstein, Norman. "Tradition and Modernity, Judaism and Objectivism: The Poetry of Charles Reznikoff." In DuPlessis, 191-209.

Fish, Stanley. *Doing What Comes Naturally: Change, Rhetoric, and the Practice of Theory and Legal Studies*. Post-Contemporary Interventions. Durham, N.C.: Duke University Press, 1989.

Foucault, Michel, ed. *I, Pierre Riviere, Having Slaughtered my Mother, My Sister, and My Brother: A Case of Parricide in the 19th Century*. Lincoln: University of Nebraska Press, 1975.

Giorcelli, Cristina, ed. *The Idea and The Thing in Modernist American Poetry*. Palermo, Italy: Ila Palma, 2001.

Goodrich, Peter. *Legal Discourse: Studies in Linguistics, Rhetoric and Legal Analysis*. New York: St. Martin's Press, 1987.

Hindus, Milton. *Charles Reznikoff: A Critical Essay*. Santa Barbara: Black Sparrow Press, 1977.

—, ed. *Charles Reznikoff, Man and Poet*. Orono, ME: National Poetry Foundation, Inc., 1984.

Hogan, Patrick Colm. *On Interpretation: Meaning and Inference in Law, Psychoanalysis, and Literature*. Athens, GA: U of Georgia P, 1996.

Hutchinson, Allan C., ed. *Critical Legal Studies*. Totowa, NJ: Rowman and Littlefield Publishers, Inc., 1989.

Lagayette, Pierre, ed.. *Strategies of Difference: Case Studies in Poetic Composition*. Madison, NJ: Fairleigh Dickinson UP, 1998.

O'Barr, William M. *Linguistic Evidence: Language, Power, and Strategy in the Courtroom*. Studies on Law and Social Control. New York: Academic Press, n.d.

— and John M. Conley. "Ideological Dissonance in the American Legal System." In Briggs, 115-134.

Perelman, Bob. "'Still Itself': Charles Reznikoff's Poetry, or, The Vicissitudes of Simplicity." In Giorcelli, 91-107.

Posner, Richard. *Law and Literature: A Misunderstood Relation*. Cambridge: Harvard University Press, 1988.

Reznikoff, Charles. *Testimony: The United States (1885-1915) Recitative*. 2 Vols. Santa Barbara: Black Sparrow Press, 1978.

Charles Reznikoff Papers, MSS 0009. Mandeville Special Collections Library. University of California—San Diego. http://content.cdlib.org/view?docId=tf0s2004ng&chunk.id=bioghist-1.2.6&brand=oac 9/2/07.

Robson, Ruthann. *Sappho Goes to Law School: Fragments in Lesbian Legal Theory*. New York, NY: Columbia UP, 1998.

Sante, Luc. *Evidence*. New York: Farrar, Straus and Giroux, 1992.

—. *Low Life: Lures and Snares of Old New York*. New York: Farrar, Straus and Giroux, 1991.

Weisberg, Richard. *Poethics and Other Strategies of Law and Literature*. New York: Columbia University Press, 1992.

*Special thanks to the National Reporter System

Deconstructing Product Design

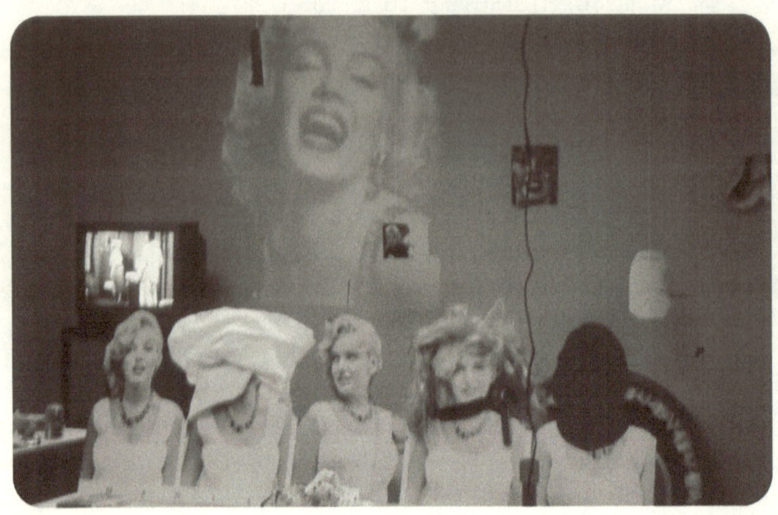

Fig. 6: *Mise en scène,* Monroe Project (detail).

4 Script 3: The Monroe Project, or, the MM Effect—Going Over—

We sat there, her tiny audience

—Jack Myers

In the critical performance The Monroe Project, a dysfunctional product design team utilizes a semiotic methodos to dis/reassemble—to remake—the pop cultural assemblage, "Marilyn Monroe." Incorporating video, computer-manipulated images, sound bites (a montage of scenes, permutations of stills, and audio excerpts, respectively, from the film Niagara*), and found cultural objects, the piece attempts to come to terms with the pervasive cultural presence of Marilyn Monroe, skipping off the properly nominal alliteration and riffing on issues of identity formation/construction and alternate modes of cultural and self (re)production along the way.*

Based on Monroe specifically as she appears in the 1953 film Niagara*, and as she is configured in various pop biographies, The Monroe Project is not a conventional analysis of her identity construction, but a creative, theoretically driven response to it—a counter or parallel enactment musing along the edges of her performance (and her identity as performed, the Monroe body serving as medium). The piece is a multimedia performance that explores various aspects of the simulated phenomenon designated Marilyn Monroe: the filmic image/presence, the significance of this image construct to codes of femininity (from the fifties to today), and the meshing of the film icon with the biographical configuration: the social/economic/ emotional/sexual/ideological nexus inscribed as the "real" Marilyn Monroe, a reality/identity effect ballasting the screen version. The Project is especially interested in the Monroe construct as a specular configuration of her audience's—those who buy and consume her— (self-sub(di)verting?) desires. The "investigation" of the pop culture icon—the observations and conjectures, analyses and theoretical day-dreaming spun around cinematic fragments and biographical inscriptions —takes the form of a brainstorming session carried out by (as noted above) a self- be-musing, procedurally challenged product development team, whose (ultimately aborted) task is to come up with a truly postmodern, yet commercially viable, "MM."*

Following the piece are an Audio Appendix and the "Monroe/Me Auto) bio," which is read, murmured at times, throughout the piece.

D = the team director

M1, M2, M3 = team members

[*The set: a bare table. On one side, a computer and monitor topped with a blue sailor's cap; on the other a podium. Behind the table, occupying a central position in the set, a video monitor draped in black stretch material; another monitor is off to the side and a third monitor, between these two, will display live video—M1 & M2 use it to "rehearse" lines and to try out bits of physical business. Marilyn Monroe Project mobiles dance on either side of the central monitor; the mobiles are fashioned from various fragmented images: photographs of MM, publicity stills from* Niagara, *graphs and charts, Niagara posters, marked over sections of the performance script, etc.; some of the images have been palimpsested. The following plot synopsis, taken from the back of a video carton, or perhaps a Netflix CD envelope, has been distributed to the audience:*

Set against the dramatic backdrop of Niagara Falls, Marilyn Monroe portrays Rose, a femme fatale possessing two of the most powerful weapons: an erotic body and an evil mind. Planning to murder her troubled husband (Joseph Cotton), Rose first uses her double-edged sword to drive him to the brink of total insanity. Then she seductively torments a series of strangers while her mysterious lover waits in the shadows.... Marilyn's classic performance... is at once fascinating and frightening, painting a powerful portrait of human sexuality and passion. 89 Minutes, color, 1953, recorded in Hi-Fi.

D enters and sits before his/her computer and monitor. M3 is standing at a podium, dressed in a conservative though insipid suit with a bright red out-of-fashion tie.]

[audio 1][32]

D: Heads! [*Enter the 5 faces of MM on two pair of legs—M1 & M2. Each head of the serial life-size stand-up strikes a slightly different pose; three of the heads have been concealed in pillow cases, on one of which is a cheap platinum wig. M1 and M2 frequently*

32. See "Audio List," p. 00

deliver their lines from behind these heads, using one head as a "home head." All prepare: lay out props—robes (draped behind), white gloves (on table in front of MM); other props are placed behind the cardboard stand-up (a small red beacon, black leather cap, fireworks, a cigarette lighter, etc.). As this transpires,

M1 or 2 [*aside to audience, fr. behind heads*]: (many of my comments on product design theory may be quoted, paraphrased, or misdirected in whole or part from Ulrich, Roozenberg, Belofsky, Boothroyd; there is a bibliography...)

[audio 2]

D: Lay out props... beauty mark! [*parts of M1's and 2's bodies or body pop out fr. behind heads as called for; M2 puts on a pair of dark blue stockings and dark blue heels. M1 gives M2 a red "beauty mark." M2 wraps a white scarf*

[audio 3]

around M1's head. M1 puts on a dark sleeveless fur vest, a pair of mirror shades, and a blue

[audio 4]

*beauty mark. D puts on the sailor's cap and speaks into a little recording machine, which s/he then places on the table in front of MM and plays back "here kitty kitty." M2 finds the machine, places it elsewhere, replays—" here kitty..." M1 finds the machine after two replays, speaks into it—" here kitty kitty kitty"—and plays it back; all look about. M1 then places it on the podium next to the prop table. M3 picks up the recording device and places it on the other side of the podium; D, M2, and M1 look, but M3 does not play it. Throughout the piece, D experiments with the MM image (*Niagara *is the source for most of the slides), manipulating/permuting it in various ways. Some of the "finished products" are displayed as large image slide projections, on either side of the central video monitor. The audio tape is composed of brief clips from the soundtrack of* Niagara, *montaged to short-circuit narrative continuity. Text, visuals, and sound bites cluster improvisationally, in a field of* *open interpretability and Inter-penetrability. What follows is just one possible synchronicity*]

***

D [*D's voice is amplified throughout the piece*]: Video, please. [*M1 turns on the marginal monitor: Stop action, blurred image swipes: walking along the Falls at night, hand-held camera. Soundless. The tape plays out during the piece, eventually going to snow*]

[audio 5]

[text slide:

After brief interrogation by a Canadian border guard, Polly and Ray arrive at Niagara Falls, Ontario, sure of their identity. Ray hopes to meet his boss, Mr. Kettering, owner of the Shredded Wheat factory at Niagara; Ray has just won a prize for a turkey stuffing recipe using Shredded Wheat. Checking in to Rainbow Cabins, they meet Rose, who claims that her husband, George Loomis, is ill. We later learn that Loomis, a failed farmer, met Rose at a bar in Duluth; her background is uncertain... She walks away; Ray's eyes, then his body, begin to follow... Polly reaches out...]

Gloves. [*all put on white film handler's gloves*] The Project Development Team [*all freeze in tableau; D continues, reading from* Production Design and Development, *Ulrich and Eppinger, New York: McGraw Hill, 1995*] "team diversity":

Successful development requires many different skills and talents. As a result, development teams involve people with a wide range of different training, experience, perspectives, and personalities [*M1 and M2 sit behind MM*].

[begin image slides: permutations of stills from *Niagara*]

M3: [*reads a few minutes of biography from one of several standard biographies of MM he has at his podium; as the piece progresses, M3 will occasionally confuse facts, and interpolate sequences of autobiography. However, by the end of the piece he is able to successfully integrate these fragments—or so he thinks—into a "Monroe ME." This pseudo characterological development is suspended between bio. segments, when the M3 member reverts to an inanimate object; when not reading, he is not*]

M1 [*interrupting M3*]: We have means of transport.

M2: Silence of the bells. Rising from shadows on the diagonal...

M1: We will spin around the cultural hot zone (knot of dialogic activity) Marilyn Monroe...

D: (MM, mmmm...) "Familiar examples of products composed of polymers are...

M2: Legs, lips, a mouth opening in laughter, a corpse...

M1: Our props cultural theory: a Deleuze cigarette lighter, a Baudrillard wig, a Sorkin backscratcher, mirrored Berger glasses, Bakhtin mobiles... [*digitized laughter*]

D: paper—cellulose, a natural polymer."

M2 [*kicking off a heel, spinning it*]: as "she" (the elusive image complex) reels off...

M1: projects through American popular culture [*M2 hands M1 one of her blue heels*] ... a second-hand shoe... [*considers the possibilities, but comes up blank*]

M2: destabilizing images of femininity.

M1 [*up*]: To codify the Monroe-event (ME) into a vacuous blonde, goldbricking, or femme fatale "stereotype" is to overcode (oversee), to reproject a projection, re-present...

[audio 6]

M2 [*interrupts, excited, head popping out the side of MM head 5*]: The King of Shredded Wheat pilots his red/white/blue motor launch into Chippewa Slip, on cue, according to script!

M1 [*forward—to live camera*]: To fabricate a stereotype is also to entangle it in all that it cannot (fore)see, its surplus valencies: The stereotype—as any product stylization—occupies only one (of many possible) discourse positionalities; absorbing a representation (as the abstraction "MM" = ME) into an image field, into variable articulations/ agglomerations of movement, light, and sound, is also to set the representation free from any single formulation, or from the mandate to "represent" at all.

M2: "Avedon yelled 'go!'..."

M1: Team! [*fist up, turning from live camera*]

M2: "and she pursed her mouth around her cigarette, kicked a balloon, shot the fan out forward—and she made a world. ... Suddenly she was all angles, suddenly the wig had become her own hair and the costume her own dress."

M1 [*trial appendage extensions*]: Her "own"? Who "owns"? We go' wheels, mon. Anthropomorphic balloons in a holiday parade, severed from their cords, colliding with lamp posts and building edges; taut skinned plastic pears of breath popped with pins or the hot coals of cigarettes. Skin grafts, silicon remodeling, celluloid reification, hermeneutical (re)fabrication:

M2: Good pitch. [*adding to above*] "Wore a latex bridge to widen the cinematic effect of her profile."

D: Ok—send it to engineering!

M2: "The way we got her shade of platinum is with my own secret blend of sparkling silver bleach plus twenty volume peroxide and a secret formula of silver platinum to take the yellow out."

M1: [*simultaneous*]: ash blonde, sliver blonde, amber blonde, honey blonde, golden blonde, smoky blonde, topaz blonde, unbleached dark blonde, platinum blonde… [*as he recites this list, M1 is lulled into a trance-like state, followed by a moment of catatonia; he slips into these states periodically throughout the piece*]

[audio 7—Maid of the Mist fog horn]

[*from within his trance state, M1 "sails" the dark blue heel across performance space into catatonia*]

M3 [*simultaneous bio., undertone, almost a murmur*]

D: MM dialogizes the stereotypes, carnivalizes them, becomes a play of pure signifiers. To take the mask at face value is not to see the mask, as put (-) on.

M2: Satisfied customer? "When you came on the screen we almost lost our eyeballs. We didn't… know who you were."

[text slide:

Polly and Ray tour the Falls on the Maid of the Mist; they kiss, their raincoats touch. Rose kisses a lover at the foot of the Falls (later). Mr. Kettering's boat—a trim red white & blue cruiser—is wrapped in celluloid, waiting...

D, M1 [*snapping out of it*]: Ha, ha. [*M3, as always, is looking through his books.*]

[image slide: black, hold]

D: Vid., please... "videotape—thermoplastic film extrusion" [*M1 removes the black stretch material from the central monitor, switches on the video, stretches the material away from the image, drapes it around himself, walks back toward MM, freezes. The video is a montage of fragments from Niagara, cut to evade narrative continuity—focusing on image rather than story or plot. There are moving shadows, moments of laughter, a stocking being put on, bands of light and dark—the striating effect of blinds—cutting across, or through (since it's all a matter of light and movement in cinema) figures, a piercing gleam of light from a lipstick case, etc.; the video bits are speeded up, slowed down, taken out of sequence, replayed, played backwards, etc. This video runs until its imagery avalanches into snow*]

M2 [*as M1 drapes himself*]: a tag knotted around the big toe.

M3: [*more bio. D stops M3 abruptly*]

[audio 8]

[continue image slides]

M1 [*flattening himself against the wall/image of MM permutations with a stagy arm gesture—Polly in bed, cabin 2, screening her eyes from intense window light*]: The filmic MM is already a doubled image--a multi-D reverberation of images, which its buxom voluptuousness teasingly acknowledges, within a 2-D image plane (in the 50s and 60s, special glasses were worn to blend the red and green, slightly offset repetition of contours--self mimicking, self-reproducing, imitation of an imitation--into a single black and white illusion of three dimensionality; what happened when the glasses were worn outside the illusionistic dark of the theater? did the real--unreeled--world seem flatter?).

D: [*simultaneous*]: 36-24-34, 36-24-36, 37-23-34, 36 1/2-23-34, 37D-24-35, 38-23-36, 35-22-35, 37-23-37, 38DD-26-37...

M1: Doubled image--the play of within through about, a certain representation, and the escape (flight) from culturally coded(codable) (i.e., culturally visible) images of femininity. It is this un(in)formed, elusive image presence "MM," dedoubled, out of phase with it - "self" (its culturally recognizable manifestations), rather than humming in the clear voice of primary colors sharply resolved into familiar contours, that our simulations here attempt to trace, to project (the unprojectable).

D: [*simultaneous*]: color graphic, head and chest of a typical MM pose; black and white graphic; color collage, using photos and headlines, charcoal and/or pencil sketching, color abstract, cartoon-like graphic, patchwork wall hanging, various larger-than-life cut-outs; semi-abstract painting featuring MM applying makeup, various oil paintings; color silk-screen, featuring eight different-colored MMs; color graphic, featuring MM getting into bubble bath....

M2: "Anybody who knows me better knows better."

M1 [*laughs*]: Could be logo?

M2: ("We" = five masculfeminine thinkers, by gender mixed.)

[audio 9: "Rose... Rose."]

M1: Wha... whose missing? Roll call!

D [*M1 & M2 gesturally mark off players, images, props*]: a boat rower, a waitress, a mistress, a burlesque queen, a fish cannery worker, a beauty contestant, a psychotic baby sitter, a girl in trouble...

[audio 10]

[image slide: black]

M3 [*interrupts with more bio.; he seems excited, or upset, and loses his place several times. M1 gets quickly behind MM*]

[audio 11]

[image slides: blank]

M1 [*popping up, stuttering*]: ki... ki...ki...k. k... kitty...
M2 [*simultaneous*]: "Here kitty kitty..."

All: Here kitty kitty...

[Tape B, from a *Niagara*
trailer: MM singing "Kiss";
voiceover—" She sang of love
just as she lived for love,
like a Lore Lay, flaunting her charms
as she lured men on and on
to their eternal destruction";
simultaneously, overhanging this last word
—" per fec tionnnn..."]

[text slide:

Rose sings along with her favorite record, "Kiss," during a patio party at Rainbow Cabins. In the window of her cabin, behind blinds, the watching shadow...

[audio 12]

M1 [*a new tack*]: MM, the image in transit. Allow us to drift for a while longer... [letting black wrap fall; *fastening on elbow and knee guards*]

[continue image slides]

[*to live camera*] A simulation, representation of a representation without a referent (an orphan? who is her mother, where is her father? her "real" changing names and the names she played with--and through--lasting the duration of a few reels: evading the articulation of them while within a film, if possible, letting others sound them...

[audio 13]

a simulacrum, yet more real than the reality-effects produced by the culturally reified images/models...

M2: the various biographical versions?

M1: All "real" [*two white fingers up like ears*] wo/men--the "everyday" woman... nurturer, domestic worker, independent professional...

D: v. the reel real?

M2: did you survey?

[audio 14]

D: Development time, development cost, development capability—are the team and the firm better able to develop future products as a result of their experience?

M1: Fashion models make the everyday seem more real, but MM's reality is not to reaffirm the "truth" ... [*behind MM, pacing*]

[audio 15]

to prove (yet again) the intractableness of the code of the "everyday" (tough this may be one of her cultural functions)—but to bring us into contact with pre-subjective lines of flight. She is a form/body all but breaking out of idealized anthropomorphic outlines [*bouncing on trampoline*], the exaggerated contours of conventional sexuality/femininity parodically stressed to the limit, un-fashionably: the dresses too tight, the lips too bright--makeup in contact with the full lips catalyzing a burning chemical image [*leaps off trampoline, disappears behind MM*].

[audio 16]

M2: "The truth was that with all my lipstick and mascara and precocious curves, I was as unresponsive as a fossil. But I seemed to affect people quite otherwise."

[text slide:

Loomis smashes the record; it cuts his hand...

D: Bakhtin heels, Baudrillard pillow cases, Sorkin Kimono, Deleuze fireworks...

[image slides: black or blank]

M1: [*assisted by M2, springs into demonstration/magician position, draped in black, with a telescoping light wand/pointer*]: Problem decomposition assuming an external energy source and commodifiable real: energy [*outside head (1)*] > convert energy to translational energy [*covered head (2)*] > accumulate translational energy [*covered head (4)*] > apply translational energy [*covered head (5)*] > altered state [*beyond head (5)*]

[audio 17]

D: Product architecture: responsibility for the detailed design of each chunk is usually assigned to a relatively small group within... careful resolution of interactions, geometric and otherwise, among components within the chunk.

[continue image slides]

M1 [*twist, torque, extreme body distortions with black stretch material before live camera, further manipulated with digital in-camera "art" effects*]: She is pure signifier, sign of excessiveness, and in her excessiveness begins to molecularize; the body flies apart, hips shoot over the dolomite shelf that shapes the flesh of the Falls--contours of waist, thighs serge through other forms—riddle the horseshoe, "thunder 160' [throwing off black cape, *M1 throws himself against a wall or door*] with annihilating force" to the talus-strewn basin [*tumbling back over himself on blue floor mat*] hidden seductively within the deadly "fluff" of spray.

[audio 18]

[image slide: movie poster]

M1: Plastic flesh over a bone frame: This is the image on the '53 poster promoting the film *Niagara*. "She" reclines quite at ease in the artificial slopes and curves of a gargantuan hypersexualized body, carefully posed on the lip of the Horseshoe, bridging the borders of two territories—a mouthful…

[audio 19]

M2: What territories?

M1: Not thrown over by the torrent (5720 m^3sec.) because its force passes through her: They are one and the same, the flesh of the Falls streaming from the rise of thigh (the power of the Falls is not diminished in the reconfiguration—its energy now relayed through the humanoid body, creating the new form body-falls) [*leaping on, off trampoline*].

M2: "I want to reproduce, such as television and all ki(n)ds of things."

M1 [*M2 "accessorizes" M1's body: black fur vest, diskette nipples, rubber "starlet" wig over crotch, telescoping pointer between legs; pushes M1 off toward live camera for feedback*]: She does not so much anthropomorphize the Falls as de(hu) manize—demanufacturize—the feminine… not "So much," but both stratagems must be actualized so that all is set (in) motion, a passing through, slipping between forms/substances, articulated stances, cultural imaginings (the equation of "nature" with sexual wild(er)ness, for example); one colossal cultural construct straddling another—the Falls, too, no more (or less) than the accumulation of its popcultural presences [*seeing himself in video monitor*]—wrong slide!—when she walks she falls…

[audio 20]

D: In product development, everything has to do with everything and everything proceeds into everything.

M2: "Why haven't I the right to grow and expand like everybody else?"

[pause image slides]

M1 [*lets all add-ons fall*]: They won't buy it.

M2: "When she's there she's there—all of her is there." [*M1 freezes*]

M3: [*more bio. M1 picks up props, positions himself before live camera, waits for cue*]

D: Hold! [*gestures to M1 to continue*]

[audio 21, 22]
[image slide: Microfluff™; hold]

M1: Analogical development: In the 1950s, a scientific wonder enters the cold war stage combat of ideologies of progress—the merging of science and fantasy not so critically assessed as in today's technoculture—: Microfluff™ [*displaying a ball of blue polka dot nylon*], a synthetic material that has no macro identity of its own, no recognizable shape; ads for the material in popular science magazines of the decade omit detailed information about its chemical makeup, so it even seems to be without articulable form or substance, truly mysterious.

[continue image slides]

It can adhere to anything--becoming all becoming it--enacting the truth of mass commodity culture, the "melting pot," endless chemical flow amassing into imagery held on the cusp of deformation...

[audio 23]

M2 [*simultaneous*]: 5454 Wilshire Blvd., Unnamed street. Los Angeles Orphans Home, unnamed street. 11248 Nebraska Ave., 4524 Vista Del Monte, Unnamed street. Hermitage St., Studio club, El Palaccio Apartments, Bel Air Hotel, Beverly Carlton Hotel... unnamed street. Outpost Estates.

D: Is this practical accessorizing? [*M1 steps away from live camera*]

M2: "It doesn't make any difference where a kid like M comes from. The shortest distance to stardom is from the screen to the seats in the first row..."

M1 [*simultaneous w/ final prepositional phrase, above*]: Marilyn Mon roe...

[audio 24]

[text slide:

Polly is in George and Rose's cabin, nursing Loomis' wound. He darkens the room to show Polly the "Illuminated Falls" through blinds. Ray enters. Loomis tells the story; he smashes the model car he's been building against the wall, kicks over a coffee table...

D: A product: an object that functions in a psychological sense and embodies cultural values. A technical-physical system that has to function efficiently and reliably. Something that can be manufactured, often in large numbers, preferably fast, cheaply, accurately and with the lowest possible number of faults... yields an attractive return... can have undesirable and often even harmful side-effects...

M1: [*simultaneously, facing wall image*]: birth, 1/26; entered orphanage

9/13/35, left orphanage 6/26/37; first screen test, 7/19/46; divorce, 9/13/46; posed nude, 5/27/49; first life cover, 4/7/52; footprints in cement, 6/26/53; 3/31/55, rode atop a pink elephant at Madison Square Garden... [*freeze*]

[pause image slides]

M3: [*quick piece of bio., statistical*]

M2: "My travels have always been of the same kind. No matter where I've gone or why I've gone there it ends up that I never see anything....

[continue image slides]

D. Gloves. [*all change gloves. M1 spins back into action*]

M1: "...the same picture layouts of yourself" ...?

M1 [*studying images*]: A search for the "real" MM... always mediated, always versions, through others' words, her "own" words—representations, reproductions, re-visions, signs without diacritical marks...

[audio 25]

M2: "I used to get the feeling, and sometimes I still get it, that I was fooling somebody—I don't know who or what..."

[text slide:

Loomis follows Rose to the Scenic Tunnels, Cave of Winds... she eludes him. He takes the elevator down to the tunnels; Rose's young, virile lover follows... Walking away, she hears their song, as planned... but the improbable has happened...]

D: Models fulfill in simulation the function of giving us a grip...

M2 [*pointing to M3*]: The box set—domestic MM, behind the scenes MM, dark mysterious MM, unspoiled Norma Jean; MM the wife, the star, the versions we create—2nd, 3rd hand.... we never touch her—can she be touched? [*M1 is preoccupied with the projected images*]

M1 [*entering the consciousness of the image-conscious images*]: "The real lover is the man who can thrill you just by touching your head or smiling into your eyes or by just staring into space." ...

[image slides: Niagara brochures
w/ aerial views;
pictographic tour maps]

M1 [*remembering the discourse, but not the job*]: Boxes in boxes.... The reel versions. The *Niagara* MM that escapes formulation—why we hover briefly over the film Falls in our hermeneutical helicopter...

[audio 26]

D: "credit cards—thermoplastic money"

M2: Let us imagine MM posing for us, in her various costumes...

M1 [*Self-involved, M1 begins to cross-dress, with M2's help; removes the black fur vest, puts on a blue kimono and the blonde wig (all three covered heads are now identically identitiless); M2 gives M1 a red dot, and takes a blue one for herself. Throughout this scene, until "Modern Housekeeping Cabins," M1 experiments with various movements inside the body-image MM*]: white sharkskin with an orange yoke, white suede shoes; sheer black negligee, blue polka-dotted cotton, tight white shorts, choker of pearls, baseball cap, low-cut blouse with tight plaid pedal pushers; a strategically placed decorative rose, gold lame, army pants and combat boots, [*toys with/stretches a black stocking*] black wool jersey with a black wool coat, white gloves, mink coat, no makeup, a Chinese Kimono, dark glasses, a white scarf, black net with a translucent bosom [*facing M2*]...

D [*simultaneous; waits for M1 to begin, above*]: How does the product smell, taste. sound?... Let us imagine her in her various roles....

M2 [*simultaneous. Props her leg on a chair—or the table—strips off one of her dark blue stockings (alternatively, she may draw one suggestively from her brief case), and, w/ M1's help, stretches it over her head and face; M1 considers, gives her a blue dot*]: Norma Jeane Mortenson—a sexy neighbor/model/ actress; Norma Jean Baker—a vulnerable divorcee, an aspiring actress; Norma Jean Dougherty—a chorus girl, a secretary; Marilyn DiMaggio—Dick Powell's girlfriend; Marılyn Monroe—a hardened nightclub singer, mistress; Marilyn Miller—an alcoholic singer/ukulele player of an all-girl band... [*M1 nets M2's head in black stocking*]

[hold image slide]

D: They won't buy it. There has to be coherence, alignment—signified with referent—phase parity... a sign wave...

[audio 27]
[image slide: blank, hold]

M2: Let us imagine the body, as it appeared at 10:30 am on august 5, 1962: "a 36-yr. old well developed, well-nourished Caucasian female weighing 117 pounds and measuring 65 1/2 inches... The eyes are blue."

[continue image slides]

M1: Let us imagine the opening of the corpse, as it took place on table #1 in the Hall of Justice, the slitting of thoracic and abdominal cavities with the "usual Y-shaped incision..." [*quick aside to audience*] Yes, a question? ...

[audio 28]

M2: "The heart weighs 300 grams, contains no excess fluid, the epicardium and pericardium are smooth and glistening... both the lungs are moderately congested... the surface is dark and red with mottling...."

M1: Hard to draw breath, to catch breath, to pass through unnoticed on an exhalation...

D: "The thyroid glands are of normal size, color, and consistency... the external genitalia show no gross abnormality.... the stomach is almost completely empty... the convolutions of the brain are not flattened; the contour of the brain is not distorted... The brain weighs 1440 grams."

M2: Lips moist even in death: "Marilyn has make-up tricks that nobody else has and nobody knows... she puts on a special kind of lipstick. It's a secret blend of three different shades. I get that moist look to her lips for when she's going to do a sexy scene..."

M1: Who knows you more intimately then your mortician...

M2: "by first putting on the lipstick and then putting on a gloss..."

M1: Fall mouth, 202, 000 cfs wet lips, sucking down into, depths of the organic, internal darkness of the creature... out again, in again...

the floor at the tip top of the bell tower, death orgasm, frozen comedrop bells—still shots in moving montage; locked in the girdered erection, a last night with the dead lover…

[audio 29]

D: 11/54, gynecological surgery; 8/57, miscarriage; 12/58, miscarriage; 6/59, 5/61—gynecological surgery; 7/62, alleged abortion…

M1 [*directly behind one MM head*]: The inability to reproduce, to let her body (any longer) be the subject of a reproduction.

M2: "Her body voluptuous and ridiculous, her face a blank negative on which male fantasies of rape and impotency were printed…"

[audio B: fade in MM singing "Kiss,"
from the soundtrack of *Niagara*]

D: Modern Housekeeping Cabins

[pause image slides]

[As Monroe sings "Kiss," M2 and M1 sheath themselves in hooded yellow rain ponchos; M2's head is still sheathed in the black stocking. Something begins to protrude from underneath…a backscratcher, from M1, and from M2 a big pencil! They mechanically caress each other—eroticism twice removed—moan, swoon… music stops abruptly; M1 & M2 throw off coverups; M2 removes the black stocking from her head with the poncho. M1 & M2 quickly disappear behind MM]

[text slide:
Polly, Ray, and the Ketterings tour the Scenic Tunnels, Cave of Winds, dressed in black and yellow raincoats. Slick catwalks. Polly falls behind; glimpses Loomis, in black

raincoat, following. She runs, slips, falls against the railing, it breaks, she grabs the splintered post, Loomis pulls her back…

D: The simulation model should be a homomorphism of the original

[continue image slides]

[audio 30]

M2 [*as if commenting on previous interaction*]: "I feel as though it's all happening to someone right next to me. I'm close, I can feel it, I can hear it, but it isn't me."

M1 [*pops up, with a heart-shaped paperweight; points it toward the audience, suggesting protruding breasts*]: Hey! honeymoon MM bust paper weight—shake it up and watch the image fragments drift down in hermetic lucidity…

D: Good accessorizing. Send it to Industrial Design.

M2: Newspaper story of the death, police photos, pointing fingers—the evidence, the window (shattered glass—through which she saw…) fragments …

D: "computer housing—thermoplastic injection molding" [*directs M3 to begin, as she/he*
continues computer manipulation of Monroe images]

M3 [*bio., daydreams. M1, about to make a point, freezes before live video camera*]

M1 [*to live camera, though he has trouble staying within the frame; may overlap M3*]: And Joseph cotton, too—fails to master the forms of successful middle-class life, is sucked into the maelstrom of culture-destroying forces, transmogrified by his proximity to the transmitter, gamma-burst MM, comet converted, his arms fly out from his body, miniature plastic replicas of the "good ole days" of western culture dashed to pieces against the walls that restrain him… spoked wheels, tiny instrument panels… what does he think the walls can save him from? these last rafterings of mid-American modular model honeymoon success stagings of domestic bliss drifting over the shattered imagery, disintegrating documents of a "life"—a veneer hypostatized by the culture, a room with a view on the brink…

D [*simultaneous*]: She drove or was driven in a Model-T, a blue 1940 coupe, a 1935 Ford spots car, a 1948 Ford convertible, a black Cadillac convertible, a black Thunderbird, a jaguar, a white Cadillac, a chauffeur-driven limo…

M2: "They've said I want to direct pictures. I couldn't direct traffic."

D: A 'man model' is a representation or imitation of ergonomically relevant features of a population…

M1 [*delayed response to joke—giddy laugh*]: "Georgie" (JC) and Rose (MM)—both brief presences, the odd honeymoon couple, masks of deterritorialization; she an (auto)biography of absence; he, a shadow of "social man"—both epiphytes living on images… so JC and MM are only superficially opposed in abstract Hollywood thematic machine meant to re- channel, categorize, contain, cordon disruptive mind trick; modular composition, suburban track homes, motel units…

D: Computer simulation is only possible if the behavior of the original can be represented in a mathematical model…

[hold image slide]

M1: Polly, and the naively resistant "Ray" (opaque illumination) ... the perfect hosts, like the motel room/representum, meme of suburban life they function within (what is it like in their room? what do they do? what do they talk about? what "happens"? the "story" is not there, simply because the narrative is too seamlessly in place: we always already know their room, their story); so they become the perfect subjects upon which to test the virus, the resilience capacity of society, the strength of the ideological coding resisting infection, infestation, infiltration...

M2: What?

D: Keep on track.

[continue image slides]

M1 [*live camera: briefly tries to recontain himself within the frame*]: The Modern Housekeeping Cabins, the familial couple [*fanning out a deck of girlie play cards, CU in video eye*], the moralized body of the woman; model cars and natural phenomena packaged as tourist attractions. MM the lower rapids; turbulent swell in the planescape of Duluth... whatever of the human her path crosses, by chance or direction, swept into the black hole, particulate cosmic humanicide...
wherrrroooorrrrr... [*flings deck of cards, freezes; M2 silently reorients...*]

[image slide: black]

D: A moment of catatonia for the product designers... [*M2 puts wig on M1*]

[audio 31]

[continue image slides]

[text slide:

Who will go over? Rose tries to escape, cross the border… "Georgie" is already there, on the deserted walkway, waiting… cigarette pressed between his lips, right hip thrown out in bitter mockery…

M2 [*to live video camera. As M2 speaks, a slow, distant smile passes through M1's features, gradually distorting into a kind of grimace; the jaws continue to stretch to the point of discomfort as M1 draws the mirror/script closer and closer to his face*]: The film, spiraling out from its empty core, images hurled down a beam of light, dashed against the metallic screen, flushing back over the tiered faces—pick one, anyone, how much does the light weigh as it passes through the cornea?—then (re)absorbed by 50's Lowe's State sham opulence. The screen is Falls, as the Falls is screen, porous screen absorbing while reflecting… the denser fabric of the movie screen—a particle weave… the screen of water rushing at such speed, force, and volume, it seems motionless—a matter of gravity… the apparently stable movie screen undergoing photon bombardment—it wails… "kiss me…" the light particles rebounding into the eyes/faces of the viewers—"kiss"—douse with illusion… Cave of Winds, repercussion of tons of falling water, air forced violently back over us, bumbling forward in the cheap futile raincoats provided for our comfort, soaked to the bone by the play of images, enraptured…

[audio 32]

D: We've got a product to get out here! [*M1 & M2 switch heads, in an excessively orderly, almost military fashion. The next several lines are played out behind the heads, letting the language rhythms carry the action*]

[slides blank, hold]

M3: [*struggles with his bio.: an intimate confessional babble*]

[audio 33, 34, 35]

[continue image slides]

M1 [*semi-trance*]: Her lips illuminate behind the screen of water; the falls itself a prop, MM a prop...

M2: "committed under restraint"!

[image slide, hold: hyper-colorized Falls & MM superimposed]

D: 200 Bengal lanterns behind a scrim of water...

M1: both driven--propelled-- by the same force...

D: Is the product exciting? Attractive? what images come to mind when viewing it?

M2: ("cascade of diamonds"?)

M1: Lip falls, pudenda lubrication, hip action, streaming libido; techni-flush of the Falls (night-lit color spectacle mimicking diurnal rainbow) rims moist lips of the lover--a clandestine kiss at the foot of the Falls, kiss of death--color coordinated excessiveness, the plunge, loss of self...

D: company policy... Team mission!

M1 [*may emerge from behind MM here*]: She is movement of passion, form of force slowed down enough (just enough), through makeup costume set direction constantly frustrated by her volatility-" too hot" to handle--and the relatively slower speed of light projecting through celluloid, to briefly irradiate a human, molar, thematically coded (codable) aggregate.

[continue image slides]

M2 [*simultaneously with M1*]: at age six, by a friend of the family; at age seven, a Mr. Litman, with his finger; at age eight, at age eight, age eight, a Mr. Ka... Ka.... Ka Ka K... at age 12, by an artist...

M1: Glacial drift grazing a '50s suburban patio party, drawing destruction in its wake. Joseph Cotton smashes the plastic disk, the codified melody of love electronically reproduced for the temporary residents of Modern Housekeeping Cabins...

D [*simultaneous with M1*]: geometric integration and precision, function sharing, localization of change, accommodation of variety, enabling standardization, portability of interfaces... [*continuing after M1 stops*] go with the flow, use visual stimuli and props, suppress preconceived hypotheses about the product technology, have the customer demo. the prod. and/or typical tasks related to the prod., be alert for surprises and the expression of latent needs, watch for nonverbal behavior... [*M1's gloved hand rises from behind MM, or, if M1 is standing, comes down with great malicious comic force to grab his crotch, as he makes his way back behind MM to work out his desires*]

M2: "A photographer once told me that my two best points are between my waist and neck."

M1 [*giddy laughter, begins to "masturbate"*]: But the refrain, abstracted from the lyrics, repeated over and over in MM's sing/talk-" kisssss me" -escapes semantic surveillance, the stability of definition...

M2: "It isn't necessary to use your voice in any special way… if you think of something sexy, the voice just naturally goes along."

M1: as does MM as a form of material culture… Georgie…

M2: "My looks are against me. They're too specific."

M1 [*laughing neurotically, masturbating fiercely; M2, not paying too much attention to M1, takes over for him—his discourse, that is…*]

D: Design methodology—how one may or must act in a certain situation…

M2 [*standing*]: The form of a cultural content and the content of that form…a flush in the cheek, Falls spray filtered through technicolor rainbow, micropolitical subversions of the radiant, erratic, nomadic body at large…

M1: "I always sleep with my mouth open. I know because it's open when I wake up."
[*Everyone has begun to laugh, except M2*]

[audio 36: Rose screams
as Georgie strangles her]

[*M2 observes M1's activity and screams, dovetailing Rose's prerecorded scream. At that moment, an explosion as M1 ejaculates a champagne popper from behind MM head, a flurry of Microfluff™; if he has been standing, M1 now collapses into his chair*]

[audio B 2, from a *Niagara* promotional trailer:
"It's Marilyn Monroe skyrocketing
to new dramatic heights

in the destructive whirlpool
of another's deceit"]

[image slides: the last few slides repeat]

D [*setting up a red flashing beacon—like a small lighthouse—in front of the head of the MM stand-up behind which M1...*]: "It was because of this violation that she began to stammer..." Gloves!... [*all change gloves; M1 and M2 also change heads—i.e., the heads from behind which they sometimes speak*] "Team Spirit": Product development teams are often highly motivated, cooperative groups. The team members may be co-located so they can focus their collective energy on creating the product. This situation can result in lasting camaraderie among team members [*M1's doctor hands, above the head, in his sterile new gloves*].

M2 [*walking to live camera*]: Reel real and real reel—the full dynamic assemblage designated MM--the MM complex, an image complex/ phenomenon of material culture that subsumes other artist formations, past and future—Mae West, Madonna, GaGa, etc— coordinates of an abstract event that can't be defined by limits--by lines limning--an actuation that is, by definition, indefinable, existing as a multi-dimensional space/time web the extensions, resonances, and molecules of which are in continuous dialogic tension...

D: a reciprocating screw injection molding machine...

M2: and exchange... (subsuming, subsumed by...)

D: "takes solid granules of thermoplastic resin, melts and pressurizes them in the extruder section, forces the melt at high velocity and pressure through carefully designed channels into a cooled mold, then ejects the finished part(s) and automatically recycles."

M1 [*stirring behind his new head*]: Better to move in the direction of less complexity... better better... they'll like...

M2: indifferent to dialectic closure. We follow the contours of MM's expanded/exploded body, cruise the margins of cultural coherence, register those points where she slips away...

D & M1 [*D ironically, emphasizing "now"; M1 sing-song*]: "yea, now, slip away ..."

[audio 37]

[pause image slides]

D: Common dysfunctions exhibited by development teams during concept generation include: failure to consider carefully the usefulness of the concepts employed, ineffective integration, failure to consider entire categories...

[audio 38]

M3 [*tries to come back with a "new" bio. entity—the Monroe "ME." He ends on his own, looking for approval; D stares, then cues to M2*]

[audio 39]

[continue image slides]

[image slide: Cave of Winds]

[text slide:

Rose flees, George follows—up the bell tower that plays tunes on request (that played "Kiss" when her lover, instead of Loomis, went over—for her, with her, without her). No more flights of stairs to run up: "Georgie" ... a stifled scream...]

M2 [*to live video; M1 reenters, out of it*]: Cave of the Winds. The husband and the lover, saturated in a becoming woman, the annihilating downpour of thigh, the thrusting out and beating down—MM's sexuality in the film always thrusting outward (even as she walks away), rather than being thrust into; she is not penetrated but engulfing—the morning after, waking late in Rainbow Cabin, it is apparent that she has taken JC for a ride in the machine of her desire...

[audio 40]

M1: The bell tower, the morning after, erect and silent. Rigor mortis. Inside, in the dry core of the tower with its seven flights of locked doors, a ray of light falling on the jeweled lipstick case, beaming back like a near star.

Ray fishing, cast...

[image slides: collages]

D: State of the world at time 1 (S1) + action = action + effect (S_2).

M1: Ray's lighted world, a clean wide plane with a bowl of shredded wheat—molded into airy bricks—and the luminous pitcher of milk...
[*as if reshaping on of MM's heads*]

M3 [*small piece of bio. Or—nothing, waiting, beaming, looking out over the audience. M1 walks toward audience, so that the live camera frames him from behind: the monitored image recalls MM's long walk, away from the camera, in* Niagara]

[audio 41]

M2 [*making her way back behind MM*]: Walk/stalk: following what?

[text slide:

Locked in. He finds the purse, its spilled contents, the jeweled lipstick case...]

M1: Walk away, lead astray.

M2 [*as M2 speaks, M1 "draws" on a MM collage projected on the wall: using a fat red phallic pen as a pointer, he connects various parts—an eye to a leg to a magazine cover, etc.—a kind of rebus message—and then invisibly writes equations or words*]: Loomis: "He came after me with a wrench; after that it was a case of who killed who." Use of a pronoun that conflates, rather than distinguishes... who is who? encased in identity-neutering rubber coats, the "I" can no longer secure itself by what it "sees," the physical no longer an adequate sign of power; in the shadow play of forces without names, faciality ceases to operate, the stops are pulled—what is what and who is who...?

M1: A problem of costumer interface...

[image slides: Cave, various superimpositions]

D [*trying it out*]: (cus...con...tomsum...?)

M2: Stairways over the Falls, catwalks of the improbable—that which cannot not happen, "happens"; desire to void the self... Cave of Winds—voice obliterating, sign obscuring blast of wind and spray through a resonant absence, black hole, vagina/cavity hidden moist risky behind the eruption, the spewing out (and "over") of all significance...

D: Still good accessorizing.

M2: battering down under its own weight onto rockfall into deep plunge pool

M1 [*simultaneously*]: Canadian curve of hip, the horseshoe that kicks, clangs; she is the foreign falling… [*slipping down wall/image*] MM fucks them all, carries them all away.

D: (We thought it best to let the designers themselves describe the case studies, and did not force them to use our terminology.)

M1: "It seems to me it's time they stopped knocking their assets around."

M2 [*M1 wanders*]: MM—the face of cinema freed from its justification in "representation"—she is pure image, all act.

[audio 42]

M1: "My work is the only ground I've had to stand on. To put it bluntly, I seem to have a whole superstructure with no foundation."

M2 [*M1 imitates MM straddling the Falls in the '53 poster*]: So what do we follow, chart, annotate? to note the whereabouts, the when, the with whom, is to drift on a circulation of signs for their own sake, to be taken for a ride, caught in a game of tracings like a riddle of catwalks over whirlpools of deterritorialization.

[audio 43]

From Polly to Ray to the Shredded Wheat King (Mr. Kettering), the characters move further into the realms of middle class dissimulation…

M1: Customer's usually right...

M2: further from contact with the white hole/white Falls; and the further "in" they get, the more packed with articulation the culture space becomes—black hole/defined Falls—the harder to escape...

[text slide:

Loomis in flight, attempts to steal Mr. Kettering's boat. Bad luck, Polly shows up. "Get off this boat." They struggle, she falls... It's red with blue and white trim... mid river, the boat runs out of gas, gets caught in the main current... The police boat turns back (deep blue?) ... "scuttle it scuttle it" ... she takes water, slows, draws toward a rock; George pushes Polly off to safety... watches, then...]

M1 [*positioning himself before live camera for a profile shot*]: Imagery stretched over a syntactical framework... *that* side of the black hole is white annihilation...

M2: The portly Mr. Kettering sketched across a verbal wall of banal signifieds. Only when he sees his little red white and blue cruiser adrift in the main current is he stunned into silence. Polly without a Ray. Georgie aft working a nylon stocking, remembering Rose... what does Polly want? ...

M1 [*simultaneously*]: "Pip pip, toodaloo... those fish are dyin' to get our bait... just tryin' to get things organized... Olive oil as the French say..." [*facing audience, with his back toward live camera*]: "Nearly every step forward in her acting seemed to require a step backward, a rehearsing of previous mistakes, a compulsion to repeat..."

D: Polly want...?

M2: So what are we following? MM effect; image, emanation, illusion of our own deconstruction. A pair of legs—whose legs? A shadow, like all shadows; a surreptitious profile, an energy without a face, pure virility/vitality…

[Text Slide: hand-written, holograph note, on Hotel Bel-Air stationary, MM to…?

"You changed my life—even though you changed it, I still am lost—I mean I can't seem to pull myself together—I think Its [sic] because everything is pulling against my concentration ["representation"? could be…]

[audio 44]

M1 [*back behind MM*]: That's not marketable.

M2 [*rising, wandering before camera. M1 experiments with various props—mirrors, shoes, writing instruments*]: —who is JC when he returns from the Falls, the Cave? His hips thrown in static unconscious imitation of hers as he stands waiting for her at the border to her full-fleshed America. By a turn of events he is now the threshold, in her name (enacting the signature icon), through which she must pass, not into cultural, ideological or political sanctuary

[audio 45: a stuck horn]

(for she was never a woman with a country), but out of her "self," her ineffectually (or futilely) politicized body (made in the image of 1950s American plentitude): out of her "Rose" subjectification (a partial identity) and eruptive body that was never completely probable, that was always movement toward designification, a passing through/veering away from the delimitable… out of, to… *rite du passage* from partial construction on a plane of stratification to greater realization as pure MM effect [*M1 shoots a pair of white-gloved "fives" over MM*], replicated as pure cinema, a rhythmic coalescing and dispersing of elements in a mixed semiotic field, a deterritorialized(ing) milieu within which he is as much her as the red/white/blue boat adrift as the running red stripes of emblematic nationhood…

[audio 46]

M1: Running off, away, a flag torn holy battle beautified—as the red lips carrying (them) all over… lips sink ships…

D: Surgeons' gloves—vulcanized latex rubber.

[text slide:

Polly is rescued by helicopter…

M2: And a piece of blue terror-struck Polly, wet blue-black hair, stranded on a spray-drenched Hollywood rock… pursued by…

M1 [*popping up*]: "True or falsie…"

[audio 47]

M2: protruding ruggedly from the torrent, lifted on what looks like a lawn chair dangling at the end of a cable into the technicolor sky—a highwire act worthy of Blondin…

D: MM's voice in a minute. But first, we should not forget to mention simulations based on stochastic models. If we take as an example somebody who is leaning completely drunk against a lamp-post. He tries to make some steps, but he sways over the street, forward, backward, to the sides—he cannot walk straight. Would it still be possible to say something about the distance the drunkard has walked (probably) after a few steps? Yes, for that purpose the Monte Carlo technique can be applied.

[audio 48]

M1 [*simultaneously, piecing it out*]: "Please don't make me a joke."

[image slide: cu of MM, hold]

M2 [*considering the video monitors; sometime previously, perhaps only recently, the video machines have automatically stopped "playing," the images dispersed into "snow"*]: Video tape is tangible, like a book, but dark and wound in on itself; the laser disk goes a bit further, toward transparency and extreme sharpness of image repro., toward the pure digital—look, an Image in the palm of a hand… then, silently, after a preset quantity of time, the image flash-dissolves into snow—a video snow whose (no)temperature is constant, comforting, anywhere on or off earth… welcome to Niagara Falls…

D: Can we project images onto video snow?

M1: "I worked with her hair till it was perfectly white—'pillow case white' she called it"

M2 [*looking at MM*]: Polly wears blue for the skies…

M1: MM's eyes… all that blue…

M2: (thoughts freed also from objects, as objects are cast into the whirlwinds of thought…)

[audio 49]

D: Profitability is often difficult to assess quickly and directly.

[image slides: blank, hold]

M1: "It might be kind of a relief to be finished."

[audio 50]

D: The mock-up. [*M2 unveils first head of MM, the stand-up, revealing a standard pose; smiles, imitating the cardboard expression, and gestures for "client" (audience) response*]: She's satisfied, she has what she wants, she lets us know…

M2: This doesn't follow… [*unveils middle head*] she looks away—at what? —just a pose… [*elicits customer response. Unveils the final head, revealing a blacked-out face, turns the pillow case inside out, and places it over M1's head. Customer response*]

M1 [*from within pillow case*]: she laughs, laughs, the teeth a cold crescent, the mouth is dark… she has begun to become…

M2 [*lighting a sparkler and mounting it in one of MM's heads*]: And so we go…

M1 [*still "body"-bagged*]: star fishing!

[slides black]

[audio 51, 52]

M3 [*searching his books*]: ummmm…

[audio B 3, from *Niagara* trailer: "She could never be his, nor any man's completely"]

[audio 53]

[M2 helps M1 out of his kimono, then puts it on him backwards, securing it like a straight-jacket; she then turns M1 around, so that his "back" faces the audience, revealing, printed on the pillow case over his head, a CU of MM, head thrown back and mouth wide and dark in laughter…]

D [*with a sense of fashion, as M2 backs M1 into a front row seat among the clients*]: "Marilyn's body was partially exposed in a solid bronze casket that was lined with champagne-colored satin. She was dressed in her green Pucci dress and a green chiffon scarf. Her hair was done in a pageboy."

[audio 54]

[All offstage. D is the last to leave, distributing xerox reproductions of one of the "final products" to the clients, along with a blank sheet of paper]

D [*amplified, from rear of performance space; pausing between each question, allowing audience time to respond, on paper or verbally*]: Postmortem project evaluation:

[audio 55]

Did the team achieve the mission articulated in the mission statement?

Which aspects of project performance were most positive? most negative?

Which tools, methodologies, and practices contributed to the positive aspects of performance?

Which tools, methodologies, and practices detracted from the project success?

What problems did the team encounter?

[audio 56]

What specific actions can the organization take to improve project performance?

[audio 57]

What specific technical lessons were learned? how can they be shared?

[audio 58-65]

Audio List

1-3: Customs Inspector: "Where do you live?... where were you born?... are you bringing in anything besides your clothes and personal belongings?... How long do you plan to be here?" [*the last three questions replay*]

4. Ray: "Honey, you can see it from here!" [*laughter*].
5. Cabin manager: "The Falls are that way..."
6. [*Parody of* Niagara *theme music, as Ray observes Rose's walk*]
7. [*Maid of the Mist fog horn*]
8. Ray [*dramatic music*] "Farther back honey" [*posing Polly at Falls*]
9. George [*Rose in shower, humming "kiss"*] "Rose... [*more forceful*] Rose?"
10. George [*to Polly, in his room*]: "I suppose she sent you to find out if I cut it off..."
11. George: "but that... song..."
12. Polly: "it's a stunning dress"
13. George [*to Polly*]: "that's some confession to make, idn' it..."
14. Polly: "What's that?" George: "It's 8:30... look out the window."
15. Polly [*peering through "Venetian" blinds*]: "OH!"
16. George [*to Ray and Polly*]: "you make different models from little kits...," followed by white water: The Falls
17. George: "Oh but she's got a reason you'd bet on that... she's got a reason..."
18. George: "occupational therapy!" [*smashing his model car against the cabin wall, kicking over a coffee table*]
19. Rose [*telephoning, a boarding house, coding ("signifying") to lover*]: "Hello is... is this the bus terminal? I'd like to know what time the buses leave tomorrow for Ottawa." "No no no! ya got the wrong number..."
20. [*Rose's lover whistling "Kiss"*]
21. Ray [*posing Polly on the chaise lounge for a typical "cheesecake" snapshot; just before Ray releases the shutter, Rose's sudden unexpected presence briefly darkens over the posed body*]: "wha... oh [*nervous laugh*] oh, just a minute please, wou..would ya mind—your shadow..."
22. Chief Inspector Starkey: "bring in the missing persons file!"
23. Inspector Starkey's assistant: "a transient..."

24. Rose [*at the entrance to "Scenic Tunnels"*]: "You've heard something about my husband." Inspector Starkey: "Just that he is your husband."
25. Inspector Starkey: "Tell me Mrs. Loomis, is there any chance he could have come here today?" Rose: "Here?" Starkey: "Yes, *here*."
26. Rose: "What are we doing here?" Inspector Starkey: "Wasting your time, I hope."
27. Scenic Tunnel Custodian: "Hello Mr. Starkey." Inspector Starkey: "Hello. Did you check again?" Custodian: "Yes sir I did, and there's still one missing."
28. Custodian: "and over here…" Starkey: "Le'me see… [*to Rose*] ever seen these before?"
29. Starkey: "Have ya got anyone to take care of ya, any friends or close relatives?"
30. Rose: "No, no one." [*Ray, in the background*]: "no one…?"
31. Rose [*bells, echoey/eerie: "Kiss"*]: "I'd rather walk." [*bells continue, sound of footsteps*]
32. Chief Inspector Starkey [*at the morgue*]: "Mrs. Loomis, can you identify this body as that of your husband, George Loomis?" [*dramatic music, sound of a body collapsing*]
33. Inspector Starkey [*visiting the recently hospitalized Rose*]: "What's all this?… I wanna talk to 'er." Doctor: "Come around in the evening, she'll be out till then."
34. Manager, Rainbow cabins: "The key's in the door."
35. [*door opening, closing, latch turning; blinds being drawn*]
36. [*eerie echoey music*]
37. [*eerie echoey music, creepy base. Peering through a window, the camera picks up an uncanny silhouette in the bushes out back of cabin 2. Inside, in bed, Polly has displaced Rose. George, returned from the "dead" is unaware… Polly screams*]
38. Ray: "Sport clothes… [*snicker*] all we needed here was a couple 'o shrouds."
39. George [*forcing Polly into a narrow hollow, Cave of Winds catwalk*]: "on the floor of the tunnel I found his claim check… th… then I could put on his shoes and walk out of there officially dead."
40. Ray: "Now get organized baby…what's wrong?"
41. George: "get a job, get organized!"
42. George: "Let me stay dead." Polly: "Take your hands off me."
43. [*dream-echoey bells and distorted lyrics—" Kiss"—MM's drugged semi-sleep in hospital bed*]

44. Rose [*on the run*]: "Say what I want to know is can you get me to the bus station on the American side?" Taxi Driver: "If you're not in too much of a hurry... they've got some kind of a road block up there at the bridge."
45. Falls Tour Guide: "Now right over there on June 30 1859 Blondin a French tightrope walker made his famous walk right over the Falls... if you follow me I'll show you a little better where it happened" [*tense creeping background music*]
46. [*foreground: tense stringy music, metallic sound of small objects falling onto a hard surface, frantic knocks on a door, footsteps running upstairs, other footsteps in pursuit, more frantic knocks on doors, music becoming more dramatic*]
47. [*sound of a body falling to the floor*]
48. Marina watchman [*"stuck" car horn—a decoy*] Hey!... What's wrong over there!... Hey!
49. George: "Get off this boat!"
50. [*sound of a boat motor idling, revving up, throttling out*] "Hey!... Hey you!"
51. Ray [*riding in police car, tracking the stolen cruiser; sirens*]: Well... where's he trying to go?"
52. [*sirens*]
53. [*Falls roar, crashing water; scuttling*]
54. George [*eerie* Niagara *theme music fading to background as Loomis, slipping quietly into bed after his dawn walk to the base of the Falls, whispers to the dissembling sleeper*]: "Rose? [*slightly louder*] ... Rose?"
55. [*Rose laughing, slyly*]
56. The Shredded Wheat King: "Well, toodaloo for now [*laughter*] pip pip, c'mon mamma" [*more laughter*]
57. Ray [*noticing a bouquet of roses on the coffee table of their cabin*]: "What's this thing?"
58. [*door slamming?*]
59. Chief Inspector Starkey: "I know you've seen enough of the Falls for one trip, but... don't cross us off your list."
60. [*tense music, Rose's breathless scream*]
61. The Shredded Wheat King [*laughter*]: "Just tryin' to get things organized" [*laughter*]
62. [*group laughter*]
63. The Shredded Wheat King: "c'mon, c'mon kids we haven't got all day... those fish are dyin' to get our bait." [*"our bait" repeated*]
64. George [*eerie Niagara theme, fading to background, as 53.*] "Rose? [*quietly*]... Rose...?"

65. White noise: The Falls

Bibliography

Baty, S. Paige. American Monroe: The Making of a Body Politic. Berkeley: University of California Press, 1995.

Belofsky, Harold. Plastics: Product Design and Process Engineering. Munich: Hanser Publishers, 1995.

Boothroyd, Geoffrey, Peter Dewhurst, and Winston Knight. Product Design for Manufacture and Assembly. New York: M. Dekker, 1994.

Churchwell, Sarah. "'The Naked Truth': Pathography and the Case (No. 81128) of Marilyn Monroe." A/B: Auto/Biography Studies, 14:2 (1999Winter):161-85.

Cohen, Lisa. "The Horizontal Walk: Marilyn Monroe, CinemaScope, and Sexuality." Yale Journal of Criticism: Interpretation in the Humanities, 11:1 (1998 Spring): 259-88.

Conway, Michael, and Mark Ricci. The Films of Marilyn Monroe. New York: The Citadel Press, 1964.

de Dienes, Andre. Marilyn Mon Amour: The Private Album of Andre de Dienes, Her Preferred Photographer. New York: St. Martin's Press, 1985.

DePaoli, Geri, ed. Elvis + Marilyn: 2 X Immortal. New York: Rizzoli International Publications, 1994.

Friedlander, Jennifer. "How Should a Woman Look? Scopic Strategies for Sexuated Subjects." JPCS: Journal for the Psychoanalysis of Culture & Society, 8:1 (2003 Spring): 99-108.

Lembourn, Hans Jorgen. Diary of a Lover of Marilyn Monroe. Trans. Hallberg Hallmundsson. New York: Arbor House, ND.

McDonough, Yona Zeldis. All the Available Light: A Marilyn Monroe Reader. New York, NY: Simon & Schuster, 2002.

Mailer, Norman. Marilyn, a Biography. New York: Grosset & Dunlap, 1973.

Niagara [film]. Dir. Henry Hathaway. Starring Marilyn Monroe, Joseph Cotton, and Jean Peters. 20th Century Fox Corporation, 1953.

Pepitone, Lena, and William Stadiem. Marilyn Monroe Confidential. New York: Simon and Schuster, ND.

Riese, Randall, and Neal Hitchens. The Unabridged Marilyn: Her Life from A to Z. New York: Congdon & Weed, 1987.

Rollyson, Carl E. Jr. Marilyn Monroe: A Life of the Actress. Ann Arbor: U.M.I. Research Press, 1986.

Roozenburg, J. Eekels. Product Design: Fundamentals and Methods. Chichester, England: Wiley, 1995.

Sexton, Richard. American Style: Classic Product Design from Airstream to Zippo. San Francisco: Chronicle Books, 1987.

Shevey, Sandra. The Marilyn Scandal. London: Sidgwick & Jackson, 1987.

Summers, Anthony. Goddess: The Secret Lives of Marilyn Monroe. New York: Macmillan, 1985.

Ulrich, Karl T., and Steven D. Eppinger. Product Design and Development. New York: McGraw-Hill, 1995.

* Special thanks to Gilles Deleuze and Felix Guittari, *A Thousand Plateaus: Capitalism and Schizophrenia*, Minneapolis: U of Minnesota P, 1987.

Theory = Motion.

(*The following essay is read at various points during the performance of the* "Monroe Project." *It speaks for itself.*)

Monroe/Me (Auto)bio (Zoe Randall, *TEZ*)

Born June 1, 1926 (in or near Los Angeles, CA), Norma Jean Mortenson (also known as Norma Jean Baker) "looked like any other baby"—" She was the same as the rest," said one Dr. Beerman, the obstetrician who delivered her. Her mother—abandoned by her husband, later to be widowed, and finally insane—was, at the time, a film cutter at R. K. O. She abandoned her child to a succession of approximately twelve (Norma Jean lost count) foster homes and several orphanages.

By the age of two, Norma Jean had survived being nearly smothered to death; by six, she was almost raped by a close "friend of the family." Story has it that the child was penetrated by a Mr. Litman's finger (Litman, a border at one of Norma Jean's foster homes) at seven—molested by a Mr. Kimmel and raped by a Mr. K at the age of eight. She began to stutter. At nine, she was interred in the Los Angeles Orphan's Home, where she earned her first "big money" working in the orphanage pantry for a nickel a month. She bought a hair ribbon with a "surplus" penny (She had to donate part of her earning to the church basket)—" So runs the legend," says biographer Mark Harris (Conroy 9).

Perhaps the legend of Marilyn Monroe began when Norma Jean was just sixteen: when an Army publicity man photographed her, thinking that her image, distributed among fighting men, would boost morale. [O]ne unit named her Miss Flamethrower, soldiers in the Aleutians voted her the girl most likely to thaw Alaska, and the Seventh Division Medical Corps elected her the girl they would most like to examine (10). Three weeks after Marilyn turned sixteen, June 19, 1942, she married Jim Dougherty (probably to escape the orphanage) and began modeling—her face and figure splashed across several magazine covers (Dougherty joined the military). By autumn, 1946, they were divorced. In 1948 Norma Jean became Marilyn Monroe, picked up by 20th Century Fox at $125 a week (renamed by Fox). She played a bit role as a farm girl in *Scuddle Hoo! Scudda Hay*, but her scenes wound up on the cutting room floor.

Marilyn continued to model, posing nude (the famous nude shot) for Tom Kelly for only $50 (Kelly sold it for $900; the photo, turned barbershop, military barracks, and gasoline station calendar, yielded three-quarters of a million dollars). According to Harris she refused to disclaim the photo (Fox afraid that it would damage her career): "Sure I posed," she said. "I was hungry."

I'm hungry....

Her first film (one can't count cutting room scraps) was *Dangerous Years*—" a very tame movie about burlesque," says filmographer Michael Conroy (16). Then Fox dropped Marilyn's contract—Columbia Pictures, picking her up for *Ladies of the Chorus* (1948). Monroe sang "Everybody Needs a Da Da Daddy" (certainly a reoccurring theme in Marilyn's life—a girl who dreamed of having Clark Gable for a father, who called her first husband "Daddy" [Doherty called her "Baby"]. Of *Ladies...*, Tibor Krekes of the *Motion Picture Herald* wrote, "One of the bright spots [of the film] is Miss Monroe's singing. She is pretty and, with her pleasing voice and style, she shows promise" (Rpt. Conroy 29).

This "promise" manifested itself time and time again: Love Happy (United Artists, 1950)—a "walk on" for The Marx Brothers; *A Ticket to Tomahawk* (20th Century Fox, 1950)—a minor "decorative" role; *The Asphalt Jungle* (Fox)—playing the seductive "niece" (the role of "mistress" was taboo in 1950) who piqued public interest (Who is this provocative, yet still naive, girl?); *All About Eve* (Fox, 1950)—a small, though showy, role; The Fireball (A Thor Production, 1950) with Mickey Rooney; *Right Cross* (Metro-Goldwyn Mayer, 1950)—no billing at all!; *Hometown Story* (1951)—her second and last MGM film; As Young As You Feel, Love Nest, and *Let's Make It Legal* (all under a new contract with 20th C Fox, 1951) launched (deliberately) M M, the sexy blonde. By the time she made *Clash by Night* (RKO, 1952) and *We're Not Married* (Fox, 1952) the public loved her (in spite of the "calendar scandal"). That same year she played her first dramatic starring role (a psychotic woman) in *Don't Bother to Knock*, starred with Cary Grant and Ginger Rogers in *Monkey Business*, and played in *O. Henry's Full House* (all for 20th C Fox).

Yet it was not until Monroe's eighteenth film, *Niagara* (Fox, 1953) that she became a full-fledged star—top billing, people pouring into the box office to see *her*. It was the public, not the Hollywood studios that made her a star. "Some stars are manufactured...the studios nurturing them along in just the right vehicles from the start," explains Conroy, "Marilyn's unique personality and special beauty drew public notice and caused the people themselves to lift her to stardom as a result of their clamor at the box office" (??).

During this time, Marilyn had also drawn the attention of Joe DiMaggio and Robert Slatzer. Why not? Lee Strasberg tells us that Marilyn had "a luminous quality—a combination of wistfulness, radiance, yearning—to set her apart and yet make everyone wish to be a part of it...share in the childish *naiveté* which was at once so shy and yet so vibrant" (Rpt. Baty 7). And she was gorgeous. Marilyn married Slatzer October 4, 1952, in Mexico. The marriage was shortly annulled. She married DiMaggio, "The Last American Hero," in January, 1954. He was her "Slugger", her "Giuseppe" and her protector (Riese 124). Less than two years later, they, too, divorced. In 1956, she married Arthur Miller. After two miscarriages and irreconcilable differences, a divorce was granted in 1961.

He told me that it was my radiance and lack of restraint that drew him to me.

> *He thought I was beautiful...sexy. He liked that other men paid attention to me, knowing that I was his.*

DiMaggio was paternalistic and jealous (Marilyn's alleged affairs with John and Robert Kennedy got to both he and Arthur Miller). Marilyn could not be contained. "Everything I have is mine," Marilyn told Earl Wilson on the subject of falsies (145). Marilyn dressed to accentuate her body: to wear on her first date, Norma Jean borrowed a red silk party dress from Beebe Goddard; she wore a black negligee for her first advertising assignment; her first date with DiMaggio—a tight blue tailored suit with a low-cut white "shantung" blouse (black silk, for the divorce); a one-size-too-small gold lame gown for the 1953 Photoplay Awards....

> *A representative of the academy, I wear my suit. You can't see the black lace—underwire gently pressing against my rib cage—my nipples piqued. "She's not merely `lovely,' she's brilliant," one colleague corrects another.*

"I like to be really dressed up, or really undressed. I don't bother with anything in between," Marilyn told *Cosmopolitan* in 1960 (147). Of the Photoplay gown, James Bacon observed, "When she wiggled through the audience to the podium, her derriere looked like two puppies fighting under a silk sheet'" (147). Marilyn wore nothing to bed. She wore gloves to camouflage aging. M M was wearing a white terry robe when her body was found—no makeup.

> *I remember Albert Murray—teasing—offering me his jacket, cover me up. My husband liked me in scanty dress.*

Marilyn Monroe and Jane Russell (all dressed up) co-starred in *Gentlemen Prefer Blondes* (1953)—never trying to outdo one another. That same year, Marilyn co-starred with Betty Grable (for years a 20th C Fox star—America's symbol of "wholesome" sex—and perhaps the reason why Fox was not so immediately anxious to nurture "blonde bombshell" M M) in *How to Marry A Millionaire*. 1954: *River of No Return*, Marilyn's first Western, and *There's No Business-Like Show Business*. *The Seven Year Itch* (1955) was filmed during a period of pandemonium and strife for Marilyn—the Joe DiMaggio divorce. Legend has it that DiMaggio no more liked Marilyn's sexy dress, than he appreciated her intelligence. Rumor has it that he hit her.

> *He knocked me against the wall for flirting with a dinner plate—letting in drop. Miscarriage. Divorce granted 1992.*

Marilyn was no dumb blonde. "Rapaciously inquisitive, her intelligence matured at an astonishing pace," writes biographer Sandra Shevey (2).

I buried my body in books.

"Both a zealous Democrat and a keen citizen, she [Monroe] followed politics and corresponded with Lester Markel, then editor of the *New York Sunday Times*, often complaining to him about news coverage and the lack of prominence give to some important stories" (2). She read Stanislavsky, Rilke, Freud, Camus, Joyce, Chekhov, and Poe. Arthur Miller took her as a serious actress—perhaps one the things that attracted her to him (along with his own intellect and power). Certainly after *Bus Stop* (1956) Marilyn wanted to be taken seriously. "Is not Monroe the image *par excellence* of this New Woman? She is voluptuous, but she admires Dostoyevsky," commented biographer Maurice Zolotow (Riese 344).

> *Not all great minds are packaged in the phallic mode or in the shape of Madame Perloff (no offense intended; appellation courtesy of Diane Wakoski).*

Monroe could also be cruel. Legend has it that she was an impossible diva on the set.

> *But even the man who (when I was in graduate school) commended my intellect said he would rather write his "marginal notes" on my inner thigh than on my paper. I smiled, watching him squirm in all his professorial prominence.*

In 1957 Marilyn formed her own production company, releasing (through Warner Bros.) *The Prince and The Showgirl* starring Lawrence Olivier and M M. She was already in her 30's (but never more beautiful), and she was determined not to spend the rest of her career (to use Eli Wallach's phrase) "just wiggling her behind" (Conroy 13). Still Monroe spent painful hours in front of the mirror—noticing various physiognomic flaws in her body.

New lover suggests silicone. I stand naked in front of the mirror—having nursed two babies.
Some Like It Hot (United Artists, 1959), starring M M, Tony Curtis, and

Jack Lemmon (Curtis and Lemmon, in drag) has become a comedy classic, and *Let's Make Love* (20th C Fox, 1960) set off some mild M M/Yves Montand gossip (Though nothing like the Kennedy brothers scandal—heightened by M M's "Happy Birthday, Mr. President" in Madison Square Garden). But *The Misfits* (United Artists, 1961), Marilyn's last completed film, is regarded by many as her best film—certainly marking M M as more than a ravishing comedienne. By then, Marilyn Monroe was indeed respected as a fine performer.

> *"So much did we think of her personal and intellectual qualities...took the unprecedented step...moving her up to the position of adjunct lecturer...first year... program...expectations well fulfilled... performance in this role."*

What happened? "In a while she'll either be dead or in a mental institution," remarked director John Huston, after the completion of *Misfits* (Rpt. Shevey ??). The death of Clark Cable and the end of her marriage to Arthur Miller (who had written the screenplay for *Misfits*) upset Marilyn terribly.

"Sit on the highway, it represents life!" Andre De Dienes (Marilyn's favorite photographer, who was also in love with her) told Norma Jean in 1945. "You have a long way to go" (19)! De Dienes arrived home the night of Marilyn's death, his telephone ringing. He dropped his keys—got to the phone too late. "Was it Marilyn?" he wondered. She often called when she was troubled.

> *I thought, first, about making love this morning. Second, about presenting this paper. I dropped my white robe. Sheets of paper. "Kiss me." My new husband, one who, at once, respects my intellect and loves the way I sit on a pool table, insisted that we rehearse. That I revise....*

"Rejected and vilified, her body lay unclaimed for days on a slab in the city morgue, with only a name tag for a talisman knotted around her big toe," writes Sandra Shevey. Shevey tells us that both Miller and DiMaggio were contacted—neither one of them making "an immediate effort to redeem the body" (3). Whitey Snyder, Marilyn's makeup man, would have claimed her except for the financial obligations that are attached to such a claim—obligations which made others reluctant, as well. Days later the Monroe estate made the formal claim for Marilyn's body. Joe DiMaggio donated the $800 bronze crypt and ordered a black vase filled with fresh roses to be placed at the grave "twice a week—forever" (126). But the estate paid for the funeral.

Marilyn Monroe as "representative character"—as symbol, a "concentrated image [embodying] the way people in a given environment organize and give meaning and direction to their lives" (Bellah 39). Marilyn Monroe was not only lifted to stardom by her public, but was forged by that public. The same public that clamored to the box office—that made Marilyn a star—thus predetermined her demise.

I only wanted to be loved....

Cultural critic S. Paige Baty asserts that the representative character of Marilyn Monroe has been further manufactured by "mass-mediated remembering" (20):

> Contestations abound in rememberings of Marilyn. She is remembered as victim, heroine, queen bitch, unattainable sex object, frigid sex symbol, dumb blonde, feminist, communist, political pawn, communist spy, photographic object, biographical subject, material object, material girl, and media manipulator. (22)

I'm not supposed to get into the theoretical stuff. Stick to the bio. Scream when he masturbates.

Norma Jean Mortenson, Norma Jean Dougherty, Jean Baker, Marilyn DiMaggio, annulled Marilyn Slatzer, Marilyn Miller, and the "real" Marilyn Monroe are all at rest. MM, the legend, is "beautifully preserved...imprinted and displayed on T-shirts, calendars, postcards, ashtrays, soap dishes...impersonated by rock stars, fans, and other actors..." (Baty 3)—even imbibed (*Marilyn Merlot*). We cannot say goodbye. "Marilyn never liked goodbyes" (Lee Strasberg).

I don't like goodbyes—can never properly conclude. I know/teach the rationale and methodology:

> An effective conclusion is as important as a good introduction...There are a variety of ways...

1.Briefly summarize the essay's main points. [**The real M M could not reconcile with her representative character**.]

* * *

2. Make and interesting comparison or image. [**An enlarged M M, accentuated hip, reclining at the lip of the Horseshoe Falls**.]

* * *

3. Suggest an action or an idea that readers should consider in light of your essay [**The nature of consumption can be devious, "insinuat[ing] itself everywhere, silently and almost invisibly, because it does not manifest itself through its own products, but rather through its ways of using the products imposed by a dominant economic order (de Certeau xiii).**]

* * *

4. Speculate about what your thesis implies for the future [**A woman's proficiency to market herself for consumption in an order that is hostile to her, will continue to foreclose the strength, desire, and ability to claim (stake a claim) for a "woman's self" outside that order.**]

* * *

5. Make a brief remark that sums up your feelings. [**The tragedy lies in the closure.**] (Greenberg 380)

"I cannot say goodbye. Marilyn never liked goodbyes, but in the peculiar way she had of turning things around so that they faced reality—I must say *au revoir*" (Lee Strasberg).

C'est tout.

Zoe Monroe-Randall, 1962.

Works Cited

Bellah, Robert, Richard Madsen, William M. Sullivan, Ann Swidler, and Steven M. Tipton. *Habits of the Heart: Individualism and Commitment in American Life*. New York: Harper Row, 1985.

Baty, S. Paige. *American Monroe: The Making of a Body Politic*. Berkeley: University of California Press, 1995.

Conway, Michael and Mark Ricci. *The Films of Marilyn Monroe*. New York: Citadel Press, 1964.

de Certeau, Michael. *The Practice of Everyday Life*. Berkeley, California: University of California Press, 1984.

de Deines, Andre. *Marilyn Mon Amour*. New York: St. Martin's Press, 1985.

Greenberg, Karen L. *The Advancing Writer*. New York: Harper Collins College Publishers, 1994.

Riese, Randall and Neal Hitchens. *The Unabridged Marilyn: Her Life from A to Z*. New York: Congdon & Weed, 1987.

Shevey, Sandra. *The Marilyn Scandal Her True Life Revealed by Those Who Knew Her*. London: Sidgwick & Jackson, 1987.

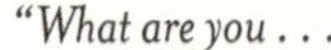

"What are you . . .

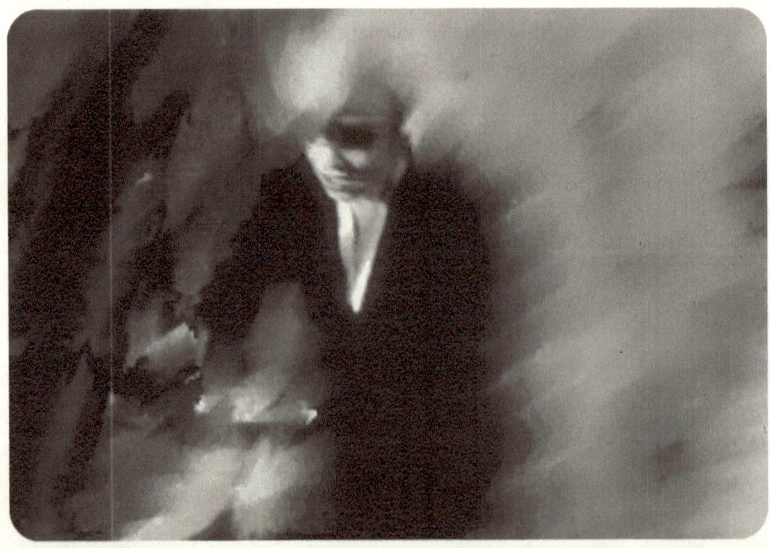

Life: 9/9/57

WILD-EYED SHOCKER
anytime, anywhere
double action hyper power wrap around red
missile—the "French look"

v.

QUIET ZONE
smooth burning veinless
careful craftsman
sani-white all-weather elegance
"beautiful"—
made from Melanine™

ROUND ONE
brought to you by

Lavoris, the Post-Toasties—
"man, they're the 'gators!"—
  and…

THE BELL

Q: "What does it taste like?"

blonde ponytail striped pajamas
perhaps fourteen, legs dangling
over arm of "dad's" overstuffed chair
sound asleep.

the little hand is on the ten and the big hand…
        "ok, but watch it—back in there!"

the match scrolls down the screen.
        "vertical hold—break it up!"
On top the TV, the box of cereal
turned on its side, wide open…

THE COUNT

Honey honey dream in black
and white with shades of pink:
no death just white's pure clean
and fragrant night's sweet breath

AND STILL

A: These days, it's just "competitive spending."

The Speed of (Re)production

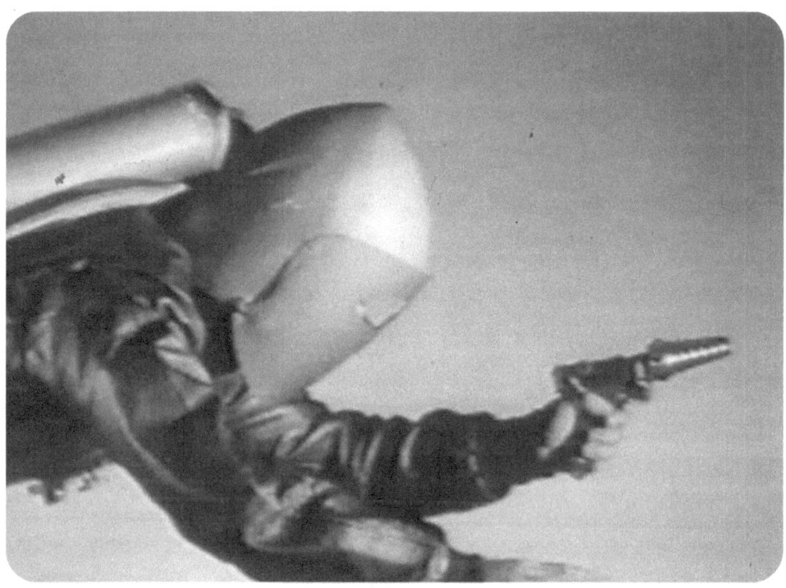

Fig. 7. In-flight imagery: Rocket Man, from *King of the Rocket Men*, dir. Fred C. Brannon, Republic Pictures, 1949-56; used by permission (see below, 'Coming Next: Feature 3').

5 Script 4: The Beat Poetry Games

{} = *music and sound cues.*

<> = *"beats" of silence: e.g.,* <3> *= three silent beats.*

audio tapes: A = bop jazz; runs continuously throughout the piece, except for brief pauses or cut outs. B = brief quotes from film soundtracks, R & B/rock riffs, misc. sound effects as indicated.

props: toys and other popculture materials "played with" during the performance are scattered about the space, on tables and the floor. They include two Hula Hoops, a Marilyn Monroe "life size" stand up, a '57 Chevy w/ moving-light pistons and working headlights, a missile-launching pen and other aerial devices, two 3-D Viewmasters (one a hand-held projector), three pair over-size "3-D" glasses, one pair "headlight" glasses, a "circus" toy with spring-mounted plastic dogs bears cats on metal wire loops and spirals, a multicolor telescoping light-up pointer, and various sound-effects devices (including MegaMouth™).

slides: advertising text and images appropriated from popular magazines of the period: Life, Look, Time, Mademoiselle, Popular Mechanics, Popular Science, Family Circle, and others; *the focus is primarily on numbers from 1955, especially October 3, 10, 17 (*Life, *39.14, 15, 16) —issues for the weeks preceding, during, and following the 6 Gallery reading.*

Other print text and image sources include Look at the USA 1955 (Look *magazine*), the San Francisco Chronicle *and* The New York Times, *both from 10/7/55 (and, for the* SFC, *from the week just preceding 10/7/55, beginning with James Dean's death on 9/30); Allen Ginsberg's* Snapshot Poetics, *Fred McDarragh's* Kerouac and Friends, *Elilas Wilnetz's and McDarrah's* The Beat Scene, *Michael McClure's* Scratching the Beat Surface, *Ginsberg's annotated* Howl (*quoted extensively in section two of the piece*), Beat Culture and the New America, 1950-1965 *(Whitney Museum of American Art)*; Lyrical Vision: The Six Gallery, 1954-1957 (*Natsoulas Novelozo Gallery*); *Rebeccaa Solnit's* Secret Exhibition: Six California Artists of the Cold War Era; *Karal Ann Marling's* As Seen on TV, *David Halberstam's* The Fifties, *William Boddy's* Fifties Television, *Robert Frank's* The Americans, The Partisan Review *19.3,5 (1952), and various holographic ms. in the Ginsberg and McClure collections at Columbia University. Film and video sources include* The Seven Year Itch, Hondo, The Stranger Wore a Gun, The Wild One, Tarzan the Ape Man, King of the Rocketmen, The Creature from the Black Lagoon, Revenge of the Creature, *and various TV commercials and serials of the period.*

computer: on-site manipulation of images occurs at various points during the performance, as noted in script.

video: ongoing nonlinear compilation of film and video sources listed above. Specific TV series deployed include The Honeymooners, I Love Lucy, The Walter Winchell Show, The Adventures of Ozzie and Harriet, Howdy Doody, *and* King of the Rocketmen. *Video clips are edited according to graphic paradigms such as cross-hatching, continuous line spirals, spirals doubling into infinity... The pace is rapid, individual clips ranging in length from 3 to 45 seconds; the compilation closes with an extreme fast motion, visually distorted presentation of all twelve chapters of* King of the Rocketmen, *intercut with three extreme slow-motion sequences, two from commercials and the third from* The Seven Year Itch. *In the first SM commercial insert, a forkful of cake gradually enters an opening feminine mouth; in the second, a shot of a woman towel-drying a dog dissolves into a shot of the dog resting on a hook carpet, slowly becoming aware of a can of Dash dog food that displaces it, filling the frame. For a description of the scene from* The seven Year Itch, *see below "Feature 3." The compilation ends with the slow-motion destruction of Manhattan, simulated with models, from the final chapter of* Rocketmen. *Though the video editor's manipulation is everywhere evident in the compilation, in this last section the interference of the electronic editing technology—and its breakdown—is pushed to the foreground. Due to the speed of the tape over the reading heads, the sensors have trouble "keeping up," resulting in distortions and glitches, the images often deteriorating into particulate streaks... with current digital technology we could go even faster before reaching a tipping point...*

We always play "behind," or immersed in, the projected images, featuring them, as our text bends itself on bop and rock rhythms...

{A low, bop}

T: The "setting" [*during this opening section—till E formulates and announces the "hook" for the "production team"—T performs as lecturer/presenter, while Z & E ignore the "stage"—any sense of staging, academic or otherwise—and move about as necessary (or not), getting things ready (or not) ... This section lays the conceptual groundwork for the Games, and proceeds as a slightly ajar lecture...*]

Z: It's 8:00 pm: *Truth or Consequences*, *Ozzie and Harriet*, and *A Century of Headlines*...

[video: test patterns]

{A fade under B: rock, layer}

T: I've finished the "Criticism and commentary" section of *A Casebook on the Beat*, ed. Thomas Parkinson, Thomas Y. Crowell Co., NY, 1961, and the cover, I thought, looked like a face--the "b" and "g" as eyes and the period between a nose (and what's the period after the G? another nose, Picasso-like?) ... The critical rhythm suggested by the cover is more Cubist than oppositional--if we don't see the breakdown as parceling--though the book presents itself as "The pros and cons of the beat movement." A "pro" is impelled by a "con" and vice versa, and this ideological pendulum is swept by its own weight toward a presupposed entitativeness on either side of a dividing line... {B pause}

[*Z distributes publicity information about the TEZ group, including group photos*]

Parkinson, like many of the critics writing in the 50s and early 60s, finds the Beats troubling, in his case pleasurably perplexing, though the *mise en abime* that his reflections on the period briefly reveal is quickly and easily resolved in a utopian vision of existential harmony (academic discourse is the game of avoiding aporias, analytical pitfalls--the shadow of larger, identity-dissolving black holes). Parkinson's "Casebook" is a "selection" of writings of key figures backed by a critical debate; as he admits in his own article (placed not in the position of final authority but second-to-last in the "Commentary and Criticism" section), from one perspective, the "Beat movement... can be assimilated into the institution of literature as generally--that is, academically--understood"; though, he says in the next paragraph, "In another sense, the experimental writers destroyed convention in order to create a completely new way of looking at experience and cannot be assimilated into the existing institution." He tries to counter the trap of contradiction that binary frameworks will always stumble over by troping it--subsuming it--in a greater dualism (note too that the greater the momentum in a binary system the more extreme its oppositions become: can the Beats be said to have invented a "completely new way,"

[slide: announcement/invitation,
6-G reading, 10/7/55]

and isn't this "new" still in dialogue with--at best a partial deterritorialization of--an "old"? The solution, says Parkinson, is "not to..." "but to..." by a turn of equations substituting one common denominator for another, not to divide to attain "a golden mean or shabby compromise," but to stand united, independent and equal in "integrity": "The solution is to be, where you are, what you are, with such persistence and courage as can be called life. The best of the beat writers exemplify precisely that state of secular grace." They "exemplify precisely," and the humanist seduction (despite the Buddhist aura of the phrasing) lies in the generality of the rhetoric, in the mask of exact demarcation, washing over the dynamic (whether conflictual or compromising) of particularity. What if this "are" is undecidable? We have to look back a few pages in the essay for a potential imaging of nondualism that jeopardizes the existential humanist surety of the closure; to a passage that windows *differance*, rather than differentiation (so instead of hybridization or mosaic, which, along with transubstantiation, are the highest forms of becoming other still based on a differentiation--but can't we multiply instead of divide, choose a different key?--we have the internal slide away from identity(ies)): ...

E: (watch the parentheticals) ...

T: thinking perhaps of Kerouac's early to mid-50's prose (& specifically *On the Road*), Parkinson comments "it is a syntax of aimlessly continuing pleasure in which all elements are 'like'.... Release, liberation from fixed categories, hilarity--it is an ongoing prose that cannot be concerned with its origins... the ideal book by a writer of beat prose would be written on a single string of paper, printed on a roll, and moving endlessly from right to left, like a typewriter ribbon."

[*demonstrate, then pass around "Beatnik Bob": iron filings sealed over a cardboard face*]:

E: Instructions: "Use the energy that flows through the wand...." [*Z demos: touches magnetic wand to her lip, eye, ear.*] And who is Beatnik Bob, you ask? Well, who are you?... [*Z moves wand on the back side of the card*] Bring Beatnik Bob to life."

T: It is this not completely controllable rehearsal of such tensions, rather than its stated contents, that accounts for my fascination with Parkinson's book, poised as it is on the cusp of hermeneutic schizophrenia. The 50s in America. A liminal period in many ways, as the rhythm of Parkinson's discourse registers after the decade's close.

{A pause}

{B: R & B}

This is the era of pop psychoanalysis, wide spread

[slides: Beats--circles and clowns]

commodification of the unconscious: effects of a shift from decades motivated by idealism, reason, or at least a sense of social responsibility, to the mid-century resurgence (all the more repressed) of spirituality and "darker forces" -the 50s sci-fi/ alien craze, the threat of the irrational rationalized; nuclear holocaust--fear of what can't be seen--the atom--or controlled; superpowers and super ids. This liminality can also be traced in the slip from the social, the public as "actual" physical performance, to simulations of the social in the proliferation, by the late 50s, of TV "families" and stylized "communities."

{B dissolve into A low}

And there are ideological retrenchments toward the rational, toward common sense, the socially responsible, etc., in literary/cultural criticism, as well as in (especially in) the sponsored versions of society programmed for mass broadcast, and a complimentary material movement toward the concrete, moneyism, the product-demonstrable "good life" ... It is in this complex dialogos of simulations and terrors that both literature and criticism--that literary discourse--become distorted practices, resisting or unable to control their own liminality, yet not knowing how not to be in control, though the vortex of the age demands it.

{A pause B: quiz show theme, fade under}

So I'm thinking of the "Beats" as competing yet inter-looping

[slides: var. ads: 50s *Life*]

circles--not of individuals but of cultural constructs, a phenomenon invented by mass media and the academy to provide an "explanation," and simultaneously a parody of, a distraction and relief from, the bottomless (if cosmetically hidden) pits and suspected breaches, the paranoias and insecurities that "subconsciously" (psychology's mask of organizations) darken the bright paradoxical face of what appears to be one of the more financially, ideologically, and socially stable moments in modern American cultural history. On the one hand, full-fleshed Marilyn Monroe cultural productions; on the other, McCarthian madness

[slide: black]

{B pause A low}

But how do the Beats play through/to/across their various academic and popculture subjectifications? Along the way to commodification, the Beat, especially as performed at 6-G and other venues, if viewed as cultural phenomena, as event, can be traced as a Deleuzian map of dislocation, as lines of deterritorialization always tremoring (or staggering) away from spikings of subjectification. From the beginning the Beat was a multimedia phenomenon, (a "mixed semiosis," to use Deleuze's phrase), not an energy/discourse containable within one semiotic system; their voices, at 6-G, playing over muslin and plaster coated fragments of orange crates (Fred Martin's sculptures) in an artificially darkened space that was formerly an automobile repair shop. This was a chance coming together of word and object (interestingly no electronic reproductions of this early reading exist--though at the Berkeley recreation of the Six Gallery reading, Bob Rosenthal has said, there were at least three machines running). At the Berkeley reading, some months later, the "found" sculptures are replaced by Robert LaVigne's poster-like nude drawings of Orlovsky and Ginsberg, related directly to the subject-content of the performers, whereas at 6-G sexuality was a chance encounter of human and nonhuman other (orange crates and visionaries on a stage of circumstances).

Z: Then this is our starting point--before the contours of the image have solidified, the Jell-O chilled...

{A pause B: rock riff, followed by *Ozzie* theme}

E: The overall pattern/process, the conceptual rhythm: flux (field) > condensation/formularization > reproduction and dissemination, or: experimentation > design/manufacture > marketing/advertising.

[*start video show: 50s TV*]

Z: experimentation leading to reduction, mass reproduction and proliferation. Once a product has been captured/packaged as a sign/template, it is possible to effect multiple embodiments/transformations of the concept package: not just via pop media spin offs (notably *Dobie Gillis*, *Johnny Staccato*, *Route 66*— all late 50s-early 60s resimulations), but through large-scale image migrations mobilizing out of (off) screen and the pages of popular magazines: everyday objects--anonymous cups, T-shirts, writing instruments--as well as public gatherings and even the creative process itself can be imprinted by the Beat logo, the Beat sign.

E: Peripheral development: file it.

T [*stepping away from lectern*]: But there are challenges to this rhythmic stabilization:

{B: Eisenhower—the "candidate for peace"—
fragments of campaign speech cut/w
"Duck and Cover" civil defense/commercial jingle}

recombination as guerrilla manufacture; permutational computer imagings, textual distortions, *mise en scene* collagings cutting across semiotic boundaries. Creation is achieved though fluidization and synaesthesia, disrupting clearly defined, semiotically stable, coherent production.

Z: To this end we will cruise 50s culture, peruse with specular pleasure its obsession with the reproducible, the transportable, the excessively embodiable…

T: while stimulating micro disruptions of its monolithic self-presence.

Z: So we have to come up with a simple template…

T: and we have to riddle it, irradiate it.

Z: We must also run our "beat" line through popular culture at large--a beat rhythm through all the images…

{B pause}
{A low}

T [*back to lectern/"drawingboard"*]: So the piece always circles back to what veers away, lines of flight vectoring through and away from modularization/ formularization, and the performance itself, in attempting to measure the fissures in particular mid-50s literary productions, in attempting to assess the potential impact of the "S/D-effect" (semiotic field-splitting, deterritorialization) working within and through the literature, continually puts in question/on trial its own statements/ subjectifications, as the bemused academic mind, in a state of anxious exhilaration, slips away from--in an out of--its own comprehensions into a mixed and unclosable semiotic field.

[A pause}

E: The windup: "We are interested in the larger semiotic arena that developed around proto-Beat scenes, such as the Six Gallery reading in San Francisco (10/55), and in bringing the language events enacted on those sites into sharper dialogue with the popculture imagery of the time. We are also intrigued by the literary/critical and pop media configurations generated by those seminal, 'hallmark' literary moments; figurations that can be seen as synthetic (re)capturings of a mythologized moment in cultural history, a moment that comes into existence only in its passage, when it takes its place in academic and pop cultural discourses (clowns and intellectual outlaws), hence becoming subject to reification (i.e., the concern for 'biography,' reminiscence, drafts, letters, memorabilia, etc.).

To thoroughly apprehend the process of identity fabrication, we should also consider how self-presentation is affected by mass reception. Taking the fall 1955 Six Gallery reading as a 'rehearsal,' and the spring 1956 Berkeley Little Theater reading as a somewhat more self-conscious restaging (reenactment), we can see the cultural industry at work in its most profoundly disturbing locale--at the seat of self-comprehension. But these are topics for further research; though we may touch on these here, we do so only residually..."

T: Work that arm... [*leaving the lectern*] let's give it another twist: "Following from Deleuze, we are primarily concerned with locating points--textual sites (in the broadest semiotic sense) -upon which to establish temporary, nomadic missions of deterritorialization--guerrilla (manu)facto(u)ries permuting the material presences of a few 'key' Beat figures."

Z [*following T*]: That's our spin: "We claim that to capture the Beat as a sign, as a transportable ideological commodity--whether a 'self'-representation or a culture production (which are anyway 'always already' enmeshed)--is to block any 'lines of flight' (Deleuze) *it* opens, to seal over the breaches, create 'black holes' of existential amnesia, even though, like the North Hollywood tar pits, 'it' [E *spits—on the "ball"*] keeps oozing through..."

T: Think of it as an Expressionist paint bomb: a central point of impact, streaks and spatters...

E: Freeze! [*pause video; end of introductory lecture. Z & T rush on stage with suitcases, open them, displaying an eclectic vivid assortment of colors and designs; these items of clothing will be used for both arbitrary and motivated costume changes occurring at regularly spaced intervals*]: Frame: The year is '55, Or '56, sometimes. The TEZ group, a somewhat dysfunctional product design team, has been hired to develop an all-new, bigger, more colorful and more "holy" ...

{A low}

T: (full of holes)

E: Beat for Berkeley, '56, and the future...

Z: It'll have to be pop, pop and bop...

{A medium}

T: Question: the benefits package...? A product is not simply an object, but "also a package of benefits, psychological as well as physical, for the consumer..."

{buzzer} {A pause} <3>

{B rock, medium}

E: It is "every want-satisfying attribute a consumer receives in making an exchange..."

T: nostalgia... nostalgia, dynamism and immediacy, and theory...

{B low}

[*out pops Z from behind a TV*] who are you?

Z: I'm nostalgia

T: no you ain't, you're... [*approaching, lustily*]

{B up}

Z: Nix! I'm on company time.

{B pause}

***

{5 rings} [*on 5th ring, images change, as below*]

[slides: wall: Popsicle^{tm} circle;
Marcel Marceau circus mime w/hoop on 5th ring;
easel: target; Ginsberg's holograph
"wake up" note to McClure on 5th ring.
Computer monitor: revolving simulated "hula hoop."
VCR monitor: Howdy Doody "test pattern."]

T: What signals there were, and what lines to receive them--antennae roof East 7th, NY, 1953: Naomi...

[slide: brief dissolve over above:
AG on a lower Manhattan rooftop]

***

E: Role call!

T: Six Gallery, 10/7/55, 8:00 pm. (for detailed accounts of the event see McClure's *Scratching the Beat Surface*, especially pages 11-33; Rebecca Solnit's *Secret Exhibition: Six Artists of the Cold War Era*, 47-49, *Lyrical Vision: the 6 Gallery 1954-1957*, 20-31, *and* the annotated *Howl*, 165-69) ...

E: No—the *primary* role.

{B: Abbot & Costello: "Who's on first..."}

Z: Lamantia's on first

{A start low}

T: but he was absent--the voice was there, the physical body, but not the textual; or let's say he enacted an interesting play of voices--John Hoffman's through his.

Z: And what about the textual Hoffman?

T: Looked for the poems--RLIN, LC, NYP, Columbia Rare--nothing, no luck.

Z: Well, Whalen's on second...
{B: Abbot and Costello: "What's on first,
Who's on second, I don't know's on third ..."
E: (That's two relative pronouns and a simple negation.)

T: "'Plus Ca Change," [*E recites the poem, in which the speakers, formerly human, are birds; see "The Poems" appendix below*] ..." Who'd recognize us now?... what *shall* we tell the children?"

Z: A possible 50s domestic situation...

T: the birds talk, and they're in color...

Z: we don't see the faces in the poem, just hear the voices...

T: the rhetoric of domestic upheaval in the throats of birds--colonization of the animal!

{A up}

Z: or the "nuclear" family transmogrified...

[slides: masked faces—
nuclear test site;
50s TV family: Ozzie & Harriet]

{A down}

T: the "nuked" family--ok... or, the problem of becoming animal, or of a becoming other possible only through split-second evasions of self-consciousness... (see Deleuze: "Becoming-Intense, Becoming-Animal, Becoming-Imperceptible...," 232...)

Z: We'll work through that later with Ginsberg-Coyote-Snyder-- actually a becoming cartoon representation of Coyote becoming the "other" ...

{A up}

T: existential loony tuning… but we're running ahead of ourselves…

{A down}

Z: So where?

E: Who's on third?

T: McClure. "For the Death of 100 Whales": "No passages or crossings / From the beasts' wet shore…" [*see "The Poems"*]

Z: Ummm, as far as the consequences of our loss of the animal, imaginative shutdowns, stoppages or blockages of lines of flight, of becomings…

{A up, down}

T: Whalen: "Pull down the shades. Turn off the lights…"

E: when push comes to shove…

T: (Deleuze on "segmentarity" here? 222…)

{B: *Seven Year Itch*-" I bother them…"}

Z: Under the flap of your… notebook?

[slide: Neal Cassady and Natalie
under a movie marquis, as described below;
the features are: *Stranger Wore a Gun*,
Wild One, *Tarzan the Ape Man*]

T: aaa… a black and white document, a movie marquis, under which Neal and Natalie, in the long coat, 2 X 2…

{A up}

Z: her teeth were buck.

E: A gun in her pocket?

T: The cigarette, just begun to burn away…

Z: midday San Francisco? -after the fog has lifted.

T: Who's walking away, in folds of gray…

Z: womannequin forlorn...

T: if we begin here, the image sinking back through grey

{A down}

layers of "Comfort" and control... [*indicating signs suspended above the street's diminishing perspective: an optometrist's shop—" Comfort"—and beyond that, the bottom half of a high vertical neon on a white ground—" PLAN"*]

Z: a well-ordered progress all ways easier to view [*on Marquis*]: Three big features: McClure Ginsberg Snyder...

{A up, down}

T: "The Wild One"?

[slide: three big colorful
ice cream cones—single, double,
and triple scoops]

Z: triple play on a triple scoop--a preview: three in one and one in three...

{A pause}

T [*quoting Brando*]: "It begins here, for me, on this road..."

[*distribute copies of McClure poem*]

***

{B brief rock interlude}

E:

Feature 1: "*Stranger Wore Gun*"
plus
King of the Rocketmen, Ch. III: "Dangerous Evidence"

[slide: Rocketman, in flight,
as sketched on title shot of series]

{B: *Stranger*: "That's a strange dog you have, mister...
I don't have'em... he stays with me"}
{A start, low-medium}

[easel slide: McClure poem,

including epigraph fr. *Time*]

T: "For the Death of 100 Whales." We enter the whale's death through a doubled inscription--*Time* magazine and McClure's poem...

Z: which means, we try to capture that death through the net of our inscriptions, which anyway come up empty...

T: but that's where we swim, in language; the whale dives out of sight through its element, as we do in ours...

Z: so do we deploy nets of hydrogen to catch a...? [*quickly inhale and hold*]

{A pause}

E: Was that a question? <2> [*exhale*]

{buzzer}

T: McClure's poem answers the pop media version exaggeration for exaggeration...

[slide: Maidenform bra
in a house of mirrors]

compare *Time*'s (April, 1954) description of the rounding up and shooting gallery extermination of 100 killer whales in the subarctic--[*zapping the projection with a laser pointer*] "as one was wounded, the others would set upon it and tear it to pieces with their jagged teeth" to McClure's--"Gnashed at their tails and brothers"--*Time* packages the "beast" in unbreachable otherness; McClure reinscribes them as a community, driven to extremes...

{A start, medium}

Z: different sentiments, but comparable dramatizations... excess...

T: aesthetic competition...

[slides: Popsicle™ "Famous—
Ranch Brand contest...
$100,000... Terrific prizes!..." (reshoot);
big finny car—lots of HP & torque,
nuzzling up to a fall-coated couple]

E: (Match the symbol with the name...)

Z: "Thirty feet long with teeth like bayonets" v. "Brains the size of a football / Mouths the size of a door"

E: "Make Big Money!"

T: Exclamation points... fascination with teeth, bayonets, fire power: a video game, an arcade simulation--virtual reel-ality 50s style

[slide: sketch of a child
peering with fascination and delight
into a Viewmaster(tm)]

played through the "real..."

Z: The world as 2-D view disk...

T: with a 3-D "lift" ...

Z: riding the 50s on a wave of color and style...

[slide: "World's Smallest
Complete Kitchen";
CU—chili corn bread upside-down pie,
thick red sauce oozing over]

{A low; rhythmic alteration}

T: an aesthetic, virtual consumerism spinning somewhere above the heated-up commodity...

Z: spinning off it: the commodity "always already" multi-dimensional, the 50s 3-D fad a parodic inflection of a specular orientation toward the "real" ...

T: (Guy Debord?)

E: "Big Money--Easy!" ...

{A medium}

[slide: "Miracle Projector,"
"electric" enlarger and copy maker]

[*during the following 2-3 lines, Z & T bring Hula Hoops close to, then away from projected images: they've jumped through; or, the hoops are enormous focusing rings*]

Z: Step right up!...

T: Where, on or before the screen?

E: "live ants, flies, bugs, small animals in action, fighting, eating, playing..."

T: Project on the screen first to rebound off?

[slide: comic strip:
as Owl holds Pogo's question
mark balloon, Pogo bats an identical
balloon fr. Owl's head]

Z: On which side of the viewreel?

E: "Project beautiful girl pictures!..." 3-D stereoscopic Hi-fidelity True-View!

Z: Doubled images, one copy on each side of a laminated disk, superimposing this side of the lens... [*pointing to head*]

E: (quantum reel!)

[slide: mirrored halves of cars]

{A low-medium}

T: (automobile prototyping--working half a 2-ton clay model along a mirror, rhyming the extent half-paradigm with its perfectly symmetrical 2-D projected completion, while its other half, other side of the doubled mirror, is half an other...)

Z: the material a copy of the immaterial reflection of the material...

[*Z balances the hoop around her head on extended arms, then lets it drop*]

T: materially immaterial immaterially material...

{A pause}

E: Get back to it!

Z, T: Picture windows!

{A start}

Z: Two-way theater! A showcase for paradigms of order...

T: glimpses of interior life within/behind the displays...

Z: and a cinema *verite* window on the "scenes" outside the domestic space...

E: Look at me.

{A quick fade, low}

T: But this is everything, this is TV. This is what the rhetoric of McClure's imaginative production does when it resonates with(in) *Time*'s: he selects a few quotes, the bulk of the article falling into the void of ellipsis... frames a world view...

Z: Then is McClure's poem a re-presentation of a representation?

{3 rings; wait}

T: Except the play is within the contours of two dominate mid-50s cultural epistemes--imaginative consumption and competition--that shape both poem and prose piece, so we can't say the game "originates" in one or the other...

{A medium-high}

Z: His blood and sperm not a counter to 2-D voyeurism?

T: No, just better dramatic technique.... A HA HA HA!

{A up}
{A low}

[*Five-line digression: A ring toss game with Hula Hoops: Z & T try for the TVs*]

Z: "Take me out to...

T: the selection was not random...

Z: all games are rigged.

T: But not baseball!

Z: At the $64,000 question, take a dive.

[slide: "humm...strum...
Butter Rummm..."
LIFESAVERS—straw
boater banjo & parasol couple
languishing in a rowboat]

{A down}

T: The poem polemicizes Anglo-gnostic literary traditions, as well, strumming and humming along with Lawrence, while out-performing a Lawrencian atavistic spiritualism...

Z: a *Time* and Western Great Books whale hunt...

{A pause}

[slide: McClure & Snyder in '58]

T: (there's the photo of you with GS, reading from a big book--that's Berkeley '58, but it works here) ...

Z: with Melville too in the "Flung blood and sperm. / incense" montage.

{A start medium}

T: So, Goya's Ahab?

Z: No, the whale.

T: *And* the whale?

Z: Ahab's in the voice ...

{B: *Stranger*: "that water sure looks inviting"}
[*Z & T try to interlink hoops, Olympic style, but they're no illusionists.*]

E: This isn't getting us anywhere.

{A pause}

T: But that's it--how fast is possible, staying in place: speed, movement as movement, not distance traveled or destination; speed is quantity, too. It's what we *do* with McClure. That's *On the Road*; also check *Aesthetics of Disappearance*, Virilio's take on Howard Hughes: traveled around the world, stayed in identical hotel rooms specially prepared with grey walls and shuttered windows...

Z: (like inside a movie camera) ...

T: only to return to the exact spot from which he departed, docking his plane in exactly the same figure/ground orientation. Speed for its own sake; "forward flair" ...

[slide: "forward flair"—
altered image of Mercury,
front end spliced in slightly out of line]

Z: that's 50s auto styling—a flash of speed while standing still...

T: Speed as excess, as style (cf. W. T. Lhamon, *Deliberate Speed*). Harley Earl for GM: "dynamic obsolescence": it's got to keep changing; the rhythm of change overrides utilitarian value of specific alterations...

[slides: Elvis Presley—reverberating—
doubled, colorized image;
Milton Berle in full flamboyant dress]

Z: This episteme of speed also colors Ginsberg's (sub)atomic condensed image juxtapositions, which he doesn't have to justify *vis-a-vis* surrealism--it's in the mid-50s cult-air.

{A start medium}
{B: *Stranger*: Indian whooping over A}

T: And in its rhythms--Ed Sullivan's Presley: lip-syncing innocuous love ballad, sense of words lost burned up in vibrato and pelvic torque, twisting like hell held in place by a static mic and camera...

E: Beat Berle and Presley: surface exuberance for its own sake: material excessiveness leads to interpretative excessiveness.

T: Black Cat, Sky Buster, Mega Magic, Galaxy Fiesta...

Z: Oh!... T!

T: Artificial Satellite!... Sorry--just thinking ahead (see below) ...

{A low, B stop}

shot above the waist, only--Sullivan's compromise. Just at the end, after the last word of the lyric, something happens...

Z: a gesture only the audience of that moment sees--a slip out of line and dip, back...

T: as if the knees give way, a switch back of the arm--a movement that escapes media surveillance...

[slides: "X Appeal"—hand-masked
peek-a-boo sheer lacy bra in mink cake;
Rauschenberg's 1955 painting...]

Z: Time for a change! [*rapid costume alteration*]

{A medium}

T: *Mother of God*! designed for flux drive outstripping cartography [*playing off painting*].

Z: In center of this rearranged 2-D topography...

T: a white hole--painted white...

Z: what color is the Masonite[tm]?...

T: the whole nothing but 2-D absence of a probable map...

Z: "no passages or crossings..."

T: becoming an N-dimensional theoretical black hole.

E: Are the whales escaping us?

{A pause}

Z: Sure, when the concerns are "destroyed thousands of dollars' worth of fishing tackle" (*Time* slots in the economic voice with the sensationalism). McClure tries to salvage the event for his own (agnostic) spiritual economy.

{A start low-medium}

T: There's the hinge, *charniere et gond*...

Z: McClure addresses economic discourse obliquely,
counter valence: "incense."

T: A glancing shot. A product used, let's say, in zazen...

[slide: "lasting, luscious color..."]

Z: or cosmetics, which *could* be made from whale sperm...

T: (spread on the face?)

[slide: "on your lips..."]

Z: Metonymic catapulting from the scent of the sperm immerses us in the spiritual play of the poem...

T: a movement antithetical to the soldier's inscribed inhumanity
(if they smell, do they think "incense"?)—the military the "bad guy" ...

Z: and the good guy? not the whales...

T: The poetic consciousness that reconfigures and

{A high}

reevaluates, imaginatively repackages... a counter or resistant or at least

unaccountable (in a monetary sense) ...
{buzzer}

E: What?

Z: (just a) ...Second!

T: literary/spiritual economy.

Z: Putting out a product that makes the dialogue possible...

[slide: "Quotes" panties—
sketch of young slim-waisted
woman wearing girdle only, reading large
tabloid, "Quotes," which conceals torso and
face—" gentle control... delightful colors...
Simply Sensational"]

E: dialogizing "ways of seeing"?

Z: The body of the animal, as quoted...

T: Throws imagistic blood and sperm...

[*E reads brief quote from poem*]

Z: Specular reenactment of what the soldiers must...

T: desire electrifying the strategic template: "rounded up into tight formation with concentrated machine gun fire, then moved out again one by one..."

Z: cued by this, the blood and guts imagery upstages—or
restages—reportage...

{A pause}
{4 rings}

T: McClure gives us tragic emotion, in answer to mere rhetoric of suspense. Finally, though, the poem is trapped by its own devices: in its final lines, the poem deploys a tactic of undecidableness which imagistically reopens--or keeps open--the abyss churning beneath the grids of strategic thinking while simultaneously enacting aesthetic closure. [*E quotes closing lines*]

OH GUN! OH BOW!
There are no churches in the
waves,
No holiness,
No passages or crossings
From the beasts' wet shore

{A start low}

Z: So *aporia* is here (aesthetic) apologia.

T: His overall strategy to channel emotion through quick, sometimes single word montages and apostrophes while channeling the whole into the resonate hole of a negative image.

{A up a bit}

Z: So we have to reopen the dialogue…

T: bring in technology from a different angle…

Z: spin off the guns? the boat? the general exotic oceanic atmosphere? Tilt it toward pop…

[slide: "Today's Mixer Sensation:
New, sparkling all chrome sliver-chef"]

slogan: "A whale of a…

{A quick fade under to pause}

[slide: fisherman in rowboat
eye-glass spying in wrong quadrant
bumps into a friendly spuming whale:
cartoon still fr. Pall Mall commercial]

E: Measuring, conceptualizing, testing the product. Is it being created according to plan (instressing the intended "self-knowledge," behavior, ideology--correct attitudinal orientation). Is it up to code? The product must be inscribed to attain mastery of form without self-reflexive edge (the "echo chamber" principle—simulated self-reflection operating within the parameters of the model): To become the product is to become the "real."

{B *Stranger*: "I can't swim…[splash]"}

Z: Let's run through this.

{A start low-medium}

E: (pell-mell)

"Brains the size of a football. / Mouths the size of a door."

[slide: big fin Dodge, from rear,
Creature from the Black Lagoon
posing beside door
(or, svelte woman posing… creature
displaces the woman… enter…)]

E: The Series 75: length--237.1", weighing in at 5,015 lbs.; turning circle radius 52'…

Z: (We've got to be amazed by the size of the creature we've stirred up.)

T: Ok, '52: "They are mostly below the surface, and it goes without saying that they are in essence resources of the spirit" (Newton Arvin, *Partisan Review*—hereafter *PR*—'52, 288).

Z [*theatrically*]: ("to wage a never-ending combat against…")

E: The "vest pocket" submarine x-1: only 5" long and accommodating 5-6 rounds; cigar shaped hull blends unobtrusively with business attire; comes with miniature conning tower, for close-in attacks.

T: In the poem, let's say… the resources are "menaces": The cultural formation congenial to *Time*… the speaker writes through the voiceless suffering of the whales…

Z: (submarine camouflage)

T: for the sake of spirit--to destabilize…

{buzzer}

[slides: a sterling fork
delicately balanced between
white gloved hands;
retouching--coordinating makeup—
"you'll hardly believe..."]

Z: "to apply the spiritual tools of traditional Western civilization to the finishing and refining of these raw--both promising and threatening--materials" (*Ibid*, 291) ...

[slide: man, partially dressed,
pulling on his face in a dark frame,
distorting his features...]

{A pause}

T: the "traditional" tools reinforced with the "raw material" to struggle against a more refined "menace" ... "Western Civilization," Ch. 23...

E: (20? Or Monroe's waist in '55? See below)

T: harboring both the menace it tactically locates elsewhere and the home-spun "promise" (Goya, Lawrence) to reconnect us with spirit (in McClure's reconfiguration, actively animal rather than abstractly moral) ... though... there's something elevating about a close shave...

Z [*sarcastic Noh*]: You're spinning out...

[slides: 2 shots fr.
Oscar Meyer cartoon commercial:
a squat singer about to take
a bite out of a whiner; his two
hotdog-skinny partners tugging him away
by the collar, a dog left spinning mid-air]

{A low}

E: The hotdog, at least, has a beginning and end; though we can't say which is which in its packaged state, when its relationship with a consumer is realized the uneaten end must always be farthest from the originary middle. But cut a slice out of the middle--that's franks and beans.

T: The terrifying "promise" of technology, fire power of a piston--during WWII GM made tanks! there's the *gond*, the torque--this is where we'll find the driving force, the "lift" ...

[slide: head of GM surrounded by his" toys"]

E: Eating your dog at both ends...

[slide: Coke, "a light little lift"—
crewcut and knee socks couple posing
on each side of the Coke machine]

Z [*to T*]: The "anima"? where?

T: Here [*indicating images, props*]

{A up, down, pause}

{buzzer}

E: Q: "In his sense of lonely horror, the writer was most one with everyone else" (Leslie Fiedler in *PR*, '52, 296). To what extent is the "lonely horror" of the writer"

{B: begin clock tick or music}

like the soldiers on a "lonely... airbase"?

{B stop}

{bell or buzz--question too long, time's up}

T [*Z, T exchange looks*]: If the airbase is "lonely," what are the soldiers?

E: Is that your answer?

Z: Human emotion displaced to landscape...

T: The writers are whales...

{A up, down quickly}

[slide: a *Look* at boxing:

a ko in round...?]

{ping or quiet bell}

Z: Wait, it's...

{B sounds from the ballpark, or
song "take me out..." etc. over A}

Sandy Amoros, deep in left field, about to make the catch that will end the Series...

{buzz! buzz!}
{B pause; A pause}

[slide: cut to blank]

E: Your consolation prize...

[slide: Heritage Books
offered by disembodied hands—
sets incl. *Pinocchio* & *Treasure Island*]

this set of beautifully bound authoritative non-variorum editions: "A lifetime of reward in the pleasure of reading."

Z: Good copy.

T [*shouting to others*]: 8:30: *San Francisco Beat*, *San Francisco Deadline* are on...

Z: "The sleek wolves / Mowers and reapers of sea kine. "

{A start medium}

E: Keep it moving.

T: "The Giant Tadpoles..."

[slides: headline fr. *Life*, 10/10/55:
"Big New Bomber Dies...";
sea-green Mercury with whale-mouth grill]

Z: Big letters, leaping out of the text, like the vocal notations (exclamation points) in the poem...

[slide: "Win $25,000"
in large red letters,
"One Great Big Prize"]

T: as text and vocal performance, outshouting the culture permeating it...

Z: the little poem with the big power pack.

T: Hey, good slogan!

Z: "(Meat their algae) / leapt"

E: Good. File it. I was about to cut...

{A low}

[slide: auto prototyping]

Z: The simplest tools shape a car body, hammering sheet metal around a wooden form to create a prototype; in this case, a gun eliminates imperfections in the system, outbreaks of "savage," perverse disobedience...

T: That's it: easy-to-use technology deployed through strategic thinking leading to a critical dysfunction...

{A medium}

[slides: *Life*: sketch of man
posed w/ hand on "head" of his big dog V-8—
a disembodied engine on wheeled display dolly;
woman sewing blindfolded—the "super-robot...
completely automatic... SO SIMPLE"]

Z: a shutdown of polyvocalism...

T: cultural obsession for testing the expedient and efficient application of a "sufficient" force (drawn from a wealthy storehouse of power) ...

E: (*Life* 1/3/55: $6.6 bill. in surplus food in gov't warehouses).

Z: 100 whales v. 79 G.I.'s with machine guns…

T: in self-confidently "small" boats…

Z: overcoding and hence demobilizing the physical and emotional impact of the slaughter…

[slide: Einstein's study,
equations on board & papers scattered on desk,
empty chair rotated away fr. desk: 4/2/55; *Life*, 61]

T: (Einstein's brain has been removed for scientific study) …

{A pause}

ALL [*differently*]: really (.,!,?)

Z: The "Savageness" of the "beast" an easy target for the well- equipped "posse" … the *Time* piece assumes control, no possibility of our not having it, just a question of how it's mobilized; the crux is, the sea "cannibals" can't be explained, only eliminated…

E: 42, 893, 550 TV sets illuminating 30, 700, 000 American homes by 1955.

T: Technology of evasion… *Time* Presents! The return of the repressed exerting pressure on a consciousness of denial--look at any mid 50s newspaper: economic hoopla and upbeat techno- propaganda side-by-side with violence, technological failure, political unrest… the drama is in our resistance to a culture splitting at the seams…

[slides: cars in formal, detached settings—
a pair of light blue Caddys in equipoise]

{A start}

E: nuclear paranoia, fear of foreign invaders, fear of the foreign within the familiar…

Z: The decoy "drama": working out of the "plan," the process of extermination…

[slide: "Sock-O" super sling shot—

"silent… powerful… accurate"]

E: "lively raw rubber… sweet shooting… 100 steel balls…
rifle fast…"

{A pause}

T: As a discourse act, the poem both accounts and (over)compensates for the reduced condition of the human that *Time*'s rhetoric elides: imaging an emphatically visceral, emotional encounter with experience as corrective to short-circuited communication, crippled crossing of animal to animal…

[slide: Browning rifle (erect)
and automatic pistol set
(3 cocks in velvet lined case)—
"for a lifetime of pleasure"]

{A start}

Z: The poem as g(ue)orilla…

[slide: a colorful line of portable radios]

E: 9:00: *Industry on Parade*…

[slide: Ban roll on—
the arm raised, in deep chiaroscuro,
the translucent ball rolling over the smooth depression]

T: ideological shell game… the cover-up… technology against the odoriferous…

{A pause}

E: This still lacks appeal.

[slides: car "on the drawing board"
being man-measured, contours templated;
profile of Ava Gardner]

Z: "A sweeping silhouette in tailored steel"

T: Now that's "forward styling" … where's my template! [*find a template suitable to Gardner's breasts*]

{A start, high}

[easel slide: poem, as before]

[*apply template to easel projection of poem*]
{B *Stranger*: "You're a strange man…." "I don't know about that"}
Ready for text: "steamers" … "door" … *Life*!

[wall slides: begin to flash a round of images
fr. *Time*, *Life*, *Popular Mechanics*, e.g.:
young couple, on their knees, measuring a car;
designing the dashboard on a clay model—
measuring the glove box closure w/ calipers;
futuristic auto bodies;]

[*computer manipulation of text, according to easel reconfiguration, giving the poem fins and sharp curves with the extra material*]

Z: *Time*, 10/55: "Leapt" … "bore" … "incense" …!

[slide]

T: "floor" … "bridges" … "BOW!" … *Partisan Review* '52….

[slide]

Z: Let's take it for a spin…!

{A fade under}

[slide: blank]

Hung midsea
like a boat mid-air
The Liners boiled their pastures:
The Liners of flesh,
The Arctic steamers.

E: Change! [*costume alteration*]

[slide: B-52 in the hangar,
hung up]

T [*simultaneous*]: "Big New Bomber Dies A Sacrificial Death": "Engineers... were hard at work tearing one of their B 52s to pieces..."

Z:

Brains the size of a football.
Mouths the size of a door.

T: Massive front end, twin tower headlights that say stop with great authority...

[slide: labeled sketch of TV—
"biggest picture... dark-toned safety
glass... 'golden throat' fidelity..."
illuminated "king-size" numbers]

Taut-muscled, forward thrusting... no dead-air bulges...

Z:

The sleek wolves
Mowers and reapers of sea kine
THE GIANT TADPOLES

[slide: TV—the big picture:
woman demos. w/ her hands,
measuring the screen]

T: Looks big, feels big, acts big, is big...

(meat their algae)
Leapt

T: Now, back to the *Review*: "In the administration, there is hardly a man with a political position independent of Eisenhower's."

[slide: a mechanical cow udder]

Z:

Like sheep or children
Shot from the sea's bore

[slide: labeled diagram
of missile—" warhead," "target seeker,"
"guidance," "telemetering," "control,"
"propulsion"]

T: "Yet neither the fact of his illness nor the prospect of his retirement jolted..."

[slide: sketch of air captain
demonstrating w/ hand gestures
to a boy & his young pretty mother
how smoothly the planes takeoff & land]

Z

Turned and twisted
(Goya!!)
flung blood and sperm.

T: "The web of committees and the pressure of agenda hold it tight..."

[slide: safety razor—
3 frames: "presto" (loading),
"twist" (closing), "safe" (dispose of used blade)]

E: It's hanging out in too many places.
{A up to pause}

[slide: baseball—
a Dodger sliding into base... safe]

T: (In a moment, the game will be over; in less than two years, they will have been sold off, lost among the image factories of Southern California...)

[slide: black]

Z:

incense.
{A start}
flung up...

[slide: red negligees
modeled by four young women,
one side-saddled on a blue marble pony]

T: America--a gory enactment of its frantic self-obsession!

E: Off course! wheel it in, man!

[slide: blank]

T: Discipline the rhizome, eh...

Z: 10:00: *Wrestling Workout!*

T: Hey: "The stock market ducked for a day, then bobbed up. Elsewhere the momentum..."

[slide: architectural rendering—
50s style ranch house,
no human presence detectable]

Z

Gnashed at their tails and brothers,
Cursed Christ of mammals,
Snapped at the sun,
Ran for the sea's floor.

T: "The democratic values which America either embodies or promises are desirable in purely human terms."

[slide: "'finger-tip' cleaning...
'it's so easy to use'"]

Goya! Goya!

Oh Lawrence,
No angels dance those bridges.

T: "We are certain that these values are necessary conditions for civilization and represent the only immediate alternative..."

[slide: blank]

{A pause}

E: Problem with you is, you got no style.

Z:

OH GUN! OH BOW! {A start}

T: "As long as Russian totalitarianism threatens world domination...."

[slide: Rocketman
in flight, ray gun drawn]

Z: The whales are...

T: the Russians!

[slide: blank]

Z, T: Goya Goya... Oh, Lawrence

E: I want it on my desk!

{A pause}

Z: Straight, or at an angle.

T: "Governments, as governments..."

Z: "as governments"?

T: "should, express the society."

E: Back off the *Partisan Review*. We need a new track.

[slide: Bucky Beaver
orbiting on a tube of Ipana™]

T: Let's go back to Howard Hughes, piloting a smaller version of the Comet II...

{A start low}

Z: The "Rome jinx," 1954: The Yoke Peter and the Yoke Yoke, disappearing into the Tyrrhenian and Mediterranean seas, respectively, only months apart...

T: What technology could achieve that?

Z: They considered it failed technology: metal fatigue, problems with the fuselage, too much interior pressure...

T: That's what they said, but in actuality they had found the *charniere* of aviation tech. [*gesture with hand*]

Z: Now you're just flapping... but you're on to something. Try this cut: "if the shock area were visible, the plane would appear to be flying through the center of a huge phonograph record" (*NYT*, 10/2/55).

[slide: Ipana™ on radar]

T: "Rear drag forces"

E: "Wasp-waist" it!

{A medium}

Z: We can get to, say, 800 mph with a straight fuselage, but 1000+ with the middle tucked...

T: The "Coke bottle," the "MM" effect...

Z: So it is: we can appear to take away by adding to, fore and aft...

T: If only I had a template...

[slide: nude curve of back,

waist, hip on a mattress—
"a level spine is the secret..."]

AH... [*makes template by tracing projected image on poster board, cuts, applies to poem-image projected on easel*]

{A low}

[*E reimages poem on computer according to easel sketch*]

Z: No "dead air bulges."

T: Let's run it!

[slide: labeled sketch
of proposed space vehicle
at moment of liftoff, *Science & Mechanics*]

E: Vertijet™!

T [*heading out runway*]: "For the Death of 100 Whales"

{A pause}

Time, 11/54: "...Killer whales... Savage sea cannibals up to 100 feet long with teeth like bayonets... one was caught with 14 seals and 13 porpoises in its belly... often tear at boats and nets... destroyed thousands of dollars' worth of fishing tackle... Icelandic government appealed to the U.S., which has thousands of men stationed at a lonely NATO airbase on the subarctic island. Seventy-nine bored G.I.'s responded with enthusiasm. Armed with rifles and machine guns one posse of Americans climbed into four small boats and in one morning wiped out a pack of 100 Killers...
...First the killers were rounded up into tight formation with concentrated machine gun fire, then moved out again one by one, for the final blast which would kill them..."

{A start, low}

The technique demonstrates the "perfection" of a logic of order and technological control: the system works, no matter what the material; the whales a convenient testing ground, a foreign site for the specular working out of experiments in socio-political control.

E: sounds like…?

{A pause} <3>
{buzzer}

[slide: blank]

T: The whales are the other, as are the Russians, as are the "masses." Weapons and TVs…

{A start}

Z: No time for this now.

T: what's being rehearsed is faciality: the right positioning of the camera, composition of a shot, evincing the faces of authority, of cultural value: a parade of redundancy, puppets of a coded significance…

{A medium}

slides: CU: pretty posing, politicians;
Hi-fi™ "fluid make-up"—CU lips, face—
sharp image in a mirror/screen]

Z: You should have come up with that earlier.

T: There are plays on these faces…

[slide: removing the black mask
she holds up a tapered glass
in a gloved hand
for more]

E: Get out there! [*T strips down to red and white starred silk shorts with black infinity symbols, or figure 8s, attached one to each buttock*]

T: "as one was wounded, the others would set upon it and tear it to pieces with their jagged teeth…"

{A low}

[*T puts on Texaco baseball cap, slowly*]

{B *Stranger*: "a long time ago I made a rule: let people do
what they want"}

E: Vertijet!? [*T heads out runway*]

[slide: "revised" poem, reshaped as below;
see "The Poems"]

Z: We've got cognition… Freeze!… [*pause video*]

{A pause}

[*E, Z, T put on "3-D" sunglasses; the glasses are marked "2 D," "+ D," and "N D," respectively*]

[easel slide: airborne car,
fins in cloudless blue,
and/or sketch of missile/Vertijet]

[*T sets up 4th of July skyrocket*]

Z [*referring to poem*]: Looks like a "giant tadpole" to me…

E: "Greatest Experiment Ever: Space Blast: Radar and Radio Disrupted: Shots undetected by World…"

{B rock medium}

[*reinscription of McClure's poem read by Z and T, T as Rocketman. T reads his lines in flight, discovering marks in aerospace. "Original" poem, in italics, recited by Z* {5 rings} *punctuate first stanza*]

Hung midsea
like a boat mid-air
The Liners boiled their pastures:
Big New Bomber Dies A Sacrificial Death
Engineers were *The Liners of flesh*, hard
at work tearing *The Arctic steamers.*
one of their B 52s to pieces…

Z: Tuck that.

{B pause; A medium}

E [*simultaneous*]:

"sorry we can't take your call;
we've slipped between the lines"

massive front end, twin tower headlights that say
stop *Brains the size of a football* with great authority
Mouths the size of a door. looks big feels big acts big
{A pause; B start}
taut-muscled, forward thrusting *the sleek wolves*
trigger torque *Mowers and reapers of sea kine*
THE GIANT TADPOLES obey your commands
in an instant *(meat their algae)*
Leapt in the administration

E:

aaaaaa...
{B pause; A medium-low}
the momentum of U.S. life
carried on without a jar.

Like sheep or children
Shot from the sea's bore

Yacht calls for help

Turned and twisted
(Goya!!)
flung blood and sperm.
becalmed 150 mi. southwest

San Francisco. *Incense.* Truce:

{A pause}

600-man battalion, 2 medium tanks
Gnashed at their tails and brothers,
four half-tracks mounted with 50-m. machine
guns took over the task of enforcing law and
order in this strike-torn *Cursed Christ of mammals,*
steel-helmeted troops, armed with rifles, *Snapped at sun*
in Indiana. Salable hogs 11,000 head *Ran for the sea's floor.*
It is not merely a capitalist myth... the democratic values which
Goya! Goya!
Oh Lawrence, Viscose
Corporation expects sales

to total $225,000,000 this year
the securities and exchange commission
No angels dance those bridges. Barrows and
guts, sows and 280-pound butchers *OH GUN! OH BOW!*
Boy, 13 years old, saw an arm reach through a broken
kitchen window. He grabbed his bow and shot an arrow into the
arm. *There are no churches in the waves,*
Henry Ford Claims Biggest Profit Year

No Holiness
wandered into white house
by mistake with a loaded gun,
was fined $25 The satellite, which
government scientists believe will be
about the size of a basketball, will definitely
contain data reporting instruments *No passages or crossings*
4 types of Beats Noticed in Heart *From the beast's wet shore.*
Women prefer white soap to gray 12 to 1 rigid price supports for
agriculture is like spinning the wheels of an automobile stuck in
mud

Z: He's connected...

E: We "could achieve a record breaking $400,000,000 economy 'in the near future'"!

Z [*Z & T communicate via walkie-talkies*]: How's it look out there?

{B start}

T: It's a 260 HP Super Red Ram... a 265 cm labium... pair 'o dem...

Z: What?

[slide: ad: soldier
with a flying helmet]

T: No, he's not on second anymore...wait, it's the man with the "$70,000 hat"!

[easel slide: reshaped poem,
as before]

Z: That's just a recruit... T, come in, it won't go, I'm worried: we forgot about the top [*pointing out unaltered prose epigraph*] it's as square as ever... [*aside*] I can't read him...

{B stop}

T: That's just a decoy: it's designed to look like it will blast hell hog through the dense rhetoric of the upper atmosphere, but in actuality it's already instressed those discourses--geared them down within its own energy matrices... the competition, the tension, is its internal dynamic--a fully functioning machinic assemblage...

Z: That's engineering! so it already is what it would pass through...

E: That's not motion as we know it

{B clock}

Z: But can you make it home?

<3> {buzzer}

[slide: holograph note,
McClure to Ginsberg:
"burn all my letters and poems"]

[*All remove "3-D" glasses, regroup*]

T: "How the Beat Generation Was Born..."

E: Well...*NYT*, 10/7/55: Article 2: Functions of the Atomic Energy Agency (hereinafter referred to as the Agency): A. 1. To encourage and assist world-wide research on and development of peaceful uses of atomic energy and to serve as intermediary.... 2. To make provision... of nuclear materials... for research in and application of atomic energy for peaceful purposes.... 3. To foster the interchange of scientific and technical information and the development of standards in the field of peaceful uses of atomic energy...

[slide: blank]

Z: We need more details.

[slide: black]

***

Interlude Riffs

[*T dresses. Z & E hand out hyper-colorized xerox facsimiles of color-retouched magazine images of TV dinners. Jazz or rock between textual "riffs"*]

{A, low-medium-fade under}

{B over A: cafe ambiance}

[slides: auto-image drift;
E scatters some images on walls
with hand-held projector;
the slides specifically noted below
are easel slides]

[*Z, T, E stretch, walk about, mingle with sounds and sights*]

T: Tables pushed back, mic & stool, cat blowing his axe into the corner--it's a dark inside cool brick slightly subterranean place... {A pause}

Z,T [*chant, fade under music*]: on tape: "the beat, yeah the beat, uhhuh the beat beat, ehh the beat...

{A start low}

Z: the beat, yeah the beat beat... AAA the beat, uhhuh the beat beat...

E [*simultaneous with "chant"; wait for music. T puts on Mickey Mouse suspenders, changes hats, and "plays" with props*]: How to dress them in? Let them explode onto, then off stage--into a kaleidoscope of spin-off products:

{A fade under}

like subatomic particles in a TV bubble chamber. Let the media make them into buffoons; the "craze" will generate quick millions, the counter-culture identity eventually flatten out around an easy refrain, then dissipate... "rear drag"; some will contract for more stable positions, others may vector off into nascent counter movements... the point is, whatever force hits consumer culture will be absorbed by its fleshy boundaries, channeled to sustain it, then redirected into planar stability allowing underground currents to continue, underground: what's down there doesn't matter; whenever a tumescence "pops" up, it'll make a buck--so long as you don't aggravate the assault by imposing a code of containment... stay alert, ride it out, and let it dissipate over the social field...

{A up, medium, brief, fade under}

*

[slide: Sta-Flat girdle—
the model instructed—
methods and measures]

T: Clothing as technology...

Z: alteration of the body...

T: the science of altering appearances...

Z: paradigm self-modeling...

{A up medium, brief, fade under}

*

[slide: *Life*: "star" cover, 10/3/55]

T: (see Del.): eyes, looking beyond the frame... a contour, gesture, or a sound, phoneme, fragment of syntax, particle of language, of discourse--casting out toward something else... Rock Hudson's hands, hooked into his belt, while the eyes engage...

Z: we can't see the hands...

T: could just as easily unclasp the belt...

Z: the eyes don't close...

E: What are you driving at?

Z: Away from...

T: Deleuze, 224: "What is a center...of power?" ...

Z: a game of holes.

{A up louder, fade under}

*

[slide: see below]

Z [*during the rather lengthy popculture analysis that follows, Z displaces easel; T "beatifies" Z by affixing large sheet of newsprint to her (see "Quotes" slide, above) and tracing the "Beat" image projected on her: a computer manipulated Ginsberg as Trident, wearing BG "necklace" (a miniature of a group shot), or, hypercolorized MLS of svelte hipster "chic" in full dance-trance (still fr. '61 film* The Beat Generation). *Meanwhile, E manipulates an image on computer--a scratch-and-make Jell-O spiral*]: It began with Disneylandia: A proto Disneyland travelling exhibit. The "old West" on wheels: a miniaturized, automated, overcoded representation of a fictionalized American "way of life"—little 3-D model environments set within painterly frames—that served as a pop rendition of an "historically" based text as exemplum for current lifestyle. Disney's genius, when he finally realized his theme park in 1955, was to immerse visitors in the simulation--they performed within its space, moved according to its rules over a highly seductive, carefully programmed surface. Main Street U.S.A.: pastoral revisioning of rural America--"Dis-America" (dizzying, if you need the ballast of a reality-effect); a semiotic sleight-of-hand (the step-back reproductions of buildings from Disney's Midwest birthplace skews perspective, makes them appear taller than they are); Peter Pan magic coaxing visitors toward a misrecognition, troping them out of their roles as consumers at a commodity exchange/(re)distribution site: i.e., Disneyland is a shopping mall, pushing all kinds of consumer items "authenticated" by the Disney logo; the "face" of Disney metonymic for the ur-product Disney sells--fantasy. (The sharpness and stillness of the model-effect is especially impressive in the old 3-D Viewmaster[tm] reels—life as a becoming scale model) ...

T [*picking it up, placing drawing over monitor image—static cling; Z retrieves a Marilyn Monroe multiple (see E, below)*]: What's most significant, however, in assessing its semiotic valence as cultural discourse, is the fact that Disneyland's grand opening occurred on television: It is first and last a media event. A special "preview" opening, arranged for newsmen and television cameras, was broadcast coast-to-coast; so it seemed to be a Disney animation coming to life (the way Betty Boop and Coco create themselves from fluids of the draftsman's pen in some of the old Max Fleischer cartoons). Potential visitors were "prepped" by a media pre-simulation, a re-presentation of a representation, perhaps to enhance the "reality-effect" of the fantasy in the "real," walk through simulation. And entry into the "magic kingdom" required a special sort of "spiritual" preparation: families had to become mobile, put themselves on wheels, "liberate" themselves from their daily routines in order to reach the site of imaginative dis-location. This of course supplements the illusionistic ruse that the package is not...no... Disneyland's TV opening, and its "setting" in the suburbs of Southern California were just clever sweeps of the showman's arm, displaying dazzling surfaces of a box each side of which is (always already?) doubled... trick is to evade recognition of package as package, in all the specificity of its social-economic function: that's what you buy (into) at Disneyland.

[slide: blank]

E: Good riffs, up to jargon... [*demonstrating on serial Marilyn Monroe life size stand up (5 MCU's, each striking a slightly different pose)—see the "Monroe Project"*]: Problem decomposition assuming an external energy source and commodifiable real: energy [*outside head 1*] > convert energy to translational energy [*head 1*] > accumulate translational energy [*heads 2-4*] > apply translational energy [*head 5*] > altered state [*beyond ultimate head*].

{A up, medium, fade under}

*

T: Line 25, "For the Death of 100 whales": "No angels dance those bridges." A few more lines, then a pause, a break. Kerouac turns sliver alloy into wine. The murmur settles, and the tones that would spin the century on its axis...

Z: Hey!...
T: begin to sound... In approximately 10 minutes, Ginsberg arrives at *Howl*, strophe 25: "Who loned it through the streets of Idaho seeking visionary Indian angels..."

Z: This is no Main Street U.S.A.

T: That's the (spirit) bridge: across this span of time--maybe 45 minutes?

-through the discussions, flirtations, buying of wine, stepping out into the street, commenting on Fred Martin's orange

[slide: the "crates."]

crate sculptures--whatever--through all this uninscribed "mundane" activity these lines tensed--from line 25 to strophe 25--taut as a cable of the Golden Gate Bridge, sketching angels in the air...

[*the flash and positioning of slides around the room has created the impression, or vague dream-like reminiscence, of Six Gallery*]

Z: Ready to be packed in "orange crates of theology."

{A up, low, brief, fade under}

*

E [*Z & T "dance" with hoops*]: For extensive descriptions of the event, see...

Z [*Z & T continue dancing*]: The world coming at the poet, poets coming at each other, poetry coming at the critic; theory, discourse, and jargon coming back at the poet...

T: a sphere traversed by circles...

Z: and the yin yang of the stitch lines...

T: and who is throwing the masculfeminine ball?

Z: It is light spinning over and into dark spinning over and into light...

T: At night, the ball's dark core spins unseen under arc lights.

{A up, fade under}

*

E: What's Walt Disney's favorite car?

{A pause}

T [*read rapidly*]: You think the 50s is flat bland Perry Como? Little Richard and Allen Ginsberg are both messing with our (cultural) minds you might also look at the 100,000 psychiatric patients in NY's hospitals alone to chart the tension the well-ordered exterior of Levittown a mask, evasion, strategic maneuvering around that which cannot be "secluded" without rupture are Ozzie & Harriet on Serpasil? certainly they live in Miltown.

[slide: automobile dashboard,
part of a steering wheel,
a finger extending from a poised hand...]

Z [*tense hush*]: While a gloved feminine hand pushes a button for "drive" (R, N, and L are also choices), under hood things are explosive--all power directed by the engineers, of course, into a "safety surge..."

T [*Extra! Extra!*]: "New chemical agents might revolutionize the treatment of...mental affliction... reducing the use of restraints and seclusions by 50... some patients, formerly hospitalized without improvement despite extensive conventional treatment (electro-shock, insulin and all other types of therapy) have been released after using the drugs and have made adequate social adjustments in their communities..." (*NYT*, 10/7/55).

Z: Answer: the '56 Dodge with Magic-Touch Push-Button Automatic driving!

{A up, medium, fade under}

[slide: Dodge, full view]

*

E: What does Allen Ginsberg fielding the streets of SF have to do with Rosa Parks waiting for a bus Montgomery, AL, 12/1/55...?

{A pause} <3>

Z: Or beat women, including those who were killed...

T: or sold themselves into stereotypes...

Z: executive marriages...

T: memories...

Z: institutions...

[slide: Jay Defeo's painting *The Rose*]

T: or saw the immense flaming roses of their visions sealed behind 20 yr. walls...

Z: Volmer Kendel Cassady Glassman Adams DeFeo

{2 buzzers} <4}>

{A start low}

T: each player a ring, interlinked (syn- and diachronically) in trans-text-sexual orgy...

Z: Or, Willy Mays: "I don't make history, I catch fly balls..."

{A, low, brief}

*

E: Question...

{A quick fade to pause}

[*a runner is caught between "bases." E & Z throw a small red beacon back and forth, the runner (T) following mechanically, while reading aloud the following newspaper story. Toward the end of the story, E dissimulates; the runner, thinking she/he missed the throw, turns back: Out.*]

T: *New York Times*, 10/7/55: "McArdle said the trouble began when the three approached him and several friends and asked for a piece of paper. 'We told them we didn't have any paper,' the youth explained. 'They got nasty and we told them we'd meet them tomorrow [yesterday] to discuss where we should fight.' Instead they came back an hour or so later with the gun."

{buzzer}

{B: "Take me out to the ball game, take me out with the crowd.
Buy me some peanuts and cra ker jack,
I don't care if I ever get back. Let me root root root
for the home team--if they don't win it's a shame,
but it's one, two, three..."}

T [*simultaneous, from "Let me..."*]: Serpasil, Thorazine: Chlorpromazine; Miltown, Frenquel, Meratran, Raudixin...

[slide: Ipana[tm]: cartoon target
zeros-in on what appears to be
an astral whale]

***

E:

Feature 2: *The Wild One*
plus

[slide: *Rocketmen*—
Ch. IV title shot]

King of the Rocketmen, Ch. IV: "High Peril"

Z [*fr.* Wild One]: "Where do you go?"

T [*quoting Brando*]: "Oh, man... we just go..."

E [*simultaneous*]: blow.

[slide: view of Ginsberg's room,
San Francisco, as below]

{A start medium, fade under}

T: Let's name what we can [*studying the image*]: From a POV either lying in bed or squatting beside it, over blurred seat of stool (foreground), groin-level of chair where Ginsberg (not included) drafted *Howl* Part I summer '55: LaVigne's Orlovsky framed leaning against desk, Bach's Mass in B Minor in cardboard cover (thin symphony), front street window shade drawn... *Howl* typewriter, hot flash just above desk on window shade [*suddenly turning to face audience*]... "What?" ... something heard or imagined. Shot from desk [*describing room from the opposite POV*], what would have been behind the writing: a fire in fireplace? Checkered blanket over alley window, LaVigne's "Cezanne-like" watercolor cityscape and portrait of A G squared above un or roughly made bed;

stool, big dark armchair, "Bach & clock," portable Hi-Fi, clock atop letters or essays by E P bound at bed head… Hot spot at joint of wall and ceiling… These overexposures irradiating space [*gesturing an arc from screen to audience*]: "Blessed be the muses / for their descent / dancing round my desk / crowning my balding head / with laurel."

E: (1010 Montgomery as Orgone Collector, *Howl* as product of Orgasmatron…)

{A up medium, fade under}

T: And Berkeley (sometime before 4/26/56): the reenactment: seated in a semicircle of thrones in theater twilight, impressions of linear intimacy shooting Toulouse Lautrec across the walls (jetting, compacting, thickening, suddenly veering off, knotting again, shooting free again… Ginsberg and Orlovsky… rhythm of slowness and speed…) …

Z: And before it all, Lionel Trilling's letter to Ginsberg, 8/9/45: "Rush of sound… together with relative obscurity of thought… a good deal of Shelley here—are you aware of it?"

E: (*PR*, '52, 565): "American art and thought must become awkward again."

{A up slightly}

T: These reworkings, should we choose to deploy them, should carry us across many potential self-stratifications…

* * *

[*T reads from '55 draft of* Howl *as Z reads simultaneously from final draft: "citational" v. "poetic" presentational styles; T also imports commentary from Ginsberg's annotations*]

Z, T [T]: "I saw the best minds of my generation destroyed by madness, starving hysterical [mystical] naked…"

E: "hysterical naked"?

{A pause} <3> {buzzer}

T: "Crucial revision… key to poem's tone… empathy and shrewdness… darkly comic realism… shadows of Chaplin…"

Z: Cosmetics, gone wild:

{A start low}

"I dreamed I was---starving mystical beatified in my Maiden
form bra!"

[slide: bra in fantastic surroundings]

Z, T: "dragging themselves through the negro streets at dawn looking for an angry fix"

T: cf. Huncke Harlem morning, sunless Times Square junk hunt...

Z, T: "Angel headed hipsters burning for the ancient heavenly connection to the starry dynamos in the machinery of night"

T: Deleuze:

{A pause}

literary machine whirring on the code of juxtaposition; techno-cosmic puppetry vectoring...

{A start}

Z: but those "long, low, breath taking lines... so completely responsive"

[slides: a Mercury inclining,
passing a powerfully built mountain goat
on a rocky pinnacle;
oats boiling in a glass pot]

T: In lab tests supercharged spiral nebulae heat up space in a Pyrex[tm] pot, "boiling" the oat stars into turbulent chaotic patterns... a cosmic light show

{buzzer}

{A pause}

E: "Who"!

T: 's on first....

Z, T [Z]: "poverty and tatters and [fantastic] hollow-eyed and high sat up smoking in the supernatural darkness of cold-water flats floating across the tops of cities contemplating jazz"

T: late Bowery loft bop jams...

Z: "Hollow-eyed smoking" takes us further away; with "fantastic" we get something else happening in the eye...

{A low--medium}

[slide: eyes in "living colors"]

T: "pretty please," "pink queen," "rhapsody in red..."

{A up slightly}

but this eye is as it is, a black hole in faciality that carries all away--bop annihilation...The witnessing eye of Reznikoff's *Testimony*.

E: (not yet)

Z: loss of parameters...

T: being hollow, the eyes are...?

Z: a zero ground still framed by a face... if the face implodes?

T: (See Deleuze, 167—, "Year Zero: Faciality")

E: Change! [*costume alteration*]

{A pause}

Z: But what's "floating"?

T: The mind, as quadrilateral locator set adrift--adjusting sites over foreign territory...

{A medium}

Z: Don't forget to set parallax for a balanced picture.

T: 230, 000 HP; 1, 036 ft. long "with weapons of awe-inspiring speed, range, and lethality"; a 4-acre deck and 7 AC systems--enough cooling capacity for a space bigger than Radio City Music Hall... "If our way of life is to survive we must." (*NYT*, 10/2/55).

Z, T: "Who bared their heads to Heaven under the EL and saw

Mohammedan angels staggering on tenement roofs illuminated"

T: Spring Lamantia comatose spiraling over Koran couch: "I floated toward an endless-looking universe of misty, lighted color forms: green, red, blue, silver... suddenly the outline of a benign bearded face..."

{A pause}

E: Q: cf. *NYT*, 10/7/55: How is a religious system like an economic system?

<3>

[slide: perfect hair—
the head targeted in a thin red circle
as a feminine hand, gloved to the elbow, smooths the lapel]

{A medium}

T: Brylcream[tm] angels assembled on tenement roofs "lustrous and immaculate" ...

Z: "Red Majesty..."

T: at ease in their signifying halos, blowing bubbles over cloverleaves of a limited access highway... {buzzer}

Z: sulfurous star gleams among the furrowed stripes of husbandry...

T: redundant and transportable face of power--this man is our man...

Z: 50, 000, 000 tubes and bottles a year sold over the drug counters of America.

[slide: Gillette shaving
serial: before and after]

{A low}

T: The process. A sequence of rectangles; the sixth one--the face almost ready, groomed to the micro edge of a concept, "thinner than this page" ...

[slide: ghostly arc of electric razor,
on chin, extreme CU]

E: (this is *Life*, 10/10, 104).

T: it's the circles, the arcs themselves that signify. It doesn't matter what's inside or outside the span, what degree the arc; the fragment contains the whole and vice versa…

Z: meta geometry…

T: the hollow-eyed machinery of abstraction…

{A up slightly}

Z: circles whirring in circles…

T: engineered illusions, a staggering collusion of technology and metaphysics…

Z: an outgrowth on faciality requiring a precisely machined surveillance…

T: The machine as ontology, gesture of an arc… as if the whole thing operated on a spiritual current…

Z: "cy."

{A Pause}

T: Yes [*"seeing" image*] … as if mechanical parts were no longer necessary…

Z: shaving on faith…

T: and so the old angels stagger.

Z: It's the after image that gets me.

[slide: Lanolin fairy
sparks her wand on
sleeping beauty]

E: Veer off! Compact!

Z: Play ball!

{B: crowd sounds over
A: start medium}

E: Freeze! [*pause video*]

[slide: blank]

[*T tries the runway; pitches a strike or two but winds up walking the "hitter"; Z is not always sure when to swing or at what, exactly, she's swinging*]

T [*pitching*]: Brylcream duplicating angels bypassing air-glide tenements, thruway sweep of hair, smiles stenciled onto vivid complexions in the pentacolors of faith really one--Red Majesty gay red pink queen... [*Z doesn't swing*]

E: He must have... strike!

{A pause}

Z: We weren't ready...

E: What's the market objective?

T [*T looking about, as if for potential steals*]: Ditto.

[slide: ditto machine]

Z: What?

{B: begin cut from "All Shook Up," low over A}

E: 's on second.

T: Ditto! the five-color duplicator!

[slide: fauve cigarette ad—
multicolor face of young woman,
ribbons of smoke]

E: Who's the audience?

{A up medium}

T [*winding up*]: Suzuki bucket seats, four-barrel consciousness Kenosis, 23 cents a gallon vision...

E: (this is not obtainable from a single master)

T: French pressed cocksucking high octane Latin [*the pitch*] blues daydream… [*Z doesn't swing*]

E: Ball!

{A low}

[slide: looping baseball Cheerios]

He's out there…

T: (impossible sound contours sifting through early morning cafe muddle…)

[slides: Ginsberg's holograph recipe
for spaghetti with clams ("1 can *snow* clams /
2 cubes margarine," etc.
"Simmer 10 minutes");
Mixmaster™ in action;
easel: beans w/ alarm clocks,
spaghetti w/ "Super Royal 8"s
and other kitsch-surreal food collages]

Z: He seems to be mixing Kerouac, Lamantia, Snyder, Ginsberg…

T [*out on the mound, in self-dialogue, blending*]: Beat Monroe, beat Barbie, Betty Crocker…

Z: Kerouac cocktail, bunless Ginsberger, Whalen split, Snyder sweet and sour, Ferlinghetti primavera, Jell-O™ laminate…

{A up medium}

[slide: holograph McClure note:
"I don't think too much of these—
The Bop Wino"]

{B stop}

T [*simultaneous*]: Ride-a-Beat, Rent-a-Beat, Beat Disney, Atomic Beat,

3-D Beat, Beats run the bases; a mini tour of Beatsville in a Beatmobile, nobody beats the… [*quick wind up and pitch*]

E: Watch your zone limits!

[slide: blank]

T: walls of signs; 20 suitcases filled with collapsible visions, stackable delusions, nervous tics, febrile tight-wound clocks giant Mexican jumping beans rattling still lives of florid decay in vaults of…

{B: crowd cheering and radio sportscaster
as Dodger's win 1955 World Series:
"I don't believe it… I don't believe it…"}

Z [*can't find the ball--it's everywhere and nowhere*]: knowledge?

E: Strike!

T: "Poseidon Flop House": hot blood infusions, libido injected techno-cosmic doughnut revelations…

{A pause}

Z: I don't remember that…

{A start}

T: millennial strophes burning in sunless morning studio windows like movie credits of infinity…

E: high and away! [*Z swings at it*]

T: each life individually packed in tissues of concern all for one low price in the dollar stores of morality?

Z [*E, as catcher, signals "no"*]: No!

T: Contraband self-help guides through "Chaos Wonderland," rubbing boys somnambulistic chewing the fat on Coney Island bound tongue twisters… [*windup and release*]

Z: torque twisters?

{B: brief riff from "All Shook Up"

superimposed over crowd sounds}

E: Low and inside... passed my stop, man

{A low}

T: rain mirror pavement, slick expression corner 83rd and Broadway (3333! -that key wasn't working a minute ago!) "I understood all too well the sentiment that the poet was expressing"

E: [*Z forgets to bat*] Out! -the line!

{A pause}

Z: He is "always already" out.

{B stop}

E: But perhaps a crossword cutup would work... columns of words perpendicular to rows of words, nonsense in certain directions...

Z: each word resonating with its own clue as the puzzle builds antisemantically...

{A medium}

T: breasts clues in the grid of dreams, nipple bottles sealed around bicoastal stairways spiraling into dunes of shifting logic, granite carrousels of surf riders, who deep sucking fears explains this is binding holy body self into books of alienation...

{A pause}

E: sounds like...?

<3> {buzzer}

T: costumes of terror jostling in ammonia stairways Happy Birthday Horny Death!...

[*Z: a you-better-stop-before-it's-too-late look*]

{A low}

T: Meanwhile, somewhere just off zero ground, a left field stretch for mushroom highballs...

E: Ball!

Z: come on in now, T

E: His head's gone all a loose--he needs...?

{A pause}

[*Z & T look at each other, searching each other's eye for clues*]

[slide: Anacin,
the suffering & the happy masks—
"get FAST relief with..."]

{B: Anacin commercial: "sure you're upset,
but don't take it out on the children"}

{buzzer}

T [*hands to head*]: cyber-coded flies...

{A low}

[slide: commercial surreal:
man sipping vodka on a carousel pony
dislocated to seashore—the bottle, along w/
a screwdriver & a bloody Mary
in the sand in the foreground]

[*coming in, headed for the dugout*] simple... simple syrup... that's how you make a Manhattan... simple syrup...

Z: As Yogi Berra says, "it ain't over till it's over."

T: (Or, the Whale[n]: "Quit trying to stop!")

E: I admire the torque, but can't travel on that output.

{A fade, pause}

T: I walked'em

*

Z: Torque? Just listen... why V not Y-8...

[slide: sketch: engine cutaway,
pistons to cam]

T: I don't know...

E: Third!

Z: No--the engine. The piston drives in at a 33.333 degree...

{A low—medium}

T: (I knew someone at that address)

Z: acute angle...

T: depends...

Z: down into the center of the block, whipped back by cam momentum...

T: the 8-fisted groin-al twist...

Z: back and forth: that's the shaft...

T: the hot rod...

Z: and circularity...

T: what we need's Bataille overdrive...

E: Reel it in!

{A low}

T: How does that go with razors?

Z: We're not talking razors, here; we're talking transport.

T: I dig.

E: Stay on task!

Z: Ok, let's run through this again.

{A pause}

[*partially rewind video*]

[slide: Marcel Marceau pointing
through hoop]

[*during the following, E may "call" rhythms-"* tuck *it in... let it out.... run with it... elongate.... spread and twist... haul up..." etc.*]

T [*picks up toy '57 Chevy, starts a metronome*]: riding a fix from negro streets at dawn to starry dynamos to hollow-eyed highs in supernatural darkness of cold-water flats (the mind sailing beyond physical circumstance) to neon visions ... you catch the oscillation?

{A low—medium}

[slide: *Popular Science*: do-it-yourself
magnetic pendulum—arrow shows the arc of travel]

T: The vast swings...

Z: The mind, traveling "across the tops of cities"—well above tenement roofs—stumbles on its 3-D illuminations...

T: as tubed neon washes cool bricks and dark windows in a haze of lost...

E: the zone limits!

T: names. From tenement roof top visions to universities, impossible degrees, without a lilt...

Z, T: "with radiant cool eyes hallucinating Arkansas and Blake-light tragedy among the scholars of war"

{A pause} [*stop metronome*]

T: In the final draft of section I, the break between strophe 5 and 6 images the confrontation of opposing socio-economic realities, tenements and universities (Columbia University on the cusp of Harlem); the high-octane irradiated state of mind eliding the stark gap in physical realities, drifting out floating

{A start low-medium}

over tenement rooftop visions enrapt--(unwrapped), raptured, rapturously transported in the beatific horror and delight of its own spectacles...

[slides: frame fr. Pogo
comic strip, as above—
question mark emerges, in a balloon, fr.
Pogo's head, drops to ground;
Marcel Marceau frames himself in hoop
with a roar]

[*start metronome*]

Z: anaphora and chanting rhythm yields sustained propulsion; not Brecht Tech—the machine runs too smoothly ...
E: Is this indictment?

T: This is torque, the convulsive force that delivers the smooth ride...

[slide: sketch: little worker man climbing
on wide flanges, w/huge wrench, torquing down]

Z: experiential tensions, dislodged syntax, rollercoaster shifts in place, compact juxtapositions: "starry dynamos," "supernatural darkness," "roofs illuminated," "radiant cool," "Arkansas and
Blake-light"/ black-light....

[slide: ads: hoops w/in hoops—
necklaces, earrings, & a white glove,
a velvet heel, a black bag]

{A pause}

T: The two machines—the language/literary machine and the social/ experiential machine operating within a larger multi- or inter-semiotic machinic assemblage: working by transsemiosis, the semiotic systems resonate within each other, translate into each other... [*pause metronome*]

[slide: comic strip:
Cicero's cat becoming Cicero]

E: The means of propulsion...? [*start metronome*]
T: Internal dynamics

{A low}

of sound and image and structure... fracturing, jeopardizing, overwriting...

Z: (riding)...

T: conventional syntactical codes...

Z: Overall conventional structure; within strophes all hell breaks loose...

{A up medium}

T: That's the power base, the accumulative system not an entropic cataloguing—closure, definition, stable differentiation, death (end) as goal...

[slide: frame fr. Pogo—
Pogo sees balloon emerging fr.
Owl's head, bats it]

{A pause}

but a series of high energy impacts and exchanges, relays: each strophe empowered out of the entropy of the preceding one, the whole amassing toward....

Z: the high pitch of the voice, when read...

T: "who... who... who..."

Z: return stroke and recombustion;

{A start low}

we cycle through each strophe—recycling culture...

[slide: Marcel Marceau w/ circus hoop]

T [*as if seeing Super(pheno)men(a)*]: Look!...

{A medium}

on a tenement roof! a gaseous mixture of imagistic and conceptual substances gathers from the chemical pools of culture.

[slide: automotive combustion chamber diagram—
arrows chart direction of flow]

Z: In the "wedge shaped turbulence chamber" of the poem, several sparks bolt... one or more strike...

T: blast us into the next ideogram

{A low}

—the milieus always recognizable, but torqued into distorted semblances. [*stop metronome*]
Z: We can't easily set mind on any of the poem's places...

T: a marvelous experimental poem machine...

{A pause}

E: All right... accumulate, disarrange, compact, regather...
something like that, that's the momentum...?

Missive: USNS Sgt. Jack J. Pendleton (T-AKV-5). 7/10/56. Dear Gene: ...The lines were printed wrong due to my negligence & publisher here negligence in instructing printer to line up like prose, each long line, and make even margin on right hand. As result lines chopped off in middle."

[slide: Toro Power Handle—
one man & one motor,
five different assemblages]

T: It's not a question of entitativeness, but a mobile center of power...

Z: "The Liners of flesh" ... "Shot from the sea's bore"

T: I saw the best minds of my ge ge ge [*hard starting: "generation"*]

[slide: "100,000 starts per
month"—automotive "torture tests"
("by authorized member of
American Council of Commercial laboratories")]

Z: "brains the size of..."

T: destroyed by madness, starving hysterical naked, / dragging themselves through commuterless aquarium light of dawn / lurching after visions tattered arms useless as fins...

E: Problem with you is, you got no rhythm.

*

T: Let's go back to the '56 Ford:

[slide: autos on interchanges]

three of 'em—

{A low}

a Thunderbird, a Victoria, and a Parklane; the T-Bird in the background at mid-loop, the other two passing on a curve; we're on the bend, down low, Victoria just about to swoop past on 'er way off the page...

Z: "Think of your spine..."

T: a dream vision...

Z: what a template it was...

T: a desire to collide with...

Z: to consummate your relationship with...

T: the vehicle... [*studying image*] the skies are clear orange sherbet...

Z: I checked the weather: 3/7/55: "spiraling highs expected over much of the west and Midwest today..."

[slide: multicolor Jell-O spiral]

{A pause}

E: Let's play... loops and overpasses!... [*puts on Headlight*[tm] *glasses—two small flashlights mounted on eyeglass frames*] White noise—top 40!

[slide: "Which one
of these sport models
would you rather have fun with?"—
autos in recreational settings]

{B: begin to fade in R & B}

T: "If trouble strikes..." [*gets Hula Hoop and '57 Chevy—
real working headlights and light-up engine!*]

E: Don't worry,

[slide: man, w/ troubled expression,
in a red space, reads over his policy—
Americana Fore insurance]

we've got you covered...

[slide: airborne car—
'55 Chevy, in blue space
seen fr. below,
tires just touching tops of clouds]

Z: "Angel-poised suspension..."

T: To fall in love with...

E: *NYT*, 10/7/55: "authority to haul dangerous explosives over the Nation's highways was given to Specter Motor Service..."

[slide: night shot of
overpasses & merges,
forming an abstract design]

T: the means of transport.

{B: var. R & B, medium—high, continuous}

[*E raises and lowers the pitch of her voice as she rides the cloverleaves; Z's and T's voices stay at the same low pitch, but vary in volume according to the Doppler effect as they "pass" each other on the freeway—stepping through a* Hula-Hoop. *Cloverleaves and overpasses are built from the* Partisan Review™*, *1952*]

E: (Perhaps we'll find something on this exit…) [*slowing, as if to exit on an overpass; voice rises*]

[slides: begin billboard barrage
of ads & highway intersections]

PR, '52: "Must the American intellectual and writer adapt himself to mass culture?

[slide]

[*voice drops, heading down*] If he must, what forms can his adaptation take?"

[*Z & T simultaneous, fast, as forces passing under/through the questions*]

[slide]

Z: "Storefront boroughs…"

T: 10th St. discount rack hallucinations…

Z: "of teahead joyride…"

T: Kerouac Cassady Brooklyn early morning jazz rides…

Z: "neon blinking traffic light…"

T: Huncke…

Z: "chained to subways Battery to holy…"

T: Dr. Morphine…

Z: "Bronx…"

T: 1945.

Z: "Benzedrine Zoo…"

T: A to Z in associative flash breath extension…

[slide]

E [*up*]: "Or do you believe that a democratic society necessarily

[slide: Pepto-Bismol[tm]]

[*down*] leads to a leveling of culture,

[slide]

to a mass culture which will outrun…?

[slide: invisible man as carburetor
w/ little mushroom of combustion flowering on lapel]

(it's "Mr. Vacuum" who clarifies vision)

Z [*Z & T simultaneous, as above*]: "who sank all night in submarine light of Bickford's…"

T: 42 St. mopping…

Z: "floated out…" "stale beer afternoon Fugazi's…"

T: phrasing added to accommodate…

Z: "crack of doom hydrogen jukebox…"

T: cafeterias had no jukeboxes.

Z: "lost battalion of platonic conversationalists…"

T: dreamy Jewish woman salvation army to Bellevue…

Z: "jumping off fire escapes Empire State…"

T: Atoms for peace! Atoms for Peace!

E [*up*]: "Where in American life can artists and intellectuals find

[slide]

the basis of strength, renewal, recognition…?"

[slide—heavy traffic
on loops & merges—aerial view]

T: Party in the Village! Party in the Village!

Z [*passes, exits to normal speaking voice*]: according to *Beauty and Power News*: "… being thrown against the steering post, striking hard surfaces within, or being thrown from…"

T [*simultaneous, dashing back and forth*]: "yacketayacketayacketayakking" Neal Cassady non-stop "in boxcars boxcars boxcars" Crane's "Hobo-trekkers" "racketing through nowhere Zen New Jersey" career failures "imagining postcards of Atlantic City Hall" family's 1930s summers Belmar "to a vanishing point…"

[slide: highways—aerial view]

Z: the smooth flow of energy through the interchanges…

T: Atoms for Peace!

{B: Pause}

E: I need more details. [*voice pitch still high*]

Z: The story's being told. It's *your* trip…

[slide: —woman in driver's seat
of convertible, about to start,
looking back over her shoulder
w/ worried expression—" brake service" …]

E: (am I in…)

Z: car, heart trouble?

{B: Start}

T: Atoms for Peace. "goonight grandfather bop kabbalah"—Americana esoterica…

[slide: red-turbaned
man w/ black beard, shouldering a valise]

E: "Can a tradition of critical non-conformism..."

Z [*simultaneous*]: ("even in strange, exotic lands, your Hartman luggage marks you instantly as one accustomed to gracious living")

E [*normal voice*]: be maintained?

T [*fast talk, slow pass through hoop*]: "naked in Kansas Idaho" vision quest "Baltimore" brick house Poe "supernova ecstasy" cosmographic human form East Harlem Blake illumination "in the Chinese" Reichean "dust [*pause, normal voice*] of Oklahoma"?

[slides: little Royal Pudding king
flying upside down;
suburban home—architectural rendering]

Z: "What are you rebelling against, Johnny?"

E: "What have you got?"

Z: *SFC*, 9/30/55: Young actor dies driving sports car: his German-built Porsche collided with another vehicle at highway intersection...

[slides: cu of nuclear mushroom;
Neal Cassady looking over used cars]

E [*another overpass*]: "To what extent have American intellectuals actually changed their attitude toward America and its institutions?"

T [*cutting through E's semi-circle*]: "howled on their knees in subways... fucked in the ass by saintly motorcyclists... "

[slides: woman
making a face—" stomach upset?";
still fr. *Rocketmen*—a building exploding
into a swirl of flame; optional—cartoon

of a child wearing part of
his parent's disemboweled TV set,
which he has made it into a space ship]

Z: Reenter! Reenter!

T: "hiccupped endlessly trying to giggle" ... Cannastra Christ Brando Kerouac and the French sailors... [*begins a silent slow pass through*]

[slide: Mercury—big "M"—CU fr.
squatting POV, wide front end
fills frame]

Z: Turn around, please...

[slide: large finned Dodge,
rear, from below—woman in green dress
w/ fur muff posing near door]

Z: Now, bend over...

E: Rear entry! Rear entry!

{B pause}

T: "faded out in vast sordid movies...

[slide: cartoon sky writing—
"Royal Instant..."
as little king's plane dives for ground]

Z: (Reprocessed vision, rearticulation through the technology of surveillance...)

[slide: woman peers w/
wide-eyed excitement
through viewfinder of movie camera,
important parts numbered—
5, 6, & 7
point to her middle finger (10/10, 56)]

T [*normal voice*]: stumbled to unemployment offices shoes full of blood"

Rikers Island prison homeless Huncke at the door, winter, 1948…

[slide: bon voyage—
in the stateroom enjoying a convivial
last drink w/ the board… through the
porthole, the city skyline

& a ship under full steam

Z: (It's on the tour) …

E: "broken neck… lacerations over entire body… terribly battered by impact… Killed instantly."

*

T: Entering a tunnel…

[slides: Brando on motorcycle;
motorcycle flying through night sky
sans Brando]

Z: Is there a tunnel?

T: stops me midword; during the gap, might lose track; when I come back, it may be something else…

*

[slides: hidden underwire highway bra or
magic floating bra—pulling a rabbit
out of a hat—" abracadabra";
Marcel Marceau w/ hoop
coaxing an imaginary animal;
frame fr. Pogo—Owl
throws Pogo's question balloon back
at him;
car, on expressway, low, from side—
"wait till you feel…"]

{A start low}

T: We're down on all fours, on the side of the road...

Z: "Looks big, feels big..."

[slide: refrigerator, loaded,
from below—plenty red meat]

T: in the kitchen...

Z: "Teen Girls Flee..."

E: Stay on track.

{A pause}

Where's the *Howl*?

[slides: as if fridge
had spilled out its contents
into a variety of ads— "Popsicle"tm;
"100 famous foods... colorama and VALUES"]

T: It's these slides... too many slides!

[slide: abstract sketch
of gloves in var. positions
& gestures, each price-marked—
"you owe it to your audience"]

E: Maybe try a template...

T: These templates, these metapatterns...

Z: That's science...

T: No, that's technology.

E: No, that's ideology.

T: prefabrication

[slide: sketch/diagram
of throat & stomach—coating action]

Z: That's overcoding, the Pepto-Bismol[tm] effect...

[slides: Marcel Marceau w/hoop;
CU of tire—a Royal 8]

T: ("circles that form, dissolve... aborified v. rhizomatic segmentarity..." also coils, springs, Cheerios. See Deleuze, 209: Circles of closed segmentarity and passages through: 1. creative work 2. family life (interior domesticity); this circle spirals into the first when creative work becomes collaborative/domestic 3. Seasonal. E.g., Spring: interface of family life with the landscape (gardening, mowing, sprinkling, etc.); plants territorialize bits of interior space in their rounded pots of soil 4. nomadic circle, briefly inhabiting the other three, at different stages, its path a coiling line of flight, kept on the move as it accumulates incrementally on its way toward outer circles of denial: garbage...)

{buzzer}

Z: We want a geometry taking place, "operative geometry" (*Ibid*, 212) ..."

T: Roundness v. concentric circularity—

{A low}

targets, test patterns— sphericity with a boundary thinner than this page...

{A up medium}

[slide: earth seen from MOUSE[tm]—
Minimum Orbital Unmanned Satellite of Earth]

E: But this is all rhizodrive, eclectomatic... each line a flight, not a sequential progression. A multivectored, multidimensional scribble masked by the clean face of a page.

{A pause}

Enticing theory but not good product

<2>

[slide: radio schematic]

T: But the refrain,

{A start low}

the anaphora, the rhythm: pulse beats in the rhizomatic flux, a calling together of the continually fleeing...

Z: Each strophe a power stroke, a poem in itself...

T: a reassemblable whole, perpetually mobile...

Z: the tension between stratification and destratification the driving force...

[slide: pair of stockinged legs
rise monolithically in foreground,
gradually closing the inverted "V"—
between the legs, a night-lit highrise,
its rain slick reflection pegged under black heels]

T: the tension between top and bottom limits of the stroke and the vectors of continuity....

{A pause}

E: I can't see what shape this has, the paradigm... [*popping some Cheerios in mouth from a cup; E may do this periodically*]

T: No templates. We have to take this locally, pulse by pulse...

[slides: blank;
a boy reading in his white attic study,
telescope aimed through skylight,
sketch/poster of "Space Ranger" rocket on wall,
featuring bright red linoleum floor w/ ab-ex design]

Z: Look, pop aesthetics dialogue in the 50s is something like this: abstraction is "good for linoleum"; realism, representation, attention to detail, real-time simulation—that's TV, Disney's participant-activated modeling; then the movies cut in with hyperreal effects—3-D and monolithic drive-in images—to compete with the real-time simulations of TV. We can refigure the Ginsberg of *Howl* as nomadic guerrilla raider—at least, from a theoretic POV—not so much coopting from these discourses (though he does do) as bemusing them by producing, and turning loose on the voice, an abstract realism, precise in detail but without narrative continuity (or, let's say, mobilizing fragmented flash or micro-narratives, little entropic flows...)

E: So where's the linoleum?

{A start}

[slides: woman demos
a hide-away TV console]

T: "Premiering: a show about a government ornithologist living in a trailer with a talking dog" ... I think we missed it...

Z: (The speechless other cruising below the surface...)

E: But the market value...

T: The third voice, running the others through each other... moment by moment, line by line, strata by strata, gesture by gesture, thetic position by thetic position...

E: Paint by number! color area by color area: strophe by color?

T: "Tone-o-strophe"?... no, no templates...

[slide: newspaper puzzles—
flying creatures (see below)]

Z: "Arithmetricks": solutions to arithmetic problems produce images when assigned points of reference in a draw-by-number format.

{A pause}

E: What is the answer to this image?

<2>

{buzzer}

T: Well... that would give us transsemiosis, too...

E: Frrreeeeze! [*pause vid.*]

[slide: page from *Howl* with crayon-by-number image of Coyote chasing Road Runner superimposed as template... his feet have just run out of ground, Road Runner off free: see "Road Runner/Wile E. Coyote Template" appendix]

{A low—medium}

T [*Z colors in area of poem corresponding to numbered area(s) on template; T reads the captured words or parts of words, reinforced with A G's annotations*]: One—peach: landscaping: "ping-pong table, resting briefly in catatonia" ... hydrotherapy, psychotherapy, occupational therapy (oil painting), and Psycho-tonic Ping Pong; N. Y. State Psychiatric Institute 7/48-3/49. Solomon: "This sounds good but the catatonia I doubt..."

E: *NYT* 10/7/55: "mattresses are growing in length and width..."

[slide: Physician w/ a bit of "distinguished grey" at the temples examines young negligeed woman beside a bare mattress—slight pressure of his hands-on stomach and bare small of bare back as she turns her head away...]

What do you suppose sold her?

T: At the Psychiatric Institute what the doc's recommending...

E: paint by number—Eisenhower does it!...

T: ping pong—take a bath! [*Z begins coloring coyote's breast*] The peach is running to plush gold narcosis...

[slide: secure, successful, fascist-looking father in smoking jacket relaxing in overstuffed gold armchair with pipe and baseball bat, day-dreaming of Books of Knowledge...]

E: This is how we hope to remanufacture them—notice he holds—does not clutch—the bat... and no fire in the bowl... Still, a fili/philo/philia-cidal look...

T: Cannastra's alcoholic death windows flung open to Brecht-Weill arias; Cassady's and friends' return journeys to west coasts w/in themselves, Lead Belly rhythm: peach: stroking the breast:

T: "next decade… fashion & nitroglycerine…

[slide: explosive, or desperate fashion, or
the inflatable man[tm?],
umbilical leading off frame fr. throat
of a man in a protective suit]

ballot for eternity…" come in come in…. quick freefall drama: Louis (Simpson): Do you have a watch? Walter (Adams): Why, Yes. Louis: let me have it. Walter: Here! Louis [*throwing watch out window*]: We don't need time, we're already in eternity." 1946.

[slide: watches arranged on a
Southwest sunburst design]

Coyote's feet race to beat the clock [*template image—spinning blur of feet*], but in cartoon desert air it's eternally… 8 to 2 8 to 2 8 to 2…

Z: And peach tongue? [*coloring in Road Runner's tongue*]

T: That's just "who."

ALL: First!

T: (What, below…)

E: Second! Yellow.

T: This section of the poem garbles history completely… "ping pong… amnesia… metrazol… insanity… Woodlawn…" no metrazol or electricity for me (Solomon).

[slide: concentric Anacin[tm] radiations from head]

E: Spiral out.

{A up slightly}

T: Bowery bums... Naomi Chaplinesque Lower East Side N.Y. 1905...

E: (see Kaddish IV) ...

T [*simultaneous*]: Harpsichord Orgone Accumulator boxes, cosmic energy monad symphonies...

[slide: architectural rendering: suburban home, "without a shadow of doubt"]

E: (see Reich's *The Function of the Orgasm*)

T [*simultaneous*]: or else large crates adapted for closets beds etc... scene of *Vanity of Duluoz* 12, VIII... also summer sublet 321 East 121 St. East Harlem 1948: theology, Blake, wooden orange crates; lease holder's tubercular chest filling with celluloid balls...

[slide: a handful of flash bulbs]

E: The color is yellow.

T: Onions, Hudson River sunsets, orange crates of theology and Blakean orgasms in wardrobe style boxes... the celluloid balls little worlds of cinema where the "bums" wear top hats... cartoon desert sand. Lemon Jell-O yellow. A young lover wooing his Woodlawn sweetheart on the cliffs of the Hudson while a vision of ping pong balls dances over the verbiage in his head...

E: (necrophilia!?)

{B over A "take me out....; film: *Revenge of the Creature*—
love talk between two scientists,
scholars of the Creature}

[slides (still fr. vid.): appliances appear
in the swelling dot
over the "i" in "Hotpoint";

Z, T: The dancing Hotpoint ball! —

{A low}

T: Take this bright yellow Stratoliner—" the first step toward modern electric living"

[slide: oven, door open
to knees of woman in red dress
coyly posed w/ potholders]

Z: I could quantum leapfrog through my affairs in that one…

T: Don't jump your orbit yet: florescent lamp over cook top, focused heat, and independent: boils, fries, warms without attention…

{A medium}

Z: dream date…

T: the "Liberator"—available in double-oven version, too…

Z: ummm… and handsome starlight gray fashion liner inside…

T: and…?

Z: automatic floodlight…!

[slide: superimposition:
baseball player in
"stadium" size *Life* oven 10/10/55]

T: (over Ebbets field—trickster Robinson stealing home!)

Z: WoW! in 3-D, too? How many seconds should we give him…?

E: Back to the story…

{A low}

T: Her alluvial grace…

Z: even living in an appliance box…

E: I don't see how to package this.

{A pause}

Z: The weird yellow-green tint on photographs of atomic explosions…

[slides: study shots
of test sites, as described page left
and below]

{A low}

T: shadows of gamma rays…

[slide]

Z: a dummy house, built on the test site, a mile from zero ground, blown apart in the first half sec…

[slides: dummy house;
viewers ogling the mushroom, in dark glasses]

E: Is this post-nuclear family living?
"the first step…"

T: Yellow Naomi, staring out Bronx window overlooking Woodlawn cemetery, circa 1953…

[slide: background—
nuclear explosion
rhyming palm tree in foreground]

Z: and don't forget the yellow of Coyote's eyes, set on "cried Madison Ave…"

T: as he looks down, realizes what's not there—gay old peach face and sand beard, doesn't see his desire for the bird is displacement of autoerotic urge… ion & nitrog… on Ma… ments of fash…

Z: in a specular economy…

T: (aut-onomy) …

Z: running after his own image between Saturday morning TV commercials—that's Madison Ave.

{A pause}

T: Unless it's his feminine other he's blundering into, out there...

Z: Let's not essentialize...

E: Well... three: follow out orange a bit.

T: Let me see...

Z: No—I don't know.

E: What? [*silence*]

{A low-medium}

T: Desert rock and sand hills, Road Runner's beak...

Z: Trickster Robinson heading for home...

[slide: *Popular Mechanics*:
multidirectional antennae—"TV reception in all directions"]

T: what Coyote looks back for, flying off the edge...

E: 10:00, *City Detective*, *Lineup*, and *The Hunter* are on...

T: "Three big sticks," "three big sticks" planted down Naomi's back during insulin and electric shock treatments as antennae... she swears...

E: 10:30 *D.A.*, 10:45, *The Visitor*...

T: hygienic cathode ray therapy: to see is to receive, to become medium...

[slides: tire mold w/its rubber product;
girl instructed, under hypnosis,
not to collect $10,000 offered her
in post-hypnotic world;
blind reading machine—a man "reads"
a newspaper w/ an electronic scanner pen
in one hand & the other on a sensor/decoder;]

"demanded sanity trials... and were left with their insanity & their hands..." (AG: rhythmic substitute for idiomatic "on their hands"): leaves their hands as free of their sanity as... Coyote's feet? —each segment of the incomplete circle pushes toward transformation/self-transgression, the probability of which plummets when cartoon logic sets back in.... vectors of futile motion... so many feet, suddenly, all useless... But for the moment, she's left spinning in liminal purple haze between zero ground of scientific logic and deterritorializing lines of flight...

E: Super Fleetway, Air Ride, and the Royal 8 = infinity"

[slide: array of tires
in abstract *Life* ad space (5/4/55)]

{A low}

Z: except that "demanded sanity trials" is really brown, not orange...

E: 11:00 *Gangbusters*.

T: Let the hands do as the feet...

Z: (Tune in?)

{A pause}

E: "Fissionable materials within the meaning of the present statute shall include uranium-enriched isotopes U-235, U-233, plutonium 239 and alloys and compounds of the foregoing materials and such other materials as the board shall from time to time determine."

T: The daisy chains we weave glow orange...

[slides: a "parade" of radios,
helter-skelter;
3 in 1 combo. —cosmetic case,
radio, overnighter...
a face making itself up in the pop-up mirror]

E: Four.

T: there is no color four…

E: Five!

{A low-medium}

T [*Z & T color*]: Brown. The groundwork, principal bedrock and sediment…

Z: "who in humorless protest… concr… heads… dadaism… hypnotism… and… and… presented themselves… suicide… &…"

[slide: canned food,
pictorial/editorial labels—" crop values"]

T: We keep coming back to—the container, as paradigm: what does the container contain? The package an image and the image a contents (and an imaging of a content made in faith of the image). A taste of color. Consumer as co-creator, easy as a twist of the wrist… Pream it.

Z: "Explosion Angles Baffle Experts" (*SFC*, 10/1/55)

E: Give me more data points!

T: In the rapidity of separations, positional shifts, the old-world view hangs on, for perhaps…

[slide: cartoon of a child w/
coconut cakes as eyes, one slice missing
to mark the pupils—a frazzle of the "actual"
cake brushes his cheeks in the margins]

Z: I… I… I can't.

E: Pream it!

{A pause}

T: passes over into the moment of its annihilation for a liminal fraction of a moment suspended—not even the length of a phoneme, a few frames of vision… in that moment s/he has all and nothing at all, is neither here nor there—the condition of Coyote in the world… let's trace it: (when we finish, you'll see, we'll have filled in much of the ground, and the body that will bring Coyote to ground—completely colored—but none of the infinity "8" or the tail wing and breast of Road Runner, whom we must leave unfinished, suspended...) the poem, at once hurtling us to ground while incessantly yaketychanting through the *mise en abime* of material culture... let's face it...

[slide: little woman
showing off guts of a TV
fr. rear—her techno-mate, much
bulkier than she is]

Z: "The question is, what blew up?"

[slide: Hypercolorized
TV dinner—the corn is pink
& the yellows "really" yellow]

T: We're free to drift through the silver linings of the image tube... no effort at all to serve you... now, remember... what is it you're eating?

{B: Jell-O theme}
{A medium—high}

[*Z & T quickly color in the legs of Coyote and feet of Road Runner*]

[slides: girls in pink
making pink Jell-O]

{A pause}

T: Isn't pink yummy?

E: This poem is in the can, triangulated in aluminum... colorize it! [*computer manipulation of templated poem*] Wheel it out! Go go go!...

* * *

{B: *Rocketmen* theme music}

T: "Coyote's *Howl*" [*shouted over music. T holsters a Viewmaster*[tm]*: Rocketman suiting up, adjusting controls. Test run.*]

[slides: uniforms "fit for action"—

"stretch, stoop, squat, stand!...
cut to curve & move with your body!";
blank]

{B: music stops abruptly}

T: Wait!... it's breakfast time... [*unstraps Viewmaster*] Hey, here's an interesting game! [*Z & T read from large flat cards representing cereal boxes*]

Z: Mine has quotes from literature.

T: Q: What happened or was *about* to happen on these dates (match right with left column) ... Brooklyn, NY: 10/4/55, 3:42 pm... In approximately one minute (providing J. W. Milam's pickup starts promptly and doesn't die) 14-year-old Emmett Till will be kidnapped...

Z: 4/56. "Dear Louis: The Reading was pretty great..."

T: There was a bullet hole in his head, which had been bashed in.... No, that's got to be...

Z: "We had travelling photographers who appeared on the scene from Vancouver to photograph it..."

T: 37-23-34... MM's measurements in 1951?

Z: "A couple of amateur electronics experts appeared..."

T: Washington, DC, 5/31/55: Chief Justice Warren orders the integration of public schools with "all deliberate speed..."

Z: "with tape machines to record..."

T: 37-24-35: ummm... I'll say MM's measurements in '54...

Z: "request from State College for a complete recording for the night..."

T: Rosa Parks is waiting for a Montgomery bus; In a few minutes—exactly when depends on whether or not the buses are running on schedule—the Civil Rights Movement will be born... well, has to be...

Montgomery, AL, Thursday, rush hour, 12/1/55...

Z: more requests for copies of the recordings, ...

T: 36 1/2-23-34... let's say, MM's measurements 1952...

E: This is non-(con)sequential.

Z: "even finally organizaions [sic] of bop musicians who want to write music..."

T: In one minute, the Dodgers will win the world series .... *that's* Brooklyn, 10/4/55, 3:42 pm... 38-23-36...

Z: "and give big west coast travelling tours of *Howl*..."

T: 38-23-36! MM's all new and biggest body 1955! ... Buffalo, NY: New Year's Eve, 11:59 pm, 10, 045 BC?... got to be birth of Niagara Falls, comparing the geologic history of earth to a 12-month calendar year...

Z: as a sort of Jazz Mass....

T: Money, MS: Saturday morning, 8/27/55, 1:59 am... that's Till... The body was so badly mangled... it was identified primarily from Emmett's ring... Sunday, 7/17/55, Anaheim, CA: the television opening of Disneyland.

[*Z has become interested in T's box, so T takes a look at Z's*]

T: (typos left unemended to mark speed of writing.)

Z: In approximately one minute, if the reading begins on time, the Beat Generation will be born... well, that leaves Friday, 10/7/55, 7:59 pm.... [*looking up at the blank squared sun projected on the wall*] T?...

* * *

{B: Superman theme, fade under}

E: "Coyote's *Howl*" [*T on runway*]

Z [*Z & T communicate via walkie-talkie*]: This is a test.

T: This is not a test.

Z: Check stator and impeller.

{B: weird Rocketman takeoff music}

[slide: "Go power"—
Cheerios kid running bases]

E: "a ring-shaped vortex shock wave"

[slide: Rocketman taking off
in a sugar-hyped blur]

T [*pops a few Cheerios, simulates take off; once "airborne"*]: "No kidding. You have no idea what a storm of [aerostatic] lunatic-fringe activity I've stirred up."

{A low-medium}

E:

ON HIS HAUNCHES, WHITE GRIN,
LONG TONGUE PANTING, HE WATCHES:

[slide: Rocketman, airborne,
looking about]:

[*T circulating among props*]

T: One—Code Peach. Citing: ping pong table, resting briefly in catatonia…

[slide: cartoon Cheerios
arc through space]

Z: Forward thrust… strophe crossing…

T: Journeying… their… German… on broken… window… trucks

Z [*simultaneous w/ above*]: Steady…easy glide…

T: happened… intelligent editors… fashion & nitroglycerine… Avenue amid… Avenue… cried… gave up… on Madison… regiments of fashion

ion & nitrog… on Ma… ments of fash…

sa oug th!

Z: Planet gear to sun gear—cite it!

T [*looking in Viewmaster*]: old … suits… regim…";
xt dec… allot for eternit…!

E: "Fallen friend in reflective suit shines"

Z: "Who"

T: Cried Madison Avenue!

Z: Yellow two! —Powerflite!

[slide: orbiting Jell-O spiral]

T: Ohhh!… and who… therapy ping pong and amnesia protest overturned only one symbolic concrete void of insulin hea dadais hyp ism Metrazol electricity d d d th uic presented elves sanity…

Z: Woo! [*phew!*] … command responsive power!

E: "Smoother going down"

[slide: Calvert[tm], being poured
over the rocks, as the copy
(E, above) arcs over the glass]

T: Woooo…dla… iers"

Z: Spiral out!… watch that astral spaghetti of intersections…

[slide: plate of astral spaghetti
with sauce (recut)]

T: digested crab at muddy Bowery bottom… Chaplinesque pushcarts full of onions and bad… laurel; crowned with oblivion… er the bridge, and rose up to build… cliff-banks of Hudson Vanity… crowned with flame under tubercular theology

E:

FUR THE COLOR OF MUD, THE SMOOTH LOPER
CRAPULOUS OLD MAN, A DRIFTER,
PRAISES! OF COYOTE THE NASTY…

[*see "The Poems" appendix*]

Z: Orange Three! Reverse planet gear…

[slide: auto transmission diagram]

T: wh… who sa? who southern Pacific hypnotic daisy chain or grave…
[*pick up speed*]
and who… therapy ping pong &… hyd… ed… hydrotherapy… demanding… themselves… insanity

Z: Map it. Four…

[slide: *Popular Mechanics*: woman blowing
a strange homemade instrument]

T: Five. Brown. Groundwork bedrock sediment: "who in humorless protest… concrete… head…ism… ism… d… and… d th… suicide… &… presented themselves on… demand…"

daisychain… who demanded sanity [radio not ant. imp.] … who threw potato salad at granite steps of the mad… instantaneous lobotomy… trials trials!

Z: Retro Blast!

T: [*heading back in*] en inst

{A pause}

[slide: airborne glasses
of Hamm's beer, gliding over
an island-dotted lake to a
safe landing in a well-manicured hand]

E
COYOTE: SHOT FROM THE CAR, TWO EARS,
A TAIL, BRING BOUNTY.

[slide: "Power Protein"
nuclear spiral above a bowl
of Cheerios]

Z: G-spin Brown!

{A low—high}

leg One:

[slides: baseball action shots,
players in mid-air—some shots repeated,
torqued in different directions, free space tumble]

T [*working back up runway*]: Journeying vision… you… other's hot-rod… blast of colossal finished whine-glasses?

Z: leg Two:

T: Journeying… I… back… and others… finally went… Denver… or you"?

Z: leg Three:

T: Journeying… out… who…

E: ('s on first)

T: heroes praying… second…

Z: (What?)

T: for impossible blues… each other's

Z: Leg Four:

T: Journeying… find… Denver loaned for cathedrals… hair in jail… hearts who sang… a habit or rocky… black locomotive

Z: Leg Five:

T: past journeying… incarnation hours… died in… seventy-two… eternity jazz highways?

Z: Leg Six:
T: Chinatown… bridge… in despair fell… all over the… European… moans… of the past journeying…

Z: Entropic stretch…

[slide: last pitch world series
10/4/55, 3:41 pm?]

T: their ears… 1930s German… danced on… subway window and firetrucks and walked away…

E: "Free beers!"

Z: Image fix

E: "teenagers snake-dancing in streets"

[slide: young boy gazes amazed
into unlikely Viewmaster]

T: or were… nitroglycerine shrieks / amid blasts… of leaden… open / open antique… vegetable… alarm clocks…

E: "12 false alarm fires"

Z: Slip of the signified away from the signifier? nothing but an afterimage to hold to… the ears getting it:

E: "radios, factory whistles, church bells, horns,
Yankee effigies hung from lamp posts..."

[slide: the catch]

T: Avenue... up... eternity... egg... unsuccessfully... growing...

[slide: magnified cell cluster]

{A low}

E: "Artificial Life, 3 Days Old"

T: Dancing Butterfly, Two-stage Chrysanthemum, Artificial Satellite...
Z: Page? [*Z retrieves and sets up 4th of July skyrocket*] or next script...

[slide: painting (below), tilted 160°]

{A pause}

E: Question: What is *Satellite* doing in deep space?

T: The difficulty of locating Rauschenberg's canvases—spatially or as discourse constructs. He collages with everyday objects—

{B rock riff}

newspaper comic strips... have less three dimensional presence than ...impasto paint embedding... lace doilies... slight three... dimensionality... flatten on canvas... scraps of wallpaper printed abstract floral... painted pheasant in dead strut across... upper stretcher strip... rustic found environment... dead D the pheasant three dead... space out of which it can now... temporal atemporal temporal atemporal... space out of which it can now... the pheasant the pheasant 3 dead... now no longer be said to be...

{B stop}

E: Is this your answer?

T: framed—3 dead D. The pheasant.

[*T moves back into position for power run lift off*]

Z: Peach orange yellow brown...

T: There's got to be a little something for everybody…

E: A hue family?

{A low—medium—low}

T: The colors of earth in the body of Coyote, the solar spiral [*point to Road Runner*] one body of desire… "past journeying"—the transcendent…

Z: elusive…that's 5…

T: phallus.

E: Keep it up!
T: and Coyote's many no-feet (whose else?), the lost footing—follow brown—looking back—his heart leapt… a dusty rose, wishing on a blue tale…

Z: that's 7, and 2—"peach"—away from the legs, bodies, 5—both for the moment suspended—

T: When you put two tricksters together, Coyote always takes the dive—through herself…

[slide: *Life* 10/17/55—
Eureka Roto-Matic™ vac. w/ Roto-Dolly]

Z: His rotor's in the wrong place…
"It beats, it sweeps," it sucks. Fun with vacuums…

E: "So easy…you can sing 'goodbye forever'…"

{A pause}
{B: Rock riff}

[slide: *Life* 5/2/55, 1/24/55—
vacuum vision—woman vacuuming,
manic smile, a bare rug
dissolving into a blank horizon]

[*T puts on pajamas, tux tails, and Hula Hoop capsule; holsters a long-draw hand-held Viewmaster proctor*]

Z: so *you're*...

{B stop}

T: Rock it, man... I guess you had to know, sooner or later... but I'm more than an estranged mind in a bullet shaped helmet chasing after my decimator to keep it from falling into the wrong hands... [*tossing out a diminutive American flag on a stick, prepares for take-off*]

Z [*lights skyrocket*]: Power stage 12! Dynaflow! lift off! [*fizzle*]

{A low}

E: "Deep in the Dynaflow unit, little propeller-like blades bite into swirling oil..."

[slides: var. artifacts of 50s *Life*
in orbit, free tumbling...
including a Royal pink typewriter!]

Z: Prepare for transmission!

E: (he's already long gone...)

T: Watch barreled groaning phonograph leap sang... [*lift off*]

T: jumped who... [*orbiting*] drunken fairies burned the tanked-up advertising taxicabs... [*spin into higher orbit*]

[slide: transmission diagram
turned on end]

Z, E: Transmission!

{B: Abbot & Costello}

T [*over walkie talkie*]: who... who... who... who... [*orbiting, drawing projector from holster, flashing Road Runner cartoon images randomly, over other images*]

[slide: boy, mid-air leap
w/ spoonful of Jell-O]

Z: He's out among the images... [*singing into talkie*] "take me out to the..." with you!

[*projectors on automatic function, flashing random images—all that didn't get used*]

E: "Like nothing you ever felt before in commanding an earth-bound vehicle..."

T: The planets have been tossed, but where's the juggler?

E: Don't take your eyes off'em!

T [*noting the uncolored clouds of the template*]: From the "floor of Harlem" through the purple sky of Coyote... "crates of theology... light and breasts... yellow morning..." of the black on white signifying clouds. Just look up, Coyote, while there's still a thought...

Z [*caught in the line of random cartoon image fire*]: T, guess who I am...

T: "...don't care if I ever..."

Z: 8,000 mph spinner and takes all year to get home...

E: I'm not sure what game we're playing.

Z: fastest slow ball ever...

[slide: MOUSE in orbit—labeled]

T [*over walkie talkie, spelling out*]: It's M O U S...!

E: (Minimum Orbital Unmanned Satellite of Earth)

Z: I'd say these trips are affecting you, but you're always so spacey... You moon rider... my Happy Lamp™... you solar eyes... my Cloud Dragon™... honey honey...

T [*mumbling nonsense to Mickey Mouse Club melody*]: stumble bomb... leaping color... instant sex... Screaming Demon™... illusion roll on... strato-streak... black diamond... attach-o-matic... slip-a-rung... Whistling Cicada™...

[slide: *Life* 10/3/55—
life insurance—
young family climbing a ladder]

E: Keep those balls up!

T:

"FUCK YOU," SANG COYOTE
AND RAN.

[*Mouse Club rhythm—M O U S... M O U S...*] My dri ving mem ber my driv en mem ber! who who who who

[slide: wall: hold: Robinson
coming in]

Z: Can't read you... home home home home... come on in now: look what I've got for you! {A slow fade}

[slides: wall: spaghetti, 10/17/55!
w/ bright red sauce!
ground beef in bread slices w/melted cheese;
cartoon worker swinging in fr. an I beam for
his lunch, or for Ava (see below);
chili dogs w/ Dinty Moore™.
Easel: elevated cake;
Jell-O swirl 1/24/55;
Ava Gardner in profile;
silverware wedding—
a monolithic place setting dangles
above a stairway leading into space—
the knife cutting down between the bride & groom
the fork aiming at the bride's head—
as the diminutive couple prepare to ascend...]

T: "P.S.: You are my Shelley on earth..."

E [*aside*]: Gregory Corso, from Venice, to Ginsberg, in another space, February 1958.

Z: "The more you'll eat the higher you'll jump..."

T [*read as poem*]: Sweet Beats (surplus, some damage)

visions (heads smashed in)

Glucose syrup, sugar water, gelatin,
cornstarch and artificial flavor

—of beatitudes—

Red #3, Red #40, F D &

{B: five rings}

C Yellow # 5... [*after 5th ring*] Blue #1...

{A off}

{B Jell-O theme, merging w/ rings}

Z [*answering*]: T, it's for you!

T [*as if answering*]:

Beatrice!

***

E

Coming next: Feature 3: *Tarzan the Ape Man*
plus
King of the Rocket Men, Ch. V: "The Dive"

[slide: wall: Rocket Man
displaces Robinson, in powerless free fall;
other images fade]

Z: Road Runner, man, you may be fast, but nothing beats this... poem.

***

[slide: wall: fade Rocket Man.
Easel: Beat group shot
outside City Lights bookshop—

sun, shaded display window,
parking meters... as below]

E: Arms around shoulders, waists... on his left, the artist, who sketched the lovers nude on a theater wall, and the Producer, resting his arm on time and money; on his right, two who rode it out... Bob, Neal, Allen, Robert, Larry: Spring, 1956. We're *all* in... The circle's open...

[slide: fade Easel.
Final wall slide: *Life* 10/10/55—
inside back cover—
Mr. I. W. Walker
(Kentucky Straight Bourbon)
tipping his hat.
Fade...]

T [*tipping*]: "... it's always / a pleasure." [*countdown*] 10? 9—down to black
[video: pause or snow]

***

E: You should see the following video now: the design team has reproduced itself as a talk show, with some of the following monologue [*canned laughter on B tape*].

T [*as MC, w/mic*]: Ever notice how planes seem to be getting smaller, seats a little cheaper—like airborne VWs... [*laugh*] Hey! I'm the last clown on board! [*more laugh*] (I only ride peanut airlines you understand...) Flight attendant, I can't find my seat. Yes, we meant to add those rows, but... [*laugh*] Never mind the carry ons: "There's a teeny space up there..." Do you get service up there? [*laugh*]. First time in my life I wished I was my underwear... [*laughter and applause*]

Speaking of getting high—does that explain it? —Ever notice how slow elevators can be... I was on one yesterday that was so slow I changed my life on the way up... [*laugh*] yea... relived it on the way down... but that's another story... I'd better get off here. "Please be aware that your closest exit may be behind you." [*mild laugh*]

Well, we've got a great show tonight—a talk show, we're gonna talk about... well our first guests are product designers; they're gonna tell us how we got where we are today, or how we can remake what we are, or how we're not what we are—I don't know...

E: 3rd! {B: canned laughter quick fade to silence}

[slide: wall: still fr.
Seven Year Itch—movie marquis
"Creature from the Black Lagoon,"
fade to black]

{B: "The Great Pretender"}

T [*reading from notebook as "Pretender" plays, T provides narrative context for the still; the scene described also occurs, in extreme slow motion, toward end of compilation video (see introductory comments)*]: Freeze!... From *The Seven Year Itch*. On the marquis, life-size stand up of the Creature; pan down to... MM and Ewell, walking away. Cut: two CUs of MM, as she stands over subway grate. 1. Profile. Intense physical pleasure. The "A" line has just passed, at great rackety careless speed, through the erogenous zones... Bernoulli's principle. 2. Looking at—through—the camera into space—vague vast post-orgasmic seductive contentment... desire propelled, projected, reenacted (by the viewer) at the moment of its just having been...

Z: MM as desiring machine...

E: "Endsville." *Time*, 12 December, 959.

Appendices

Howling Hollywood: Road Runner/ Wile E. Coyote Template

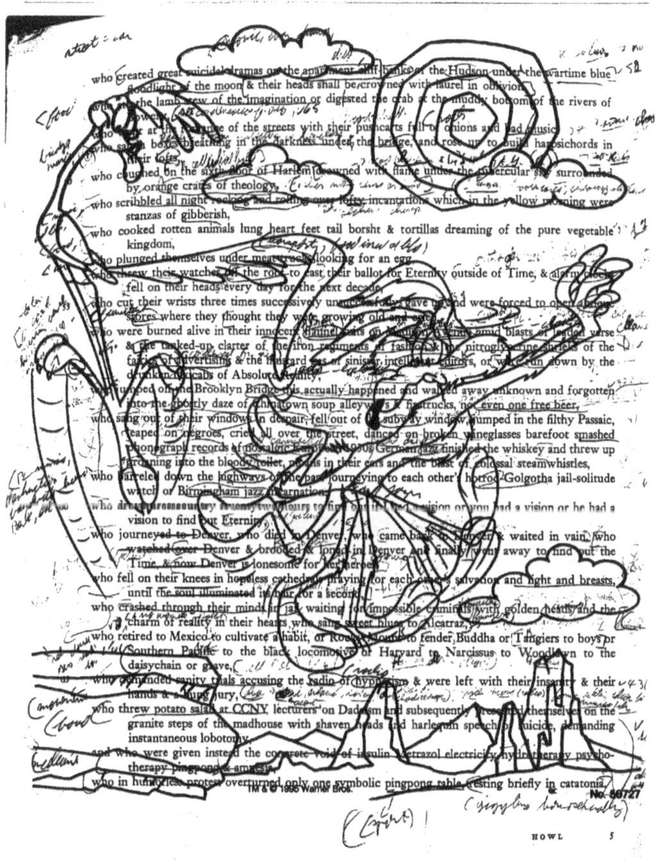

Fig. 8: numbered Wil e Coyote interpretive template/exegetical aid as applied to a page from *Howl* bearing my illegible annotations. c. 1995 by Warner Bros.; c. 1995, New York: Harper Perennial; c. 1995 by author. Used by permission, used by permission, used by author, permissively.

1 = Peach 2 = Yellow 3 = Orange 4 = Red 5 = Brown
6 = Green 7 = Blue 8 = Purple 9 = Black

The Poems

from "'Plus Ca Change...'" (Philip Whalen)

What are you doing?

. . . . .

Tell me what we're going to do.

That's what I'm coldly calculating.

You had better say "plotting" or "scheming"
You never could calculate without a machine.

. . . . .

(SILENCE)

Listen. Whatever we do from here on out
Let's for God's sake not look at each other
Keep our eyes shut and the lights turned off—
We won't mind touching if we don't have to see.

I'll ignore those preposterous feathers.

Say what you please, we brought it all on ourselves...

Who'd recognize us now?

We'll just pretend we're used to it.
(Watch out with that goddamned tail)
Pull the shades down. Turn off the lights.
Shut your eyes.

(SILENCE)

There is no satisfactory explanation.
You can talk until you're blue

Just how much bluer can I get?

. . . . .

Will you listen, please? I'm trying to make
A rational suggestion. Do you mind?

"For the Death of 100 Whales" (Michael McClure)

"...Killer whales...Savage sea cannibals up to 30 feet long with teeth like bayonets...one was caught with 14 seals and 13 porpoises in its belly... often tear at boats and nets... destroyed thousands of dollars' worth of fishing tackle... Icelandic government appealed to the U.S., which has thousands of men stationed at a lonely NATO airbase on the subarctic island. Seventy-nine bored G.I.'s responded with enthusiasm. Armed with rifles and machine guns one posse of Americans climbed into four small boats and in one morning wiped out a pack of 100 Killers......First the killers were rounded up into tight formation with concentrated machine gun fire, then moved out again one by one, for the final blast which would kill them...as one was wounded, the others would set upon it and tear it to pieces with their jagged teeth..."

Time,
April 1954

Hung midsea
Like a boat mid-air
The Liners boiled their pastures:
The Liners of flesh,
The Arctic steamers.

Brains the size of a football.
Mouths the size of a door.

The sleek wolves
Mowers and reapers of sea kine.
THE GIANT TADPOLES
(Meat their algae)
Leapt
Like sheep or children.
Shot from the sea's bore.
Turned and twisted

(Goya!!)
Flung blood and sperm.
Incense.
Gnashed at their tails and
brothers,
Cursed Christ of mammals,
Snapped at the sun,
Ran for the sea's floor.

Goya! Goya!
Oh Lawrence,
No angels dance those bridges.
OH GUN! OH BOW!
There are no churches in the
waves,
No holiness,
No passages or crossings
From the beasts' wet shore.

from "A Berry Feast" (Gary Snyder)

1
Fur the color of mud, the smooth loper
Crapulous old man, a drifter,
Praises! of Coyote the Nasty, the fat
Puppy that abused himself, the ugly gambler,
Bringer of goodies.

In bearshit find it in August,
Neat pile on the fragrant trail, in late
August...
Bear has been eating the berries.

. . . . .

"Where I shoot my arrows
"There is the sunflower's shade

—song of the rattlesnake
coiled in the boulder's groin
"K'ak, k'ak, k'ak!
sang Coyote. Mating with
humankind—

The Chainsaw falls for boards of pine,
Suburban bedrooms, block on block
Will waver with this grain and knot,
The maddening shapes will start and fade
Each morning when commuters wake—
Joined boards hung on frames,
a box to catch the biped in.

. . . . .

2
Three, down, through windows
Dawn leaping cats, all barred brown, grey
Whiskers aflame
bits of mouse on the tongue

. . . . .

Creeks wash clean where trout hide
We chew the black plug
Sleep on needles through long afternoons
"you shall be owl
"you shall be sparrow
"you will grow thick and green, people
"will eat you, you berries!
Coyote: shot from the car, two ears,
A tail, bring bounty.

Clanks of tread
oxen of Shang
moving the measured road

Bronze bells at the throat

...the bright Oxen
Chanting...

        Fat-snout Caterpillar, tread toppling forward
Leaf on leaf, roots in gold volcanic dirt.

When
Snow melts back
        from the trees

.....

Green shoots of huckleberry
Breaking through snow.

3

. . . . .

"You can't be killers all your life
"The people are coming—
        —and when Magpie
Revived him, limp rag of fur in the river
drowned and drifting, fish-food in the shallows,
"Fuck you!" sang Coyote
                and ran.

. . . . .

                "Stopped in the night
                "Ate hot pancakes in a bright room
                "Drank coffee, read the paper
                "In a strange town, drove on,
                        singing, as the drunkard swerved the car
Wake from your dreams, bright ladies!
"Tighten your legs, squeeze demons from
        the crotch with rigid thighs
"Young red-eyed men will come
"With limp erections, snuffling cries
"To dry your stiffening bodies in the sun!

Woke at the beach....
...One naked man
Frying his horsemeat on a stone.

4
Coyote yaps, a knife!
Sunrise on yellow rocks.
People gone, death no disaster,
Clear sun in the scrubbed sky
                    empty and bright
Lizards scurry from darkness
We lizards sun on yellow rocks.

          See, from the foothills
          Shred of river glinting, trailing,
          To flatlands, the city:
                    glare of haze in the valley horizon
          Sun caught on glass gleams and goes.
          From cool springs under cedar
          On his haunches, white grin,
                    long tongue panting, he watches:

Dead city in dry summer,
Where berries grow.

McClure Makeover: "For the Death of 100 Whales" (as re(con)figured by the Product Design Team...)

"...Killer whales...Savage sea cannibals up to 30 feet long with teeth like bayonets... one was caught with 14 seals and 13 porpoises in its belly... often tear at boats and nets... destroyed thousands of dollars' worth of fishing tackle... Icelandic government appealed to the U.S., which has thousands of men stationed at a lonely NATO airbase on the subarctic island. Seventy-nine bored G.I.'s responded with enthusiasm. Armed with rifles and) machine guns one posse of Americans climbed into four small boats and in one morning wiped out a pack of 100 Killers...

...First the killers were rounded up into tight formation with concentrated machine gun fire,

then moved out again one by one, for the final blast which would kill them...as one was wounded, the others would set upon it and tear it to pieces with their jagged teeth..."

Hung midsea
like a boat mid-air
The Liners boiled their pastures:
Big New Bomber Dies A Sacrificial Death
Engineers were *The Liners of flesh*, hard
at work tearing *The Arctic steamers.*
one of their B 52s to pieces...

massive front end, twin tower headlights that say
stop *Brains the size of a football* with great authority
Mouths the size of a door. looks big feels big acts big

taut-muscled, forward thrusting *the sleek wolves*
trigger torque *Mowers and reapers of sea kine*
THE GIANT TADPOLES obey your commands
in an instant *(meat their algae)*
Leapt in the administration

the momentum of U.S. life
carried on without a jar.

Like sheep or children
Shot from the sea's bore

Yacht calls for help

Turned and twisted
(Goya!!)
flung blood and sperm.
becalmed 150 mi. southwest

San Francisco. *Incense.* Truce:

600-man battalion, 2 medium tanks
Gnashed at their tails and brothers,
four half-tracks mounted with 50-m. machine

guns took over the task of enforcing law and
order in this strike-torn *Cursed Christ of mammals,*
steel-helmeted troops, armed with rifles, *Snapped at sun*
in Indiana. Salable hogs 11,000 head *Ran for the sea's floor.*
It is not merely a capitalist myth... the democratic values which

Goya! Goya!
Oh Lawrence, Viscose
Corporation expects sales
to total $225,000,000 this year
the securities and exchange commission
No angels dance those bridges. Barrows and
guts, sows and 280-pound butchers *OH GUN! OH BOW!*
Boy, 13 years old, saw an arm reach through a broken
kitchen window. He grabbed his bow and shot an arrow into the
arm. *There are no churches in the waves,*
Henry Ford Claims Biggest Profit Year

No Holiness
wandered into white house
by mistake with a loaded gun,
was fined $25 The satellite, which
government scientists believe will be
about the size of a basketball, will definitely
contain data reporting instruments *No passages or crossing*
4 types of Beats Noticed in Heart *From the beast's wet shore.*
Women prefer white soap to gray 12 to 1 rigid price supports for
agriculture is like spinning the wheels of an automobile stuck in
mud

*Sources for the reconstruction include *Life* (1/4, 10/3/55), *New York Times* (10/2, 10/7/55), *San Francisco Chronicle* (9/30, 10/7/55).

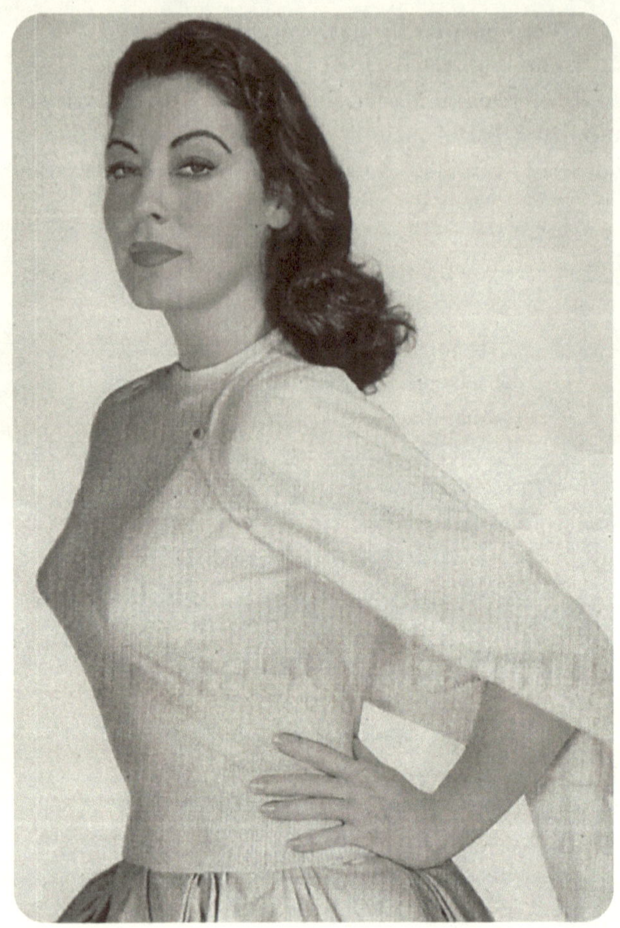

Fig. 9: Potential reconfiguration template for McClure Makeover.

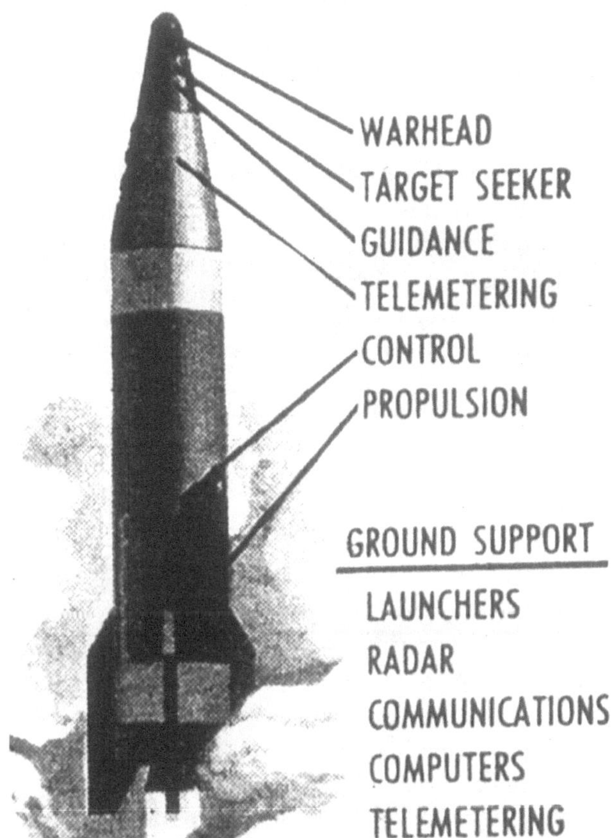

Fig. 10: Potential reconfiguration template for McClure Makeover.

Works Cited

Ginsberg, Allen. *Howl*: Original draft Facsimile, Transcript & Variant Versions, Fully Annotated by Author, with Contemporaneous correspondence, Account of First Public Reading, Legal Skirmishes, Precursor Texts & Bibliography. Ed. Barry Miles. New York: Harper Perennial, 1995.

Deleuze, Gilles and Felix Guattari. *A Thousand Plateaus*. Minneapolis: University of Minnesota Press, 1987.

Lahmon, W.T. Jr. *Deliberate Speed: The Origins of a Cultural Style in the American 1950s*. Washington: Smithsonian Institution Press, 1990.

Looney Tunes Crayon by Number. No. 50727. Toledo, Ohio: Craft House Corp.

McClure, Michael. *Scratching the Beat Surface: Essays on New Vision from Blake to Kerouac*. New York: Penguin, 1982.

Parkinson, Thomas, ed. *A Casebook on the Beat*. New York: Thomas A. Crowell, 1961.

McClure, Michael. "For the Death of 100 Whales." *Hymns to St. Geryon, and Other Poems*. San Francisco, Auerhahn Press, 1959.

Snyder, Gary. "A Berry Feast." The Back Country. New York: New Directions, 1968.

Virilio, Paul. *The Aesthetics of Disappearance*. New York: Semiotext(e), 1991.

Whalen, Philip. ""'Plus, Ca Change...'" *Collected Poems of Philip Whalen*. Middletown, Conn.: Wesleyan University Press, 2007.

*Holographic material courtesy the Columbia University Library, New York.

Select Bibliography (listed in introductory note)

Boddy, William. *Fifties Television: The Industry and Its Critics*. Urbana: University of Illinois Press, 1990.

Frank, Robert. *The Americans*. 4th ed. Washington, D.C.: SCALO, 2000 [originally published as Les Americains. Paris: R. Delpine, 1958].

Ginsberg, Allen. *Snapshot Poetics*. San Francisco: Chronicle Books, 1993.

Halbersrtam, David. *The Fifties*. New York: Fawcett Columbine, 1993.

McDarragh, Fred and Timothy McDarragh. *Kerouac and Friends: A Beat Generation Album*. New York: Thunder's Mouth Press, 2002.

Marling, Karal Ann. *As Seen on TV: The Visual Culture of Everyday Life in the 1950s*. Cambridge: Harvard University Press, 1994.

Natsoulas, et al, eds. *Lyrical Vision: The Six Gallery, 1954-1957*. Davis, CA: Natsoulas Novelozo Gallery, 1989.

Phillips, Lisa, et al. *Beat Culture and the New America, 1950-1965*. New York: Whitney Museum of American Art, 1996.

Solnit, Rebecca. *Secret Exhibition: Six California Artists of the Cold War Era*. San Francisco: City Lights, 1990.

Wilentz, Elias and Frank McDarragh. *The Beat Scene*. New York: Corinth Books, 1960.

Select Bibliography (Other Sources)

Allen Ginsberg Reads Howl and Other Poems. Compact CD Set. Liner notes by Anne Waldman and Allen Ginsberg. Santa Monica: Rhino Records, 1998 [remastering and reissue of Allen Ginsberg Reads Howl and Other Poems, Fantasy Records, 1959].

The Beat Generation. Compact CD Set. James Austin, Producer. Santa Monica: Rhino Records, 1992.

Charters, Ann, ed. *The Portable Beat Reader*. New York: Penguin, 1992.

Cook. Bruce. *The Beat Generation*. New York: Charles Scribner's Sons, 1971.

Davidson, Michael. *The San Francisco Renaissance: Poetics and Community at Mid-Century*. New York: Cambridge University Press, 1989.

Johnson, Ronna C., Nancy M. Grace and Ann Charters, eds. *Girls Who Wore Black: Women Writing the Beat Generation*. New Brunswick, NJ: Rutgers University Press, 2002.

Kinght, Arthur and Kit, eds. *Kerouac and the Beats: A Primary Sourcebook*. Foreword by John Tytell. New York: Paragon House, 1988.

Miles, Barry. *Ginsberg: A Biography*. New York: Harper Perennial, 1989.

New York Times Book Review: "Beat Movement Concludes." 13 February, 1972

Panish, Jon. *The Color of Jazz: Race and Representation in Postwar American Culture*. Jackson, MS: University Press of Mississippi, 1997.

Perloff, Marjorie. *Radical Artifice: Writing Poetry in the Age of Media*. Chicago: University of Chicago Press, 1991.

Raskin, Jonah. *American Scream: Allen Ginsberg's Howl and the Making of the Beat Generation*. Berkeley: University of California Press, 2004.

Sanders, Ed. *Tales of Beatnik Glory: Volumes I and II*. New York: Citadel Underground, 1990.

Skerl, Jennie, ed. *Reconstructing the Beats*. New York: Palgrave, 2004.

Sterritt, David. *Mad to Be Saved: The Beats, the'50s, and Film*. Carbondale: Southern Illinois University Press, 1998.

—. *Screening the Beats: Media Culture and the Beat Sensibility*. Carbondale: Southern Illinois University Press, 2004.

Timm, Robert C. "Unleashing Language: The Post-Structuralist Poetics of Gregory Corso and The Beats." *Kerouac Connection*, 27 (1995 Winter): 34-41.

Watson, Steven. *The Birth of the Beat Generation: Visionaries, Rebels, Hipsters, 1944-1960*. New York: Pantheon, 1995.

Womack, Steven. "Popular Media Representations of Beat Culture; or, Jack Kerouac Meets Maynard G. Krebs." *Studies in Popular Culture* 24.3 (April 2002):" 17-24.

Excess Material / Outtakes / Notes

(re)sourcing and continuation of "Sweet Beats" found poem:

Lyric ingredients (coagulated in transit)

Sugar, cocoa butter, milk chocolate, lecithin—an emulsifier, salt, dark sweet chocolate, partially hydrogenated soybean and cottonseed oils, cocoa processed with alkali, fructose, dried egg, hydrolyzed soy protein, whey, antioxidants, brazil nuts; almonds, cashews, walnuts…

glycerin monostearate, sodium hexametaphosphate, propyl gallate (antioxidant), sodium lauryl sulfate, a whipping aid (may also contain nuts) …

+ broken hearts

(my? al, be m??e, ?rue love)

reduced, priced as marked

cinnamon imperial (expired dates)

shimmering heart confetti, shredded metallic heart filler: 50 cents off

becomes:

Sweet Beats

(surplus, some damage)

visions (heads smashed in)

Glucose syrup, sugar water, gelatin,
cornstarch and artificial flavor

—of beatitudes—

Red #3, Red #40, F D &
C Yellow # 5, #6,

and (of course) Blue #1…

Beatrice!

"*tri-ce*"

(that trace)

"Be Mine."

Happy

after hearts.

***

phrases:

it needs more theory / it needs more color / I don't like the styling (i.e., the way something's going. Var.: your problem is, you got no style) / I've got to change (i.e., an article of clothing) / I don't have the right one (template) / Beatify it! / Daddyo™ it! (originally a font style) / who's Beatnik Bob? (var.: whose Beatnik Bob) / customer survey! / you're killing me! / keep those balls up! / I can't get the figures right... we need Eniac, Uniac, etc. / fusion piano / this is not a test / this is a test / play here / that's a straight six (not much Go power) / that's a V8, or, a super 8, or super V (it moves) ...

* * *

fireworks:

black cat, sky buster, desert storm, proud glory, galaxy fiesta, mega magic, big shot, big thunder, golden waves, star burst, Texas giant, spirit of America, jumbo carnival, dancing butterfly, killer bee, Phoenix, tall howl, tiger roaring fountain, autumn drizzle, screaming demon, garden in spring, flying dragon and jumping tiger, fairy with flower, two stage chrysanthemum, blue stars with reports, jumping wheel, kaleidoscope, cloud dragon, big snow, green bamboo, moon festival, victory celebration, happy lamp, climbing panda, hen laying egg, artificial satellite, star cruiser, black diamond, music man, whistling cicada, frightened bird...

* * *

lines/bits:

Blank models. Actors wrapped in paper sheets ("cocoons"). We can project on them, color them, molest them...

*

if a phone rings five times, it should be answered, but too late. If it rings three times, we should wait for the other two.

*

T [*pitches*]: Whew! what a workout. I did better with cigarettes and booze. Z [*swings*]: Each one's ok, on its own rhythm, if you keep the momentum up... T: It's when the Pall Malls and the Chivas hit the treadmill the trouble begins.

*

It's 10/7/55, 7:59 pm. in one minute (if they start on time), the BG will be born; compare this with the formation of the earth compared to a

12-month calendar year, compared to the development of MM's bust line... this is nonsequential.

*

The family eating cereals, reading cereal boxes, as a report of Emmett Till's murder is heard

*

Q: how are religious systems like economic systems? A: "They both compete in seeking members, give people what they want, produce saleable and attractive packages, enter into the nooks and crannies of life..." (*NYT*, 10/7/55)

* * *

headlines selected from the *New York Post*, including a special series on the Beats, by Al Aronowitz, that ran for several consecutive issues in the spring of '59:

Inside A City Hospital: A Day in Ward 4

Inside Fordham Hospital: A Reporter Turns Nurse's Aide

The Beat Generation

Insists Cash Was Mother's
"The Beat" on the Campus

The Ex-Cop's Mystery list: Probe New Names

The Beat Generation: The Poet and Prophet

Rackets Jury Calls 16

Snow, Sleet, Freeze

* * *

more fr. *NYT*, 10/7/55:

"bank of New York reported total deposits $462, 361, 654; assets $517, 786, 008.... State municipal long-term financing $389, 848, 781..."

"Aluminum Adds $17 Million to Expansion Drive... Aluminum, Ltd., plans to nearly double its capacity for producing alumina—or semi-precious bauxite—in Jamaica, BWI, at a cost of $17 mill."

"$51 Million Added to Armco Buildup"

"20 Chinese girls, all over 16 and unmarried, will pass before judges in Chinatown's... Mott St."

"a committee of children's doctors today issued a warning on competitive sports as a means of improving the physical fitness of American youth. ...two members said they did not know 'exactly what the president had in mind...'"

***

Life Ads

10/10/55:

6: Hotpoint^{tm} electric range coral pink sunburst yellow seafoam blue meadow green woodland brown push button cooking handi-raise broiler new time center controls both ovens both broilers, surface unit, barbecue, thrift cooker Super 2600 Calrod impartial speed tests fastest burner in any kitchen heats a can of soup piping hot in 65 sec. Harriet Nelson in white apron green dress holding bowl

16: Marcel Marceau w/ hoop, as lion tamer—5 frames: theatrical greeting, command to jump, lion passing under instead, Marceau pleading for low jump, and finally enacting lion, framing his head in hoop (what is it that passes under, that won't do as we command, though we were confident it would. A compromise perspective? We create the worlds we can't find). As balloon vender—pulled off balance, lifted—almost—off ground.

20-21: Looks big—feels big—acts big—is big: two tone red white Mercury Montclair, CU, diagonal, dark trees behind; we look from wheel level, as if crouched or kneeling at roadside—woman passenger looks out, awed/delighted, red lips white teeth, by the bigness, man driver's head only partially visible, mouth merged with the forward thrusting hood in the radiated darkness; the trees, whiteness of woman's teeth, chrome grill...*manage a trois* Merc-O-Matic, Safety Surge V-8, 225 HP, "the big move will be to the big M..."

56: Bolex movie camera, woman wildly enthusiastic amazed, slight up-angle, features of camera numbered—what's she gazing at?... "you'll be amazed at the reproducibility," the drop-in spool loading, the instant stops the ratchet winding 3-4 scenes per winding...

90: an array of flash cameras
192: Royal typewriter: suit feel of the machine to any touch—heavy light or in between scientifically designed keyboard preferred 2 1/4 to one

*

10/17/55:

35: X appeal. She stands in what looks like a mink layer cake, the fur almost liquid X= glamour + comfort—formula for commodified sexiness hand playfully seductively bewitching mask face all trace of nipples has been airbrushed away flat flexible superhighway ribbon wire "lifts you into rounded beauty curves" lip overpasses dead man's curve around the ghosted nipple U.S. 101 NJ (the "killer" highway) X-ray book *Xurbanites*: who controls the way we think, act, consume…

36-37: two bewitchingly sexy housewives having fun with laundry, tying sheets into knots "six pressure wash rinses plus deep agitated rinse"

40: the last pitch and the catch and the double play Johnny Podres Sandy Amoros Gil Hodges outs McDougald at first ball a split sec. after Podres releases it, looking down, not at ball the ball just as Amoros catches it just short of 301 ft. mark #12 heads back to first…

51: Swanson TV dinner. Painterly butter pads the red nailed hand taking it to the wheeled cart "no cooking for you no dishes to do" "perfect for sudden guests keep several in your freezer" looks like three separate images superimposed in tray compartments the three potatoes one in each corner of the main triangle the pads of butter like sad melting irradiated eyes, beef mouth and the glutinous Jell-O like gravy "savory slices of Swanson roast beef with little brown potatoes swimming in a rich beef gravy" the aluminized face of nuclear family Lucy light dis/ transfunctionalism

56: tire—the mold (paradigm) and the product… out of this mold, with rubber-gloved hands… the precision bladed mold intricate tread pattern… "safety tensioned gum dipped cord"

?:

n.p.: hunter w/ gloved hand &

quiver of arrows
sips a Hiram Walker[tm]—
in background, at his ear, a diminutive
version of himself draws bow for a kill…

Antic Politics

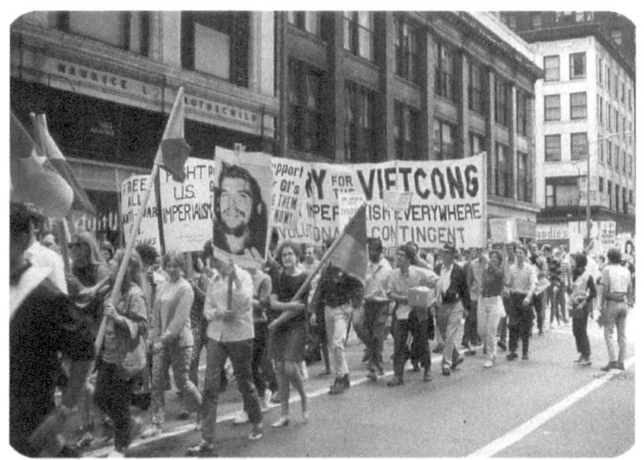

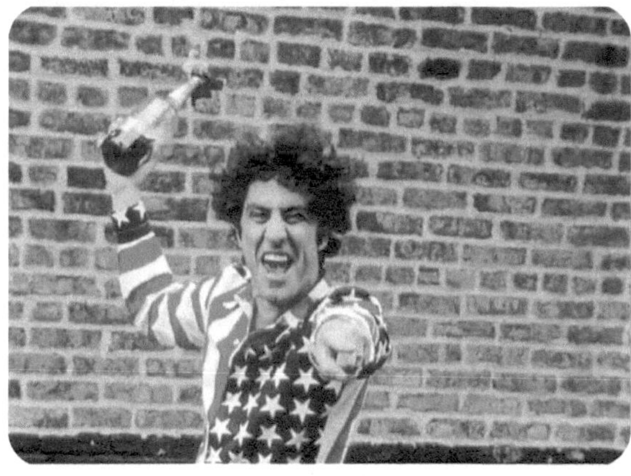

Fig. 11: (x)—protest actions (as this anti-war march, 8/10/68, leading up to the Chicago DNC) f (as function of) Fluxed resistance (Abbie Hoffman's symbolic molo-toss one member of such a set) = Fluxed protest, as, for e.g., Jerry Rubin's nomination of a pig for POTUS during convention wk. '68—pictured next page, an effigy of "pigasus" is carried before the federal courthouse, Chi., during the Chicago 8 (-1) trials, autumnal equinox, 1969)

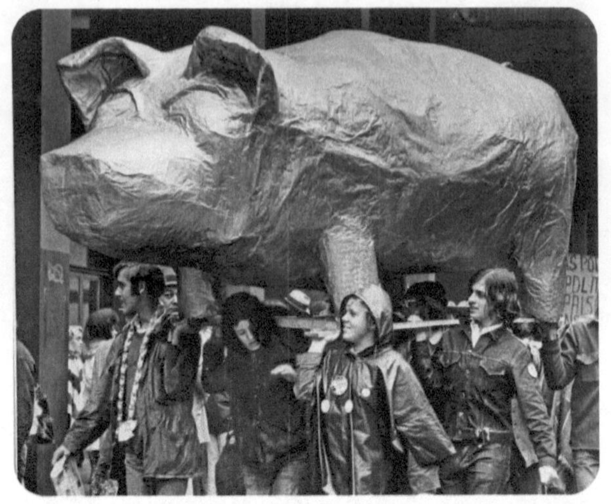

6 Script 5: Poetics of Protest: A Fluxed History of the 1968 DNC

Commentator/Over Voice (*CO*; as described below)/*Conductor* (*Panel Chair*)
Documents ("objective")
Fluxedout (*Fluxed*; Fluxus attitude)
New Historical Left (*NHL*; based on "old" and "new" New Left and New Historicist voices)
The Institute for Cultural Studies (*TICS*; an institutionalized postmodern academic voice)
Yippedout (*Yipped*; Yippie!)

Poetics of Protest is staged as a typical (atypical) academic conference panel presentation. At the front of the room are two long tables, one for the panelists and another for props. Props overflowing the table may also be ranged around the room, redeploying chalkboard ledges, windowsills, and floor margins, marking the space's boundaries. Redeployed, theoretically fortified cereals (i.e., empty boxes)—Žižek Os™, Blau Pops™, Lucky Deleuze, Baudrillard Puffs™, Foucault Flakes, etc.—are suspended from the ceiling. There is also a podium, a data projector and projection screen displaying an interactive image map of Chicago, circa 1968, highlighting the Amphitheatre and key riot and protest sites, and, optionally, a video monitor on which the audience may view muted interviews with Yippies. Projected on the podium and the floor directly in front of the podium—slow motion and stop-action scenes from Brett Morgen's animated documentary of the Chicago 8 trial, Chicago 10[33]*; the panelists pause, at intervals, to act out—or rather, act with, re-act (to), comment on via serial* tableau vivant*—fragments of these scenes, some of which include archival footage of events at the '68 DNC as well as mo-cap animation. The central performers in the piece are the panelists and the audience/participants, who double as session attendees. An enumerated list of Fluxbits[34] is hand printed on a long scroll, or cue sheet, hanging from the ceiling (or attached to a wall). The number of the Fluxbit corresponds to a group of props arrayed with others around the performance space. Descriptions of the bits, and corresponding numbers, are printed on 4 X 6 index cards, which are distributed to the audience. Blank, unnumbered cards are also distributed to the audience/participants, encouraging them to develop their*

33. CO: Morgan: the Yippies were a "cartoon show"; animation as critical commentary—see Anderson…

34. CO: (De)formation from "Fluxkits." Mini-scripts (playings within the "play") performed by the panelists and audiences—see the "Fluxbits" appendix.

own Flux scripts, in addition to or even as comments on assigned scripts, though not as substitutes for them; the blanks may also be used to jot down scripts for deployment in other, similar contexts (conference sessions, lectures, business meetings, debutante balls or other exclusive gatherings...).

When a Fluxscript/bit is called out by the panel Chair (or otherwise), functioning as Conductor, performers (audience members along with panelist(s) indicated on the card) should either perform suggested action(s) (preferable), or read the script aloud. If a Flux card reads "Discard Props," after the event is performed, the props may be added to one of the onstage piles; otherwise, they should be returned to the prop table, window sill, chalkboard ledge, etc.

The Panel Chair may also double as the CO *(though this role may also be played by a "respondent," or an amplified and unidentified "offstage" voice), shifting roles as necessary, surveying, supervising, policing, and conducting within the spirit of the whole—creative resistance, not chaos. She/he may also select hotspots on the image map, allow video voices to be heard at relevant moments, and direct the panelists to act out scenes from* Chicago 10.

When conducting panelists, the following signals will be used: rolling wrists suggest speed of delivery; hands pushing forward (toward panelists) indicate softer speech, hands drawn toward Conductor, louder; baton raised up, higher pitch; lowered baton, lower pitch; baton moved horizontally means sustained syllable; smacking baton in hand, stop. Pointing the baton at a particular panelist while another is delivering her/his lines cues that panelist to begin delivering the same lines, according to the actions indicated (if no action is indicated, then she/he should deliver the lines in a conventional manner). If the Conductor calls out a speaker (e.g., "Fluxed, pickup"), that speaker should begin with her/his next scripted lines, even though they may overlap or run simultaneous to another performer's. Pointing the baton at a particular speaker followed by one of the actions noted above indicates that only that performer performs the action. When more than one performer is delivering lines simultaneously, the Conductor may indicate, through a sweeping motion of the baton, that the action following is to be performed by all who are currently reading (thus, for example, a baton sweep followed by a slower, horizontal movement of the baton indicates presenters sustain whatever syllable they happen to be speaking at the time).

Though the placement of Fluxbits in the (mega)script is determined dramatically and associatively, the selection and order, with the exception of the opening, middle, and closing bits, are determined aleatoric ally, through one hand of three card draw (Gut) Poker played by the panelists at the beginning of the session. As the panel Chair/CO tends to some final stage management business, the panelists/players are seated, the scripts are shuffled and dealt, each player allowed one discard, after which the game proceeds in the following manner: Fluxed: "I'll raise ya" (no levitation occurs); TICS: "I'm out"; NHL I'll see ya" (gets up and leaves game); the remaining players match hands, then disperse to their opening positions. All hands and discards are gathered by Chair/CO, counterclockwise,[35]*and, unless there is audience intervention, will be called in this order (i.e., the holder of bit #2 may or may not be the second to perform). Players disperse to their opening positions; the performance begins.*[36]

[Fluxbit 1: *Opening*. Performed by **Fluxed**, aided by **Documents** and **Yipped**, who provide the props—an ongoing event]

* * * * *

Yipped: Let's try it this way:

Lecturer (that would be me) (**Yipped**, *awkwardly making his/her way to the podium, bumping the heads of the other panelists with his old suitcase full of props*): Pardon me, did I hit you?... Excuse me I didn't mean to, did I? No I did not. (*Reaching podium*) Well (*suitcase regurgitates contents*)... oh... I guess you can see it better that way anyhow... I realize this is an academic conference, not a circus sideshow... you've come with certain expectations... so rather than assault you, perhaps a symbolic member... if you'd like to volunteer, please raise... yes (*looking down at the floor in front of audience*), you sir, good (*picks up a flat cardboard standup, w/raised arm, that has been lying face down—though when it is lifted to view, it has no face*). And you might tell us a bit about yourself (*pause, silence*). Yes, that should do it. Now my assistant (**Fluxed**, *costumed as Catcher*) and I and this dumm... representative of the People—Everyman but also the Candidate for Everyone—will demonstrate... just what I'm not sure... actually we're going to play a game. You're the spectators. But you're also directly involved, metonymically speaking. We'll be talking about demonstrations and you're the demonstrators; you're the resistance and that which resists the resistance, the enforcer. You're a bystander or passerby in the downtown Chicago Loop on a Tuesday

35. **CO**: The current grouping determined by a game of "52 Pickup."

36. Performance Studies International, Brown U., 0...

or Wednesday evening in late august '68 who becomes radicalized—" come join us..." You're the delegates at the Amphitheater behind the stockyards who don't yet know (*lowing & mooing from the panel, conducted by* **Fluxed**) ... you're the TV audience at home sitting around the set with the "kids-go-into-the-other- room-for-a-minute-get-a-Rainbow-pop" anxieties watching Wednesday evening's broadcast of mayhem in the streets. You're McCarthy workers on the 15th floor of the Hilton overlooking Grant Park; he's (*gesturing toward the faceless standup*) Humphrey Johnson Daley Deputy Mayor Sthal Chief Conlisk the Chicago PD the National Guard an FBI special detachment Chicago PD undercover the 113th Military Intelligence Film Unit... could also be, from a slightly different perspective, McCarthy, McGovern, various convention podium speakers. We're (*including audience*) Yippies MOBE activists SDS Chicago street kids with no exit who have found a target Hoffman Rubin Gregory Dellinger Hayden Seale, and the Media. Ginsberg Sanders Burroughs Genet Southern the MC5, Phil Ochs. Journalists Lane, Schlutz, Gitlin are somewhere, observing... that could be you, too, or if you like you could be the drafters of *Strategy of Confrontation*, a report prepared by the City of Chicago Corporation Counsel (9/6/68), based on skewed second-hand evidence and selective statistics (though that's probably *his* job); or, the co-creators of our "unofficial report" based on second and third hand evidence skewed another way; or, members of the Chicago Study Team submitting *Rights in Conflict* (11/18/68), a report penned with a more objective, critical eye... (*"smack" of a hand in baseball glove from the impatient "catcher"; speaker reacts, in a choreographed manner, as if punched in stomach*)

Fluxed [*as Catcher*]: "Work that frame!"

Documents: No, wait... I think we should begin,

"Convention Week '68: An Overview"

Pre-convention week, MOBE (National Mobilization to End the War in Vietnam) set up organizational centers to discuss strategies and methods of realizing an overall theory of nonviolent demonstration in the streets of Chicago during the final week of August, 1968. During the Convention, conflicts arose between the MOBE and SDS (Students for a Democratic Society), more militant agitators pushing for direct confrontation as it became clear that nonviolent protest wasn't working. Meanwhile, Yip continued its more rhetorical, imaginative forms of provocation, including a mock convention and an LBJ un" birthday party" during which Pigasus the ("real") pig was nominated for president. When riots broke out, and the nonviolent-oriented MOBE Marshals lost control of the demonstration, it was the street-wise kids (many newly "radicalized" from working class Chicago street gangs as well as from middle class homes, including the 14-year-old who "liberated" the statue of a civil war general in Grant Park) who maneuvered most adroitly. Make shift weapons included (metal) spiked golf balls, nail-studded park bench slats, bags of excrement, bottles, broken tiles, bricks, rocks— [*glove smack*] whaaaa…tever refuse could be gathered from the parks and gutters and recycled—radicalized—into protest material; trash barrels were overturned and set on fire and windshields of patrol vehicles smashed. On the other side were tear gas canisters, tear gas-converted flame throwers, billy clubs, rifle buts, and at one-point gloves filled with bird shot. The Chicago PD and U.S. National Guard (barb wired vehicles, gas masks, helmets, and a show of artillery—tanks, bayonets, grenade launchers) v. the demonstrators (wet handkerchiefs, makeshift helmets, bottles of water, blinking eyes and fast legs). There were several attempted peaceful marches toward the International Amphitheater (the Convention site), which rarely lasted more than a few blocks, and ended in police and National Guard blockades, failed negotiations, forced retreats, blocked exits and riots (many of these provoked, as it came to light later, by police plants). There were evening raids to clear Lincoln Park of sleepers (the Yip had applied for grants, but were denied), and orders to clear the streets of demonstrators (one of which resulted in the infamous, nationally broadcast Hilton Hotel "police riot"). Despite Daley's attempts to prevent direct reports of street activities from reaching the delegates at the Amphitheater (not to mention the larger national TV viewing audience) by refusing network connections to the media workers on the scene, the Convention had its own tensions, protests, and guerrilla theater actions [*Catcher throws in his/her glove*], including floor scuffles among antiwar and pro-Humphrey/Johnson delegates and plainclothes thugs hired to "preserve order" (beating newsmen who happened to be in the way), staged walkouts over the refusal to seat minority delegates (Julian Bond and the Loyal Georgia delegates), and protests staged by antiwar delegates after failure of the Peace Plank, including a "march" beneath the podium. After the Peace Plank went blank (like the amphitheater movie screen after a tribute to Bobby Kennedy) ...

Yipped: Yes...

Fluxed: and after the first broadcast images of riots penetrated the nomination process, the larger dialogos of "convention week" became clear, as the boundaries between outside and inside, street theater and riots and the internal dynamics of the "authorized" convention space collapsed (guerrilla tactics and confrontations on the "inside" mirrored—or, more accurately, were charged by the same field of energy—as struggles on the "outside").

Yipped: Doubly ironic that Wednesday night's media spotlight highlighted an event that took place outside—in the street—crashing (literally) *through* the plate glass window of a commodified allusion to the city's early labor riots—the Hilton's Haymarket Lounge?

Documents: Even the smoothly channeled flow of main stage convention rhetoric was disrupted after broadcast of the "Haymarket" riots: Abe Ribicoff's politically expedient commentary—" with George McGovern for president, we wouldn't have Gestapo tactics in the streets of Chicago"—abutted by Daley's guttural response from the Chicago delegates' section—" Fuck you you Jew son of a bitch..." brought the podium to the floor.

Yipped: The parallel becomes most apparent when "inside" (legitimized by convention pass and delegate badges) and "outside" (repressed, unauthorized, rebellious) literally merge, as in the Thursday evening's candlelight march of the delegates to Grant Park.

Fluxed: The city of Czechago brings you... The Drama of Convention Week: a complex, dialogic interplay of events, often distant in space and time (though broadcast 40 minutes after they occurred, the Wednesday night riots not only had a condensed symbolic valence for the delegates, but also charged subsequent "real"-time street theater events); rhizomatic flows of radicalized thought and their attempted blockages...

Documents: And *that* is the central concern of our present enactment. From this expanded perspective of the '68 DNC, there is no "offsceen" space.

NHL: Hmmm...I was just dreaming... I like the performative, situationist, recontextualizing effect of the Yipped beginning... how about starting out with a persona piece, a set up to get us into the mindset without actually having to stage it.

We sketch the aging newscaster in his media booth: earphones, telephone, monitor, high windows, trying to deal with the realization of the falseness of his own position; that newsmen could be treated so disgracefully—in America!— and how to come to terms with this, through the images, videos, photos, reports—nothing first hand; alone with representative fragments of a shattered world—"nothing but wreckage..." (as a Humphrey advisor summed it).

Or this:

McCarthy and son, high in a hotel room, playing catch with an orange—why did the scripts fail? Who's at the other end? Hoffman's wry wit and clowning, and the raw energy of the kids in the street—perhaps that's it. McCarthy who, as police donned masks in Lincoln Park, deserted his own campaign, conceding that Humphrey had secured the nomination; who, looking down on the Wednesday night's aborted marches and chaos and from his 21st floor suite commented "The country's like that. Milling around, ready to march, nowhere to go... a battle of purgatory"; and who (with at least some sense of neglected responsibility) addressed the protesters the following afternoon from the Grant Park bandshell: You, my government in exile... (Witcover, 334, 339). A demonstrator raises a Vaseline-coated hand, giving the sign... Meanwhile, Humphrey meditates on his campaign memorabilia...

Documents: Yes, and the final count? McGovern 146 1/2, McCarthy 601, Humphrey...

Fluxed: HHH (the initials like barbed wire, as Gitlin notes) (*The Sixties*, 324) ...

Documents: 1, 761 3/4.

NHL: A first ballot victory!

Documents: Others, 114 ½ (including 67 ½ for Reverend Channing E. Phillips).

Yipped: And LBJ, the sly so and so, in cahoots with Texas governor and ranch buddy John Connally, kept just enough southern democrats dangling till the last minute, just to keep the Hump from slumping (Kaiser 222).

TICS: What we need is a properly academic, but mildly intellectually kinky, beginning...

Punching the Line: Fluxus, Yippie, and the 1968 DNC

New Year's Eve, 1967; Abbie Hoffman, Jerry Rubin, Ed Sanders, and Paul Krassner gathered in rented rooms of Hoffman's Lower East Side loft—Louisaida, Alphabet city. Hoffman picks a letter—" Y"? (Kaiser 232)—and the Hip is Yipped, or flipped; "Yippie," the "Youth International Party," as Paul Krassner dubbed the movement, began as a joke, a bit of Fluxus-like *detournement*, with perhaps a tip of the hat to the "Fluxus International Party," a like-minded art movement that predated Yippie by nearly a decade. The half-serious series of events that would be scripted for that summer were still a fold in the imagination, yet at the 1968 DNC (8/22–29), Yippie would find its shape, rebus-like, dialogically, through a partly impromptu, "de-coll/age" reworking of "Convention City" (cf. Fluxus artist Wolf Vostell's "civic" installations of the same period—"de-coll/age" works through de(con) struction to (re)construction). Staged on the cusp of turbulence that would radicalize not only many who took part in the marches and were victims of the riots in Grant Park and surrounding streets during the demonstrations of convention week, but also those displaced witnesses of the televised "revolution" and even the media itself, which at that moment (if only for a moment) became empowered as a vehicle of critical consciousness, Yippie carnivalizations of convention ideology, of the officially constructed convention space—an emblem of smooth, controlled transitions of power, of all-American processed democracy (rather than live process)—would register higher on the scale of ideological impacts than its founders could have envisioned....

Fluxed: I like the metaphor, but would rather take it to SOHO (circa 1960), and so:

Yipped [*as Lecturer*]: You have your script cards—you can call out the card at any time and we will attempt to perform the event; if not, the Chair will call. Or, if I'm up here alone, or not really here, which it may appear, you can read the description of the event or if you want come up and act it out with me or someone else—one of the other panelist... (Ideally, I would have a plant in the audience who would enact the skits as you called them out, and who would circulate, trying to involve you in events, and/or offering peep views of eccentric parodic pornographic cultural commentaries taking place in nominees' and delegates' hotel suites—or there could be a separate "room"/stage level/mezzanine of mini-TV monitors set up for this purpose—then, my assistant/plant would be limited to throwing words and things at me). The whole performance would be divided into 5 or 6 segments, the rhythm of happenings in each scored according to that day's event, and here is (*indicating dumped contents of suitcase*) this accumulation of de-contextualized, dysfunctionalized (or differently functioned) objects, to be re-piled elsewhere after (re)use... take this radicalized golf ball, refashioned to do the work of social consciousness—tee off with this and you'll really tear things up... but I must inform you that the text of my presentation provides much of the context and commentary that may give more meaning—more theoretical continuity—to the events, so the more you call out scripts—and you can call them more than once—the less background/theoretical context I'll be able to provide and the less sense things will make, so I do hope you'll call out frequently. I have quite a bit of material, quite a bit of it is redundant, we will stick to a 20-minute limit...

Fluxed: Or simply:

Yipped [*Lecturer*]: (Craig Saper on Fluxus): "participants interact with the ideas, playing through possibilities rather than deciding once and for all on meaning" (Saper, 80).

Documents: Hmmm... Or: "a simple vehicle for playfulness, humor, open-ended speculation, and presentation of the concrete"? (I noted that in Smith, Jenkins, 30...)

Catcher [Fluxed, taking up the glove]: (meaning of the product is determined by the processes of production?).

Yipped [*as Lecturer, becoming **Yipped***]: It's all up for grabs. Try the position of the Other, from the position of Another...

Fluxed [*glove smack* [: "Play...!

Yipped (*feigning stomach punch*): Step right up, attempt your own Flux-Yipped antics...

[*fluxed Catcher lobs something in the direction of Speaker*]

Yipped [*observing projectile where it lies*]: Daley—old school, production economics; what you can see hear touch—no image/symbol bullshit.

Fluxed [*growing impatient of awaiting the signals, or even knowing who the pitcher is*]: Batterrrrup![37]

[Fluxbit 2: Fluxed and volunteers]

TICS: Poetics of Protest: A Fluxed History of the DNC,

Or

Fluxed: "With McCarthy for President, we wouldn't have Gestapo tactics in the streets of Chicago..."

37. CO (*as Chair/Conductor signals audience*): Now, the game really begins...

NHL: "Fuck you you Jew son of a bitch you lousy motherfucker go home"
Documents: (Mayor Daley's response to Sen. Abe Ribicoff 8/28/68, approx. 8:45 PM)

Yipped: Watch the throws, as they go up, how they arc and turn in the diffuse semi-academic light, hard to fix for a moment's contemplation…

Fluxed: And so they go…

Yipped [*noting projected map*]: As they could be imagined, from any AAA approved map: Out below the Loop, Over Balbo—right over the heads of the Guard (through gridded nominations of the Symbolic Order—E Congress, S State, South Federal; W Madison, W Adams, East Monroe; S Columbus and the Eisenhower Expressway) to Michigan, south down Michigan—past Central Police Station, past Dunbar Park—a right after the Illinois Institute of Technology (do you follow, Flux?), not even a short stop at Comiskey Park (running white with the Sox) before we hit the tracks at the 35th St. Yard, then somehow up over or down under to Halstead singing blues, left, south again to the International Amphitheater one "unholy" animal "yell" from the old stockyards… no blockages this time (out). Press: pass. Pink avenues and green parks, blue numbered and lettered borders all around but somehow, what's significant has been left behind… in Cicero, a stiletto-sharp park played like a Club in the middle of Ogden avenue, Al Capone's paper clip of a dog track to the south—just images on a map—Chicago, city of train yards and slit bellies; grey streets and greyer institutes with black names—all part of the scheme; the "sanitary and Ship canal" draining blue to the Chicago River… AAA approved.

Fluxed: Goin' my way? Click: pass.

TICS: Virtual relocation. But this isn't the story—that story begins, as I've said, with a yip and a flux in "rented rooms in Manhattan's Lower East Side…" Though many factors and groups unintentionally collaborated to produce the political "Happening" of the '68 DNC (including, in addition to Old and New Left protesters,[38] the Chicago police department and even—or especially—Mayor Daley, neither of whom were in the mood for jokes), I want to consider the role of the political "jest," as theorized and practiced by Yippie and informed (perhaps unwittingly) by Fluxus conceptual clowning, in radicalizing convention "participants" (those directly involved in protest events during convention week and, less directly, witnesses/viewers—including the TV audience) and in opening a space for the development/ deployment of critical consciousness.

Fluxed: (I think we may push you beyond the "jest" to the radically performative *gest* (gesture).)

Documents: and so, off, to... Chicago, '68: Land of Lincoln, of steel, of the smelly onion and packing houses; nation's leader in production of telephones, radios, television sets, and mirrors; plastic products, electrical machinery, sporting goods, picture frames and tin cans. Home of the Bulls, the Bears, the White Sox and the Cubs; the Black Hawks, Mustangs and Spurs; home of 58 colleges and universities, a 200-billion-volt particle accelerator, the first nuclear chain reaction, the "river which flows backward" and leading producer of methane from some of the biggest butts in America whose per capita income is 28.2% above the national average? ("gem in the lake," city in a garden," *Checagou*..." I Will!")

Yipped: and as three men, gathering momentum, orbit the earth, splashing down into the Atlantic, then 3 again (for symmetry's sake) this time ringing the moon before plunging into the Pacific, to be fair, as a hydrogen bomb explodes undercover of the deserts of Nevada, rattling nickels in Las Vegas, and a 28-million-year-old ape scratches its petrified skull at the opening of "Dada, Surrealism, and their Heritage"

---

38. **CO**: If I may amplify: Demographically, the list of "radicalized" groups represents a socio-economically and ideologically diverse cross/inter section of mainstream and sub cultures, some members of which experienced the other end of the stick of authority perhaps for the first time, including, in addition to Yips, Hips, MOBE and SDS activists, working class street gangs, "authorized" convention delegates and attendees, ministers, WWII and Vietnam vets, media personnel, resident bystanders and the more or less "tuned in" (cf. Leary's *Politics of Ecstasy*) youth who came in hopes of free music, free love and dope.

at the Museum of Modern Art (MoooMaaa) and Mickey Mouse celebrates his 40th birthday (Hey hey LBJ!). Meanwhile, listening to Pulsars, voices of the stars, as Soviet tanks rumble the Czech night 78 million times simultaneously on the TV sets of America... an A train speeding beneath Neil Simon's *Plaza Suite*. Edward Albee: *Box—Mao—Box*.

Documents: You're drifting... Death of King March '68, riots in Chicago ghettos, death of Bobby K. June 68, labor strikes—taxi, bus, telephone, electrical workers

Fluxed: And now the influx of Yip-Flip whip fire heating up these normalized left-overs (as easy as TV dinner—the "Pig" is well thawed), teasing them out, making them flow so we can see the lines of repression underlying productive order; a motile force v. petrified form, drawing it out to clarify its substance (Daley's jowls flush lobster-red)... a resistance, yes, but that begins with a taunt and a hoax.

TICS: Through the (at times dark) humored fissures of Yipped protest the spectacle of glitz and solidarity bled and distorted...

Fluxed: (Liquid heated to a boiling point changes state. Apply pressure; get it hot. Altered state. The gas is everywhere in this piece, wafting through the lines. Let it pass...)

[Fluxbit 3. Performed by volunteers]

Yipped: In year '00, clean red white blue insignia mark multilane freezones cutting through incorporated territories, deadsure speed, erasure, echoless continuous crack of rubber on pavement...

Fluxed: In yr. '00, in the unreal weather of southern California, far from the muggy impulsive explosiveness and molecular rabidness of Midwest late 60s August, then again in the year '04, in the eclectic heat of resistance, another convention in another city, the RNC... and in the year ____ worse, much worse, yet to come.

Yipped: Not to mention, in the same city, the '96 DNC, lacking the dialogic, contact-zone charge of Chicago '68, all high-tech smooth flowing party-line show; digital art, games and video on the Convention '96 web...

Documents: Though Andrew ("YIPPIE, SON OF ABBIE") Hoffman's

World Wide Web Site of the Festival of Life *and* America's Soup Kitchen on Wheels

did promise a renewal of the Festival of Life (focused on "a democratic agenda for peace and social justice for the environment"— "combat racism...keep everyone healthy" and "save the environment") so "rudely interrupted by spies and thugs" 28 years earlier...[39]

Fluxed: No LSD in the city water supply, seduction of delegates wives, or "fuck-ins" on the beach? Tame, tame.

NHL: *Meanwhile*, back at the Amphitheater, home of the annual International Live Stock Exposition, the DNC is well underway...

Fluxed: Yaow—plenty of BS and fodder, lowing and mooing at the podium....

NHL: Documents?

[Fluxbit 4. Performed by volunteers]

Fluxed:

> Hello Panelists:
>
> Qualities that distinguish Happenings from conventional theater, according to Allan Kaprow...

NHL: I meant...

Fluxed:

---

39. **CO**: both seem to be dead links now...

> fluid, open-ended form; a site-specific nature; lack of plot—actions improvised from a jotted down score; use of chance as a structuring principle; language play; lack of separation between "audience" and "actor"; the "impermanence," or perishability, of materials; most importantly, for our purposes, the potential for—and acceptance of—failure (Kaprow, *Essays on the Blurring of Art and Life*, 16-20).

Documents: Tempting, but I believe this is my dance.

Political context of the '68 DNC (which may help account for its so-called "dialogic charge," or momentum): Pre-1972, fewer states had primaries—15 as compared to 35 today—so conventions were used as stages for nomination process, making for a more dynamic event, but also allowing for potential dissention (as one teenage woman tried to explain to an officer during one of the futile "negotiations" between police and protesters during the '68 DNC, "You see, many of us come from states without primaries. The only way we can vote, can hope to influence the delegates, is to be seen at the Amphitheatre") (qtd in Lane 52). This voice...

Fluxed: Try this step (from the same email):

> We must think counter, athwart, through our core presentations; what could be happening in the margins of the discourse? This leads to associative, disruptive or complementary actions that will require gesture/movement, word/sound, and (though not necessarily) simple props.

Documents: Not my style.

This voice of youthful angst highlights another wrinkle in the process: pre '72, in addition to the exclusivity of the primaries, delegations were not always representative of their constituents' views. Cases in point: in '68 80% of the popular vote went to antiwar candidates (Kennedy, McCarthy, McGovern), but a Johnson man was nominated (Gitlin, *The Sixties*, 331) (it's hard to say how things would have added up if primaries were more inclusive, but this condition of being out of touch with the pulse of American concerns is the point); the convention at first refused to seat the Georgia Loyal delegates, headed by Julian Bond, who sought to split the Georgia vote with the (essentially all white) Georgia Regulars.

We know how the turmoil in Chicago, the broadcast clips of riots in Grant Park, and the defeat of the peace plank fractured the Democratic party, turning away many voters, enough so that Nixon, by contrast, seemed the safer bet (winning by a narrow margin—1%).

Yipped: Got it!

[Fluxbit 5. Performed by Yipped & volunteers]

Documents: Well…

TICS: Here, let me [*striking a self-consciously academic pose*]. In terms of the connection to Yippie actions, it is also important to note that many Fluxus performances are collaborative and interactive in nature, "decentering the role of the artist and artwork"; as art historian Owen Smith emphasizes, "ultimate power lies with the audience" (Smith 170). Fluxus founder George Maciunas calls these events "art-amusements," which are often "a simple natural event, a game or a gag. It is the fusion of Spike Jones, Vaudeville, gag[s], children's games and Duchamp" (Maciunas, "Fluxus Broadside…"; qtd. in Smith 181). The linking together of "gag" and "Duchamp" strikes a keynote for the activities of both movements: jokes, yes, but with a conceptual and critically conscious kick.

Documents: And, if I may add, excerpting from George Maciunas's 1963 letter to Emmett Williams, as he planned the New York launching of Fluxus (the first Fluxus festival took place in Weisbaden, Germany, in the *final week of August*, 1962—nice coincidence? —followed by the Festum Fluxorum in Copenhagen that same year): "Our activities…" and "PROGRAMMING… which must…" (Williams, 168-9). So it was never meant to be disengaged conceptual play…

Fluxed: I, docu:

> Large amounts of hair spray were sold in the Old Town area stores during the time of the Convention. The expulsion of

> hair spray from a can when set fire to works as a home-made flame thrower. Royal Blue Food Store at 744 Fullerton Avenue reported large groups of Yippies purchasing large quantities of hair spray. It is common knowledge that Yippies have no use for hair spray or other cosmetics for personal use. (*Crisis in Chicago*, np.; qtd. In O'Brien, par. 2)

[Fluxbit 6. Performed by Fluxed & volunteers]

Documents [*seeing what the game is, attempts dialogic confrontation, weighing in with statistics and a document and larger font*]: Every academic wo/man for her/himself....

Johnson: 500,000 soldiers to Vietnam by 1968.

Daley: 7,500 U.S. Army troops and 6,000 National Guardsmen beefing up a force of 12,000 police officers.

Martin Luther King in 1967: "We spend $322,000 for each enemy we kill, while we spend in the so-called war on poverty in America only about $53 for each person classified as 'poor.'" (Phinney, ABCNews.Com, 1998)

Yipped: Perhaps what was so unsettling was not only that most Americans most have at some level known that the protesters were right about the war, but a step away from that—to admit that would also raise the specter, as a kind of question mark written in tear gas snaking through the indignant crowds, that we might be wrong about a lot more...[40]

---

40. **CO**: Ironically, the list of 82 protest groups represented at the DNC—some "of a permanent nature, some temporary, ad hoc types, some large, some small"—compiled by HUAC staff researcher James Gallagher and presented at the HUAC October '68 hearings as evidence of the attempted "radicalization of America" seem to also make this point. Can so *many* folks—from established Old Left groups such as the Socialist Workers party and the Progressive Labor Party to New Left groups like the National Unity for Peace, People Against Racism, and Women for Peace to groups of concerned citizens such as the Catholic and Episcopal peace fellowships, the W.E.B. DuBois Clubs of America, Parent School, and even the High School Union

Documents [*trying a different rhythm, adding a step*]: FLUXUS BEGINS Weisbaden Germany the final week of August 1962; CONTINUES as Festum Fluxorum, Copenhagen, Sweden, the same year; in a 1963 letter preceding the movement's launching in New York, George Maciunas to Emmett Williams (I paraphrase)—OUR CLOWNS ARE BARBED.

[Fluxbit 7. Performed by **Fluxed & Yipped**]

TICS: Ok… [*choosing an authoritative block font,* sans serif] **Franklin Gothic Heavy! Yippie Movie Presents Clear Challenge to Mainstream Image of "Radical" as Humorless, Dehumanized, Militant "Other."** Yes, the '69 film *Yippie* begins with a borrowed ("detoured," as Guy Debord would have it) bit of silent-era footage juxtaposing Yips to keystone cops—as if to say, "look at yourself and laugh"; the comic cops also parody the Chicago PD's (by extension, Daley's) fumbling, misdirected rage. **To think of authority this way is to give it up.** The film also montages snippets of early Hollywood spectacle (i.e., images in "public domain," but also out-of-date/out-of-tune with current spectacle) to comment on the **"revolutionary" rabble**, as the sound tract detours Zenned utopianism (Ginsberg's **"Om"** morphs—with a twist of Lacan, as the signifier slips away from the signified—to pop middle-class escapism **"dreaming of a white Christmas"**). The film closes with the nomination of Pigasus as democratic candidate for president at a can-can LBJ birthday bash in full costume. **Nothing is sacred in the film.** Hierarchies (cultural, social, intellectual) are leveled as the imagery revels in serious buffoonery. Like Fluxus performances, **the self-parody in *Yippie* implies that "radicalism" is not an uncommodifiable lesion in the social tissue: it can be *thought*, and it can achieve a state of *communitas* through (critically torqued) laughter.**[41]

all be *worng*? (*Subversive Involvement in Disruption of 1968 Democratic Party National Convention*, 2245-46).

41. **CO**: If TICS is going to move in this direction, he/she/it could also point out how the Yip MO even infects Hollywood productions of the period. In a scene from *Medium Cool* (directed by Haskell Wexler), a pre-war recording of "Happy Days" counterpoints shots of riot and wounded protesters at the DNC, staged here for Wexler's lens as the "actual" protest events were staged for the media (the protesters aware that their "real" actions were part of a

NHL [*getting into the act*]: Right! In Yippie spirit—Jokerman: In a filmed interview, Hoffman, conscious of being cast as the "radical," adjusts his image to counter expectations; we can read the key critical points: The New Left has become too academic, perhaps too dogmatic, so instead of offering a clear, if jargon-ridden, Marxist influenced, utopian reconfiguration of society as an answer to the interviewer's query ("Why are you [i.e., the Yippies] here [in Chicago]"), he says simply, "you'll have to ask each person."

---

media show, a guerrilla put-on—"the whole world is watching..."). Wexler's film raises the complex (irresolvable?) question of the art/life boundary, as the line between "actual" event and "reenactment" is blurred (are these "real" or "representative" cops? following a fictional or "real"—i.e., social—script?) That these scenes are the (philosophical) center of the film is emphasized by the negligible, add-on feel of the "story" line. Everything is self-consciously framed for media consumption: especially, for example, the opening discussion among reporters—"we don't explain, but provide images"—and the closing scene, zooming into the dark box of a camera glare shade to the credits (or does it zoom in on us?), along with whatever questions, conflicts, and continued discussion these scenes dreg up. In the fatal finality of its closing sequence, the film's would-be heroine, who helps the "cool" cameraman find the value of human life beneath media images of suffering, is DOA and the cameraman left in critical condition after his media-marked station wagon crashes (a "white-trashy" family drives by in a beat up wagon from the previous decade and snaps pictures, drives on). In addition to making the viewer aware of the media's "dramaturgical" role in (re)presenting events, the low budget texture and downbeat ending reenact the depressed mood at end of convention week—the defeated peace blank, the nomination of a "Johnson man," the shattered Yip vision (like the glass front of the Hilton) and the apparent triumph of anti-creative forces. All come to nothing more than the lukewarm shutter click of a forgettable photo...

George Romero's *Night of the Living Dead*, by contrast, whose popularity feeds off deep-seated fears of the (unknowable/untouchable) other, is a coterminus cultural production that lacks the self-reflexive edge of *Medium Cool*: A terrifying force is on the march, a threat to all ("natural," normal) life, the disinterred upturning the comfortable conventions of suburbia; the lost numbers, thirsting for what they've been deprived of, are driven by desire, insatiable and insistent. We can't rest secure, nothing stays in place: On one side, irrepressible, uncontrollable desire; on the other, insecurity, the base ontological binaries that frame a rational world—life v. death—overthrown. But not a shred of critical consciousness; at no point does the narrative step back to reveal the *real* forces at play—the vapidness of a middle class existence must reenact what it denies...

Documents: Rephrasing his manifesto of 8/22, which opens with the epigraph "Be realistic—demand the impossible" (slogan borrowed from the May '68 Paris student protests): "This is my personal statement. There are no spokesmen for the Yippies. We suggest to all reporters that they ask each and every Yippie... why they have come to Chicago. We are all our own leaders" (qtd. In Farber, 55).

NHL: Read as: *I won't counter one ideology with another that could become equally hegemonic/oppressive; I can't speak for others, who have their own acts, thoughts, agendas; what I say may be only partly relevant to what happens; I prefer to remain fluid, open—not commit the potential flux of events to a single meaning or direction*. So, like Zen k ans, the statement is deceptively simple, and infinitely unpackable.

Documents: Recall George Brecht's 1964 comment on the MO of Fluxus: "Fluxus encompasses opposites"; if you think it's Fluxus, "there is someone associated with Fluxus who agrees with you" (David T. Doris, "Zen vaudeville: a medi(t)ation in the margins of Fluxus," *Fluxus Reader*, 94-95) (and, Doris points out, someone who disagrees). And in 1978: "Each of us had his own ideas about what Fluxus was and so much the better. That way it'll take longer to bury us" (qtd. in Smith, Jenkins, 24). Or, as he flipped the adage in *Flash Art*, nos. 84-5 (October-November 1978): "If the flux fits, wear it: (qtd. in Simon Anderson, "Fluxus, fluxion, flushoe: the 1970s," *Fluxus Reader*, 30).

TICS: The emphasis is on lack of closure, on supplementarity, current and future readers, critics, artists (the distinction blurs in Flux) being part of the act; on continuing the dialogue and being unable—or in Flux spirit, unwilling—to reduce Flux to an easy definition or set of goals...

Yipped: is also what makes Yip Flip and what makes this (current) project *happen*.

[Fluxbit 8. Performed by **Yipped** & volunteers]

TICS: Hoffman's self-presentation in the interview, like the *mise en scene* of the film ***Yippie***, invites sustained, non-reductive interpretive play with/through the "text" (the text in this case being Hoffman himself). (Britannia Bold.)

NHL [*continuing*]: His manner, too, during the interview, plays against the militant stereotype of the political "radical" speaking with a distancing, anti-capitalist rhetoric: "Call me Abby"; (the sense that the New Left has become detached—from its own emotions, and others—can be read through the intimacy, informality, and ease of interaction.)[42] No wonder the media loved Hoffman. He gave us something else—something essentially human—to ponder; he wasn't all legislation, principles, politics, morality and agenda-driven activism, but figured a creative, upbeat side of the "revolution." Consider his *Look* magazine "fashion" photo op: as if to say, "*look*, I'm a radical, but I can also cut a pleasing image on the popular scene"; the change has to occur right there, in the practice of everyday life, in and through the terms of our (mediated) world; Yip's particular alchemy was its ability to make those images speak in richer, more meaningful, resonant ways, and to seduce the general public into relation with the unapproachable/untouchable "other:" "This is a "radical? But he looks so well adjusted, self-confident, and nonantagonistic...so *adorable*" "Celebrity" leaders like Hoffman and Rubin were, as Gitlin observes, "colorful and symbolic" and "guaranteed good copy" (*The Whole World Is Watching*, 176; *The Sixties*, 233), while presenting the intellectually playful side of radicalism.

Fluxed: Though Hoffman could be provocative, too—wearing a torn American flag during the Chicago Seven trials: the point is, he could shift positions, keep us moooving/thinking about what "radical thought" (Baudrillard) means, realizing that its main component is fluidity, unde(con)finability; that the movement itself between stances—working the frame—*is* the essence of radical.[43]

---

42. **CO**: Both Hoffman and Rubin showed how Yip could also offer a corrective to "old new left" theorizing. Rubin declaimed "[New Left] ideology a brain disease," exhorting youth to "act now, analyze later" (Gitlin, *The Sixties*, 237). At the Drawing Board, for example, the Diggers conference at Kalamazoo in '67, Hoffman presented, as he recalls in *Revolution for the Hell of It*, this counter scenario: "They do socialism, we blow pot in the grass; they do imperialism, we go swimming; they do racism, we do flowers for everybody...." Gitlin, *The Sixties*, 231)

43. **CO**: Consider, too, Rubin's media posturing during the House UnAmerican Activities Committee hearings: an (anti)colonial America-era revolutionary (i.e., clad in an American Revolutionary War "costume") (Gitlin, *The Sixties*, 233; *The Whole World Is Watching*, 171)—is he "serious," just "playing"? Yet what sort of play is it that placed him before the HUAC?

Yipped: and that "practical" political consequences—closure—were not the ("real") goal: "demand the impossible..."

Documents: Let me see...what was that step again? (*quoting him/herself*):

> As for exploiting the media, Yip had its precursors: In New York, in 1967, San Francisco Digger Peter Berg appeared on a talk show hosted by Alan Burke. When an older woman in audience stood up and asked what American youth stood for, Berg asked "Emma Goldman" (a Digger plant in the audience) to answer the question. The woman walked up and smashed a pie into the questioner's face; Berg then demonstrated how people could walk out of the "box" (the confining mind-space of TV) by standing up and walking out the exit ("now turn off your TV's and go to sleep") (Gitlin, *The Sixties*, 231).

Fluxed: Yeeeaaaaa! That Digger was on (rhetorical) point.

[Fluxbit 9. Performed by **Fluxed** & **Documents**].

TICS: But while Berg used the media self-reflexively, to criticize media manipulations, Hoffman and Rubin were more expedient, (re) tuning the media to a "revolutionary" program. (Impact, 12, 14pt.) The Yips, especially, Hoffman, were both dramatists and publicists. Before dropping dollar bills on floor of New York stock exchange (1967), Hoffman sent out press releases (by contrast, Digger events were often unannounced and anonymous). For Hoffman and Rubin, cultural intervention, or what Situationist founder Guy Debord called *detournement*, was the key to social change; knowing they lacked the support for a "real "revolution, they were fighting a "revolution of the mind" (Poet Gary Snyder's phrase). Detouring the popular media was a key element of this strategy, diffusing a heavily symbolic imagery through the usually vapid medium. Though Gitlin suggests the opposite may have been the case, media standards coopting radicalism, reducing it to just another digestible packaging, for Hoffman and Rubin, Yip politics was, as Hoffman figured it, an "art form... part vaudeville, part insurrection, and part communal recreation"; an exercise of the imagination; a playful working out of possible alternative ideological and lifestyle positionalities. For Hoffman, if you can get the "right image, the details aren't that important"[44] So, though the revolution may not be televised, it could be partially fought through the media: "We are living ads, TV movies, Yippie." (Gitlin, *The Sixties*, 236) [45]

Fluxed: As *via* Flux artist Wolff Vostell's TV "de-collage" (circa 1963) which could bring the inside (what's hidden) out (expose, an exploded TV, as if caught in the act), split seams (what *seems*), invert, overturn, denaturalize and generally complicate the picture of things/ situations/events/social forms/ideologies.

Documents: But what Vostell actually did was "prepare" TVs, de-programing them at the consumer end—distort the reception, take them to bed, burn and bury them...

Fluxed: Give me a Bit

[Fluxbit 10. *Performed by volunteers*].

Documents: (Hanhardt, 123).

Fluxed: Convention week as decollage, imaginatively reconfigured with Brechtian/Frankfort School critical consciousness; in other words, decollage (re)performance produces critical consciousness. In Fluxus performance, Happenings, the activities of convention week, our work here, the important thing is process, focusing on

---

44. **CO**: [9] For Rubin, too, it was important for the late 60s activist to include the media as part of his methodological terrain; in planning for convention week, Rubin stressed it was important to "conjure images" and construct scenarios—make "myths"—to bring about desired changes (see Gitlin, *The Whole World Is Watching*, 175); Rubin and Hoffman began with "as if propositions," as Gitlin theorizes it: "act as if" the young were dropping out and heading for the "land of Lincoln", "as if" the state were collapsing and the "reality" would follow (Gitlin, *The Sixties*, 236).

45. **CO**: Hoffman: Chicago was an "advertisement for revolution" (Gitlin, *The Whole World Is Watching*, 186). But I think TICS misses a beat, here. Hoffman may have been a more penetrating media critic then Gitlin allows: Hinting at TVs seductive fictionalization of reality through a myth of objectivity, Hoffman observes "the media in a real sense never lie when you relate to them in a non-linear, mythical manner"(ironically, after the events in Chicago, three advertising agencies offered positions to Hoffman and Rubin) (Gitlin, *The Sixties*, 236).

doings and our own doings; as in Marx's definition of the ideal commune (i.e., community, society), *labor* is value and the basis of social relations (what we *do*, individually and together), rather than commodities/products (i.e., the objects of labor, bought and brought along; or, as Kristine Stiles puts it, "meaning of content is determined by the processes" that produced them (95). For TV viewers during convention week, conflicting images, especially Wednesday night's *mise en scene*, enacted a TV decollage right in their own "living" rooms (the synthetic light emanating for the image-box irradiating the room with politicized "life").

Documents: Or Henri Michaux's Schi[zzz]zophrenic ta [AAA]ble? In his imaginative reworking of the utilitarian object "It had been desimplified in the course of its carpentering... As it stood, it was a ta[ba]ble of additi[ti]ons, much like certain schizophrenics' drawings, described as 'overstuffed,' and if finished it was only in so far as there was no way of adding anything more to it, the table having become more and more ['n more an] an accumulation, less[less] and less a [(t)]able" (Henri Michaux, *The Major Ordeals of the Mind*, 1974, 125-27. *Anti-Oedipus*!). (Matisse ITC, curlz MT, Gigi)

Yipped: Yopp.

[Fluxbit 11. Performed by **Yipped** & volunteers]

NHL [*getting more into the swing of things, quotes her/himself*]:

And the New Left started to catch on. At least Tom Hayden, seeing his plans for more direct intervention strategies were on the Lake's rocks (due to lack of numbers), eventually glimpsed the symbolic beauty of the Yip's Zen-lit banana peel neon (though he didn't see through to its full implications: that *Daley's* Keystone Cops wouldn't "distinguish 'straight' radicals from newspapermen... rumors about demonstrations from the *real* [italics mine] thing"); attuned to the phantasmic dimensions of the conflict, Hayden projected the consequences: "Threat of disorder, like all fantasies in the establishment mind, can create total paranoia... at a minimum, this process will further erode the surface image of [smoothly operating] pseudo-democratic politics; at a maximum, it can lead to a closing of the convention... for security reasons" (qtd. in Gitlin, *The Sixties*, 315). Though from a Yip-Flip POV the "Convention," as decollage, should—could—not be "closed" (i.e., could not as Happening, reach a state of intellectual or emotional closure), at least the MOBE was tuning in to the performative vectors of the event. Gitlin, too, catches the drift. Listen, as the observer with New Left sympathies, covering daily events for the *Wall Poster*, describes on Tuesday night's standoff between protesters and the National Guard in Grant Park (the first action of the Guard as stand-in for the police): they "materialized, in full battle dress.... My feelings cascaded: astonishment... then fright, then euphoria—the late Sixties' definitive sequence of feelings. We had outlasted the cops...." And another image: "we were like the Czechs, at that moment confronting Soviet tanks" (rather than the outdated troop carrier the protesters actually faced—it also more of a set piece than serious fighting machine—its guns were never loaded)"; Gitlin terms it a "storybook confrontation" ("comparably noble" protesters v. a "comparably bankrupt" social "machine") (*The Sixties*, 331). His allegorical and allusive re-construction/re-scripting of events moves toward (counter)image play, sketches the event over a larger cultural field—perhaps the most vital way to go once one realizes the self-delusive stance of "real" revolution in post-modern America.

Yipped: Revolutionary change, too, has come up short in its accounts?

NHL: The Lincoln Park Monday night barricades were, Gitlin observes, "part Eisenstein, part Paris—so what was real?" (*The Sixties*, 329). But the Yipped lesson is clear: We have to take society where we find it; it can only be detoured by/through its most seditious, subtle, and seductive means of reproduction: the spectacle itself. The MOBE had been...

Fluxed: Say/Do it!

NHL: za(yi)pped by a line of flight, become (Flux-)radicalized!

[*midpoint* Fluxbit 12, Ring Around—Question.
Performed by **NHL** *& volunteers*]

Documents:

> Theater can be used as an offensive and defensive weapon, like blood. We had a demonstration in New York. We had seven gallons of blood in little plastic bags. You know, if you convince 'em you're crazy enough, they won't hurt ya. Cop goes to hit you, right, you have a bag of blood in your hand. He lifts his stick up, you take your bag of blood and go whack over your own head. All this blood pours out, see. Fuckin' cop standin'. Now, that says a whole lot more than a picket sign that says end the war... (From Hoffman's Lincoln Park speech, Tuesday, 8/27/68; qtd. in Sloman 149).

Fluxed: Though key New Left ideologues (Dave Dellinger, Hayden and Renee Davis) agreed all along that the demonstration would be billed as "nonviolent and legal" (Gitlin, *The Sixties*, 320), Yip antics, refusing to operate at a (merely) literal level and to stay in (a practical) place, carnivalized and evaded the whole system of protest and defense (i.e., authorized, state- and federally-enforced "law and order" v. political protest—violent or nonviolent). Yip overshot this binary and gathered its forces in another realm. Only in this way, from this perspective—by getting out of our (cultural) selves—could boundaries be worked, frames flipped and examined, creative mind stimulated to bring a dialogic wealth of associations and interconnections—a vaster, more dynamic assemblage—into play. Yip was in an elusive, liminal, not completely self-coherent place, between "revolutionary" social and aesthetic praxis; part performative put-on (like current *haute couture*) and part bodily, blood-in-the-street performance, one perhaps "commenting" on the other.[46] It's all, after all, ideologically driven theater—perhaps if that were understood, a de-reification of the theater of war and political confrontation would follow... [*to him/herself*] (*pause here, if necessary, to allow more time for the parade of inquisition—"Ring Around..."*)

[Fluxbit 13. Performed by **Documents** & **Fluxed**]

Yipped: Unlike Wexler's dialogically directed lens in *Medium Cool*,

46. **CO**: Yip Marx's ideal commune: their social relations are based on their labor of protest, which involves permuting and/or "throwing away" various concrete and ideological commodities.

mainstream media coverage of the convention was "radicalized" despite itself. By staying on point during the events surrounding the defeat of the Peace Plank, what the media caught, by chance—like skirmishes on a football field—not only dramatized the ideological rift in the democratic party, but also lifted the convention out of itself (its self-image of harmonious convening) and dropped it right on the shaggy green polyester turf of middle America's rec. rooms; everybody stopped crunching Chez-Its™ and watched. First, the numbers of defeat appeared graphically on the screen. Then, a group of delegates began slowly waving flags, side to side, singing "We shall overcome." Immediately, the convention band struck up "Happy Days." The delegates, radicalized (by proxy), become actors in real contestatory (if not yet guerrilla) acts, rather than merely performing the conventional Convention roles of roll call, vote casting, and cheering or booing at appropriate points; the eruption of such conflictual interactions are what work the cracks in the system, pry it open. Dialogical moments like this make the Convention scene improvisationally performative, rather than mechanically reiterative, following a pre-inscribed script. With the defeat of the Peace Plank, the formal/formularized *mise en scene* of the Amphitheatre began to transform, tracing the confrontational dynamic of the protests nearly 40 blocks away in Grant Park; mirroring marches in the streets, the peace delegates threaded through the seating area and beneath the podium holding a long black cloth, still chanting "We Shall overcome" (somewhat echoing, also, the trance-like chant-ins led by Ginsberg in Lincoln and Grant parks). So even though radicalized groups (protesters and delegates) did not (yet) share physical space, they communed through an experience/performance "braid" (Richard Schechner's term).

[Fluxbit 14. Performed by **Yipped** and **Documents**]

Fluxed: (*To Yipped*) You, my comrade, have a bit of TICS in you, enticingly torqued. (*To audience*) Both met resistance from the dominant power base, and, like the Yips, the delegates co-opted theater as a way of "overcoming" (troping, if not over overpowering), hegemonic blockages. The March as a symbolic protest form had been prevalent throughout 60s; deploying it here, wormholing, as it were, the conservative (i.e., not yet radicalized) convention space, plugged that scene into a kind of seismic line of flight running from Grant Park to the

Amphitheater (and beyond, diachronically, to other protest marches), the node of transference—the moment of (dis)charge— being the *collapse* of the McCarthy candidacy and the Peace Plank (McCarthy, curiously detached from his own campaign, perhaps unaware of or untouched by its dialogic momentum, or simply accepting a *fait accompli*)…]

Yipped: Ginsberg said—since it's all about (ideo)theater, changing mind(set)—just say the war is over. And Ochs sang:

> So do your duty boys and join with pride
> Serve your country in her suicide
> Find a flag so you can wave good-bye
> But just before the end even treason might be worth a try

Documents: (*aside*) (Composed for the '67 War Is Over rally, Ochs' and producer Larry Marks march-like arrangement, *a la* John Philip Sousa, "radiates Americana.") (68a) [*To Yipped and Fluxed*] Maybe you could do this… [*To audience*] from Hoffman's testimony under examination during the Chicago seven trial:

[Fluxbit 15. *Performed by* **Documents** *and volunteer(s) as* **Yipped** *and* **Fluxed** *read following excerpt*]

> THE WITNESS: Well, I had cowboy boots, and brown pants and a shirt, and I
> had a grey felt ranger cowboy type hat down over my eyes, like this.
>
> MR. WEINGLASS: What, if anything occurred while you were sitting there
> having breakfast?
>
> THE WITNESS: Well, two policemen came in and said, "We have orders to
> arrest you. You have something under your hat."
> So I asked them if they had a search warrant….
>
> I lifted up the hat and I went "Bang! Bang!"
> They grabbed me by the jacket and pulled me across the

> bacon and eggs
> and Anita over the table, threw me on the floor and out the door and threw
> me against the car, and they handcuffed me.
> I was just eating the bacon and going "Oink Oink!"

NHL: V. mainstage acts, the Broadway of political theater as it continues still (media critic Norman Solomon on the '96 DNC): "Scripted events like photo-ops and televised speeches are shadow plays, diverting attention from what occurs far from media spotlights "(684sol7).

Yipped: But the *Grand mise en scene* of '68, bounded to the north (stage Left) by Lincoln Park, and the south (stage Right) by the stockyards and the Convention site.... (*excerpt read by* **Documents** *and* **Fluxed**)

> MR. KUNSTLER: Now, Mr. Ochs, do you know what guerrilla theater is?
>
> THE WITNESS: Guerrilla theater creates theatrical metaphors for what is going on in the world outside.

Yipped: It's all a-Happenin', beyond anyone's intentions...

Documents: [*aside*] (the foregoing form Phil Ochs,' and following from Ginsberg's testimonies during the Chicago Seven trials)

[Fluxbits 16 and, time permitting, 17—including "(Un)self-defense censoring," recalling Rezkinoff's *Testimony... are performed by* **Documents** *and volunteer(s)*
as ***Fluxed*** *and* ***Yipped*** *read excerpts*]:

> MR. WEINGLASS: What was occurring at the park as you got there?
>
> THE WITNESS: There was a great crowd lining the outskirts of the park and a
> little way into the park on the inner roads, and there was a larger crowd
> moving in toward the center. We all moved in toward the

center, and at the
center of the park, there was a group of ministers and rabbis who had
elevated a great cross about ten-foot high in the middle of a circle of
people who were sitting around, quietly, listening to the ministers conduct
a ceremony.

MR. WEINGLASS: And would you relate to the Court and jury what was being
said and done at the time?

THE WITNESS: Everybody was seated around the cross, which was at the center
of hundreds of people, people right around the very center adjoining the
cross. Everybody was singing, "We Shall Overcome," and "Onward Christian
Soldiers...."

[*volunteers perform self-censoring acts using black carboard rectangles*]

I was seated with my friends on a little hillock looking down on the crowd,
which had the cross in the center. And on the other side, there were a lot
of glary lights hundreds of feet away down the field. The ministers lifted
up the cross and took it to the edge of the crowd and set it down facing
the lights where the police were. ....

MR. WEINGLASS: And after the ministers moved the cross, what happened?

THE WITNESS: ... there was a burst of smoke and tear gas around the cross, and the cross was enveloped with tear gas, and the people who were carrying the cross were enveloped with tear gas which began slowly drifting over the crowd.

MR. WEINGLASS: And when you saw the persons with the cross and the cross
being gassed. what, if anything, did you do?

THE WITNESS: I turned to Burroughs find said, "They have gassed the cross
of Christ."

MR. FORAN: Objection, if the Court please.

Fluxed: There will be none, I think, here.

TICS: OR there will; your own scenarios suggest it [*sings*] "The young land started growin' / The young blood started flowin..."

Documents: [*aside*] (Ochs, "I Ain't Marching Anymore").

TICS: Try putting this in Playbill

[*during* **TICS** *summation, midpoint* Fluxbit 18—A Moment for Artaud—
19 and 20 *are performed by volunteers*].

Hoffman's mode of "comic "intervention in the political process often walked the line between the hilarious (or insane) and the deadly serious; not even fellow radicals always knew how literally to take his scenarios. *Seed* publisher and Chicago Yip Abe Peck recalls that in the planning stages for convention week actions, on "Wednesday, Abbie penciled in a riot. He was talking about twenty to thirty killed, six thousand wounded. Was that a prediction, a caution, a desire, an obituary, gallows humor?" (Sloman 127). Jerry Rubin made some equally disconcerting remarks, seeming to mix symbolic and literal blood: "My plan in Chicago was we want good to be facing evil, we want young white kids beaten by the cops" (Dream 122). Of course, such a dis-easing response is exactly what Hoffman and Yip's rhetoric was deployed to provoke; yet, despite his off-hand militant posturing ("well, maybe a few people will be killed in Chicago, but it will save thousands of lives in Vietnam") (Sloman 122), what finally "happened" in the radicalized space of the DNC was not Hoffman's kind of theater.[47]

Documents: Will you try? Just give me some space…

we instantaneously threw up a marshal line and locked arms. … And then the command was given to charge us with blue helmets and swinging batons. There were policemen literally chanting "Kill Davis" as I was being attacked. I was the first one to be hit. The first strike brought me to the ground, opening my skull (Rennie Davis, testimony, Chicago Seven trial).

[*excerpts read by* ***Fluxed*** *and* ***Yipped***]

THE WITNESS: Well—[sings] "Where have all the flowers—
THE COURT: Just a minute, young lady. THE WITNESS: [sings] "—where have all the flowers gone?"
DEPUTY MARSHAL JOHN J. GRACIOUS: I'm sorry. The Judge would like to speak to you.
THE COURT: We don't allow any singing in this Court. I'm sorry
(Judy Collins testimony, Chicago Seven trials)

TICS: Huh! In his book-length narrative poem, *1968: A History in Verse*, Sanders states that he "wanted to get the Hell out of Chicago / to the safety of Avenue A." Out of the "hasty signs" and "hasty props" of Convention week, he comments (echoing Blake and quoting Yeats' "Easter Sunday 1916"), "a terri-

---

47. **CO**: Hoffman's schedule of events for the week included workshops in self-defense, but even these tactics were vehicles for a counter-symbolic offensive: Japanese snake dancing, for example, v. Western style military/police lines.

ble beauty was born" (203), a striking image of which might be Abe Peck's grotesque rewriting, *in true Yip-flux spirit*, of a pop/Hip song lyric as warning to prospective Festival attendees: "if you're coming to Chicago, be sure to wear some armor in your hair" (qtd. in Farber, 49).

[*excerpts read by* ***Fluxed*** *and* ***Yipped***]

The Hilton bar was right there. A guy had combat boots on, kicked the window, broke it, and everybody went storming through the plate-glass window into the bar.
(Jeff Nightbyrd, Sloman, 154)

Everybody's hands and face were cut, their hair was full of glass and there was no place to hide. So you got beat up and then dragged through revolving doors. I don't know if you've done that but the human body is not designed to be pulled through a revolving door.
(Tom Hayden, Sloman, 154)

MR. WEINGLASS: Directing your attention to the morning of August 24, 1968, where were you?
THE WITNESS: I was on a plane coming from New York to Chicago.
MR. WEINGLASS: Now, *en route* to Chicago while you were on the plane, what if anything, did you do?
THE WITNESS: **I wrote poetry....**

I am the Angel King saying the Angel King/As the mobs in the Amphitheater, streets, Coliseums, parks and offices/ Scream in despair over meat and metal Microphone.
(Allen Ginsberg's testimony, Chicago Seven trials)

TICS: And I (still) say (*quoting him/herself*):

"Part of the reason behind the escalation of violence throughout the week was that Daley didn't fully comprehend—and hence couldn't intelligently counter—the subversive force in all its modulations: The Yip actions—symbolic/activist, parodistic interventions; the MOBE/SDS brand of practical, nonviolent resistance/protest; the youth who came mainly for the advertised festivities and to be part of the 'scene'—direct, explosive, many of them street smart, influenced as much perhaps by Up Against the Wall Motherfucker's aggressive posturing[48] as Rubin's Zenned "act first, analyze later" activism—but not necessarily motivated by a clear political agenda; and the 'legal,' 'respectable,' symbolic, and controlled actions of the McCarthy delegates.[49] To meet these various modes of resistance with the unreflective response of a billy club and tear gas canister said a lot about the lack of suppleness of the forces for 'law and order,' how easily they could be provoked, but also to what extent they would go to protect that order and to the limits of a Yip-fluxed political theater, of radicalized laughter, in defusing those forces."[50]

Documents [*aside*]: Somebody throw in a Fluxbit, please!

---

48. **CO**: Yes, the UAWM connection works, here. Their slogan was "Armed Love"; they ran recruitment ads juxtaposing the image of a revolver with middle class cultural illusionism—"We're looking for people who like to draw"; at a March, '68, SDS National Council meeting they karate-chopped a gold foil packaged brick, stating "We're going to smash capitalism" (Gitlin, *Years of Hope*, 240)

49. **CO**: Once they moved beyond the territory of the Symbolic Order (offscript, so to speak, and into the streets), they were quickly assimilated into one disruptive mass with the other protesters that had to be disciplined. Never mind the delegate's badges—though these labels of apparent legality did "mean," to the police, linking up to an appropriate response of preferential treatment, at least to a point; beyond that point somehow their meaning became altered, the codes malfunctioned (though there were still plenty of "delegates" who were what their badges said) and they were "marked" as "other" (police slashed the tires of McCarthy delegates' cars). In the heat of some early frays, the cops removed *their* nameplates and numbers, so it was fist to fist—and who were they then? But I digress...

50. **CO**: Interestingly, the System partly orchestrated its own decollage upheaval. According to a 1978 CBS News special, army sources boasted that "about one demonstrator in six" at the '68 DNC had been an undercover agent; some were Federal agents, and others were Daley's men—police officers doubling as "demonstrators" (Gitlin, *Years of Hope*, 323).

[Fluxbit 21 *performed by volunteers as* **Documents**, ***Fluxed*** *and* ***Yipped*** *continue to read excerpts*]

THE WITNESS: I was referring to defending myself.
.....

R. SCHULTZ: To kill the policeman.
THE WITNESS: To defend himself.
MR. SCHULTZ: And that means if necessary to kill that policeman, does it not?
THE WITNESS: If that policeman is attacking me, if he is violating the law, if he is violating the law unjustly, attacking me, —I am not talking about a policeman down the street stopping somebody—
MR. SCHULTZ: That means killing, if necessary, doesn't it?
THE WITNESS: No.
MR. SCHULTZ: You will not kill a policeman, is that right?
THE WITNESS: It is not the desire to kill, and that's what you are trying to put in the tone of it, and it's not that—
(Bobby Seale, cross examination, Chicago Seven trial)

> MR. SCHULTZ: In Mr. Stahl's office on August 7, did you hear Hoffman say that the Festival of Life that you were discussing with Deputy Mayor Stahl and Al Baugher would include nude-ins at the beaches, public fornications, body painting, and discussions of draft and draft evasion? Did you hear that?
> THE WITNESS: Nudism, draft counseling, the beach thing, but he didn't use the word "public fornication."
> MR. SCHULTZ: He didn't use that word. What word did he use in its place?
> THE WITNESS: Probably fuck-in.

(Ed Sanders, cross examination, Chicago Seven trial)

MR. SCHULTZ: When you told the people in Lincoln Park, "Pick up a gun, pull the spike from the wall, because if you pull it out and you shoot well, all I'm gonna do is pat you on the back and say, 'Keep on shooting,' "That was part of your revolutionary tactics too, was it not, sir?
THE WITNESS: Yes, sir, and if you look generally—

MR. SCHULTZ: Please, that is all.
THE COURT: You have answered the question.
THE WITNESS: I strike that answer on the grounds that that particular
question is wrong because it ain't clear.
THE COURT: I have some news for you, sir.
(there is applause in the courtroom)
THE COURT: I do the striking here, and will the marshals exclude from the courtroom anyone who applauded. This isn't a theater. Anyone who applauded the witness may go out and is directed to leave.
(Bobby Seale, cross examination, Chicago Seven trial)

TICS: This simply supports my point...

Fluxed and **Yipped**: More Flux!

[Fluxbits 22 & 23. *Performed by volunteers*]

TICS : [*continuing to quote himself*]: "Though Yip may have pre-conceived the DNC as an opportunity for large-scale *detournement*, for a city-wide happening—bigger even then the '67 symbolic siege of the Pentagon—they may have overlooked that their unwitting audience/participants—the Chicago PD (the "pig") as well as some of the protesters—were not SoHo aesthetes and may not have quite been "in tune" with the symbolic, Yip-Flip intentions of the event's designers, even though many events leading up to and during the first part of convention week were obvious symbolic carnivalizations of 'official' culture:... [*excerpts read by* **Documents** *and* **NHL**]

MR. WEINGLASS: Now you also indicated that Mr. Rubin mentioned nonverbal education. Will you explain what that is to the Court and jury?
(Allen Ginsberg, testimony, Chicago Seven trial)

MR. WEINGLASS: As you were running, what if anything were the police doing?
THE WITNESS: They were beating people, pushing peo-

ple up against the doorways of buildings. And, I mean, we couldn't get any further onto the sidewalk we were on. And there were masses of people on the sidewalk, and some people were trying to get into building and others were being beaten into doorways. And I saw a policeman coming towards me, and I motioned to him with the microphone, that I had turned it off, and the camera was behind me. I thought he would understand I wasn't a demonstrator, and he hit me.
MR. WEINGLASS: What happened?
THE WITNESS: He hit me across the neck and shoulders.
MR. WEINGLASS: What happened to you as you were hit?
THE WITNESS: I went down, and a man, there was a man standing in the doorway where I fell, he reached down to help me up, and the policeman hit him across the bridge of his nose and knocked his glasses off.
MR. WEINGLASS: And this man who attempted to assist you and was struck himself, was he filmed?
THE WITNESS: Yes, my husband filmed him sitting there with his head in his hands and a bloody wound on his head.
(Sarah Diamant, testimony, Chicago Seven trial)

We were tear gassed and there was a girl crying to her boyfriend,
"They can't do this, this is my world."
(John Sack, Sloman, 152)

TICS: the election of a pig—Pigasus—as presidential candidate at a mock convention cum celebration of LBJ's birthday; a Yip woman costumed as a "Native American" (punningly named "Helen Running Water"—run for water, piss on your grass, no running water in the parks) presenting a Lincoln Park sleeping permit application to Deputy Mayor Sthal, the permit wrapped in a Playboy Playmate of the Month foldout (signifying on Chicago's publishing industry and the ribald, (self)exploitative, "PR" nature of the whole event). Despite such parodic actions and the Yip's exaggerated rhetoric—"We will burn Chi to the ground," "we will fuck on the beaches," "we demand the Politics of Ecstasy," Acid for all!"—and other agitprop scenarios, such as spiking the Chicago water supply and delegates' drinks with LSD and sending out Yip "chics" (and "hyperpotent" young Yip men) to seduce delegates and their spouses, Daley took the Yips on their word[51]: the police and guard were ready to trade real beatings, split scalps, and gassings for symbolic testing.[52] Showcard...

Documents: Gothic! (*aside*) Fluxbit!

[Fluxbit 24. *Performed by volunteers*] (*inserts read by* **Documents** *and* **NHL**]

---

51. **CO**: Paul Krassner points up the difference—the slip or mis-phasing—between what the Yipped radicals thought they were up to and how Daley envisioned it: during negotiations for protest permits, Krassner remembers having this exchange with Stahl "'What do you guys plan to do in Chicago?' I said, 'Have you seen *Wild in the Streets*?, the film where teenagers took over the government and put acid in the water supply.' He said, 'No, We've seen *The Battle of Algiers*.' *Battle of Algeirs* is guerrillas blowing up ice cream parlors. So what was gon'a happen in Chicago was a clash between our mythology and their mythology" (Sloman 128). Other typically outrageous Yip scenarios planned for convention week—the "dummy agenda," Gitlin calls them—meant to be understood as imagery, as figures of desire, rather than literal "plans," incled a mass nude float-in in Lake Michigan, roaming the streets costumed as Viet Cong, and a mass draft-card burning spelling "beat army' in flames.

52. The New York Yip should have guessed (if not smelled) the gas coming, sobered by the March '68 fiasco in NY's Grand Central Station, which was billed, in a clash of symbols typical of Yip socio-political irony, as a media event in celebration of the spring equinox: the phrase "Peace Now" was inaugurated on the four faces of the terminal clock, imaginatively juxtaposing natural rhythms to the time-clock driven, anonymous movement of labor in service of capital. In an inspired moment, one of the 6, 000 demonstrators who turned out to "occupy" this node of practical transit "detoured" it into a space of desire, ripping (capturing?) the hands from one of the information booth clocks. Foreshadowing things to come in Chicago, fifty cops gathered outside the station and charged the crowd with clubs, beating generally (including non-mainstream newspersons from the *Village Voice*), but especially Yips (Hoffman was beaten unconscious). Daley, too, had shown his true colors in his brutal responses to ghetto uprisings and protests following the King murder in March '68 (white supporters marched in sympathy with the black Americans) and to a peaceful April 27 anti-war March in downtown Chicago. But perhaps Yip thought that this time in Chicago, because the "whole world [would be] watching," things would be different.

THE WITNESS: Most of our consciousness, since we are continually looking at images on television and listening to words, reading newspapers, talking in courts such as this...prevents us from breathing deeply in our bodies and sensing more subtly and sweetly the feelings that we actually do have....

(Allen Ginsberg, testimony, Chicago Seven trial)

R. WEINGLASS: What was your purpose in filming these events?

THE WITNESS: To use them as research material for my doctoral dissertation.

(Sarah Diamant, testimony, Chicago Seven trial)

TICS: The logic?

NHL: Yes...but, I can see a point: the goal was to be a "Cultural Revolutionary"—it's the only thing that makes it all worth it. Even a courtroom could be shown up as a stage for set pieces, a THEATER OF PROCEDURAL CONVENTIONS that misses the reality of the "evidence." Consider Phil Ochs testimony (aborted by the Court) as witness for the defense during the Chicago Seven trial [*excerpt read by* **NHL** *and* **Documents**]:

> MR. KUNSTLER: Now, Mr. Ochs, I call your attention to sometime in the vicinity of 6:00 p.m. Tuesday, August 27...
> ....
> Did you sing a song that day?
> THE WITNESS: Yes, "I Ain't Marching Anymore."
>
> .....
>
> MR. KUNSTLER: Now, would you stand and sing that song so the jury can hear the song that the audience heard that day?
> MR. SCHULTZ: If the Court please, this is a trial in the Federal District Court. It is not a theater. We don't have to sit and listen to the witness sing a song. Let's get on with the trial. I object.

MR. KUNSTLER: Your Honor, this is definitely an issue in the case....

NHL: The "case" to which Kunstler refers is defendant Jerry Rubin's intent and the "mood of the crowd," since Rubin requested Ochs to sing that particular song at the Lincoln Park rally; it is also the case we are making here of performative intervention...

TICS: (well, we can all agree that precedence for such exists—see "Legal Discourse v Poetic Discourse..."above...)

NHL: in *all* cases, that which the court refuses to hear, as did the Democratic political machine in Chicago... [*excerpt read by* **Documents** *and* **NHL**]:

> THE COURT: I sustain the objection.
>
> MR. KUNSTLER: Your Honor, he is prepared to sing it exactly as he sang it on that day.
> THE COURT: I am not prepared to listen, Mr. Kunstler

NHL: The Defense's dramaturgical challenge to the hegemonic discourse marks the disavowal necessary to maintain conviction (the ability to "convict," but also to believe in the system—of jurisprudence, in this case); marks also how (any) authoritarian discourse must (forcibly) exclude under the guise of inclusiveness ("hearing" all the "evidence"), of finding "Truth," in order to sustain power—the "Jury" (read populace, citizenry, *audience*) is only allowed to *hear* what the Court *allows*...

Fluxed: Whose italics? You're beginning to sound like me.

[**Fluxed** *and* **NHL** *try to beat each other to the props to do* Fluxbit 25, *exchange a smile, while* **Documents**:]

Documents:

Hi Panel—

I'm attaching the original proposal so we can begin thinking about what might take place. I'd like this to be collaborative, dialogic and somewhat improvisatory, with surprises (for all). My idea is, in addition a central discourse (or set of discourses), to have some pre-scripted, Flux events (mini conceptual performances) that could be brought in a spontaneously, in the manner of (Bop) jazz performance (i.e., in tune/tempo with the whole, and the tempo can change according to...), or as a 60s-like "Happening." This would require some attentive listening, though we can also agree on a kind of rough script, once we see what we have, and/or the panel "chair" could function as director/conductor, giving cues. Also, the process (even the proposal, even this note, even your responses to this note) can be part of what *happens*. So this will be as much performance as panel. So please look over the proposal and let's start gathering materials/ideas. I already have a collection of bits which dialogue with/play on/through the Chicago '68 events and riots (including maskings and "throws" of various sorts, and other disruptive counter-discourse events), and we can certainly use these and variations of these. I'll send them to you soon. Events don't have to be specifically related to '68—but in spirit of, and contemporary connections, etc.

Fluxed: The dynamics of convention week—at least *this* (re)presentation of it as a perhaps unwieldy, tension and conflict riddled structuration (rather than clearly established structure) and what this means, in terms of Fluxed/Flipped awareness...

Documents: tttttttttttghhh [*drat cat on the keys*] "Psychic guerrilla warfare now" (Keith Lampe, "On Making a Perfect Mess," September, 1967; Albert, 405-7).

Fluxed: —is perhaps best expressed by Erving Goffman's definition of "negative experience": "If the whole frame can be shaken, rendered problematic, then this too can ensure that prior involvements—and prior distances—can be broken up and that, whatever else happens, a dramatic change can occur in what it is that s being experienced" (VL 82). This problematizing of perception and experience, defamiliarizing the ordinary by tilting it toward the absurd is what "happened" in Chicago, and is happening now as we bring these cultural materials into dialogue;

Documents: "Picture W. C. Fields announcing: 'You don't *decide* something is absurd—you *recognize* it.'" (Paul Krassner, "The Birth of the Yippie Conspiracy," January, 1968; Albert, 411) (italics imagined to be W. C. Fields')

Fluxed: this relatively (deceptively) simple *detournement* is a consequence of no single force/confrontation, not just MOBE and Yip *vis a vis* each other and Daley's knee-jerk reactions, but the whole situation, including the critical work we do here now. As Flux artist George Brecht images this nonlinear mode of thought, referring to what he calls the "Duchampian paradigm" of art-making, the artist's "works are like points scattered off into many different directions... like a spiral" (Martin 40-42; qtd. in Smith, 20).

Documents: "the Buddha nature / of everyone...like a million earthworms / tunneling under this structure / till it falls" (Diane Di Prima, "Revolutionary Letter # 7, "1971; Albert, 394).

TICS: Hmmm. And so you might say—may I? [*quoting* **Fluxed** *doing himself—i.e.* ***TICS*** *—as* **Lecturer**]:

[Fluxbit 26. *Performed by volunteers*]

Lecturer: The goal of Fluxus performance, as the Yip-Flipped/Fluxed DNC and of this critical reenactment, is to raise questions, to open and extend the dialogue rather than seek resolutions. Yip antics attempted to screw the DNC toward political comedy by transmogrifying some of its major symbols (i.e., the nomination of a pig as presidential candidate),[53] by

53. **CO**: An event that uncannily foreshadowed the Chicago 8 trial, which became the Chicago 7 trial after Bobby Seale was removed for contempt of court and tried separately—following the mock nomination, on the Friday

> attempting to de-nominate the place of the master signifier (and certainly de-humanize it) as much as replace it with ridiculous meaning. Their goal, that is, was primarily toward emptying, toward anti-meaning, then toward reconstitution/ revisioning of the symbolic order; Derridean laughter rather than Shakespearean comedy. A major method of such madness, of such decollage critical consciousness, as in the messy product we are dealing with here, a legacy of late 60s volatile and multifarious radical thought and action...

Fluxed: You said it...

Documents: "This is a period of emergency. Therefore emergency theatre is the theatre of awareness" (Julian Beck, "Notes Toward a Statement on Anarchism and Theatre," 1972; Albert, 408-10).

TICS: *is*, as John Hanhardt says of Wolf Vostell's early 60s TV "de-collages," to "erase and recompose imagery" to "destabilize the institutionalized codes and meanings of the dominant culture" (Milman, 124).[54]

---

before the opening of convention week, seven Yippies, along with the Pig, were arrested. [Fluxbit 27 *is performed by volunteers during the following note*]

54. **CO**: **TICS**, or perhaps **Documents**, or **TICS** as **Lecturer** could bring up some other points of connection among Yip, Fluxus, and Happenings. In the months before the DNC, for example, Hoffman envisioned convention week as the site for a "Community of Consciousness," a gathering of "technologists and poets, of artists and community organizers, of anyone who has a vision" who would strategize a prototype for the "New Society" (Albert, 424). One way to view Convention Week, then, is as a kinetic "social sculpture" (Beuys' phrase). A (somewhat less idealistic) social vector resonates through many Fluxus events, as well: "Fluxus anything... is a voluntary association that emphasizes certain qualities, values, and social practices in the world" (Stiles, 70). Coming close to the intentions of protest leaders during Convention Week, in April '63 Maciunas proposed several socially disruptive "propaganda actions," blockages intended to draw attention to the operation of the "machine" and stimulate critical self-reflection (literal "break downs," in some cases—jammed transit on bridges and in tunnels). In a less direct interventionist vein, Maciunas' 1966 *Multicycle* emphasized the social valence of aesthetic performance by literally linking together a number of bicycles, necessitating co-responsive group action, a kind of jazz ensemble

Documents: "Nobody could explain what it all meant yet everyone was fascinated. It was pure information, pure imagery, which in the end is truth" (Hoffman, "Revolution for the Hell of It," February, 1968; Albert, 420).

Fluxed: We do Flux: "work the frame" (Milman, 82).

Documents: "The goal now is to disrupt an insane society.
We've already applied for the permit" (Krassner, *op cit*, 416).

TICS [*finally giving in(up)*]:
vvvvvvvvvvvvvvvgggggggggggggggggggggggggggggggggggg'; //, msebnnnnell... [*Get rid of the cats; keep the doors closed!*] In that case...

[Fluxbit 28. *Performed by* **TICS** *and volunteers*]

*****

---

with training wheels, or a kinetic, graphic representation of the interpersonal tuning collective action requires (the cycles were joined by bars in a way to leave open rectangles between linkages—a spectacularly tongue-in-cheek instruction book for political demonstrations) (Stiles, 86). Convention Week as a Whole, however (i.e., in the historical moment of its initial performance), may be closer to a Happening than a collection of Flux events. In a lyric passage in *Assemblages, Happenings, Environments* (1966), Allan Kaprow envisions the movement of "art" from conventional framed (off) space to a social space where it is no longer clearly distinguished from human action, and where imaginary ("dream") and social space merge:

"The pieces of paper curled up off the canvas, were removed from the surface to exist in their own, became more solid as they grew into other materials and reaching out into the room they filled it entirely. Suddenly, there were jungles, crowded streets, littered alleys., dream spaces... people moving" (165; Stiles, 93). Recall Michaux's table.

Putting this notion of an expanded, socially engaged art more bluntly, and in a spirit of guerrilla agitation closer to the experiential texture of the DNC, in 1960 Claes Oldenburg rallied for a de/recrowning of ["high art"] aesthetic hierarchies: "I am for... an art that embroils itself with the everyday crap & still comes out on top... an art that imitates the human, that is comic, if necessary, or violent" (Stiles, 93).

Think now again of the fluxed, de-collaged inflection of Convention Week limned above, while politically disastrous, made good art.

Yipped: The following scenes, emblematic of the disillusionment broached by collapse of the Peace Plank—or, more accurately, the failure of the democratic will and the loss of surety in a morally, spiritually inhabitable future—some, caught by chance in the camera eye, due to the loosely scripted nature of media coverage; others unrecorded or unrecordable—hybrid events of imagination and reality; mass movements, demonstrators and delegates—the Living Theatre of Convention week—balanced by individual actions; Happenings that, reproduced (on video, in this text), stick in the mind as the (anti)images of what could no longer be articulated: ...

[*several* Fluxbits *are performed by volunteers during the following—as many as time allows...*]

Documents: "In point of fact nothing happened" (Hoffman, *Ibid*, 420).

Yipped: A priest, standing in the midst of the New York delegation, offering a prayer.

NHL: After a film honoring Bobby Kennedy, a standing ovation to a blank screen.

Fluxed: Delegates taking their protest theater to the streets: as I (inspired by CBS news editors) juxtapose them, the theatrical black cloth Amphitheater march transforms into the delegate's candlelight street march to Grant Park (a subsequent enactment of shifted solidarity that bears the trace—is overdetermined by—protester's marches throughout the week), symbolic continuities eliding spatio-temporal discontinuity as the ribbon of black cloth threading the brightly lit but emptying Amphitheater becomes suddenly pervasive as the night, punctuated by 500 wavering points of candescence; or, we might say, the cloth, spooling out like a sinuous dividing line, disenchants, as if drawing our attention to bright but flattened, meaningless frames of a discarded film on the Convention cutting room floor (the obverse of protesters' idealistic inscriptions chalked on the dividing line of Michigan Avenue at week's end), followed by black leader, the film's end...

Yipped: Protesters facing the lines of National Guard—blockages, "negotiations" (empty processes) collapsing into raw repression and resistance—what "works"—

CO: V (v.?): Peace! Victory! Lines, dark runnels—flecked with light...

NHL: The detachment of Democratic candidates: McCarthy and son playing catch with an orange; looking down on the riots and, casting allusions (it "looks like a Breughel," "like the battle of Canae") (Farber, 201; Kusch 103); a whiff of tear gas; HHH kissing the TV screen of his nomination.

Yipped: A Barricade—built to defend against a blockage? Though alluding to the May '68 French students' barricade (and co-opting some of its symbolic value), the Chicago protesters' "barricade," in the middle of a park, blocked nothing, was pure allusion and impromptu, site-specific Happening. It was not so much a barricade...

NHL (*fading under what follows*): as a piling up of references to commodity culture, the stuff of leisure/evasion—a flimsy assemblage of picnic tables, benches, trash receptacles, whatever came to hand, including what both emblematizes and in public events literally governs authorized uses of culture—police lines...

Fluxed: (we could lend an imaginative hand...)—all under the sign of a crude cross, also erected in Lincoln Park, the cross forming an assemblage with the barricade that metonymically "sanctions" other pilings...

Documents [*reading a city tour blurb*]:

> Besides seemingly countless bars frequented by young, upwardly-mobile professionals and DePaul University students, Lincoln Park provides many theatres and cinemas, trendy boutiques, coffee shops, restaurants, and SUV dealerships.... It is... undeniably the current yuppie Mecca of Chicago. (*All Chicago,* www.all-chicago.com/attractions.html#british, 1/12/05)

CO: The barricade and cross were gassed.

Yipped: The gassing the cross, staged with long shadows, compared to the lackluster barricading in *Medium Cool*, like custodians stacking chairs.

Fluxed: The Tuesday night gassing in Lincoln Park: Club Police State. A "primitive," disturbing, percussive beat of clubs against hands as masked disco cops emerge from clouds of gas. An S/M writhing out into the "audience." The gas as "thick as milk" (MLK?) (Chi in 68, 154). Black whipped.

CO: "Beautiful... beautiful..." (John Schultz; qtd. in Gitlin, *The Sixties*, 328)

NHL: Yip and MOBE initiators comment from the sidelines, unable to keep pace with what was set in motion.

Yipped: Lying in the grass, I note
a lilt in the branches;
slight tremor beneath

TICS: Dialogic shot groupings: tight shot of delegates in heated argument on the convention floor after news of street riots v. shots of mass street actions v. Marx Brothers crowded into a ship's cabin.

CO: Street protests as a backdrop for pre-nomination cocktail parties at the Hilton.

Documents: Working class gangs, Yips, Hips, MOBE, Old & New Left; liberal delegates, ministers, WWII and Vietnam vets; media personnel, bystanders—all bleeding. Rivulets of...

Fluxed: Graffiti—"Break in Break in" on Yipped maps of the International Amphitheatre (Farber, 166)

NHL: Park chant-ins v. "patriotic" sing-ins...

Yipped: Pilot's voice over the intercom of McCarthy's charted plane, lifting away from Chicago: "We are leaving Prague" (Witcover, 344). Applause. Maps of the two cities.

Documents: Phil Ochs anti-war "commercial" (reconstructed):

> Now, I enjoy violence as much as the next guy, but enough is enough. Five seasons is plenty for the most exciting series.
>
> On Saturday, November 25, we are going to declare the war over and celebrate the end of the war in Washington Square Park at 1 p.m.
>
> That's right, I said declare the war over from the bottom up.
>
> This simple remedy has provided relief for countless frustrated citizens and has been overlooked for an amazingly long time...

(Albert, 398)

TICS: A minister down, head bleeding, skull fractured by a carbine...

***

CO: **Om...Arrrr...**

Catcher (Fluxed): Batterrrr up!

All: The whole world is watching!

Join us!

Yipped: travel in pairs and wear riot helmets

Documents: "half of us thought we were in Germany and half of us thought we were in Russia" (Elinor Langer, qtd in Gitlin, *The Sixties*, 336).

All: *This land is your land...* (Mary Travers & Peter Yarrow; Farber 202)

Yipped: don't get caught in a large action. See you in the streets.

TICS: "We were all going... to heaven... going... the other way"

(Dickens, qtd. in Gitlin, *The Sixties*, 335).

Fluxed: get the cameras and beat the press

Documents: this orderly city Chicago's lovely parks

TICS: more pay for cops

CO: this is not an authorized march

Documents: "they were a mixture of horses and whatever else they could find, chairs and crap from all over the place" (Jacques Levy, Sloman 146)

All: *mine eyes have seen the glory*

NHL: hired historical phantom…

Fluxed: You shoulda been there, man, we exposed them, we exposed them (Hoffman, Sloman, 159)

CO: he got no chance anyway

TICS: if I let anyone else across, I'm going to lose this bridge

All: *oh beautiful for spacious skies*

Documents: "I got my sharkskin pants on, got my dago tee… my Cuban heels… and I'm going, this is fucking fantastic!" (Bob Zmuda, Sloman 144)

NHL: welcome to Chicago, "the city that works"

Documents [*aside*]: (From Daley's DNC opening night "welcome" speech)
Documents: make love, not war

All: Join us! Join us!

CO: get the fuck back, I'm telling you!

NHL: what do we want? Peace. When do we want it? Now

All: oink oink!

Yipped: blink your lights...

Documents [*aside*]: (or "flick your lights"—street protesters calling for support from McCarthy workers on the upper floors of the Hilton, Thursday night)

All: **America America**

NHL: the streets belong to the people

Documents: "so I probably was the fastest radicalized [eighteen-year-old] you could ever see" (Yamuda, Sloman 144)

All: The whole world is watching!
From the...to the shining sea...

Fluxed: this is the way we will go on from here (McCarthy addressing protesters)

CO: you are a bunch of motherfuckers!

TICS: Father, semantics won't save you from the cops (92)

All: *for amber waves of grain*

join us! (95)

Yipped: why, I hardly recognize you without your helmet (94)
CO: Stop! Proper citation!

TICS: you can't go on (96)

NHL: You can't be revolutionary without a TV set (Jerry Rubin, in Albert, 443)

CO: liberals go home (any page)

All: *where have all the flowers gone?*

Documents: look, I'm no leader (102)

Yipped: Don't leave us! (103)

TICS: hell, I'm taking off my badge and going to dinner with Gregory (118)

CO: I would like to invite you to *my* house this evening (*not* 109)

All: arrest us all! (122)

Yipped: stay out of the alleys (132)

All: **Oh say can you see**

CO: stop, or I'll shoot! (op cit., 134)

NHL: those incredible scenes on television (139)

All: "*Kick Out the Jams, Motherfucker*" (MC5) (Farber, 177)

TICS: you can listen to them but don't talk to them (137)

Fluxed: wouldn't you rather hold a girl than a gun? (137)

Yipped: what's wrong with taking your picture? (134)
Documents: I'm shocked beyond belief (McCarthy on Hilton raid) (141)

Fluxed: why don't you put that thing down and join us? (137)

All: Hell no, we won't go! (Farber, 181)

NHL: well, I mean, how can you stop the cops? (143)

All: **America America**

Documents: "Makes us want to pack up our cameras and go home" (Walter Cronkite, Kusch 103)

CO: ok, wise guy, let's have the camera (Ibid., 135)

TICS: Please excuse our digressions.

CO: **Long time passing...**

Catcher [Yipped]: Out!

***

All: Join us?

[*the closing* Fluxbit, Second Line (Show Me Your Tits!), *performed by panelists and volunteers*]

Bibliography

Albert, Judith and Stewart. *The Sixties Papers: Documents of a Rebellious Decade*. New York: Praeger, 1984.

All Chicago. www.all-chicago.com/attractions.html#british. 1/12/05.

Allsopp, Ric, Ken Friedman and Owen F Smith. *On Fluxus*. London: Routledge, 2002.

Anderson, John. "Bringing a Political Trial to Animated Life." *New York Times*. *Arts & Leisure*. 2.9.1. 11/26/06. Abstract at *NYTimes.com*. http://select.nytimes.com/gst/abstract.html?res=F30917F-D395A0C758EDDA80994DE404482. 7/25/07. See full article at *Curious Pictures*: http://www.curiouspictures.com/chicago10.htm 8/27/07.

Atack, Margaret. *May 68 in French Fiction and Film: Rethinking Society, Rethinking Representation*. Oxford, England: Oxford UP, 1999.

Chicago 10 [animated documentary film; 103 minutes, color, b/w]. Dir. and written by Brett Morgen. With Hank Azaria, Dylan

Baker, Nick Nolte, Mark Ruffalo, Roy Scheider, Liev Schreiber, Leonard Weinglass, and Jeffrey Wright. Participant Productions, 2006.

Cohen-Cruz, Jan, ed. and introd. *Radical Street Performance: An International Anthology*. London, England: Routledge, 1998.

Crisis in Chicago, 1968: Mayor Richard J. Daley's Official Report—the Untold Story of the Convention Riots. Report compiled by the Chicago Illinois Law Department. New York: Beeline Books, 1968.

Danto, A. C. *Unnatural wonders* [see especially "The world as warehouse: Fluxus and philosophy"]. New York: Farrar, Straus and Giroux, 2005.

DeKoven, Marianne. "Psychoanalysis and Sixties Utopianism." *JPCS: Journal for the Psychoanalysis of Culture & Society*, 8:2 (Fall 2003 Fall): 263-72.

—. *Utopia Limited: The Sixties and the Emergence of the Postmodern*. Durham, NC: Duke UP, 2004.

Di Prima, Diane. *Revolutionary letters, etc*. San Francisco: City Lights Books, 1971.

Farber, David. *Chicago '68*. Chicago: University of Chicago Press, 1988.

Fluxus. White Walls: A Magazine of Writing by Artists, 16 (Spring, 1987).

Friedman, Ken, ed. *The Fluxus Reader*. New York: Academy Editions, 1998.

—, Owen F Smith, and Lauren Sawchyn. *The Fluxus performance workbook*. Fortieth Anniversary ed. Great Britain: Performance Research e-Publications, 2002.

Ginsberg, Allen. *Collected Poems: 1947-1980*. New York: Harper & Row, 1984.

Gitlin, Todd. *The Sixties: Years of Hope, Days of Rage*. New York: Bantam, 1987.

—. *The Whole World is Watching: Mass Media in the Making & Unmaking of the New Left*. Berkeley: University of California Press, 2003.

Hanhardt, John C. "De-Collage and Television: Wolf Vostell in New York, 1963-64." Milman, 109-24.

Higgins, H. B. "Critical refluxtions" [Recollections of Fluxus performances]. *New Art Examiner*, 21 (March 1994), 17-23.

Higgins, Hannah. *Fluxus Experience*. Berkeley: University of California Press, 2002.

Higgins, Dick. *Modernism since postmodernism* [see especially "Fluxus: theory and reception"]. San Diego State Univ. Press, 1997.

Hoffman, Abbie, Rennie Davis, David T Dellinger, John Froines, Tom Hayden, Jerry Rubin and Lee Weiner. *Conspiracy* [interview with the Chicago Seven, 1/12/70]. VHS tape 1 videocassette (59 min.): sd. col.; 1/2 in. San Francisco, CA: Monaco Video, 1990, 1970.

—. *Revolution for the Hell of It*. New York: Dial Press, 1968.

Isenberg, Noah. "Critical Theory at the Barricades." *Lingua Franca: The Review of Academic Life*, 8:8 (1998 Nov): 19-24.

Jenkins, Janet, ed. *In the Spirit of Fluxus*. Minneapolis: Walker Art Center, 1993.

Kaiser, Charles. *1968 in America*. New York: Grove, 1988.

Kaprow, Allan, and Jean Jacques Lebel. *Assemblages, Environments & Happenings*. New York: H.N. Abrams, 1966.

—. *Essays on The Blurring of Art and Life*. Jeff Kelley, ed. Berkeley: University of California Press, 1993.

Kershaw, Baz. "Fighting in the Streets: Dramaturgies of Popular Protest, 1968-1989." *New Theatre Quarterly*,13:51(1997Aug):255-76.

Kotz, Liz. "Post-Cagean Aesthetics and the 'Event' Score." *October*, 95 (Winter 2001), 55-89.

Kusch, Frank. Battleground Chicago: *The Police and the 1968 Democratic National Convention.* Westport, CT: Praeger, 2004.

Lane, Mark. *Chicago Eyewitness*. New York: Astor-Honor, 1968.

Lebel, Jean-Jacques. "Notes on Political Street Theatre, Paris: 1968, 1969." Cohen-Cruz, 179-84.

Leary, Timothy. *The Politics of Ecstasy*. New York: College Notes & Texts, 1968.

Linder, Douglas O. *Famous Trials.* "Famous American Trials: The Chicago Seven Trial (1969-1970)." "The Chicago Seven Trial: Excerpts from the Trial Transcript." University of Missouri-Kansas City School of Law. 1995-2007. http://www.law.umkc.edu/faculty/projects/ftrials/ftrials.htm 9/14/07.

McDonough, Tom, ed. *Guy Debord and the Situationist International: Texts and Documents*. Cambridge, MA: MIT Press, 2002.

Motta, Carol Rogers. *Poetics of the 1968 Student Revolutions in France, Brazil and the United States*. *Dissertation Abstracts International, Section A: The Humanities and Social Sciences*, 61:2 (August 2000).

Milman, Estera, ed. *Fluxus: A Conceptual Country*. *Visible Language*, 26.1,2 (Winter/Spring, 1992).

Mailer, Norman. *Miami and the Siege of Chicago: An Informal History of the Republican and Democratic Conventions of 1968*. New York: Dibakd I. Fine, 1968.

Michaux, Henri. *The major ordeals of the mind, and the countless minor ones*. New York: Harcourt Brace Jovanovich, 1974.

O'Brien, Ellen and Lyle Benedict, comps. "*1968, August: Disturbances at the Democratic National Convention*." Chicago Public Library. November, 1996. http://www.chipublib.org/004chicago/disasters/1968dem_convention.html. 17 August, 2005.

O'Dell, Kathy. "Fluxus Feminus." *TDR: The Drama Review: A Journal of Performance Studies*, 41:1 [153] (Spring 1997), 43-60.

Ozersky, Josh. *Archie Bunker's America: TV in an Era of Change, 1968-1978*. Carbondale: Southern Illinois University Press, 2003.

Perloff, Marjorie. "Fluxier-than-Thou." *Modernism/Modernity*, 11:3 (September 2004), 581-87.

Phinney, David. "A Storm of Protestors..." *ABCNews.com*. 1998.

Romero, George, dir. *Night of the living dead*. Image Ten production. DVD video 1 videodisc (96 min.): sd., b&w; 4 3/4 in. New York: Elite Entertainment, 2002, 1968.

Rubin, Jerry. *Do it! Scenarios of the Revolution*. Introduction by Eldridge Cleaver. New York: Simon and Schuster, 1970.

Rush, Bobbie, Jerry Rubin, Phil Donahue, Eugene J McCarthy, Abbie Hoffman, Bob Green and Abraham Ribicoff. *SDS Weathermen* [includes audio of the '68 DNC, Donahue's 1969 interview with Jerry Rubin, comments by Abe Ribicoff and Gene McCarthy]. Sound Recording; 1 sound tape reel (25 min.): 3 3/4 ips, mono.; 7 in., 1/4 in. tape, 1984.

Sanders, Ed. *1968: A history in Verse*. Santa Rosa, CA: Black Sparrow Press, 1997.

Saper, Craig. "Fluxacademy: From Intermedia to Interactive Education." Milman, 79-96.

Sayres, Sohnya, Anders Stephanson, Stanley Aronowitz and Fredric Jameson, eds. *The 60s Without Apology*. Minneapolis: University of Minnesota Press, 1984.

Shaw-Miller, S. "'Concerts of everyday living': Cage, Fluxus and Barthes, interdisciplinarity and inter-media events." *Art History*, 19 (March 1996), 1-25.

Sloman, Larry. *Steal This Dream: Abbie Hoffman and the Countercultural Revolution in America*. New York: Doubleday, 1998.

Smith, Owen. "Fluxus: A Brief History and Other Fictions." Jenkins, 22-37.

—. *Fluxus: The History of an Attitude*. San Diego, CA: San Diego State University Press, 1998.

Stiles, Kristine. "Between Water and Stone; Fluxus Performance, A Metaphysics of Acts." Jenkins, 62-99.

The Strategy of Confrontation: Chicago and the Democratic National Convention—1968. Report prepared by Raymond F. Simon, the City of Chicago Corporation Counsel, and the City of Chicago Law Department; the Chicago Police Department, and the United States Attorney's Office, 6 September 1968.

Subversive Involvement in Disruption of 1968 Democratic Party National Convention: Hearings before the Committee on Un-American Activities. Compiled by HUAC staff researcher James Gallagher. House of Representatives (90th Congress, 2nd Session). Washington, D.C.: U.S. Government Printing Office, 1968.

Television Coverage of the Democratic National Convention, Chicago, Illinois, 1968. Special Committee on Investigations, Committee on Interstate and Foreign Commerce, House of Representatives. Washington, D.C.: U. S. Government Printing Office, 1969.

Walker, Daniel. *Rights in Conflict: Convention Week in Chicago, August 25-29, 1968*. Report prepared by Chicago Study Team to the National Commission on the Causes and Prevention of Violence (Daniel Walker, Director). New York: E. P. Dutton, 1968.

Waxler, Haskell, dir. *Medium Cool*. VHS tape 1 videocassette (111 min.): sd., col.; 1/2 in. Hollywood, CA: Paramount Pictures, 1994, 1969.

Williams, Emmett. *My Life in Flux and Vice Versa*. Stuttgart, Germany: Edition Hansjorg Mayer, 1991.

Witcover, Jules. *The Year the Dream Died: Revisiting 1968 in America*. New York: Warner Books, 1997.

Yippie. VHS tape 1 videocassette (12 min. 12 sec.): sd., b&w; 1/2 in. Berkeley, CA: Quest Productions, Catticus Corp. [re-release of Documentary Interlock Production], 1980, 1968.

Poetics of Protest [Conference Version]

[Fluxbit 1: *Opening*. Performed by **Fluxed**, aided by **Documents** and **Yipped**, who provide the props—this is an ongoing event]

T [*panel chair, as himself*]: This Critical Dialogue is based on the '68 DNC in Chicago; the voices are Documents, Fluxed(out) (Fluxed), New Historical Left (NHL), The Institute for Cultural Studies (TICS), Yipped(out) (Yipped), and CO (commentator/over voice, commanding officer, code officer, etc.)

They argue for several pages about how to begin the piece— Yipped and Fluxed want a more performative beginning, NHL wants to ease us into the historical mindset; then documents...[55]

Documents: No, no... I think we should begin,

"Convention Week '68: An Overview"

[*digital projection: detoured Mapquest*[tm] *map of Chicago, mouseover hotspots revealing protest history*]

T: Then TICS suggests:

TICS: What we need is a properly academic, but mildly intellectually kinky, beginning...

Punching the Line: Fluxus, Yippie, and the 1968 DNC

New Year's Eve, 1967; Abbie Hoffman, Jerry Rubin, Ed Sanders, and Paul Krassner gathered in rented rooms of Hoffman's Lower East Side loft—Loisaida, Alphabet city. Hoffman picks a letter—" Y"? (Kaiser 232)—and the Hip is Yipped, or flipped; "Yippie," the "Youth International Party," as Paul Krassner dubbed the movement, began as a joke, a bit of Fluxus-like *detournement*, with perhaps a tip of the hat to the "Fluxus International Party," a like-minded art movement that pre-

55. CO: see the "expanded version" for the elided content, here and elsewhere...

dated Yippie by nearly a decade. The half-serious series of events that would be scripted for that summer were still a fold in the imagination, yet at the 1968 DNC (8/22–29), Yippie would find its shape, rebus-like, dialogically, through a partly impromptu, "de-collage" reworking of "Convention City" (cf. Fluxus artist Wolf Vostell's "civic" installations of the same period— "de-collage" works through de(con)struction to (re)construction).

T: And Yipped again:

Yipped: Or simply:

Lecturer: (Craig Saper on Fluxus): "participants interact with the ideas, playing through possibilities rather than deciding once and for all on meaning."[56]

[*to Fluxed*] Catcher?

Fluxed [*T becoming Fluxed*]: (meaning of the product is determined by the processes of production?).

Yipped [*becoming* **Lecturer**]: It's all up for grabs. Try the position of the Other, from the position of Another...

Fluxed [*as Catcher*] (*glove smack*): "Play...!

Yipped (*feigning stomach punch*):[57] Step right up, attempt your own Flux-Yipped antics...

(**Fluxed** *lobs something in the direction of* **Yipped**/*Lecturer*)

Yipped [*observing projectile where it lies*]: Daley—old school, production economics; what you can see hear touch—no image/symbol bullshit.

56. **CO**: for complete documentation, see bibliography, original script...

57. CO: Dan Rather takes one to midriff on the Convention floor—Mayor Daley's thugs.

Fluxed [*still as Catcher, growing impatient of awaiting the signals, or even knowing who the pitcher is*]: Batterrrrup![58]

[Fluxbit 2: Fluxed and volunteers]

TICS: Poetics of Protest: A Fluxed History of the DNC,

T: or

CO: "With McGovern for President, we wouldn't have Gestapo tactics on the streets of Chicago."

NHL: "Fuck you you Jew son of a bitch you lousy motherfucker go home"

Documents: (Mayor Daley's response to Sen. Abe Ribicoff 8/28/68, approx. 8:45 PM) ...

Yipped: Uhuh, watch the throws, as they go up, how they arc and turn in the diffuse semi-academic light, hard to fix for a moment's contemplation...

Fluxed: And so they go...

T: skipping down...

Documents: and so, off, to... Chicago, '68: Land of Lincoln, of steel, of the smelly onion and packing houses; nation's leader in production of telephones, radios, television sets, and mirrors; plastic products, electrical machinery, sporting goods, picture frames and tin cans. Home of the Bulls, the Bears, the White Sox and the Cubs; the Black Hawks, Mustangs and Spurs; home of 58 colleges and universities, a 200-billion-volt particle accelerator, the first nuclear chain reaction, the "river which flows backward" and leading producer of methane from some of the biggest butts in America whose per capita income is 28.2% above the national average? ("gem in the lake," city in a garden," *Checagou*..." I Will!")

---

58. **CO** (*as Chair/Conductor signals audience*): Now, the game really begins...

Yipped: and as three men, gathering momentum, orbit the earth, splashing down into the Atlantic, then 3 again (for symmetry's sake) this time ringing the moon before plunging into the Pacific, to be fair, as a hydrogen bomb explodes undercover of the deserts of Nevada, rattling nickels in Las Vegas, and a 28-million-year-old ape scratches its petrified skull at the opening of "Dada, Surrealism, and their Heritage" at the Museum of Modern Art (MoooMaaa) and Mickey Mouse celebrates his 40th birthday (Hey hey LBJ!). Meanwhile, listening to Pulsars, voices of the stars, as Soviet tanks rumble the Czech night 78 million times simultaneously on the TV sets of America... an A train speeding beneath Neil Simon's *Plaza Suite*. Edward Albee: *Box—Mao—Box*.

Documents: You're drifting... Death of King March '68, March riots in Chicago ghettos, death of Bobby K. June 68; taxi, bus, telephone, electrical workers strike in the Second City...

T: Lurching ahead several pages...

Fluxed: In Fluxus performance, Happenings, the activities of convention week, our work here the important thing is process, focusing on doings and our own doings; as in Marx's definition of the ideal commune, *labor* is value and the basis of social relations (what we *do*, individually and together), rather than commodities/products (i.e., the objects of labor, bought and brought along).[59]

Yipped: Yopp. [Fluxbit 3. Performed by **Yipped** & volunteers]

NHL [*getting more into the swing of things, quotes her/himself*]:

> And the New Left started to catch on. At least Tom Hayden, seeing his plans for more direct intervention strategies were on the Lake's rocks (due to lack of numbers), eventually glimpsed the symbolic beauty of the Yip's Zen-lit banana peel (though he didn't see through to its full implications: that *Daley's* Keystone Cops wouldn't "distinguish 'straight' radicals from

59. **CO**: The play is not out of bounds: Yip Marx's ideal commune: their social relations are based on their labor of protest, which involves permuting and/or "throwing away" various concrete and ideological commodities.

newspapermen... rumors about demonstrations from the *real* [italics mine] thing"); attuned to the phantasmic dimensions of the conflict, Hayden projected the consequences: "threat of disorder, like all fantasies in the establishment mind, can create total paranoia... at a minimum, this process will further erode the surface image of [smoothly operating] pseudo-democratic politics; at a maximum, it can lead to a closing of the convention... for security reasons." Though from a Yip-Flip POV the "Convention," as decollage, should—could—not be "closed" (i.e., could not as Happening, reach a state of intellectual or emotional closure), at least the MOBE was tuning in to the performative vectors of the event. Journalist Tod Gitlin, too, catches the drift. Listen, as the observer with New Left sympathies, covering daily events for the *Wall Poster*, describes Wednesday morning's pre-dawn standoff between protesters and the National Guard in Grant Park (the first action of the Guard as stand-in for the police): they "materialized, in full battle dress.... My feelings cascaded: astonishment... then fright, then euphoria—the late Sixties' definitive sequence of feelings. We had outlasted the cops...." And another image: "we were like the Czechs, at that moment confronting Soviet tanks" (rather than the outdated troop carrier the protesters actually faced—it also more of a set piece than serious fighting machine—its guns were never loaded)"; Gitlin terms it a "storybook confrontation" ("comparably noble" protesters v. a "comparably bankrupt" social "machine"). His allegorical and allusive re-construction/re-scripting of events moves toward (counter)image play, sketches the event over a larger cultural field—perhaps the most vital way to go once one realizes the self-delusive stance of "real" revolution in post-modern America.

Yipped: Revolutionary change, too, has come up short in its accounts?

NHL: Consider the Lincoln Park Monday night barricades: Gitlin observes, "part Eisenstein, part Paris—so what was real?"

Documents: Not so much a barricade as a piling up of references to commodity culture, the stuff of leisure/evasion—a flimsy assemblage of picnic tables, benches, trash receptacles, whatever came to hand...

NHL: But the Yipped lesson is clear: We have to take society where we find it; it can only be detoured by/through its most seditious, subtle, and seductive means of reproduction: the spectacle itself. The MOBE had been…

Fluxed: Say/Do it!

NHL: za(yi)pped by a line of flight, become (Flux-)radicalized!
[Fluxbit 84. *Performed by* **NHL** *& volunteers*]

Documents:

> Theater can be used as an offensive and defensive weapon, like blood. We had a demonstration in New York [Grand Central Station]. We had seven gallons of blood in little plastic bags. You know, if you convince 'em you're crazy enough, they won't hurt ya. Cop goes to hit you, right, you have a bag of blood in your hand. He lifts his stick up, you take your bag of blood and go whack over your own head. All this blood pours out, see. Fuckin' cop standin'. Now, that says a whole lot more than a picket sign that says end the war…

(From Hoffman's Lincoln Park speech, Tuesday, 8/27/68).

Fluxed: Though key New Left ideologues (Dave Dellinger, Tom Hayden and Renee Davis) agreed all along that the demonstration would be billed as "nonviolent and legal" (320), Yip antics, refusing to operate at a (merely) literal level and to stay in (a practical) place, carnivalized and evaded the whole system of protest and defense (i.e., authorized, state- and federally-enforced "law and order" v. political protest—violent or nonviolent). Yip overshot this binary and gathered its forces in another realm. Only in this way, from this perspective—by getting out of our (cultural) selves—could boundaries be worked, frames flipped and examined, creative mind stimulated to bring a dialogic wealth associations and interconnections—a vaster, more dynamic assemblage—into play. Yip was in an elusive, liminal, not completely self-coherent place, between "revolutionary" social and aesthetic praxis; part performative put-on (like current *haute couture*) and part bodily, rage-in-the-street performance, one perhaps "commenting" on the other. It's all, after all, ideologically driven theater—perhaps if that were understood, a de-reification of the theater of war and political confrontation would follow...

[Fluxbit 5. Performed by **Documents** & **Fluxed**]

Yipped: Mainstream media coverage of the convention was also "radicalized" despite itself. By staying on point during the events surrounding the Wednesday night's defeat of the Peace Plank, what the media caught, by chance—like skirmishes on a football field—not only dramatized the ideological rift in the democratic party, but also lifted the convention out of itself (its self-image of harmonious convening) and dropped it right on the shaggy green polyester turf of middle America's rec. rooms; everybody stopped crunching Chez-Its™ and watched. First [*as if pitching a ball*], the numbers of defeat appeared graphically on the screen. Then [*a second pitch, low underhand*], a group of delegates began slowly waving flags, side to side, singing [**Fluxed** *sings, softly*] "We shall overcome." Immediately, the convention band struck up [*singing*] "Happy Days" ("are here again..."). The delegates, radicalized (by proxy), become actors in real contestatory (if not yet guerrilla...

Fluxed [*simultaneous*] rrrrrr)

Yipped: acts, rather than merely performing the conventional Convention roles of roll call,[60] vote casting, and cheering or booing at appropriate points; the eruption of such conflictual interactions are what work the cracks in the system, pry it open... 40 blocks away, in Grant Park, marching in the streets, rhymed at the Amphitheater by peace delegates threading through the seating area and beneath the podium bearing a long black cloth—[*sings*] "We Shall overcome" ...[61]

Dialogical moments like this make the Convention scene improvisationally performative, rather than mechanically reiterative...

[Fluxbit 6. Performed by **Yipped** and **Documents**]

---

60. **CO**: On a roll...

61. **CO**: Line drive: protesters to delegates, and back; Schechner's experience/performance braid

Fluxed [*To Yipped*]: You, my comrade, have a bit of TICS in you, enticingly torqued. [*To audience*]
Both met resistance from the dominant power base, and, like the Yips, the delegates co-opted theater as a way of "overcoming" (troping, if not over overpowering), hegemonic blockages...

And the TV viewers? Wednesday night's *mise en scene* enacted a TV "de-collage" right in their own "living" rooms (the synthetic light emanating for the image-box irradiating the room with politicized "life").

Yipped: Ginsberg said—since it's all about (ideo)theater, changing mind(set)—just say the war is over. And Phil Ochs sang:

> So do your duty boys and join with pride
> Serve your country in her suicide
> Find a flag so you can wave good-bye
> But just before the end even treason might be worth a try

Documents: [*aside*] (Composed for the '67 War Is Over rally, Ochs' and producer Larry Marks march-like arrangement, *a la* John Philip Sousa, "radiates Americana.") [*To **Yipped** and **Fluxed***] Maybe you could do *this*...? [*To audience*] from Hoffman's testimony under examination during the Chicago seven trial:

[Fluxbit 7. *Performed by* **Documents** *and volunteer(s) as* **Yipped** *and* **Fluxed** *read excerpt*]

> THE WITNESS: Well, I had cowboy boots, and brown pants and a shirt, and I
> had a grey felt ranger cowboy type hat down over my eyes, like this.
>
> MR. WEINGLASS: What, if anything occurred while you were sitting there
> having breakfast?
>
> THE WITNESS: Well, two policemen came in and said, "We have orders to
> arrest you. You have something under your hat."

So I asked them if they had a search warrant....

I lifted up the hat and I went "Bang! Bang!"
They grabbed me by the jacket and pulled me across the bacon and eggs
and Anita over the table, threw me on the floor and out the door and threw
me against the car, and they handcuffed me.
I was just eating the bacon and going "Oink Oink!"

NHL: V. mainstage acts, the Broadway of political theater as it continues still (media critic Norman Solomon on the '96 DNC): "Scripted events like photo-ops and televised speeches are shadow plays, diverting attention from what occurs far from media spotlights. "

Yipped: But the *Grand mise en scene* of '68, bounded to the north (downstage, or stage left) by Lincoln Park, and the south (upstage, or stage right) by the stockyards and the Convention site.... [excerpt *read by* **Documents** *and* **Fluxed**]

MR. KUNSTLER: Now, Mr. Ochs, do you know what guerrilla theater is?

THE WITNESS: Guerrilla theater creates theatrical metaphors for what is going on in the world outside.

Yipped: It's all a-Happenin', beyond anyone's intentions...

Documents: [*aside*] (the following from Ginsberg's testimony during the Chicago Seven trials)

[Fluxbits 8 and, time permitting, 9 *are performed by* **Documents** *and volunteer(s)*

As **Fluxed** *and* **Yipped** *read excerpts*]:

MR. WEINGLASS: What was occurring at the park as you got there?

THE WITNESS: There was a great crowd...and at the Center... a group of ministers and rabbis who had elevated a great cross about ten-foot high....

MR. WEINGLASS: And would you relate to the Court and jury what was being
said and done at the time?

WITNESS: Everybody was seated around ...singing, "We Shall Overcome," and "Onward Christian Soldiers...."

I was seated with my friends on a little hillock looking down on the crowd....
And on the other side, there were a lot of glary lights .... The ministers lifted
up the cross and took it to the edge of the crowd and set it down facing
the lights where the police were. ....

MR WEINGLASS: And after the ministers moved the cross, what happened?

THE WITNESS: ... there was a burst of smoke and tear gas around the cross, and the cross was enveloped with tear gas...which began slowly drifting over the crowd.

MR. WEINGLASS: And when you saw the persons with the cross and the cross
being gassed. what, if anything, did you do?

THE WITNESS: I turned to Burroughs find said, "They have gassed the cross
of Christ."

CO: [as MR. FORAN]: Objection, if the Court please.

Fluxed: There will be none, I think, here.

TICS: OR there will; your own scenarios suggest it [*sings*] "The young land started growin' / The young blood started flowin..."

Documents: [*aside*] (Ochs, "I Ain't Marching Anymore").

TICS: Try putting this in Playbill

[*during* **TICS** *summation, midpoint* Fluxbits 10 and 11—
a combination of Ring Around *and* A Moment for Artaud—
are performed by volunteers;
for the midpoint bits, the text of A Moment for Artaud *may be read as pieces of textual/other object evidence are highlighted in the parade of interrogation*]

Hoffman's mode of "comic "intervention in the political process often walked the line between the hilarious (or in-sane) and the deadly serious; not even fellow radicals always knew how literally to take his scenarios. Seed publisher and Chicago Yip Abe Peck recalls that in the planning stages for convention week actions, on "Wednesday, Abbie penciled in a riot. He was talking about twenty to thirty killed, six thousand wounded. Was that a prediction, a caution, a desire, an obituary, gallows humor?" Jerry Rubin made some equally disconcerting remarks, seeming to mix symbolic and literal blood: "My plan in Chicago was we want good to be facing evil, we want young white kids beaten by the cops. Of course, such a dis-easing response is exactly what Hoffman and YIP's rhetoric was deployed to provoke; yet, despite his off-hand militant posturing ("well, maybe a few people will be killed in Chicago, but it will save thousands of lives in Vietnam"), what finally "happened" in the radicalized space of the DNC was not Hoffman's kind of theater.[62]

Documents: Will you try? Just give me some space... [*collaged excerpts read by* **Documents, Fluxed, Yipped**]

we instantaneously threw up a marshal line and locked arms. ... And then the command was given to charge us with blue helmets and swinging batons. There were policemen literally

62. **CO**: He's on: Hoffman's schedule of events for the week included workshops in self-defense, but even these tactics were vehicles for a counter-symbolic offensive: Japanese snake dancing, for example, v. Western style military/police lines.

chanting "Kill Davis" as I was being attacked. I was the first one to be hit. The first strike brought me to the ground, opening my skull (Rennie Davis, testimony, Chicago Seven trial).

THE WITNESS: Well—[sings] "Where have all the flowers—
THE COURT: Just a minute, young lady.
THE WITNESS: [sings] "—where have all the flowers gone?"
DEPUTY MARSHAL JOHN J. GRACIOUS: I'm sorry. The Judge would like to speak to you.
THE COURT: We don't allow any singing in this Court. I'm sorry
(Judy Collins testimony, Chicago Seven trials)

TICS: Huh! In his book-length narrative poem, *1968: A History in Verse*, Ed Sanders states that he "wanted to get the Hell out of Chicago / to the safety of Avenue A." Out of the "hasty signs" and "hasty props" of Convention week, he comments (echoing Blake and quoting Yeats' "Easter Sunday 1916"), "a terrible beauty was born" (203), a striking image of which might be Abe Peck's grotesque rewriting, *in true Yip-flux spirit*, of a pop/Hip song lyric as warning to prospective Festival attendees: "if you're coming to Chicago…

Fluxed [*picking up the song, keeps singing, over following excerpts, read by **Yipped, Documents***] be sure to wear some armor in your hair."

The Hilton bar was right there. A guy had combat boots on, kicked the window, broke it, and everybody went storming through the plate-glass window into the bar.
(Jeff Nightbyrd)

Everybody's hands and face were cut, their hair was full of glass…

Fluxed: Be sure to wear… [excerpts read by **Fluxed**, **Yipped**, **Documents**]

and there was no place to hide. So you got beat up and then dragged through revolving doors. I don't know if you've done that but the human body is not designed to be pulled through a revolving door.

(Tom Hayden)

MR. WEINGLASS: Directing your attention to the morning of August 24, 1968, where were you?
THE WITNESS: I was on a plane coming from New York to Chicago.
MR. WEINGLASS: Now, *en route* to Chicago while you were on the plane, what if anything, did you do?
THE WITNESS: **I wrote poetry....**

I am the Angel King saying the Angel King/As the mobs in the Amphitheater, streets, Coliseums, parks and offices/ Scream in despair over meat and metal Microphone.
(Allen Ginsberg's testimony, Chicago Seven trials)

TICS: And I (still) say (*quoting him/herself*):

Part of the reason behind the escalation of violence throughout the week was that Daley didn't fully comprehend—and hence couldn't intelligently counter—the subversive force in all its modulations: The Yip actions—symbolic/activist, parodic interventions; the MOBE/SDS brand of practical, nonviolent resistance/protest; the youth who came mainly for the advertised festivities and to be part of the 'scene'—direct, explosive, many of them street smart, influenced as much perhaps by Up Against the Wall Motherfucker's aggressive posturing as Rubin's Zenned "act first, analyze later" activism[63]—but not necessarily motivated by a clear political agenda; and the 'legal,' 'respectable,' symbolic, and controlled actions of the McCarthy delegates.[64] To meet these various modes of resistance with the unreflective response of a billy club and tear gas canister said a lot about the lack of suppleness of the forces for

63. **CO**: Yes, the UAWM connection works, here. Their slogan was "Armed Love"; they ran recruitment ads juxtaposing the image of a revolver with middle class desire for cultural illusion—"We're looking for people who like to draw"

64. **CO**: Once they moved beyond the territory of the Symbolic Order (offscript, so to speak, and into the streets), they were quickly assimilated into one disruptive mass with the other protesters that had to be disciplined.

'law and order,' how easily they could be provoked, but also to what extent they would go to protect that order and to the limits of a Yip-fluxed political theater, of radicalized laughter, in defusing those forces.[65]

Documents [*aside*]: Somebody throw in a Fluxbit, please!

[Fluxbit 12 *performed by volunteers*
as **Documents** *reads excerpts*]

THE WITNESS: I was referring to defending myself.
.....

MR. SCHULTZ: And that means if necessary to kill that policeman, does it not?
THE WITNESS: It is not the desire to kill, and that's what you are trying to put in the tone of it, and it's not that—
.....
[MR. SCHULTZ: When you told the people in Lincoln Park, "Pick up a gun, pull the spike from the wall, because if you pull it out and you shoot well, all I'm gonna do is pat you on the back and say, 'Keep on shooting,' "That was part of your revolutionary tactics too, was it not, sir?
THE WITNESS: Yes, sir, and if you look generally—
MR. SCHULTZ: Please, that is all.
THE COURT: You have answered the question.
THE WITNESS: I strike that answer on the grounds that that particular
question is wrong because it ain't clear.
(there is applause in the courtroom)
THE COURT: I have some news for you, sir. I do the striking here, and will the marshals exclude from the courtroom anyone who applauded. This isn't a theater.... (Bobby Seale, cross examination, Chicago Seven trial)]

TICS: This simply supports my point...

65. **CO**: All good moves. According to a 1978 CBS News special, "about one demonstrator in six" at the '68 DNC had been an undercover agent—the System partly orchestrated its own decollage upheaval.

Fluxed and **Yipped**: More Flux!

[Fluxbits 13 & 14. *Performed by volunteers*]

TICS [*continuing to quote himself*]: "Though Yip may have pre-conceived the DNC as an opportunity for large-scale *detournement*, for a city-wide happening—bigger even then the '67 symbolic siege of the Pentagon—they may have overlooked that their unwitting audience/participants—the Chicago PD (the "pig") as well as some of the protesters—were not SoHo aesthetes and may not have quite been "in tune" with the symbolic, Yip-Flip intentions of the event's designers, even though many events leading up to and during the first part of convention week were obvious symbolic carnivalizations of "official" culture:... [*excerpt read by* **NHL**]

MR. WEINGLASS: Now you also indicated that Mr. Rubin mentioned nonverbal education. Will you explain what that is to the Court and jury?

TICS: the election of a pig—Pigasus—as presidential candidate at a mock convention cum celebration of LBJ's birthday; a Yip woman costumed as a "Native American" (punningly named "Helen Running Water"—run for water, piss on your grass, no running water in the parks) presenting a Lincoln Park sleeping permit application to Deputy Mayor Sthal, the permit wrapped in a Playboy Playmate of the Month foldout (signifying on Chicago's publishing industry and the ribald, (self)exploitative, "PR" nature of the whole event). Despite such parodic actions and the Yip's exaggerated rhetoric—"We will burn Chi to the ground," "we will fuck on the beaches," "we demand the Politics of Ecstasy," Acid for all!"—and other agitprop scenarios, such as spiking the Chicago water supply and delegates' drinks with LSD and sending out Yip "chics" (and "hyperpotent" young Yip men) to seduce delegates and their spouses, Daley took the Yips on their word: the police and guard were ready to trade real beatings, split scalps, and gassings for symbolic testing.[66] Showcard...

---

66. **CO**: Double play...

Documents: Gothic! [67] [*aside*] Fluxbit!

[Fluxbit 15. *Performed by volunteers; excerpts read by* **Documents** *and* **NHL**]

We were tear gassed and there was a girl crying to her boyfriend,
"They can't do this, this is my world."
(John Sack, Sloman, 152)

THE WITNESS: Most of our consciousness, since we are continually looking at images on television and listening to words, reading newspapers, talking in courts such as this...prevents us from breathing deeply in our bodies and sensing more subtly and sweetly the feelings that we actually do have....
(Allen Ginsberg, testimony, Chicago Seven trial)[68]

MR. WEINGLASS: As you were running, what if anything were the police doing?
THE WITNESS: They were beating people, pushing people up against the doorways of buildings. And, I mean, we couldn't get any further onto the sidewalk we were on. And there were masses of people on the sidewalk, and some people were trying to get into building and others were being beaten into doorways. And I saw a policeman coming towards me, and I motioned to him with the microphone, that I had turned it off, and the camera was behind me. I thought he would understand I wasn't a demonstrator, and he hit me.
MR. WEINGLASS: What happened?
THE WITNESS: He hit me across the neck and shoulders.
MR. WEINGLASS: What happened to you as you were hit?

---

67. **CO**: Paul Krassner points up the difference—the slip or mis-phasing—between what the Yipped radicals thought they were up to and how Daley envisioned it: during negotiations for protest permits, Krassner remembers Deputy Mayor Stahl asking "'What do you guys plan to do in Chicago?' I said, 'Have you seen *Wild in the Streets*?, the film where teenagers took over the government and put acid in the water supply.' He said, 'No, We've seen *The Battle of Algiers.*' *Battle of Algeirs* is guerrillas blowing up ice cream parlors.

68. **CO**: Yes, but he also meant...

> THE WITNESS: I went down, and a man, there was a man standing in the doorway where I fell, he reached down to help me up, and the policeman hit him across the bridge of his nose and knocked his glasses off.
> MR. WEINGLASS: And this man who attempted to assist you and was struck himself, was he filmed?
> THE WITNESS: Yes, my husband filmed him sitting there with his head in his hands and a bloody wound on his head.
> (Sarah Diamant, testimony, Chicago Seven trial)

TICS: The logic?

NHL: Hmmm...but, I can see a point: the goal was to be a "Cultural Revolutionary"—it's the only thing that makes it *all* worth it. Even a courtroom could be shown up as a stage for set pieces, a THEATER OF PROCEDURAL CONVENTIONS that misses the reality of the "evidence." Consider Phil Ochs aborted (by the court) testimony as witness for the defense during the Chicago Seven trial [*excerpt read by* **NHL** *and* **Documents**]:

> MR. KUNSTLER: Now, Mr. Ochs, I call your attention to sometime in the vicinity of 6:00 p.m. Tuesday, August 27...
> ....
> Did you sing a song that day?
> THE WITNESS: Yes, "I Ain't Marching Anymore."
>
> .....
>
> MR. KUNSTLER: Now, would you stand and sing that song so the jury can hear the song that the audience heard that day?
>
> **CO** [*miced, deadpan, as* MR. SCHULTZ]: If the Court please, this is a trial in the Federal District Court. It is not a theater. We don't have to sit and listen to the witness sing a song. Let's get on with the trial. I object.
>
> MR. KUNSTLER: Your Honor, this is definitely an issue in the case....

NHL: The "case" to which Kunstler refers is defendant Jerry Rubin's intent and the "mood of the crowd," since Rubin requested Ochs to sing that particular song at the Lincoln Park rally; it is also the case we are making here of performative intervention; in *all* cases, that which that the court refuses to hear, as did the Democratic political machine in Chicago… [*excerpt read by* **Documents** *and* **NHL**]:

> THE COURT: I sustain the objection.
> MR. KUNSTLER: Your Honor, he is prepared to sing it exactly as he sang it on that day.
> THE COURT: I am not prepared to listen, Mr. Kunstler

NHL: The Defense's dramaturgical challenge to the hegemonic discourse marks the disavowal necessary to maintain conviction (the ability to "convict," but also to believe in the system—of jurisprudence, in this case); marks also how (any) authoritarian discourse must (forcibly) exclude under the guise of inclusiveness ("hearing" all the "evidence"), of finding "Truth," in order to sustain power—the "Jury" (read populace, citizenry, *audience*) is only allowed to *hear* what the Court *allows*…

Fluxed: Whose italics? You're beginning to sound like me.

[**Fluxed** *and* **NHL** *try to beat each other to the props to do* Fluxbit 16*, exchange a smile, while* **Documents**:]

Documents:

> Hi Panel—
>
> I'm attaching the original proposal so we can begin thinking about what might take place. I'd like this to be collaborative, dialogic and somewhat improvisatory, with surprises (for all). My idea is, in addition a central discourse (or set of discourses), to have some pre-scripted, Flux events (mini conceptual performances) that could be brought in a spontaneously, in the manner of (Bop) jazz performance (i.e., in tune/tempo with the whole, and the tempo can change according to…), or as a 60s-like "Happening." This would require some attentive listening, though we can also agree on a kind of rough script, once we see what we have, and/or the panel "chair" could function as

> director/conductor, giving cues. Also, the process (even the proposal, even this note, even your responses to this note) can be part of what *happens*. So this will be as much performance as panel. So please look over the proposal and let's start gathering materials/ideas. I already have a collection of bits which dialogue with/play on/through the Chicago '68 events and riots (including maskings and "throws" of various sorts, and other disruptive counter-discourse events), and we can certainly use these and variations of these. I'll send them to you soon. Events don't have to be specifically related to '68—but in spirit of, and contemporary connections, etc.

Fluxed: The dynamics of convention week—at least *this* (re)presentation of it as a perhaps unwieldy, tension and conflict riddled structuration (rather than clearly established structure) and what this means, in terms of Fluxed/Flipped awareness... [*excerpt read by* **TICS** *and* **NHL**]

R. WEINGLASS: What was your purpose in filming these events?

THE WITNESS: To use them as research material for my doctoral dissertation.

(Sarah Diamant, testimony, Chicago Seven trial)

Documents: "Psychic guerrilla warfare now" (Keith Lampe, "On Making a Perfect Mess," September, '1967).

Fluxed: —is perhaps best expressed by Erving Goffman's definition of "negative experience": "If the whole frame can be shaken, rendered problematic, then this too can ensure that prior involvements—and prior distances—can be broken up and that, whatever else happens, a dramatic change can occur in what it is that s being experienced."

Documents: "Picture W. C. Fields announcing: 'You don't *decide* something is absurd—you *recognize* it.'" (Paul Krassner, "The Birth of the Yippie Conspiracy," January, '1968) (italics imagined to be W. C. Fields')

Fluxed: this relatively (deceptively) simple *detournement* is a consequence of no single force/confrontation, not just MOBE and Yip *vis a vis* each other and Daley's knee-jerk reactions, but the whole situation, including the critical work we do here now.

Documents: "the Buddha nature / of everyone...like a million earthworms / tunneling under this structure / till it falls" (Diane Di Prima, "Revolutionary Letter # 7, "1971)

TICS: Hmmm. And so you might say—may I? [*quoting* **Fluxed** *doing himself—i.e. TICS— as* **Lecturer**):

[Fluxbit 17. *Performed by volunteers*]

Lecturer (*TICed off*): The goal of Fluxus performance, as the Yip-Flipped/Fluxed DNC and of this critical reenactment, is to raise questions, to open and extend the dialogue rather than seek resolutions. Yip antics attempted to screw the DNC toward political comedy by transmogrifying some of its major symbols (i.e., the nomination of a pig as presidential candidate),[69] by attempting to de-nominate the place of the master signifier (and certainly de-humanize it) as much as replace it with ridiculous meaning. Their goal, that is, was primarily toward emptying, toward anti-meaning, then toward reconstitution/revisioning of the symbolic order; Derridean laughter rather than Shakespearean comedy. A major method of such madness, of such decollage critical consciousness, as in the messy product we are dealing with here, a legacy of late 60s volatile and multifarious radical thought and action...

Fluxed: You said it...

Documents: "This is a period of emergency. Therefore, emergency theatre is the theatre of awareness" (Julian Beck, "Notes Toward a Statement on Anarchism and Theatre," 1972).

TICS: *is*, as John Hanhardt says of Wolf Vostell's early 60s TV "de-collages," to "erase and recompose imagery" to "destabilize the

69. **CO**: Another curve: seven Yippies, along with the Pig, were arrested—here come the Chicago Seven.[Fluxbit 27 *is performed by volunteers during the following note*]

institutionalized codes and meanings of the dominant culture."

Documents: "Nobody could explain what it all meant yet everyone was fascinated. It was pure information, pure imagery, which in the end is truth" (Hoffman, "Revolution for the Hell of It," February, 1968). [70]

Fluxed: We do Flux: "work the frame."

Documents: "The goal now is to disrupt an insane society.
We've already applied for the permit" (Krassner, *op cit*).

TICS [*finally giving in(up)*]: In that case...

[Fluxbit 18. *Performed by* **TICS** *and volunteers*]

*****

Yipped: The following scenes, emblematic of the disillusionment broached by collapse of the Peace Plank—or, more accurately, the failure of the democratic will and the loss of surety in a morally, spiritually inhabitable future—some, caught by chance in the camera eye, due to the loosely scripted nature of media coverage; others, unrecorded or unrecordable—hybrid events of imagination and reality; mass movements, demonstrators and delegates—the Living Theatre of Convention week...

[*several* Fluxbits *are performed by volunteers during the following—*

as many as time allows...]

Documents: "In point of fact nothing happened" (Hoffman, *Ibid*).

Yipped: A priest, standing in the midst of the New York delegation,

---

70. **CO**: **TICS**, or perhaps **Documents**, or **TICS** as **Lecturer** could bring up some other points of connection among YIP, Fluxus, and Happenings, such as Joseph Beuys' notion of "social sculpture," George Maciunas' '63 proposal for several socially disruptive "propaganda actions" (literal "break downs," in some cases—jammed transit on bridges and in tunnels), and Claes Oldenburg 1960 call "an art that embroils itself with the everyday crap & still comes out on top... an art that imitates the human, that is comic, if necessary, or violent."

offering a prayer.

NHL: After a film honoring Bobby Kennedy, a standing ovation to a blank screen.

Fluxed: Delegates taking their protest theater to the streets: as I (inspired by CBS news editors) juxtapose them, the theatrical black cloth Amphitheater march transforms into the delegate's candlelight street march to Grant Park (a subsequent enactment of shifted solidarity that bears the trace—is overdetermined by—protester's marches throughout the week), symbolic continuities eliding spatio-temporal discontinuity as the ribbon of black cloth threading the brightly lit but emptying Amphitheater becomes suddenly pervasive as the night, punctuated by 500 wavering points of (in)candescence; or, we might say, the cloth, spooling out like a sinuous dividing line, disenchants, as if drawing our attention to bright but flattened, meaningless frames of a discarded film on the Convention cutting room floor (the obverse of protesters' idealistic inscriptions on the dividing line of Michigan Avenue at week's end), followed by black leader, the film's end...

Yipped: Protesters facing the lines of National Guard—blockages, "negotiations" (empty processes) collapsing into raw repression and resistance—what "works"—

CO: V (v.?): Peace! Victory! Dark river flecked with light

NHL: The detachment of Democratic candidates: McCarthy and son playing catch with an orange; the Candidate looking down on the riots, casting allusions (it "looks like a Breughel," "like the battle of Canae"); a whiff of tear gas; HHH kissing the TV screen of his nomination.

Yipped: A Barricade—built to defend against a blockage? Unlike the May '68 French students' barricade, the Chicago protesters' "barricade," in the middle of a park, blocked nothing, was pure allusion and impromptu, site-specific Happening.

Fluxed: all under the sign of a crude cross, also erected in Lincoln Park, the cross forming an assemblage with the barricade that metonymically "sanctions" other pilings...

Documents:

> Besides seemingly countless bars frequented by young, upwardly-mobile professionals and DePaul University students, Lincoln Park provides many theatres and cinemas, trendy boutiques, coffee shops, restaurants, and SUV dealerships.... It is... undeniably the current yuppie Mecca of Chicago.

CO: The barricade and cross were gassed.

Yipped: The gassing the cross, staged with long shadows.

Fluxed: The Tuesday night gassing in Lincoln Park: Club Police State. A "primitive," disturbing, percussive beat of clubs against hands as masked disco cops emerge from clouds of gas. An S/M writhing out into the "audience." The gas as "thick as milk" (MLK?). Black whipped

CO: "Beautiful... beautiful..."

NHL: Yip and MOBE initiators comment from the sidelines, unable to keep pace with what was set in motion.

Yipped: Lying in the grass, I note
a lilt in the branches;
slight tremor beneath...

***

CO: **Om...Arrrr...**

T [*as himself*]: See appendices for quoted material used in the Fluxbits and spin off scenarios for Brown Campus events...

Fluxed [*as* Catcher]: Batter rrr up!

All: The whole world is watching!

Join us!

Yipped: travel in pairs and wear riot helmets

Documents: "half of us thought we were in Germany, half of us thought we were in Russia" (Elinor Langer, qtd in Gitlin, 336).

All: *This land is your land...* (Mary Travers & Peter Yarrow)

Yipped: don't get caught in a large action. See you in the streets.

TICS: "We were all going... to heaven... going... the other way" (Dickens, qtd. in Gitlin 335).

Fluxed: get the cameras and beat the press

Documents: this orderly city Chicago's lovely parks

TICS: more pay for cops

CO: this is not an authorized march

Documents: "they were a mixture of horses and whatever else they could find, chairs and crap from all over the place"

All: *mine eyes have seen the glory*

NHL: hired historical phantoms

Fluxed: You shoulda been there, man, we exposed them, we exposed them (Hoffman)

CO: he got no chance anyway

TICS: if I let anyone else across, I'm going to lose this bridge

All: *oh beautiful for spacious skies*

Documents: "I got my sharkskin pants on, got my dago tee... my Cuban heels... and I'm going, this is fucking fantastic!"

NHL: welcome to Chicago, "the city that works"

Documents [*aside*]: (From Daley's DNC opening night "welcome" speech)

Documents: make love, not war!

All: Join us! Join us!

CO: get the fuck back, I'm telling you!

NHL: what do we want?

ALL: Peace!

NHL: When do we want it?

ALL: Now!

All: oink oink!

Yipped: blink your lights...

Documents [*aside*]: (or "flick your lights"—street protesters calling for support from McCarthy workers on the upper floors of the Hilton, Thursday night)

All: **America America**

NHL: the streets belong to the people

Documents: "so I probably was the fastest radicalized [eighteen-year-old] you could ever see"

All [*chanted*]: The whole world is watching...!

From the...to the shining...

Fluxed: this is the way we will go on from here (McCarthy addressing protesters)

CO: you are a bunch of motherfuckers!

TICS: Father, semantics won't save you from the cops

All: *for amber waves of grain*

join us!

Yipped: why, I hardly recognize you without your helmet

TICS: you can't go on

NHL: You can't be revolutionary without a TV set (Jerry Rubin)

CO: liberals go home

All: *where have all the flowers gone?*

Documents: look, I'm no leader

Yipped: Don't leave us!

TICS: hell, I'm taking off my badge and going to dinner with Gregory

CO: I would like to invite you to *my* house this evening

All: arrest us all!

Yipped: stay out of the alleys

All: **Oh say can you see**

CO: stop, or I'll shoot!

NHL: those incredible scenes on television

All: *"Kick Out the Jams, Motherfucker"* (MC5)

TICS: you can listen to them but don't talk to them

Fluxed: wouldn't you rather hold a girl than a gun?

Yipped: what's wrong with taking your picture?

Documents: I'm shocked beyond belief (McCarthy on Hilton raid)

Fluxed: why don't you put that thing down and join us?

All [*chanted*]: Hell no, we won't go!

NHL: well, I mean, how can you stop the cops?

All: **America America**

Documents: "Makes us want to pack up our cameras and go home" (Walter Cronkite)

CO: ok, wise guy, let's have the camera

TICS: Please excuse our digressions.

CO: **Long time passing...**

Yipped [*as Catcher*]: Out!

***

All: Join us?

[*the closing* Fluxbit, Second Line (Show Me Your Tits), *performed by panelists and volunteers*]

Fluxbits, or (Anti)Terrorist Scripts from YSS (Yip Strategy Session)

All the following event pieces, listed semi-randomly, are based on happenings in and around the DNC convention site, 8/25-8/30, 1968 (including, for our purposes, the morning after the Convention officially closed). Any similarities to Real persons, places and events are indefinitely refractable. If no end point is noted in the event, a smack of the night stick or other terminal sound or action—flashing light, "move along" command from the panel CO—will signal the end of the event; in the absence of such terminal punctuation, the event continues indefinitely, or to a point of exhaustion.

* * *

Opening: miniature black box theatre: open the door, draw back the curtain, place a can of shaving cream in the box, depress the button, close door.

Flamethrower: juxtapose a can of Rediwhip™ and a Bic™ lighter

Revol(ve)ution (for three) Stand back to back, holding hand(cuff)s; rotate *en masse* one full turn to right; turn individually to the left to face each other, still in tight formation, keep rotating one more full turn.

**Digital Pieces*: Create interactive image maps based on convention photos, Chicago city maps, Hilton Hotel floor plans, etc., with hotspots linking to digital sound/image documents and/or virtual Fluxbits. Click on the corner of Balbo and Michigan—what happens?

**Take Over Piece (site occupation)*: outline a space; respond to its cultural contents. Attempt to expand your territory. Deterritorialize.

(Pop)Culture Wars (for two): P1: select an item (object, clothing, etc.) from suitcase (or box) 1 (to your left on floor as you approach front panel); P2: select a textual item from suitcase (or box) 2; P1 & P2: juxtapose the two items for audience view; add them (one at a time or simultaneously) to the "barricade" adjacent to the boxes (or start a barricade if none exists). Repeat two more times. Divide the pile of symbols into two. Scatter and/or re-disperse one pile.

Chant-in (Wrigley's) (for two): chant the following, in round: double, double trouble, trouble rubble, rubble bubble pleasure gum gun (seizure erasure)

Chewing Event 1 (for two): P1 standing, P2 squatting: P1: place a piece of gum on P2's tongue; make the sign of the cross; As P2 chews, repeat, in various intonations, the words "pleasure" "penance."

Chewing Event 2: Give each other a stick of gum; while chewing, say "Daley's doubles" in chorus, putting on (and off) various "faces" (a Groucho Marx mask, the drama double—" happy"/" sad"—injured protestor v. pundit, etc.); gestures may accompany "masks."

It's a gaaasss (two or more): put on (gas) masks; blow up and release balloons

Dance Piece 1 (Commune) (for two): P1: walk in an attempt to communicate (tracing out a word, letter, or other cipher, for example, with your footsteps); P2 attempt to block and/or obliterate the message

Dance Piece 2 (commute) (for two): P1: attempt to walk single-mindedly from point A to point B. P2: deflect, detour, distract, decoy.

Nightstick Symphony (for one, two, or more): Use toy billy clubs and/or bats to beat out rhythms on various hard and soft surfaces.

Ya Ya (for any number): Ring bells, as commentary, at appropriate moments during the session.

Riot Piece 1 (for three or more): charge against the odds.

Riot Piece 2 (for two): Put on toy helmets; remove and toss helmets toward each other, attempting to catch them with bright plastic toy bats.

Riot Piece 3 (Handicap) (for one or two): Attempt to "tee off" with toy golf club, bat, or lathing strip and spiked golf ball.

Riot Piece 4 (Seize and arrest) (for 2-6 performers): Each pair of performers struggles to rip an oversized T-shirt while shouting/chanting some or all of the following: pig! librettist! fascist! Streets litter! monitor maker! peace! free love! Target! dinner at eight! seven of hearts! Squad! Be mine! jack of clubs! no more leftie Hamlets! Trope! Troupe! Tromp! Etc. The piece concludes when the shirt is town in half.

Lecture Tableau 1 (for one): Stand in front of the panel, deadpan, wearing a Groucho mask, deadpan, holding up the bird

Lecture Piece 1 (The___$ Question) (for one): Wearing a Groucho mask and holding up a bird, interrupt ongoing presentation saying "listen to the birdie."

Roll call Event (for two or more): P1: calls out nouns and noun phrases; other performers answer the calls ("yes" or "no"): erector sets yes, bacon yes, penile enlargement no, mass sterility yes, Texas toast no, bag of clubs yes, charades yes, turn off the TV no.

Cod(e) Piece 1 (spread the Word) (for two): P1: drop seven toy alphabet cubes through a square frame, then lower the frame to genital level. P2: catch the first cube and turn it over on each of its sides on the floor, letting the other cubes hit the floor, deflecting some of them. After all the cubes have been dropped and the original side is facing up on the first, throw it back through the frame, which has now been lowered to genital level; P1: attempt to catch the cube between your legs.

The McCarthy Candidacy (or, Florida '00) (for two): P1: throw an orange (or orange ball) to P2; P2: attempt to catch the orange in a small cereal box, then toss it back to P1; P1: attempt to catch the orange with a patriotic hat. P1 & P2: put on the Humphrey, Bush, or Hoffman image "gloves" and continue the game of catch for three more rounds, using masks or other discarded props from the barricade pile; if there are no discarded props, select throws from Suitcase (box) 1, and return them to the box when finished.

The Humphrey Candidacy 1 (for two): P1: using a toy bat (or golf or billy club) "tee off" (swing at, but don't strike) a projected image (video monitor, computer screen, or slide). P2: punch a baseball glove, saying: "but real scalps were split in Chicago."

Chant Piece 2 (Stats of disunion) (for one or more): Read out/chant various statistics from the Fact Sheet[71] handout (facts about the '04 RNC protests, facts about current presidential administration) and/or from the 1968 Walker Report; the City of Chicago, Corporation Counsel Report, etc.

Throwing Events and Pieces:

Throw a Party: [Performed in conjunction with *The Party Rhetoric*; *Throw a Party* must be acted out before *The Party Rhetoric* is performed] (for two): P1: pitch the contents of a bowl containing a baggie (or baggies) of "shit" (i.e., tootsie rolls), along with champagne popper confetti, torn up academic conference paper pages, cut-up fashion ads, paper flowers, etc. all of which flutter down as the solid shit sails. P2: observe

The Party Rhetoric (for two): P2: "recycle" (i.e., throw back) the bag of "shit" (*Throw a Party*, above) in a fast food or Party Store bag. P2: Dump the contents of the Fast food bag on the conference table—shredded political

71. CO: See the "Fluxbit Protest Fact Sheet" following...

slogans and other ideological refuse, along with the recontextualized shit.

Overthrow (for two): P1 and P2: Standing on opposite sides of the panel, throw various discarded props (from the barricade pile) to each other over the speakers' heads (and/or over your own heads), stage left to right, to the rhythm of "Revolution," "Jumping Jack Flash," "If You're Going to San Francisco" and/or other pop rock tunes of the period; if there are no discarded props, select throws from Box 1, and return them to the box when finished. P1: "flying objects caused 63.5% of the known police injuries"

Throw(up) (for one): cup hands around a small toy TV (or other commodified representation of a representational commodity) and hold to mouth as if calling out.

Ideo Juggle (or, a significant slip) (for one): Hold a small plastic toy TV and an American flag in your right hand; toss up the TV, quickly shift the flag to the left hand, and catch the TV again with the right.

Play Ball! (or two): P1: throw a bag of "shit" (i.e., Tootsie rolls). P2: fist smack a baseball glove, or the palm of your hand, as if punching yourself in the stomach.

____*f (or, throw-away charade)*: P1:" you told me this would make a difference" (mime throwing away the "lie"—the script). P2: "you told me no more leftie Hamlets" (mime lying—looking for the right quote— to live). P1 & P2: "Live?!"

Evidentiary (for one): Select a text from the crate at the front of the room; show the book to the audience, reading the title; toss the book on the barricade near the suitcases (or begin the barricade of none exists).

So, there is air in here (for one): throw unthrowables—light plastic containers, pieces of paper, feathers

Throw (Back) the Other (for one): take a digital snap of the audience; "throw" the image back at the source: "Here, catch!"

Cross the Line: (for two): P1 (*squatting, as* Catcher, *slides a bra across the floor to* P2): "In Atlantic City, women burn these. (*verbal throw*): Tell the truth." P2 (*standing, as* Pitcher, *responds with verbal throw*): "In Atlantic City women burn patriarchy..." P1 (*verbal throw*): "The Truth!" Pitcher (*rolling up the bra*): "In Atlantic City, women burn away the skein of identity (i.e., self-immolate)."

(Pop)culture Wars 2 (Forfeit) (for two): P1 (Catcher): "And the Barricade?" P2 (Other): "What barricade?" P1: "Pile of... we've been circumlocutioning it." P2: "A detective threw a section of police line into the crowds" (*select an item from one of the suitcases, walk to the "barricade," freeze, drop the item on heap*).

Smile (for two): P1: using a flashlight as, keep the spotlight on P2. P2: flash the two-fingered "peace ("V") sign into the media light; move your head into spot (*ambiguous smile*), and the peace sign behind your head to become impish horn (sign of the cuckold?); invert the "V" and hold it between your legs, which also mimic a "V". Perform all these actions slowly and deliberately. P1: As P2 points his/her two fingers downward between his/her legs in an inverted "V," consider a moment, then quick hike the media light to P2. P2: catch the flashlight, point it at the audience, then out.

SOS (Symbolic Order Survives) (for one or more): Imaginatively, verbally and/or in pantomime, attack the representation of a police car (and / or projected ads for the latest car models, 60s and today).

Editorial Considerations (to be performed by panelists): When this bit is called, panelists will "shred," or throw away, one of their precious script pages.

Ring Around—Question (mass action, for seven, or any number; to be performed near the midpoint of a session): P1: Select an item from the "barricade" (i.e., discarded props); select a "factoid" (small text card) from the police cookie jar (lift and replace red the lid—a small siren sounds as the lid is lifted); slowly march around the conference table, clockwise, as the other performers line up behind you. P2-7(...): follow P1's lead. Select a prop from the barricade, a factoid from the cookie jar, and fall in behind P1. *All performers:* when you reach the podium, after circling the table, hold up and verbally identify the piece of "evidence" (the prop you selected), then, "ring it out" (i.e., comment on it) by reading the factoid out loud. The first person to read (P1) should remove the lid from the cookie jar and place it (flat side down) on the table. After reading factoids, discard into the open cookie jar; return items to the barricade. The last person to read (P7) should replace the lid on the jar. For *any* conference session, including this one, you may also quote or refer to theoretical and other textual bits from the panelists' presentations, provide your own factoids, state your own feelings and/or critical comments concerning the issues brought up in the session as well as the presentations themselves—everything comes under indictment.

(Un)self-defense Censor: practice logo/ego (un)self-defense by "Censoring"/ blocking out various parts of text and body with black cardboard rectangles; a whole body may be blocked by the faceless black cardboard figure from the beginning of the performance

A Moment for Artaud (for seven): Pick one of the text cards from the patriotic hat; slowly circle the conference table until you reach the podium; read the quote, discard it, select another from the hat; as before, circle, and read the new quote when returning to the podium. Follow this procedure until the hat is empty (a total of three rounds). As each person reads, the others may groan, scream, shout (as protesters and police):

> "Ohno, not mace!!"
>
> cutting through, "like a scythe through grass" (Mailer)
>
> percussive thudding of billy clubs on body drums, cymbals—bodies flying through glass "An atmosphere of unreality" (Hugh Hough)
>
> nightsticks and blood, overturned tables, Bloody Marys dripping from barstools
>
> "I can't walk" drumbeat to the head
>
> "Prague Prague Prague"
>
> drug by the shirt across the floor hotel bedsheets for bandages (Kusch 100-101) bricks through car widows sharpened tiles slicing air oven cleaner sprayed in the face billy club in the groin
>
> "Ommmm"
>
> "One two three four" (Kusch 98-99)
>
> ice picks and bayonets
>
> "Kill kill kill kill"
>
> "a razor cutting a channel through a head of hair" (Mailer,

Kusch 100-01)

A girl drug across an embankment by *her* hair, her boyfriend clubbed as he tries to reach her

"Move! I said move, goddamnit!"

running, choking, vomiting, arms covering faces

"Pigs Pigs Pigs"

"I stopped at a water fountain to dab at my eyes, soaked my handkerchief, wrapped it around my nose" (Gitlin; Kusch, 97-98)

"tear down the flag!"

flaming rags, razor shoes, urine balloons, human shit bags, bloodied sanitary napkins, flying

"We have two more days to burn Chicago down" (94-95)

"Be calm... don't be violent" (Dellinger)

"Move your fucking ass!" (98)

"men, women, clergymen, newsman—some were beaten and clubbed while on the ground" (Kusch 95)

"Let's get the motherfuckers!"

thewack wack, the wacka wack, thethunkwack the wack thunk, thunk

Historical Materialist Authorization Relay (for three): P1, P2, and P3 relay a series of objects. The object relayed may be any commodity, including a printed text, spoken word, or reproducible sound; objects may be selected from the onstage suitcases or the "barricade," or you may provide your own. P1 select an object and toss it to P2, the middleman. P2: briefly highlight the object, or not, in a square frame before passing it on to P3. P1, P2, and P3: comment on the object, or not, when framed. P3: return the object to its source.

Throw yourself (any number).

Procedural Piece (for one): (*to anyone*) "Excuse me, have the time?"

Abbie's New Year's Eve Piece (for one-four): place two New Year's Eve blow-out noise makers in mouth to form a "V"; as you blow, make the "peace" sign.

HHH (barbed wire, or Barbie's Wire) (for three): P1: sketch the letters ("HHH") in continuous linked sequence across a blackboard until the event concludes. P2: "Fuck you you Jew son of a bitch you lousy motherfucker go home." P3: facing audience, lip sync as P2 reads the above. P2:" Daley to Ribicoff 8/28/68" P3: facing audience, do not lip sync as P2 reads the above. P2 (faux-femme *voice*): "And I just came genuflecting from confession, twenty 'Our Father['s], Who Art in [Czechago]'." P3: lip sync, as if reading P2's lips, as P2 reads the above.

Banner Event (for 3 or more): using the paper roll near the conference table, make a banner; the banner may contain slogans, nonsense phrases, images, facts from the Fact Sheet handout, or other commentary, or remain blank. When complete, or when the "present banner" command is given, two of the performers re-roll the banner, then unroll it, as a diorama, in front of panelists' faces.

Medic! (any number): tear sheets of (academic) paper.

Blinking Eyes, Fast Legs: P1 & P2 flash lights at each other; At first, P2 mimics P1, then, as P1 becomes aggressive with his/her flashes, P2 turns his/her light onto his/her own rapidly blinking eyes, then shuts off. The piece ends.

HHH Candidacy 3 (The Nomination) (for one): kiss a TV screen.

Fire Fight Pieces:

Bombing Piece: P1 (*clicking a ball point pen*): "You're fired." P2 (*flipping a Bic lighter*): "*You're* fired."

Indecency (for one): ignite a piece of flash paper; flash the "V" sign (between legs, across genitals, etc.).

No Draft (for one): draw in and hold breath; strike a match and ignite a piece of flash paper (if available); flash the "V" sign.

Fire Power (for one): strike a match; flatulate (if available) into flame.

No (for one): shake fist in beam of projected media image.

Theory Fist (for two): P1: hold fist in beam of projected media image. P2: read from a theoretical text (social/cultural/literary, etc., provided) (about 15 secs.). P1: when P2 has finished reading, remove fist from the light. P2: sketch the absent fist and affix the reproduction to the projected image. If no sketching materials are available, a cardboard cutout, or a verbal reproduction of the fist may be substituted. (Alternately, a digital snapshot of the fist could be projected.)

Dump the Hump (for two): P1: imitate something with humps, humping, dumping—Humpty-Dumpty—until event concludes. P2 (*holding an egg*): "Chicago consumes 5 million cases of eggs a year. At 30 dozen eggs per case, that's…" (*toss up the egg*). P1: *attempt to calculate, while humping, in the time it takes the egg to hit the floor*). P2: "And all the king's horses and all the king's men…"

HHH Candidacy 4 (The Nomination) (For one): "'I came here, from the great state of California', to talk to you about a seditious repetition of signifiers— 'HHH.' Knock down the middle bars of each grapheme and what do you get? —no orange or flame thrower—*IIIIII* (italics mine)—elect the faceless dummy un-standupable with a round of champagne poppers? (*hold up cardboard dummy*). Knock away the supporting bars and what is left? Mister____? (*looking at dummy, letting it fall*) (Please cut along the dotted line)."

Daley Meets the Press (For two): P1 (Newsperson): "Mayor Daley…" P2 (Daley): "Dad." P1 (*with difficulty*): "'Dad.' What do you think the theory behind all this is?" P2 (*holding up cardboard dummy, his voice coming from behind*): "I don't think theory—how you move, your bowels, and what that means to my 72% male, 55% female, 55% black and 68 % Hispanic (which doesn't all add up right and the race and gender aspects of which I disavow) labor force that concerns me… Are you one of Daley's millions? You're either in'r y'r out!" (*throwing down dummy*)

Up Yours (for one): Raise and lower an American flag.

Peace Now (for one or more): Place blank sheets of paper along the aisles in the audience area, like a street dividing line; draw various figures, phrases, words, or fragments of text related to the core discourses, one per sheet; leave one sheet blank and let it fly (in any manner you wish) … or…

Dove (Variation of above) (for one): along the floor in front the conference table, arrange eleven blank sheets of paper to spell out the boustrophedon "won caep," with a blank sheet separating the two words. Fold the blank sheet (the space between…) into a paper airplane; write the letter "P" on one wing and "W" on the other, and sail it into the audience. Ask an audience member to unfold it and hold it up for all to see.

Under My Covers (for two): back to the audience, P1 passes a "secret" note—the script card—behind his/her back to P2, who may or may not have his/her back to the audience. Without reading the card, P2 passes it on to the panel Chair or other authority.

Disneyworld (for one or more, in succession): crouch down in the animation stand (to the right of the conference table) and say wonderful things about the current Presidential administration.

Excuse me, Would You Please Repeat the Question? (for appropriate number): Attempt to re-perform any event in reverse.

Exhibit A (B, C, D, etc.) (for two): P1: As witness, provide testimonial (or other proof) about something that has taken place during the session (e.g., "One of the panelists said" or "did" ... etc.). P2: examine/cross examine the witness (e.g., "Which panelist—do you see him/her sitting there?" etc.)

Critical Consciousness (For two): P1: write a question on the board (it may be a simple "who", "what", or "where is..." style question). P2: answer (verbally) by turning the question back to the questioner, exposing the question's underlying assumptions (e.g., Q: "When did the DNC take place?" A: Was it a "Convention"? Was it "Democratic"? What "took place"?).

Morning After (for two or more): to the sounds of shattering glass, shaking hands all around: "Goodbye, everyone, goodbye; good buy (*looking at someone, taking his/her hand and substituting a relevant abstraction or slogan for a personal name—good buy liberty, good buy freedom of speech, good buy right to protest, good buy tolerance, good buy right to be heard, good buy maimed for a cause, good buy died for no cause, good buy peace now, good buy black power, good buy dump the Hump, etc.*), goodbye, America, goodbye good buy..."

Living Theatre (for one): write on the board, "enter individually, exit *en masse*."

Second Line (Show Me Your Tits!) (mass action, to be performed at session's end): led by the panelists, marching at a funereal pace while a Kazoo chorus plays "Happy Days," session attendees/participants form a second line (i.e., fall in behind the panelists) combination festive dance and funereal march, threading through the session space, and beyond, citing/chanting facts/opinions, critical or laudatory, about the '68 DNC, the '04 RNC, the War in Iraq (and/or other aggressive, neo-Imperialistic interventions), devaluation of the dollar (or other fiscally irresponsible act, including privatization of Social Security), legislation effecting environmental policy (allowing rape/abuse of the environment by the State or individuals), globalization (esp. exploitive, neo-colonialist policies of TNCs), or other pressing issues. You may use your Fact Sheet handout as source material. All forward movement of the line should be relatively slow and deliberate, though some participants, as festive dancers, may dance in place. Bringing up the rear of the line, a second chorus chants/sings "We Shall Overcome." Once outside the conference room, at the direction of the line leader, the marchers will form a circle, bringing round the end of the line to meet the beginning, so that the two tunes confront each other. All stop.

Yippies Wild: a blank script card.

Unscripted Events:

Club Fed, Club KYA/FTA (Kick/Kiss Your Ass, Fuck the Army), Barbie's Wire 2, No Exit, Dick Gregory's Dinner Happening, Heckling Events, Yippit.

(Please add some of your own Fluxbits/props to the list, spinning out of your own related concerns, the presentation, critical responses to it, etc.)

* extra-performance bits: not included in present performance, but possible for future or past performances...

Fluxbit Protest Fact Sheet (complied by Christian Herold, *TEZ* guest)

(2nd millennium mid first-decade snap shot for use with Fluxbits as needed; to be updated as conditions worsen globally until no longer possible)

An Iraqi is 2-1/2 times more likely to die today than in the last year of the Hussein regime.

4 of the 5 Republicans investigating Rep. Tom DeLay on ethics charges have taken donations from his PAC.

Wal-Mart has received at least $625 million in subsidies from state and local governments since 1980.

It took 10 seconds for a Maryland consultant last winter to pick a Diebold voting machine's lock and remove its memory card.

The Marshall Plan spent $96.45 per European it was meant to serve. The U.S. has allocated $727.27 per Iraqi this year for Iraq's reconstruction.

40% of Palestinians in the West Bank and Gaza Strip lack regular access to food.

Average life expectancy in 22 African countries has declined since 1978.

20% of U.S. heterosexual marriages are dissolved within five years. Only 3% of same-sex unions granted to Vermont residents since July 2000 have since been dissolved

Only 52% of African-American men age 16 to 64 in New York City were employed each month last year.

Since the implementation of NAFTA in 1994, Mexico's inflation-adjusted minimum wage has decreased by 21%

29% of 2004 votes cast via a computer system produced no paper record.

5 U.S. states do not use the word "evolution" in their science curricula.

Median income of black U.S. families as a percentage of white families' declined from 60% to 58% from 1968 to 2002.

Women's earning compared to men's declined from 80.4% to 79.7 percent between 1983 and 2000.

Between 1960 and 1990, the amount of sunlight reaching the earth has decreased by 3%.

The chance that a member of New York's Army National Guard was in Iraq in June was 1 in 4; the chance that a member of Texas's Army National Guard was: 1 in 31

An estimated 61% of U.S. corporations paid no federal taxes between 1996 and 2000.

Texas has the lowest percentage of citizens of all states with health insurance.

Fresh pictures and sworn statements detailed a teenage boy being raped, prisoners being ridden like animals and other Iraqis being forced to eat pork and drink alcohol in contravention of their religion.

Businesses feel a sense of urgency to enact as many pro-business laws as possible before a fight over judicial nominees or a Supreme Court opening brings legislative action to a "screeching halt."

When he was governor of Texas, George W. Bush presided over 152 executions, more than took place in the rest of the country combined.

Shia leader al-Sistani organized large-scale protests that forced the U.S. to permit general elections to select the new government rather than through local caucuses and indirect elections, as Bush wanted.

Bush's nomination for the UN ambassador, John Bolton, said that "if the UN secretary building in New York lost 10 stories, it wouldn't make a bit of difference."

The Bush Administration underfunded Nunn-Lugar—the program intended to keep the former Soviet Union's nuclear legacy out of the hands of terrorists and rogue states—by $45.5 million.

The Bush Administration has openly opposed the Comprehensive Test Ban Treaty, undermining nuclear nonproliferation efforts

There are fewer experienced CIA agents assigned to the unit dealing with Osama bin Laden now than there were before 9/11.

President Bush is the first President since Herbert Hoover to have a net loss of jobs—around 800,000—over a four-year term.

The Bush Administration underfunded the No Child Left Behind Act by $9.4 billion

Since 9/11, Attorney General John Ashcroft has detained 5,000 foreign nationals in antiterrorism sweeps; none have been convicted of a terrorist crime

The Bush Administration has assigned five times as many agents to investigate Cuban embargo violations as it has to track Osama bin Laden's and Saddam Hussein's money.

An Al Qaeda training manual suggests that terrorists come to the United States and buy assault weapons.

The Bush Administration gutted clean-air standards for aging power plants, resulting in at least 20,000 premature deaths each year.

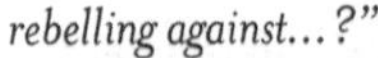

rebelling against...?"

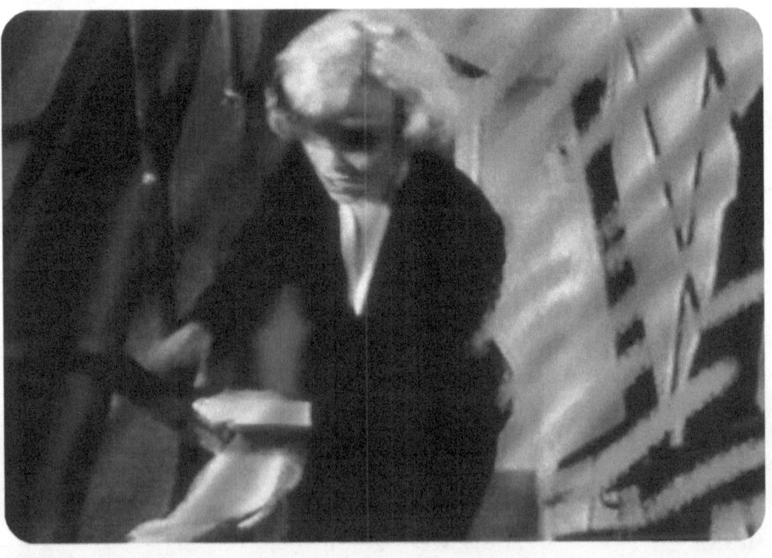

Campus Events

(site-specific extensions for the initial PSI performance, Brown University)

(See Campus Map— http://www.brown.edu/Facilities/Facilities_Management/docs/PAUR_Campus_Map.pdf or "page" search the college website from the homepage—www.brown.edu)

Site 1

Location:

lawn in front of Brown Offices.

Sign:

Overlaying a map of the Brown University Campus (not to scale) with a map of Chicago, circa 1968 (also not to scale), would locate the '68 DNC Lincoln Park riots and Festival of Life here... protesters built a "barricade"—in the middle of the park, really a heap of defiance; a ten-foot high cross was gassed... The Brown administrative offices occupy a position similar to the park cultural and arts center, appropriated by police as a command center during convention week. We are a barricade.

Activity:

attempt to establish a temporary commune in the grounds across from the Brown Office Building; seek permits to sleep overnight.

Site 2

Location:

Commons in front of Sayles Hall

Sign:

Overlaying a map of the Brown University Campus (not to scale) with a map of Chicago, circa 1968 (also not to scale), would locate the '68 DNC Grant Park riots here— "all the World Is Watching." The Grant Park bandshell served as the ideological rallying point for demonstrators. Across the grass, Sayles Hall (academic center of the PSI conference) would be the Hilton Hotel, DNC Democratic Headquarters, Humphrey in his 23rd floor suite kissing the TV screen as he wins the domination, while below, McCarthy observed, the street "looks like a Breughel." From here we pose a conference "challenge."

Activity:

While tossing a football, Frisbee, etc., indict the conference scene with various taunts: "deterrri deterri torialize" (chant), "intercourse not 'discourse'," "how many trees did you kill today—go digital!" Hey hey PSI, got no job and ask you why!" "lift your leg if you're a deconstructionist'" "Fluxup or flixout'" "wouldn't you rather hold a girl than a conference panel?" "escape now—peaces!" "PS sucks!" "don't listen to that paper—come out and play!" "throw the theory bum out!" "Abolish tenure!" "wack wack wack wack blah la blank blunk"

Site 3

Location:

Power Street, in front of the President's House

Sign:

Overlaying a map of the Brown University Campus (not to scale) with a map of Chicago, circa 1968 (also not to scale), would locate the International Amphitheatre here, approximately where the President's House is, hard by the Union Stockyards... the protest marches never made it this far. But we are here to answer the official rhetoric.

Activity:

Grouped before the President's House, narrate, in a highly rhetorical style, PR material about the University's wealth and success from the Brown website; undercut this with facts of global economic desperation and failure and "real" stories of life and study at Brown, from faculty and students, while chanting protest slogans' from the '68 DNC (optional).

Jeopardizing Academia

* * * * * (drum--Morse Code)

/p.3; 2 blank except for a crude drawing which looks like a clenched fist with pointing finger\
E. F. Grier

Everyone moving about freely

A large-square-shaped room but without any angular appearance, 2

all the light coming 3 down from ovehead,
a room full of...

Barthes' "third language"!

cheerful color

Gorilla Text!

some...reading, others writing

(through large panels of glass, forty or fifty of them.)4

a good deal of a golden hue, profusely ornamented

Don't Resist

This Text!

~~2 inserted: "a room above" ance," in "appearance,"~~
~~3 deleted: "in" ; inserted above "down"~~
~~4 subsequent entries on this page in black pencil.~~
~~5 inserted above "conver" in "conversation"~~
~~6 inserted: "muffled, yet sharp" above "sound...of". Perhaps should precede "sound"~~
~~7 inserted above "the...walls"~~
~~8 inserted above "gray"~~

the lecturer must...

subdued 5 conversation going on every where---

the lecturer must...
(grabs projector, flashes images around)

the call for one

("botanical," "critical," and "editorial"

--the lower 7 walls of the room light 6

the sound 8 muffled, yet sharp

of the clapping hands, voices throw off disguises,

run through audience

little imps of pages

gray, relieved with figures of a deeper hue--

distributing pamphlets)

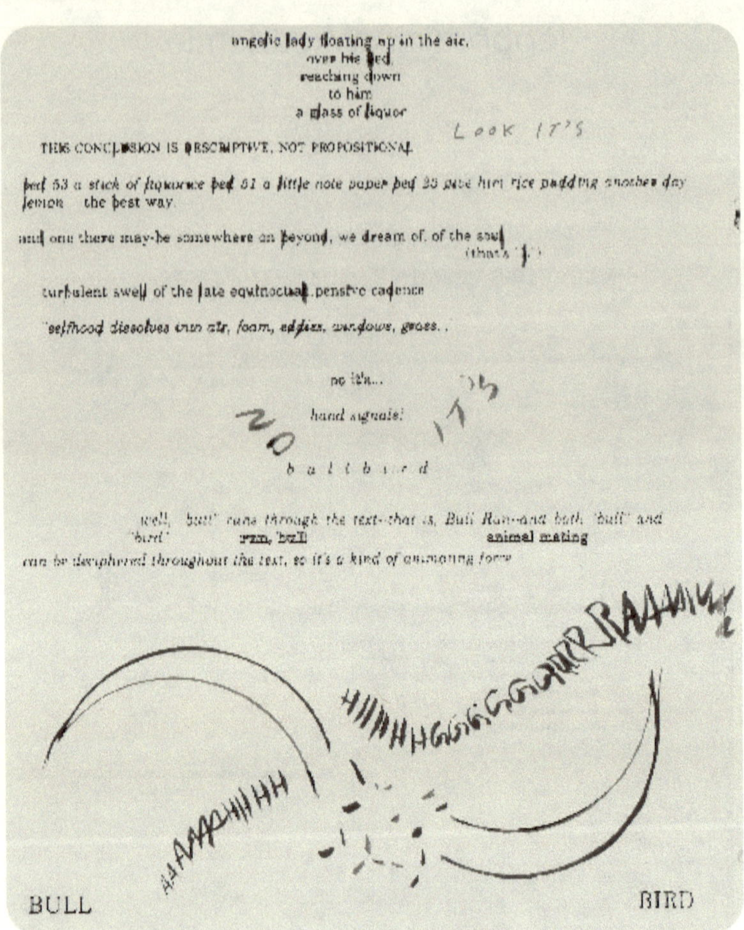

Fig. 12: excerpts from author's artist book, *Stirr'd Up Everywhere,* including hermeneutical mutinies and topsy-turviness andfirst appearance of "Bull Bird" as decoded from text and semaphoric representation)

7 Script 6: Stirr'd Up Everywhere: Whitman *en abime*

Following is a typographic transcription[72] *of the artist's book* Stirr'd Up Everywhere, *a multivoice performance collage inspired by Whitman's autobiographical, Civil War/nature diary,* Specimen Days. *The piece is intended to reenact a postmodern textual experience (what reading a text means in a poststructuralist critical, academic environment). Whitman—or any author—is not just the words on the page that we ascribe to him, but also the words of others about him (including the more or less hidden, or behind-the-scenes editorial voices that emend, comment on, and in a sense collaborate with the author, producing an "authorized" version of a text for reader consumption). Four discourse territories interact dialogically in the piece: scientific, political, academic, and autobiographical. The docu-collage incorporates material from botanical handbooks, Marx and Engels treatise on the American Civil War, critical and biographical studies of Whitman, and Whitman's correspondence and notebooks as well as* Specimen Days. *My own improvisations, based on these voices, freely traverse these territories, often overwriting them (literally, with water-color markers); I inscribe myself in the piece, then, not so much as an "author," but as an arranger/orchestrator, as* bricoleur *and originator of (extra/intra-textual) play.*

The collage, which has been presented in New York at SKEP Performance Gallery, Space 2B, and the Whitman Bicentennial Celebration (CUNY), is ideally performed by 5-6 readers/actors, representing the various discourse territories. To highlight the visual and mock-pedagogical aspects of the piece, pages of the typescript are projected on a screen or wall as they are read. Actors can memorize parts of the poem, read it from hand-held scripts, and read it across the bodies of other actors as they place themselves before the beam of the projector (at one point the image is "reduced" to a simulacrum of a standard-sized manuscript page and projected on the chest of the actor playing Whitman). The projector is the only stable (i.e., non-mobile) light source. (Toward the middle of the performance, however, even this tentative point of stasis is challenged: during a particularly wild eruption of watercolor annotations, the voices representing these annotations run through the audience tossing out pamphlets and shouting "guerrilla text!" The Lecturer grabs the projector and flashes images around the room and on the actors and audience.) Each actor/reader wears three clip-on lights. One of these lights illuminates the script, while the other two highlight parts of the actors' bodies; they can direct and redirect these lights, which are attached to flexible shafts, according to their own interpretations of the voices they are presenting (this has a Noh-like effect, keeping both actors and audience aware that what's taking place is a drama of representations, if not symbols, and not of "real-life" or life-like characters). The surrounding

72. E-version of the book with original graphics at *The Little Magazine: The Hypertext Mechanic,* 22.2 (*http://13thmoon.net/html/litmag.html*).

darkness and the fragmenting effect of the lights give an eerie, suprahuman and, at the same time, uncannily intimate quality to the piece.

The piece opens as a "lecturer" wheels in Whitman (his subject, or "specimen") on a standard-issue office chair; simultaneously, a photo-image of Whitman rolls in on the opaque projector (or fades in, if slide projectors are used). During the performance, "Whitman," who quickly undermines and detours the "lecture," wheels himself about on his chair, or is wheeled about by the other readers. Sometimes, he is compelled to jump up and guide or push the actors about, trying to "teach" them how to read or see or feel the work (i.e., the collage); at such moments, he becomes a strong physical as well as verbal presence. At one point, the projection beam is turned off and lines from Whitman's work are chanted in the dark (though the actors can turn their personal lights on and off). During this scene, "Whitman" interacts with the audience, talking to them about himself, his relationship to his actor and role, what he intends to do, and asks them for their opinions and suggestions, some of which he may incorporate in his own way; other actors may follow Whitman's lead and direct themselves to the audience at this or any other point during the rest of the show (this semi-open structure, like a jazz performance, spaces out the thematic melody to allow for solo riffs by each performer).

Throughout the performance, Whitman attends especially to the lecturer (a young, theoretically oriented, though at first somewhat too professional literary idealist). The Lecturer's voice is that of a writer surrounded by books, hurriedly jotting down notes and quotes from various sources before the library closes and the volumes are reshelved in their proper times/spaces (the job of institutional wage-earners—researchers and librarians—to maintain the order towering independently about them) ready for the next day's selective disarrangement. This persona plays off the Whitman of Specimen Days, *who is also a writer at large in the field of his sources, which are, in his case, the battlefields and hospitals of the Civil War and the surrounding natural environment. Whitman's text does not rest easily between covers. Thus the Lecturer's repetition-compulsion, displaced to harried dialogic encounters with a textual Other, cannot be reduced to a book-text situation; we all live within an atemporal abundance, a life-text that can only with great exceptions be kept in linear order.*

At the end of the piece, Whitman is "put" back into his chair by the voices of Marx and the critics, becoming a specimen again. His lights are turned off and he is wheeled off stage. The lecturer, however, is left behind, hopefully transformed by his involvement with the collage, to carry a more porous, more per-sonal message into the academic world.

The Book

The book itself, whose features include a letter-press cover, black spiral binding, found image collages printed on translucent overlays, and watercolor overmarkings (as noted above), functions as an assemblable/reassemblable collage, activated by reader participation. The pages are unnumbered, and potentially rearrangeable (a situation played upon by the spiral binding style, suggestive of a field notebook and economic expediency, as well as by the projection of individual pages during performance). Each page asserts its materiality and can be read/encountered as a serial unit with its own identity and artistic integrity, or can be read through/into an accompanying translucent overlay image page, where these occur; or each set of facing pages can be taken as a unit—where translucent pages occur, the unit becomes a variable triptych, in which the image (often a "found" photo) can be reversed and further defamiliarized with the flip of a page. Also, the front and back fly leaves are cut into five flaps; on each flap is a quote taken from a Civil War soldier's diary. These quotes may be brought in at any point during the performance of the reading, adding another layer of text to the plurilogue. Each aspect of the book's form plays on/through/exaggerates features of the close, analytical, critical, reading of texts common in academic communities—annotations, marked "bookmarks," cryptography, hermeneutical de(re)coding of text and the tracing of semantic and imagistic patterns that continually de(re)construct themselves, etc.—and on the ideological and socio-political contexts of the host text stimulating in the current text, a play of various kinds of overwriting/writings through, including color (de)codings and patterning based on semaphore transcriptions.

Both the print and web versions of the book include performance notes from the original presentation of the collage, thus documenting its pre-book existence as multimedia event; it also exists as a script for future performances, and as the vehicle for performative reading. The experience of the collage/mobile will vary for each reader, depending, minimally, on his/her turning pages, but more subliminally on the imaginative pressure brought to bear in evoking the multivoiced texture of the performance at each "turn" and on the energy of follow through, or creative play—" reading"/assembling and "rereading"/ reassembling—that the reader/co-creator carries out...

[*an offstage groan, which could perhaps be the sound of the piece of audio-visual equipment the lecturer has just moved—the performance has begun...*]

Wha...? People!

This is the 100th anniversary of Walt Whitman's death. We celebrate his death, because...

my birth...

?

I mean...

the birth of his work away from himself

well...and this is Walt Whitman...He died on March 26, 1892, but on July 2nd, in '92...

1882

sorry...on July 2nd 1882 he began to reinscribe the notes and diary entries, not necessarily in chronological order...

Run? **Bull** Run!...

*that eventually became the autobiographical work known as Spec***ssss...**

{drum—rattle}

{a spell is cast over the lecturer's slide projector}

SSSSPSSSSPSSSSPSSSSpsssss...*imen* *Days*... **?**...

SSSSpssssspssssspsss

/year in red ink\

skips and jumps...Down in the Woods, July 2d, 1882. Incongruous huddle... diary-jottings, war-memoranda, Nature-notes —If I do /in blue

it at all I must... pencil\

yes, that's how it begins...now... [lecturer's inspects the projected image—the text marked by a wild and colorful graffiti]

nowwww {pitch—low}

/~~"sending" in~~

? \

ommmm {slight vibrato} **aaaaummm aaaaummm** {drum—

when Johnny

aaaa... um...

comes marching...} aaaaummmm {drum—hurrah, hurrah}

Johnny, come...

This is a work in progress

"Autu**mmm**n Side-Bits"

Many of his aesthetic gestures are familiar ones \ (Helen Vendler): *the articulation of an individual speaking self, a visual and verbal curiosity, a belief in a possible correspondence between nature and voice, repeated allusions to past poetry, and a taste for both simplicity and grandeur*

Hummmmm

Human fragments

but it is the way Whitman combined them...

{drum-side clip}

NOT A DISSOLUTION, BUT A REORGANIZATION *That's Marx*

dissolve propositional thought into fugitive gleams, hints of sound... *I'm not sure...*

well, for instance...

shriek of a mule at night

full Under an old black oak, glossy and green—envelop'd in warmth
and *voiced,*
lyric light of noonday sun swarms of flitting insects—harsh cawing of
rise & fall crows...Battle of Bull Run, July, 1861.
...swarming wagons...men

swarming insects and... *the civil*

recoiling back, pouring over the Long Bridge
war in a gnat!

re ee treat

PEOPLE'S WARS

dust, grime and smoke, in layers sweated in, follow'd by other layers, again sweated in, absorb'd by those excited souls— *transmogrification...* their clothes all saturated with the clay-powder filling the air—stirr'd up everywhere...

(three dead men lying,)

contention!

GREAT DISGRACE OF BULL RUN...EARLIER ERROR OF ENLISTING VOLUNTEERS. each with a blanket spread over him—

...SENSELESS TO ALLOW A STRONG POSITION, ON DIFFICULT TERRAIN AND IN POSSESSION OF A FOE LITTLE INFERIOR IN NUMBERS, TO BE ATTACKED BY RAW RECRUITS return'd... **front**

front drop down any where deep **front**

front sleep profound **LINE**

in both sensual and social terms, though these soon give way to metaphysical questions

* * * {drum-slow pulse}

Like this?

My walk out around the camp, the fires burning—groups around—the merry song—the sitting *flitting?* forms—the playing light on the *cracked* faces— *like the Fall of the House of...*

PANIC WHICH TOOK POSSESSION OF THE UNION ARMY... **con-**

SURPRISE NO ONE WHO WAS IN SOME DEGREE FAMILIAR... **firmed**

(I lift one blanket and look at the young man's face, calm and yellow, —'tis strange?)

becoming...?

EXERTED A PROFOUND INFLUENCE ON... *Glicksberg?*

they would tell stories—one would tell a story of a dead man sitting on the top rail of a fence—he had been shot there at sundown, mortally wounded, clung with desperate nerves, and was found sitting there, dead, staring with fixed eyes in the morning— *wonderful!*

stories...eyes...creative...

A NATIONAL CRISIS, A LIVING EPIC, A CREATIVE FORCE...

definitely Glicksberg

swarms of dirt-covered return'd...

With few exceptions the vascular plants grow rooted in...

I don't recognize...

hurry up something

INFLUENCE ON HIS WORK CAN, THEREFORE, HARDLY BE...

"hurry up something for their"...?

what? soil, plant life?

That it is of prime importance to the human race is, of course...

baffling decon-
struction via crypto-
graphic overcoding. Who,

Ehh?...what's this...Semaphore? **or what,**
was the recipient?

the codes: the marks in the text..." If luce or ereor"?

[letters blocked out in text, revealing mysterious counter-texts, eventually leading to a primary/primal source, "Bull Bird," whose Image also appears]

ummmmmm **if**
loose

or

Is this what de Certeau meant by "la perrugue" (page 25?): the ***error***
worker's own work disguised as work for the employer—language, in this case...

Pay attention!
EYE! **con**

I...? race ***e****ras****e***

hurry up something for their grub!

recognized by the thoughtful man, and that a "love for the soil" is deeply ingrained in us clothes all saturated is also conceded.

Gibbs, Darnley, the botanist!

Then you say:
"eating the green corn—grated through tin pans with rough holes

that's reality!

pierced in them—"

(Young man: I think this face of yours the face of...)

/in red ink\
recd

through the corporeal lineaments, the spiritual...

my dead Christ

"the eclectic self is seeking types," here, "or emblems" ...I'm getting lost in this."

*** {drum—rapid}

Follow me:

sassafras **catalpas** beeches *black-walnut* holly-willow-hornbeam **mountain-ash birches** aspen hickory pine-pine *black-walnut!* **mou ma**

should we reconsider this text?

mani **maa** ni manimanimanimani **maa niii ma aaa ma nii**

at the foot of tree, immediately in front, a heap of feet, legs, *like*
arms, and human fragments, 1 **contested** *he sees it!*

split of the son into two ?

{drum—side clip}

1 Glickberg...has challenged the authenticity

cut, bloody, black and blue, swelled and sickening
pierced Christ blue

It is striking that six days after the battle amputated limbs were being left... *is it?*

The walk along the Rappahannock in front, *the mansion* a pleasant shore *converted to a hospital* See *not ten yards from* the houses *the front door, the heaps* — some with their chimneys thrown down—the hospitals—the man with his mouth blown out *nondualistic* the balloon... *the pleasant shore* **now put out the...**

LOSE IN STYLISTIC DISTINCTION, CONTINUITY, AND LITERARY SKILL...GAIN IN VIVIDNESS, CONCISION, CONCRETENESS, AND

and? Grier, Glicks...?

why did Monday, Dec. 22—forenoon very pleasant, Sun shining, a partial
this haze—Saw the balloon up—a great huge, slow moving thing, with
fascinate?

TEXT FR. GLICKBERG

these too will

a curious look to me, as it crawled up, and slanted down again, as if it were... **rise**

alive. /image in

9,600 WOUNDED... THAT'S 9 6 0 0 reddish-

yellow

unt'her'd

I sit in solitude absorbing, enjoying it all... un...
thered, hered, whered

tethered?

9 THE PRESENT STRUGGLE... *no, ALL*

exhibit A

rich coloring, yellows of all hues, pale and dark green, shades from lightest to richest red all set in and toned down by the prevailing brown of the earth and gray of the sky.

BETWEEN TWO SOCIAL SYSTEMS *between earth and...*

the fenced enclosure in the midst of the woods, 6
for butchering the beef, the just quartered cattle, in huge
pieces lying around *"the metamorphosis of the text effected by the wandering eyes of..."* —the men *gather'd around the fire, "the reader"* the play of light on the
cracked *faces* with rolled up sleeves and stained arms

the tender mother and the fierce mother, the invocation of comradeship, got the
the narcissistic turn to the body, the eerie gestures toward solitude rhythm right
and silence

Whitman as Vendler? for parallelism, see above
see here

/~~in pencil on slip~~:\
Nineteenth Century

hummm. So winter is coming **at the end of** and I yet in my sickness
the end of
WITHDRAWN FROM THE SPHERE OF DIPLOMATIC AND PARLIAMENTARY DISCUSSIONS

I sit here amid all these fair sights and vital influences, and abandon myself to that thought, with its wandering trains…

CAUSE OF WHICH…NOT CLARIFIED (*Marx*)

a fiction or series of fictions… (*Whitman*) o

AN INCREDIBLE STRAIN ON THE MEDICAL CORPS (*Grier?*)

an old black oak **a century**

I still think we should reconsider… Too Late

"*It's not until Whitman merges with the father that the types can merge*," *who says…?*

*** {drum—slow—Johnny comes}

This is later…remember? **exhibit B**
1885: "I am in my little house I told you about, not far from the river. Health pretty fair the last four months, & would be so still, except for an increasing prostration of the whole muscular system"

THE SYSTEM OF SLAVERY AND THE SYSTEM OF FREE LABOR.

o ummm…
yes

—almost a falling sickness, as at times
I cannot keep my legs.

A CASUAL VISITOR, RATHER THAN AS THE ACTIVE PARTICIPANT HE LATER CLAIMED...

—was out this afternoon in the wheel chair, the sun half-out in starts... Warren ...downstairs practicing his fiddle...

CAN ONLY BE ENDED BY THE VICTORY OF ONE SYSTEM OR THE OTHER

...ebb *edd* ing ebbing—
fairly buoyant spirits—rare egg & tea & bread
for breakfast—good bowel action—

...am floating along carried by the momentum of things I suppose
great huge, slow moving
—stupidly may be a strong word but it suggests if not describes my cond'n these times...

AT THE DECISIVE MOMENT, THE CAUSE OF WHICH
BULL
bread, swiftly cut in stout chunks

CAN ONLY BE ENDED

cold...& sunny?
.....not so bad as you might suppose...right arm giving out....

NOT A DISSOLUTION, BUT...
impotency of the individual
before a socio-politico-economic crisis?
A winged bovine? Perhaps an apocalyptic (or castration)
fantasy

"the lecturer must scream on page...?

...& they say am better...[**(stop)**

mustard plaster on my side stinging...must... [] (*stop?*)

Had a gOoD currying two hours ago—Supper of rice and mutton...

[[] (*ssst...*)

can no longer live peacefully side by...**][][**

representation of dissolution as a viable poetic conclusion

stop stew side **nonauthorial cluster as exhibit C**

must get off this line...

WHAT IS HERE SET DOWN IN BLACK AND WHITE *Glicks, or...*Mmmmarrr

IS, THEREFORE, NOTHING BUT

aesthetic images and rhetorical gestures of dispersion!

Unable [**able**] to write much stop $4 enc'd stop y'r good friend [**good letter**] good letter rec'd [**sent**] [Camd'n, 3/17/92]

—God bless you—

WW

ORIGINALLY FORGED

ON THE ANVIL OF PAIN

Death /red ink\\——————— ~~nothing~~

Is here.

12/26/62

Don't know quite how to do this... we'll help you.

"The aesthetic life—by contrast to the metaphysical life or where's the
the ethical life—gives full measure to the contradictions of rhythm
the many moods of life. It is for this reason that the aesthetic can you
moment presents itself to Whitman as a process of dissolution, sing
it?
not as one of architectonics," *she says...not as one of architectonics* **she says**
not as one of architectonics **she says** *but a process of* **diss...**

*** {drum—slow pulse}

The first shudder has long passed over, *Letter to Emerson, 1/17/63* and I must say I find deep things, unreckoned by current print or speech.

24 FROM STABS AND GUN-SHOT WOUNDS, 82 FROM FALLING OFF BUILDINGS, OR DOWN LADDERS; 22 FROM BURNS AND SCALDS

The Hospital...

R U N

Ward G bed 12 amp of left leg no. 5 ward C some ginger for diarrhea

ummmm

mottled by much light and shade...distant scream of a flock...
the hospital!

some jelly to ward B ward C bed 34 fract thigh sandy comp—good sport

he was

I desire and intend to write a little book out of this phase of America, her masculine young manhood, its conduct under most trying of and highest of all exigency, which she, as by lifting a corner in a curtain, has vouchsafed me to see **America**,
LARYNGITIS—FEVER—DEBILITY—DIARRHEA already brought to Hospital in her fair youth...

he wasn't!
DOCTOR THINKS HE IS SHAMMING *bed 13 ward G amp left leg—tooth brush*
laryngitis, fever, debility...

ground strew'd with debris...Timber creek, as I slowly pace
E R A S E *slowly*
so I can walk contrast shudder ginger
its banks, has ebb'd low... *with you* scream write America shamming
debris

But more, a new world here I find as I would show—a world full of its separate action, play, suggestiveness—

FEVER, 233; RHEUMATISM, 205; REMITTENT FEVER, 125

BIRD
surely a medium world,

ward 6 bed 52 apples a book horehound candy sweet plug tobacco

advanced between our well-known practiced one of body and of mind,
DELIRIUM TREMENS, 79; TYPHOID, 95; BRONCHITIS, 62; PHTHISIS...
and this:

angelic lady floating up in the air,
over his bed,
reaching down
to him
a glass of liquor

look it's

THIS CONCLUSION IS DESCRIPTIVE, NOT PROPOSITIONAL

bed 53 a stick of liquorice bed 51 a little note paper bed 25 give him rice pudding another day lemon the best way...

and one there may-be somewhere on beyond, we dream of, of the soul.
(that's "L")
turbulent swell of the late equinoctial... pensive cadence

"*selfhood dissolves into air, foam, eddies, windows, grass...*"

no it's...
got it...hand signals!

b...u...l...l...b...i...r...d

...well, "bull" runs through the text—that is, Bull Run—and both "bull" and "bird"
run, bull animal mating
can be deciphered throughout the text, so it's a kind of animating force...

aaahhhhhggrrrrraaawwwww

{first appearance of Bull Bird}

BULL BIRD

* * * {drum—Morse Code}

/p.3; 2 blank except for a crude drawing which looks like a clenched fist with pointing finger\ *E. F. Grier*

Everyone moving about freely

A large-square-shaped room but without any angular appearance, **2**

all the light coming **3** down from ovehead,

a room full of…

Barthes' "third language"!

cheerful color

Guerrilla Text! {"botanical," "critical," and "editorial" voices throw off disguises, run through audience distributing pamphlets}

some…reading, others writing

(through large panels of glass, forty or fifty of them.)**4**

a good deal of a golden hue, profusely ornamented

Don't Resist This Text!

~~2 inserted: "—a room" above "ance," in "appearance,"~~

~~3 deleted: "in" ; inserted above: "down"~~

~~4 subsequent entries on this page in black pencil.~~ *the lecturer must…*

~~5 inserted above "conver" in "conversation"~~ {grabs projector, flashes

~~6 inserted: "muffled, yet sharp" above "sound…of".~~ images around}

perhaps ~~should precede "sound"~~

~~7 inserted above "the…walls"~~

~~8 inserted above "gray"~~

subdued **5** conversation going on everywhere—

the call for one

—the lower **7** walls of the room light **8**

the sound **6** muffled, yet sharp

of the clapping hands,

little imps of pages

gray, relieved with figures of a deeper hue—

this is a work in progress... **I absorption**

* * * {drum—nailing down}

(scratch this page)

energy exchange!

(+) **gather'd improvis'd absorb'd dispers'd** (-)

jamm'd circl'd blacken'd strew'd

My chair!

unloos'd undream'd abandon'd revers'd

(-) **spatter'd streak'd ebb'd dash'd** (+)

Bull Horns!

dispers'd energy troops regather

momentum

WHITE WORKING CLASS WOULD GRADUALLY BE FORCED

collide alte(r(e))structure disperse

EAGLES

high-holes

bluebirds yellow birds

hen-hawks tits

tits it's

blackbirds *ravens*

eating **green corn**

white-bellied

reed birds woodpeckers

Green Bird

SANDPIPER

killdeer ring dove flicker

This is Whitman...

* * * {drum—woodpeckers, bird calls}

SSSSPssspsssspssssspssssspsssssspssssss

nature "is, yet says nothing"

I used a xerox copy of the Library of America edition of Specimen Days; *when I finished with it,*

say what?

there were places where you could barely read the text through the markings...marginal notes?...

with coffee?...not blood you?

the pages stained...I often took them outside...that's me in the old wooden chair; you can hear

all I hear is yours?

surf running up on the bulkhead, the sound of my silent reading. The house I forgot to mention.

frame! it's on wheels! will you answer?

White stucco, big "L"-shaped yard with hydrangeas, the chair, phone ringing upstairs, chain-link

careful that's me!

fence, 5' drop to the beach...that's me sitting...not quite sure why I include this, what I'm looking

aren't you? I am.

for...when I'm reading, I forget about all that...

padme pad me hum hum me flower mayweed hum-tongue
horehound pale manna mercury-millet

mock ear hobblebush paspalum hum-all
monkspa mugmud panic merry-bells

{drum—side clip}

if you insist
Scrophulariaceae, Figwort Family. the piece of board, *what*
hastily inscribed with the name—*not* in Latin—placed on *does*
it
the breast, to be ready Opposite or alternate leaves. *look*
Sepals 4-5, Petals usually 5, rarely 4, united at least at *like?*
base, usually tubular, often unequal it is (partial haze).
Stamens with fertile anthers 2-5, arising from corolla;
sterile stamen (s) padme hum sometimes present. beds 23
& 24 wants some horehound candy! Fruit dry (capsule),
several-many-seeded, rarely 1-4-seeded. *beautiful!*

Try it this way: He comes toward me through mulleins, his hands going up right alongside them, blooming verbs—L O V E S—and the other?... but the head cocked back in the dust, the lower jaw blown away... his head sunk back in the pillow, the jaw slack, unable to close around articulation.... but the eyes—still bull's eyes

Large, placid mulleins, as summer advances, velvety in texture, of a light greenish-drab color, growing everywhere in the fields *dry roads and trodden...dust...swarms* —at first earth's big rosettes in their broad-leav'd low cluster-plants, eight, ten, twenty leaves to a plant—plentiful on the fallow twenty-acre lot *improvis'd tables of rough planks...hurry up something* ...leaves as broad as my hand, and the lower ones twice as long—so fresh and dewy in the morning—stalks now four or five, even seven or eight feet high.... *couple of slices of beef, and some crackers...commenced cooking the mess in a frying pan* (... another man was waiting with similar articles to have the use of the frying pan) I've grown to a fondness for it. Every object has its lesson,

/image in yellow-green
enclosing the suggestion of everything else— brown, deep blue
and lately I sometimes think all is concentrated sparks of light\
for me in these hardy, yellow-flower'd weeds, as I come down the lane
early in the morning, I pause before their soft wool-like fleece and stem

and broad leaves, glittering with countless diamonds. Annually for three summers now, they and I have silently return'd together; at such long intervals I stand or sit among them, musing—and woven with the rest, of so many hours and moods of partial rehabilitation—of my sane or sick spirit, here as near at peace as it can be.

Emerson died, aged 79—
that's what the image refers to

/~~in red, with lines~~
~~around in red ink:~~

death of Emerson 9

~~also black ink:~~\

where is he now?

9 THE FACT THAT WHITMAN COULD WRITE THIS DOWN TWICE, AND UNDERLINE IT WITH SUCH A HEAVY MARK IS CERTAINLY SIGNIFICANT

7 talks in a whisper...would like some

* * *

{drum—improvise}

AAAAAAAAAAAA o A ha manna

Out of the cradle endlessly

AAAAAAAAAAAA o A ha manna

the musical shuttle

SSSSPSSSSSPSSSSSSPSSSSSPSSSSSssss

over the sterile sands and the fields beyond

as if they were alive

from the fitful risings and fallings I heard

AAAAAAAAAAAA o A ha manna

AAAAAAAAAAAA o A ha manna

beginning notes the thousand responses

aaaaummmmmmAH aaaaummmmmmAH

myriad thence-aroused words

AAAAAAAAAAAA o A ha manna

My point here was to have everyone talk about their

involvement with AAAAAAAAAAAA o A ha manna

of the bird that chanted to me!

SSSSPSSSSSPSSSSSSPSSSSSPSSSSSssss

a flock twittering, rising, or overhead passing

the piece. There's a need to talk about oneself, what one's doing, to define, **AAAAAAAAAAAA o A ha manna**

even though you know it can only be ended...

AAAAAAAAAAAA o A ha manna

hurriedly

UM! SSSSPSSSSSPSSSSS

I tried doing this impromptu, but then jotted some notes on the script.

UM! SSSSPSSSSSPSSSSS

I, chanter of pains and joys taking all hints swiftly leaping beyond

AAAAAAAAAAAA o A ha UM!

Someone is reading from elsewhere in the text; we won't perform that (unless

AAAAAAAAAAAA o A ha manna

peering, absorbing, translating

UM! SSSSPSSsssPSSSSS

we already have). I don't know what the other is doing. I won't ask you.

UM! SSSSPSSSSSPSSSSS

The worst thing was the fucking traffic trying to get out here.

that chanted to me!

* * *

FOLLOWING TEXT FROM GLICKBERG, 7?

Thanks, my dear friend, for the Magazine & Article...—sitting alone by my open window in part sunshine part shadow—it is unequal united, at least, at base *—but there are parts in it.*

Verbascum, Mullein slight boards, rudely inscribed with the names boxing Leaves densely white-wooly *I pause before their soft* above as well gloves! as beneath; inflorescence dense cylindric, usually unbranched; flowers sessile or nearly so. Buddha is

green corn—grated

Leaves glabrous or sparsely hairy above; inflorescence wider or looser, usually branched; pedicels of flowers distinct suggestion of everything else though sometimes short.

flying shit

Ahhh...then
voyaging done—...timbers may (or may not) hold

Corolla yellow or white

...little huts of green boughs, pine or what not—doesn't matter—impromptu shelter....10

birches aspen hickory

10 "SHEBANGS": ACCORDING TO DA, WW WAS THE FIRST TO USE THE WORD IN PRINT pine pine pine

read by fits and starts—fragments: read in moods: no sequence, no order, no nothing

damn right!

...OPPOSITION TO THE SLAVEHOLDING OLIGARCHY...

a bunch of loose leaves...tore out from some broken or cheap edition

ATTACKED BY RAW RECRUITS

blotch'd here and there with more than one blood stain, hurriedly written

an open-air formation—singly, or in clusters—wild and free and somewhat acrid-

"It is as if beasts spoke"—Emerson...

this beautiful bright forenoon...

Moth-Mullein: Pedicels 1-1.5 cm long, twice as long as fruit; flowers scattered, distant...

see?

the resolution comes, this day, this hour...

fell in love with him just from reading his...

NOoooWW**Wwwwooommmooooommmm** {pitch
—high voltage hum}

Tom *poetry* Tom *Tom?* here are some scraps and MS.... gather'd from the heap—where? *at the foot of tree, immediately in front* right—will they do?

SSSSSPssssssPssssspssssspssssPSSssssss

prepare... by the following self-teaching exercises. Abstract yourself from this book: realize where you are at present located, the point you stand that is now to you the centre of all. Look up overhead, think of... {one drum click}

OOOOOooommmmmmmmmmmmm {pitch—high}

/one word in red
black blue yellow green ink\

accepted

{drum—rattle}

SSSSSSSSPSSS**SSSSP**SSSSSSSSS**psssss**sssspssssSSSSpe*cccccimen Days...get it?* New York, Library of America, 1982, 689-926!

{second and final appearance of Bull Bird}

Voices Cited

Gibbs, Darnley. *Botany: An Evolutionary Approach*. Philadelphia: The Blakiston Company, 1950.

Glicksberg, Charles I., ed. *Walt Whitman and the Civil War*. Philadelphia: University of Pennsylvania Press, 1933.

Marx, Karl, and Frederick Engles. *The Civil War in the United States*. 3rd. ed. New York: International Publishers, 1969.

Seymour, Frank Conkling. *The Flora of New England*. Rutland, Vermont: The Charles E. Tuttle Company, 1969.

Vendler, Helen. "Whitman and the Aesthetic Life." *Democracy's Poet*. [pamphlet; distributed free during a marathon reading of Whitman's work at the Symphony Space, New York, NY, 3/28/92].

Whitman, Walt. *The Correspondence*. Vols. I and V (1842-1867; 1890-1892). Ed. Edwin Haviland Miller. New York: New York University Press, 1961.

—. *Daybooks and Notebooks*. Vol. II: Daybooks, December 1881-1891. Ed. William White. New York: New York University Press, 1978.

—. *Notebooks and Unpublished Prose Manuscripts*. Vol. II: Washington. Ed. Edward F. Grier. New York: New York University Press, 1984.

—. *Specimen Days*. Walt Whitman: Complete Poems and Collected Prose. New York: Library of America, 1982. 689-926.

Closing Gestures

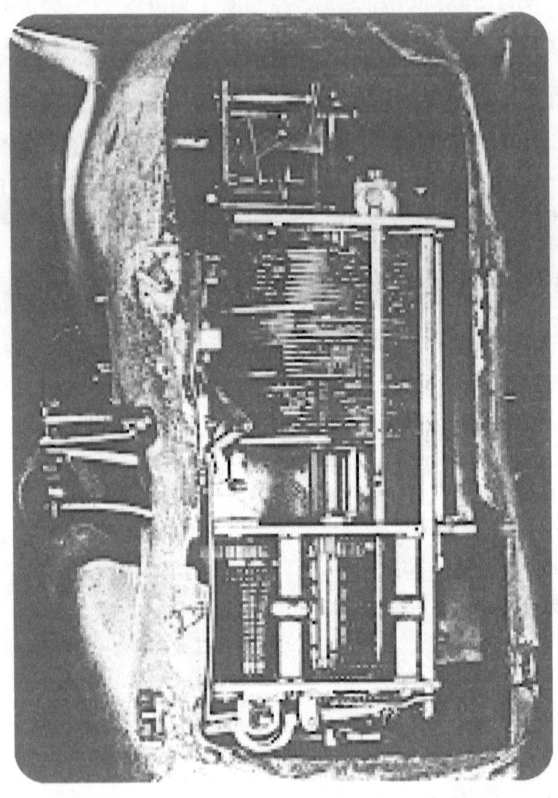

Fig. 13: The writer, writing, revealed. Image in public domain, New York Public Library.

8 Eat, Drink and be Merry, for the Food of the Performance is Inedible

(Following, performing as a self-evaluation of The Monroe Project, *is a brief self-interview by/with Team member M1 in his/her "real life" persona. This (self)critical "dialogue" is ongoing and (temporally) discontinuous, and is not necessarily oral.)*

A: I wrote it... drafted from start to finish one August afternoon on Jones Beach, outside Manhattan. Its abstract rhythms are the mood of the surf, the surrealistic qualities a result of the imagination dwelling in the abstract. The piece doesn't personify that "dwelling," but questions such metaphoric maneuvering; the seduction of Marilyn Monroe is the seduction of a metaphor. The abstraction is also a departure: I knew I was leaving New York, probably for good, moving to a city in the south that was, at the time of writing, just an image, a mirage, a spatial illusion on the marsh—a city thriving, vampire-like, on its own insubstantial self-images, hiding (architecturally, for example) behind *fin de siècle* veils, feeding off the vanished blood of the "Old South." That's some of the "personal" grounding (i.e., my liminal position at the time of writing) for the texture of the piece. I was in transit, had no place, a body— i.e., as a physical presence rooted in a place—dis-embodied.

Q: How does this tie in with the thematics of the piece?

A: Abstraction is also de-reification of the MM figure, in its various positions/ manifestations. The process of production works from the plane of ideology; there's also a system, and a technology, a methodos that guides production concepts as well as structuring and channeling the flow of material from initial design stages to finished product. So we have to remember, whenever we talk about a "cultural construct", a cultural production, we are also talking about a systemic process, and a "being", "presence", an identity-commodity that is collaboratively produced: behind every cultural product is a socio-economic-ideological "team", not necessarily of particular "people", but of the key structural elements—the voices—of the culture itself (in *The Monroe Project*, the "Design Team" represents, or is the agency of, these cultural elements/values).

Q: Let's take the *mise en scene*.

A: I think so. The primary tensions are established at the outset. There's a layering, a dialogue of images and rhetorical positions always on the verge of slipping into a reality effect: a digital head wears a sailor's cap (metonymic for *Niagara*); behind a scrim/veil of synthetic black (mourning?) stretch material, Hollywood images begin to glow and flow. Voices speak from behind a life-size cardboard serial of MM heads; team members often relate to the audience through real time synthesis—mediation of a "live" monitor—while their physical bodies are averted. The audience receives a text-Xerox of a melodramatic synopsis of *Niagara* from the back of a video box, representation of a representation of a representation: "femme fatale ... seductively torments ... mysterious lover ... powerful portrait of human sexuality and passion." The surface impact of the blurb's language is heightened by a prosody of exaggeration: alliteration and over-coded contraries held in syntactic balance. Erotic body and evil mind; a 'femme fatale' (French phraseology, stereotypically, for the *feminine* of the feminine) yielding a "double-edged sword"; a performance that is "at once fascinating and frightening." Language is itself the stage of conflicts, creating linguistic distinctions as it enacts a psychosexual doubling that troubles the boundaries of signifieds. While the excessive physicality of language is what "happens" in the blurb, the reality-claim of the language referring to an "actual" sexuality, an aestheticized cinematic representation of sexuality (the "referent" is yet another representation, continually deferred) is marked/mocked by the extreme melodramatic/surrealistic abstraction of the *Project*'s *mise en scene* (set and performance gestures). The audience reads the blurb's narrative fragments in a *bricolage* environment, a *mise en scene* of synthetic "realities" constructed of mass-produced pop cultural products (most "props" are modifications/ recontextualizations of "found" objects). The audience observes the process of Team members producing themselves as props too, costuming according to the Director's prompts; crucial, as well, is the (dis)arrangement of narrative continuity—narrative structure being the underpinning of reality effects, the experience, virtually, of "reality" as conscious codification...

Q: All this suggests why, from your point of view, criticism must be a performance— theoretically informed cultural criticism developed (produced, staged) as multi-media performance? Can you elaborate?

A: Go ahead... In the piece, the fragmentation and diffusion of image, text, and sound bits through trajectories of improvisation simulate the speed of the brainstorming session. It proceeds rapidly through a collage of quotes (sources listed in the bibliography) and theoretical speculations, the play with props and costumes playing through (against/with) the theoretical terrain. In addition to the initial synopsis distributed to the audience, bits of plot are presented on large cards and or text slides throughout the piece, with a double purpose: practically, of orienting viewers unfamiliar with Niagara (though the recut version of the film, playing continuously on the center video monitor, is a collage in its own right, obsessed with certain images, some textual references to the film are perhaps clarified), while simultaneously entering into the overall dialogos of the performance; the narrative bits are brief, familiar rhetorical nodes/islands rising out of the overall flux; all rhetorical positions are placed "on trial" (Kristeva) by the piece...

Q: And we can expand this position to say that all sign systems are put "in process/on trial"?

A: My thoughts exactly. The audio appendix more fully describes sound clips, and the script attempts to cover performative actions/gestures, but the computer-manipulated slide images (approximately 100) and the "live", improvised computer image manipulations defy adequate description and escape comprehensive encoding/re-representation, syntactic/semantic capture by another sign system (it would take many more pages to "fully" describe the images, and you'd have to continue writing, since each performance—and each potential (re)performance—alters/will alter the already said/written/seen; imagine a series of progressively more abstract Photoshop permutations of a serial image of Marilyn Monroe, veering off or back again, momentarily, to a referential stabilization, and you have a sense of one imagistic line of flight). Since *The Monroe Project* is a multimedia event, much escapes the printed text—or, put positively, much happens in the moments of performance, all of which is part of the larger, on-going "ur" text; what you read in the text version of *MP* is a script, comparable to the text of a poem in oral-based cultures. The point is that (alpha-numeric) language is never all (as Lacan says of "Woman"— consider cuneiform and rebus writing); much escapes any single sign system. Contemporary cultural criticism must find a form equal to (commensurate with) its subject (as Hartman would say), working within the flexi/fluxability of a multiplex of sign systems (consider advertising, from mail-outs to demos, and product design methodologies based on models) and maneuvering to destabilize taxonomies—the sometimes-paranoid separation of pop and academic culture, for example; the deadlock of mass-production/product design theory and high academic cultural theory.

Q: You mentioned the dysfunction of narrative earlier, but what about characterization?

A/Q: Let me reverse the question.

A: There are of course traces of characterological development—as when Team members appropriate/enter into the Monroe image-identity—cross-dressing, experimenting with the gesture and walk, acting to/for (the self-reproduction of) the camera, speaking from within the product they are attempting to (re)produce—but, like the narrative bits, these remain traces, rather than centers of structuration, and do more to de-establish, prevent, dislodge or defer than to define character—a sort of motivated anti-characterization.

Q? A? Right. (You see, even in an interviewer-interviewee situation, for example, one is self-conscious of the fabrication of the identity of a speaker or speakers... who is speaking now? It's all the same. Yes. [A?Q?] Can you be sure "I" am not interviewing "you", or someone else another?) The semantic topography of *The Monroe Project* may seem substanceless, or at least rootless, but if we view identity formation as in part a process of orchestration, or (re)arrangement of cultural givens—who am "I" as spoken, and speaking, subject? what does a signature prove? —then it becomes disturbingly, or perhaps refreshingly, impersonal in this way. From one perspective, the Monroe figure can be seen as a celebration of the disjunctive potential of a fluid sense of self—the ability to put on, and put off, eluding the limits of character definition, an ontological mode/position design team members (re)enact when entering into/testing the "Monroe Effect." Though in our "own" lives, on the contrary, we often feel (culturally) compelled to find "ourselves," and failing to reify that "self", feel lost, in a state of free fall (i.e., a falling away from coded, stabilizing positionalities), anxious and depressed—as did Monroe, in "her" life.

Perhaps the best way to "play" the piece is in this spirit of experimental self-decentering, rather than as a conclusive whole driven by plot and character, per se; or, more subtly, to play through the various discourse positionalities both the anxiety and exhilaration of the simultaneous loss of and expansion of Self.

Q: Have you encountered any difficulties realizing performances such as The Monroe Project?

A: Well, yes. Something that's always on my mind... finding an audience (i.e., the "right" one). *The Monroe Project* (like other pieces in the current collection, for there always is one...) is neither academic presentation nor performance (in the conventional sense), but somewhere between the two. It is non-theatrical performance, and we, on principle, refuse to memorize text (except a bit here and there, for performance effect): printed text is a central presence of the performances. At one point in *The Monroe Project*, for example, the script becomes a mirror/tutor ... holding it before me, I contort my face, moving on a vector somewhere between scream and laughter, keeping it mobile as I flip a page; text, too, is a prop (the slides and large cards mentioned above; in *Niagara on the Rocks*, we use overlarge cue cards, gigantic postcards, and at one point I engulf myself in a paper Falls); moreover, the texts of pieces are normally so dense as to defy memorization. So a person coming to a presentation of these critical performances expecting theatre may be put off by the experimental, impromptu, in-process, "non-professional" texture of the pieces: we make mistakes, and incorporate last-minute revisions (much in the vein say, of a 60's Jack Smith happening); we can never be more than roughly rehearsed, or rehearsed to a point of unrehearsable readiness. (And we're not "actors"; in fact, I'm quite a bad actor...) Likewise, an audience prepared for a more straightforward critical presentation may be vexed by the interdisciplinary complications. At the other extreme, viewers expecting "performance art", which is often reduced, these days, to the personal/political monologue and/or comic psychosexual rant, may also be disappointed. TEZ critical performances tend to be more conceptually based, closer to Fluxus happenings than contemporary performance art, with a carnivalistic sense of humor more akin to the former, though structurally more complex than the typical Fluxus event. The pieces also tend to be longer than the typical performance art piece, so the level of concentration demanded of a viewer can be taxing. While *The*

Monroe Project, for example, moves as a continuous modulated wave (it is just under an hour), *Niagara on the Rocks* runs almost two hours, and so the piece ... billed as an ideological tour of the Falls ... is structured as a series of thirteen (somewhat re-arrangeable) modules; we also distribute snacks twice during the tour ... synthetic "circus peanuts" and anthropomorphic jellies (it all ties in, but you'd have to see it). The closest contemporary parallels to these workings that come to mind are productions of the Critical Art Ensemble, though the events represented in the current gathering are perhaps more complicated in terms of performance, structure, and *mise en scene*. The critical performances in this volume are experimental, media-oriented, text and (ready-made) object-intensive; their venue is not properly theatre or conference hall, though they are often designed to work within, and to carnivalize, the typical academic conference environment (so when performed in a theatre setting, it's important to recognize underlying traces of the conference-style presentation). It's also important to note that there's a good deal of slapstick (physical comedy) as well as verbal clowning in the performances... comic relief indeed, given the length and textual density of some of the pieces.

Q: Is that a good note to pause on?

A: We've played it.

9 Virtual TEZ: Avatars and Acting Bodies, or Where Have All the Identities Gone? Notes Toward an Aesthetics of Liminality

Postmodern bodies in general have this in common with onstage bodies of male and female performers: as much as they may be altered by dress or cosmetics (or cosmetic surgery), there remains a perceivable tension, a lack of resolution—among put on and put off identities, "real" and "theatricalized" forms. In conventional performance, this tension is smoothed over (if not erased, as in digital alteration) or elided, silenced by the forth wall (though a sense of it can feed back over the blocked and directed presentation of these apparently differentiable bodies in space, diverting attention from the essential sameness of their position). TEZ (Techno-Eschatological Zippers)[73] critical performance group works this suture, features the tension as a function of the Real it(y) registers.

In the Monroe Project, for example, the feminine is sequenced, serialized as a range of reproductive frames, from organic entitativeness (i.e., subjectivised identity) to reproduction of the same, a yet again. "Marilyn Monroe" designates a project (MM), a conceptual palette, a work in process; no claims are made for an extant at either end (pre or postproduction); TEZ does not work with identities, which it misunderstands, but with materials, openly structural-able components. So what we mean by "woman" in the performance—in this theoretical atmosphere—is what we mean by "man" is what we mean by "self"—an open question, in-decision, consideration and trial period, a possibility of error and lack of consensus. These trans-material migrations of (mis)identity can by played (on/through) in(de)finitely in the VR realm of shifting avatars

That is, the feminine as ontological principle that slashes identity as subject formation, no longer recognizable within or delineable by the conventional terms of "femininity." In TEZ, the feminine rarely (tempo-rarily) has a chance to be (it)self. Outlines

---

73. "TEZ" is also the initials of the surnames of its founding members—T om, E llen (La Forge), Z oe (Randall)—the auto-acronym as marks of the personal, the masculine graphemic designator "feminized" by full phonemic utterance...

are blurred and anthropomorphic focus is dislocated. We may start with a shoe, the color of the lips, a footstep or phoneme—and never return (look back). What we play through is the process of rendering "one(it)self" as identity and (pre)packaged cultural commodification; one "puts on a face," makes and remakes-up. In this process of performative de/reconstruction, all presences may approach prototypes (of definition, subjectification), but can never completely "picture" themselves, or disappear into any particular figuration; fictive identity is never whole, which is an illusion-tease of the screen avatar.

Enter "Bindigirl"(www.thing.net/~bindigrl/index_refresh.html), a subcontinental, Anglo-feminized avatar complete with a VR harem of soft-porn stills collaged with Tantric sex-themed texts and an enticing, close-up slide show of part (body) objects linked to suggestively generalized phrases (for example, "doing everything" clicks to part of a naked forearm and thigh); the site also includes a "Bio" of "Bindigirl," a chat, a subscribe-to-view live cam, and purchasable souvenirs (forehead dots, socks, and goddess-print panties). Bindigirl is a commercial-commodity driven site framed as fantasy subjectification; one can buy (into) the fantasy and own RL objects as mnemonic traces of the VR experience.

Or, one can simply contract for an email order "bride," though this still does not guarantee stability through the chain of representations. Consider the Bridal Channel (bridalchannel.com). Other than the "Tuxedo" search, the Bridal Channel is all "bride"; "Tuxedo" and "Bridal Gown" both hyperlink to the same "female" virtual model. From a TEZ point of view, I am invited, as an androgynous searcher (or a non or bi-gendered one) to enter the "Virtual Dressing Room" to try various gowns on my prefabricated avatar ("Elizabeth, our generic model") whose relatively unmarked features (short-cropped hair, subdued cosmetics, and unpronounced biological designators) destabilize the conventional (i.e., Saussurian) sign system upon which the success of the wedding depends. I (re)name my "online reflection" "Pete," which, the site tells me, I can make "look as much like [me] as [I] want it to," within a dualistic, predetermined set of culturally sanctioned body specs: breasts may be large or medium—who would want to see herself as "small"?—waist well-defined or undefined—not to be misread as "indefinable"—eyes round or almond, lips full or thin, and nose narrow or wide. Hence

I'm cast in a binary, or at least reductive, milieu of racial as well as gender stereotypes; the VR here a repro of RL imaginary dualisms.

Though these are "found" sites (not TEZ productions), from a TEZ'd (i.e., critically conscious, rather than googled) perspective, the virtual remix of exotic, sexual, gender and cultural codes of the two sites is a way of playing out, experimenting with, or encountering, not unlike TEZ project(ion)s, the il(de)lusion of "male" and "female"/"masculine" and "feminine" designators, once we pass through (*pas partout*) the stagings of conventional theater (or, as in the instances above, the Photoshopped voyeurism of screenal dissimulation).

In other words...

TEZ VR, like TEZ RL, is concerned with the dis- and re-embodying of the "feminine," with what it means to perform the feminine in a VR economy driven by simulation, proliferation of desire in the imaginary, screenal subversions, the deterritorialization of difference and bleeding or co-contamination of signs via the implosion, or mutual interference, of signifiers—

M M, hmmm?):

> *There's a dialogic layering of images and rhetorical positions always on the verge of slipping into a reality effect: a digital head wears a sailor's cap (metonymic for Niagara); behind a scrim/veil of synthetic black (mourning?) stretch material, Hollywood images begin to glow and flow. Voices speak from behind a life-size cardboard serial of MM heads; team members often relate to the audience through real time synthesis—mediation of a "live" monitor—while their physical bodies are averted.*
>
> *...a melodramatic synopsis of Niagara from the back of a video box, representation of a representation of a representation: "femme fatale ... seductively torments ... mysterious lover ... powerful portrait of human sexuality and passion." ... a prosody of exaggeration: alliteration and over-coded contraries held in syntactic balance... marked/mocked by the melodramatic/surrealistic abstraction of the Project's mise en scene.... an environment...of synthetic "realities" constructed of mass-produced pop cultural products (most "props" are modifications/ recontextualizations of "found" objects) ... Team members (re)producing themselves as props, costuming according to the Director's prompts....*
>
> *bits of plot presented on large cards and or text slides—brief, familiar*

> *rhetorical nodes/islands rising out of the overall flux... computer-manipulated slide images (approximately 100) and "live", improvised computer image manipulations defy adequate description, escaping... syntactic/semantic capture... (imagine a series of progressively more abstract Photoshop permutations of a serial image of Marilyn Monroe, veering off or back again, momentarily, to a referential stabilization, and you have a sense of one imagistic line of flight)...*

—with the proliferation of images: in the minds of the audience, for example, as simultaneous multiple reception, extending the already abstracted, co-opted and pirated multiplicity of the performance. The network of the performance (through collaged texts and images, moving/performing bodies, and viewer reception) thrives in a state of interpretive elusiveness.

Though soon it may be only a difference of medium—flesh plastics or digital imaging— we are yet faced with the dilemma of apparently gendered performing bodies, as different as they are similar—performing each other through a system of differences, in a way that tilts (or torques) that system away from closure and definition (letting chips fall where they may). To ask a question about performing bodies, online and offline, is to ask a question about performance of the feminine, given the history of woman's globally "privileged" relation to representation. The male body in performance, as direct object of the gaze of the audience/" other", is brought into the position of the spectacle-ized (on or offstage) body of "woman" (though this is still not the same as the experience of the internally invaded body as direct object of the scientific gaze—i.e., as hegemonic ideology, I insert the speculum into...). Yet if we can step out of the script—step back from the agenda of conventional representation—and look at what else the representum is saying—a momentary shift of attention—we may stumble, or fall—on stage or off—out of the self into the position of the "other", leading to a bodily—i.e., performed—apprehension of that position (*as* other). It is such performed critical consciousness (which may sometimes just happen to us in a moment of insight) that effects breaks in the scripted flow—breaks that may also be scripted in, engineered—pauses that are (a)rhythmic beats.

In conventional theater, to see (oneself) or to speak (one's name) is to encounter the serialization, re-cording, (re)production, echo of one's "own" voice—the voice of a culture that owns—and to miss(understand) oneself as (an)other (one) as has never been, for the time being. TEZ's fractured performances, which deconstruct the axiom of a product as the goal of theatrical production (being about disabled—or disabling—processes of production), play in the gap, as a kind (decrowned "king") of remainder (reminder) of performance, never conclusively producing any thing. TEZ is a movement of Woman—a jostling of representational bits (that can be taken up, dispensed with, dispersed or done without), tentative structurations never settling into self-identical or pre-scripted form. To be TEZed, in a virtual environment, is to traverse the textual field with the (critical) guile of Mohini (avatar of Vishnu). Or, we might say, TEZ performance is at play in a pre (or anti)-Oedipal space that evades stable composition of a completed work with (re)cognizable contours—which is the precondition, for example, of any Imago, of attaining a "Gender," of pre- or post-pixilated identity.

PostFace

In an 1879 essay, "The Sentiment of Rationality," William James said that our language constructs (i.e., our "theoretic conceptions") are the way we think our world, standing between us and the "empirical sandheap" of reality in all its multiplicity (*The Will To Believe...*, 68, 70). By the third quarter of the 20th century, we came to realize that *because* of language our world was becoming a particle heap: as quantum physics has demonstrated (and as Lyotard points out in the *Postmodern Condition*), the closer we look at a phenomenon, the more contradictory our statements about it become. Similarly, in literary analysis, the closer we follow the language, the longer we contemplate a text, the less clear, less certain, less unidirectional/teleological it becomes; this can occur at an elemental level, at a discourse level, and at the "extratextual" level—in the social field generated around a text through reader responses (what, for example, is another reader hearing? highlighting? What text is she/he creating and how does it differ from mine?). The performative literary critic has an (anti)goal similar to both the Talmudic scholar and the student (and/or creator) of Zen kōans: to practice language to the point of exhaustion; to empty a word of fixed significance. In Zen thought, the ordinary ego is seen as a worm, not letting go its hold on one thetic position till it can grasp another; it is the interval between that is the true experience of "ego" (i.e., as positioned in non-ego). Through this interval (gap, *aporia*), the noise of poststructuralist theory rushes (Bakhtin, Clifford, de Lauretis, Derrida, Foucault, Kristeva, Lacan, Žižek, Deleuze, McGann, et al. . . . Derrida's language performances, such as *Glas*, are generated in these high-energy zones).

The floodgates are open. Territories once separate now overlap and interanimate each other. In classic postmodern literary and cultural theory we have seen an interest in performance and oral tradition (storytelling, for example, and multimedia ritual performance), a fascination with ethnography and anthropology and the function of language in those contexts (ethnography seen as a specular science, for example, built not on "objective" information but discourses—including the others' self-discourses, and the way our discourses interpret theirs); we have seen the concern in contemporary textual criticism for social Texts, and we have seen the range of semiotics expanded (as in Eco's work, and de Lauretis', who sees gender engendered in a social/historical/cultural/linguistic field—i.e., in verbal and extra verbal practices). Marxism and New Historicism have taught us lessons about the social function of language and told us stories about "texts" (films, concerts, and other cultural performances as well as written documents) maneuvering incognito (with) in a larger social/political/economic arena. The act of criticism is not a self-satisfied literary event, but takes place—happens—on several fronts.

In the aughts and early years of the 21st century, as coalitions have formed between various theories, methods, and media, it has become more and more urgent to comprehend "theory" as enactment, as praxis—a "reading" and "writing" practice engaging (and engaged in) a wide cultural field—and to re-vision "criticism" as the practice of suspending (for the nonce) critical judgment,[74]to the extent that "the critic as intermediary," as Saper frames it, becomes "merely superfluous" (*Networked Art*, 90). In the interpretative acts staged in previous chapters, my point has been to emphasize that the academic discourse is just one character, or strand (and not necessarily the dominate one) in the web of voices and sign systems that encompass text and reader (i.e., Text); a "book" is not so much a printed text snugged between covers, but a cultural text within ideological bindings, which may be expanded/exploded/imploded when embodied in the *mis en scene* of performance.

As Freud discovered over a century ago, reader reenactment is a potentially profound and much more accommodating mode of interpretation than an "objective," discursive one, which refuses to admit its own fictionalization, its dissimulation. The doxa of objective interpretation is itself a performance, a mode of self-presentation that, if it knew itself, would recognize its place. Our interpretations (of texts, of "others") confirm our ways of seeing, and, though there are many ways of seeing, ideological superstructures normally limit us to only a few. Hence, the desire of this book has been to open the text to personal encounter, to reader participation and reenactment, and to multiple interpretations that take into consideration the larger cultural landscape within which any particular text (as node) takes shape; to consider Texts not as finished products, but as always appearing in only one of their several versions; to restage

---

74. This is especially crucial in a regressive and/or "anti-theory" academic environment.

the critical act in the Textual wild; to make of the critical act a performance, an extended play, a play to the point of exhaustion (when the tired children go home, unless they have been called there prematurely, unless they are—already—homeless); to refigure the critic as a wandering (aimless?) and inspired investigator, a free agent and free lover of and in the (semiotic) open.

Thus, this book, influenced by a Zen sense of nondualism and believing in the pan-literary application of its methodos, not only straddles genres, as well as media, but also refuses to provide a unified, self-coherent theory of alternative critical writing. Rather, it is an eclectic blend of the discourses (poststructuralist literary and cultural theory, recent performance and ethnographic theory, and Zen philosophy) that internally persuade it. Nor are these scripts intended as demonstrations or examples of particular forms that can be grafted onto other works, but as bricolage practices prompting other readers to do their own work, to come forward with their own forms and techniques, inspired by the work at hand (each case is an individual case, as A. E. Houseman realized, during the first quarter of the 20th century, of textual editing). Since, as discussed in the introduction to this volume, each text presents its own discourse and subdiscourse environment, to re-present this environment as fully as possible, to reenact it, to experience it, we cannot apply a generic critical method and language but must keep our style open and versatile, in intimate contact with the texts it consumes, ready to play unusual games and risk the outrageous. Hartman puts the matter directly: the notion of a polite critic dealing with extravagant literature in tempered language is ludicrous. I press the point further: not only does "extravagant" literature require an extravagant response, but all literature, in as much as any work is always more than it—or anyone else—knows. My desire, then, in the previous chapters, has been neither to historicize or socialize texts, nor to avoid social-historical-economic contexts where such references are productive, but to establish close contact with a handful of texts through *mise en scene* re-production, and to offer these readings as records of alternative interpretative activities.

In the beginning is the Text. The Text is an Other. How do we shape it as we interpret it? To what extent is our interpretation specular? Can we be secure in our interpretation? What do we understand when we go about understanding? To what extent do we create what we analyze? Through the preceding (re)inscriptive acts, I have been promoting interpretative insecurity: we can feel something scratching at the margins; there is a residual sound in the words, a slip of signifier away from signified (or vice versa), always an echo of *differance*. As I write, the it ("you," in Lacan's formulation—the written about) becomes an inverted *I*; I will never know you while I lay claim to you, but merely re(dis)cover my "self" (the world view that foregrounds the self, its "negative space," to borrow a term from conventional picture theory). I must respond to that which *is* (a person, events, objects, language) with Zen beginner's (no)mind—expecting nothing, coming not purposefully to it (you), but *being in* the moment of encounter. I must be ready within the field of possibilities that is given, not to control it, but to act with(in) it, snap it up intuitively. (I can't explain it and still be with(in) it, unless I make of my "explanation" an answering performance.) Performance becomes, for this point of view, in Jon McKenzie's words, a "mode of experimental resistance" (235) that can take place, can happen, in the "interstices of institutions" (i.e., as TEZ performances opportunistically detour the academic conference setting), temporarily "subverting their normative functions" (8); such performances, liminal in orientation, moving between the literal and figurative, real and fictional, serious and jocular (7), can channel "mutational forces across the entire performance stratum, releasing desires and intensities from contexts that constrain them" (235).

Heteroglossic, open, or collage t_f(T)s such as those in the previous chapters make an important point clear:[75] Since all language is a matter of rhetorical positionality, no one position is absolute; there is no metalanguage. For every statement made *about* a text, a counter statement (in whatever "language") is repressed (ghosted). Realizing this, and knowing also that there is no "outside" of ideology, no ultimate or detached knowledge (we are always enacting a point of view, always *in play*), the most productive, least dissimulating stance is, as the Zen masters realize in the form of the kōan, to rest in no single position, to place the process of positionality itself in "quotes." In a famous kōan, a monk

75. And a text can be multivoiced without being a collage. As Minh-Ha has shown (*Woman, Native, Other*) other voices always already play through the voice of a writer, without having to import documentary material; there simply is no monologic or single—voiced authorship—if we look closely enough, we can always see the seams, the blend and bend of discourses that make up the authorial "voice."

enters the Zen master's chamber at a moment when the master is just about to sit or to stand; the monk makes an assumption about which it is. The master plays on this by overturning the monk's assumption; the monk, who now thinks he is onto the master's "line" of thought, is then surprised again as the master veers the situation to a third possibility (a *yet* again...). The point to be taken here is that there is no conclusive stance, no *line* of thought, but only an always on-the-alert, improvisational and indeterminate jostling among positions; to remain in play is to remain liminal, to keep the mind supple and in a state of preparedness. The exercise, the serious play of performative commentary/reading can train the mind to achieve such a state of readiness.

Experimental British filmmaker Peter Greenaway's *The Falls* (color, 185, mins., 1980), a mocumentary combining found footage and reenactments along with fictional narration, traces the bizarre after-effects of a "VUE"—"Violent Unknown Event" ("view," in French—the only language in which the acronym makes "sense," as a semanteme, though ironically the French were unaffected, according to the narrator)—on a number of fictitious persons, all of whom speak an assortment of glossolalic VUE languages: a man falls in love with a turkey, another flies planes in circles, another tries to kill himself by crashing airplanes; a women lives naked, another becomes a walking waterfall, and another collects seabird skulls; a jazz singer riffs, via an untranslatable VUE language, on a jazz standard whose (understandable and translatable) title and lyrics encode an oxymoronic, subject deformation ("The Lady Is a Tramp"), etc.—all effects that detour logical relationships, disturb (technological and other) systems, create (human-other) hybrids, assemblages... According to the narrator, there were nineteen million victims; for convenience, a representative sampling of 92, only those whose surnames began with "Fall" (arranged alphabetically from "Falla... through "Fallw...") where chosen as subjects (though the list reads like a concrete poem, generated via sound associations, the film's title the one stable semantic element, without clear referent except its derivation from the names themselves, or vice versa). The performative critical t_f(T) registers and (re)produces just such an impact on its writers/readers—is itself the VUE (just fooling?): who can tell how many its victims will be, or into what (dis)arrangement the particles will fall?

***

The form is simply a shell. An hour glass: sand leaking through a small hole into its ghosted double. Empty form waiting to become itself again, only differently, from an altered perspective, until this again must be overturned. The form, like time, is never fully present, but always turning over upon itself, in the process of emptying and filling itself. This is the hour glass belonging to a certain rōshi, who speaks sometimes in a language we don't understand, or in many different languages; often, this rōshi says nothing, or speaks like the sea, or a lover in the next room, who makes us believe that to destroy us would be as generous an act as to preserve us. Did you ever know a rōshi like that?

Index

See p. 51.

Select Bibliography

This bibliography supplements individual chapter bibliographies, though some repetition may occur.

Literary, Cultural, and Textual Criticism/Theory

Adorno, Theodore. "Cultural Criticism and Society," "The Sociology of Knowledge and Its Consciousness," "Perennial Fusion—Jazz," "Valery Proust Museum," "A Portrait of Walter Benjamin," "Notes on Kafka". Prisims. London: Spearman, 1967.

Agamben, Giorgio. *The Coming Community*. Minneapolis, MN: University of Minnesota Press, 1993.

—. *The Man Without Content*. Trans. Georgia Albert. Stanford, CA: Stanford University Press, 1999.

Allen, Graham. *Intertextuality*. New York, NY: Routledge, 2000.

Allison, David B., ed. *The New Nietzsche: Contemporary Styles of Interpretation* [especially essays by Derrida and Deleuze]. Cambridge: MIT Press, 1986.

Althusser, Louis, *et al*. *Writing on Psychoanalysis: Freud and Lacan*. New York, NY: Columbia University Press, 1996.

Aronowitz, Stanley, *et al*, eds. *Technoscience and Cyberculture*. New York: Routledge, 1996.

Austin, J. L. *How to Do Things with Words*. Second ed. Cambridge: Harvard University. Press., 1975.

Bakhtin, Mikhail. *Rabelais and His World*. Trans. Helene Iswolsky. Bloomington: Indiana University Press, 1984.

—. *The Dialogic Imagination*. Trans. Caryl Emerson and Michael Holquist. Austin: University of Texas Press, 1981.

—. "The Problem of Speech Genres," *Speech Genres*. 1st. Ed. Austin: University of Texas Press, 1986.

Balkin, J. M. *Cultural Software: A Theory of Ideology*. New Haven, CT: Yale University Press, 1998.

Barthes, Roland. "from *Roland Barthes by Roland Barthes*," "from *The Pleasure of the Text*'" "Writers, Intellectuals, Teachers," "Lesson in Writing," "Flaubert and the Sentence", "from *Writing Degree Zero*." *A Barthes Reader*. Ed. Susan Sontag. New York: Hill & Wang, 1981.

—. *Roland Barthes by Roland Barthes*. Trans. Richard Howard. New York: Hill & Wang, 1977.

—. *S/Z: An Essay.* Trans. Richard Miller. New York: Hill and Wang, 1974.

Barrett, Michèle. *Imagination in Theory: Culture, Writing, Words, and Things.* New York, NY: New York University Press, 1999.

Baudrillard, Jean. *Selected Writings.* Stanford: Stanford University Press, 1988.

—. *The Transparency of Evil: Essays on Extreme Phenomena.* Trans. James Benedict. New York: Verso, 1993.

Bediou, Alain. *Deleuze: The Clamor of Being.* Trans. Louise Burchill. Minneapolis, MN: Minnesota University Press, 1999.

Bloom, Harold. *The Anxiety of Influence.* New York: Oxford University Press, 1973.

Benjamin, Walter. *Illuminations.* Trans. Harry Zohn. Ed. and Intro. Hannah Arendt. New York: Schocken Books, 1969.

Bewes, Timothy. *Reification, or The Anxiety of Late Capitalism.* London, England: Verso, 2002.

Binder, Guyora and Robert Weisberg. *Literary Criticisms of Law.* Princeton, NJ: Princeton University Press, 2000.

Bissell, Elizabeth Beaumont, ed. *The Question of Literature: The Place of the Literary in Contemporary Theory.* Manchester, England: Manchester University Press, 2002.

Bousquet, Mark and Katherine V. Wills, Eds. *TechnoCapitalism* 3 (2003). http://www.electronicbookreview.com/thread/technocapitalism/libidinal. 10/25/2011).

Burke, Peter. *Eyewitnessing: The Uses of Images as Historical Evidence.* Ithaca, NY: Cornell University Press, 2001.

Butler, Judith, Ernesto Laclau and Slavoj Žižek. *Contingency, Hegemony, Universality: Contemporary Dialogues on the Left.* London, England: Verso, 2000.

Cage, John. *The Cambridge companion to John Cage.* Ed. David Nicholls. Cambridge: Cambridge University Press, 2002.

—. *Writings through John Cage's music, poetry, and art.* Ed. David W. Bernstein and Christopher Hatch. Chicago: The University of Chicago Press, 2001.

—. X: Writings '79-'82. Middletown, Ct: Wesleyan University Press, 1983.

Capra, Fritjof. *The Tao of Physics: An Exploration of the Parallels Between Modern Physics and Eastern Mysticism.* Second ed. New York: Bantam, 1984.

Chakrabarty, Dipesh; Bhabha, Homi K. *Habitations of Modernity: Essays in the Wake of Subaltern Studies*. Chicago, IL: University of Chicago Press, 2002.

Chang, Briankle G. *Deconstructing Communication: Representation, Subject, and Economies of Exchange*. Minneapolis: University of Minnesota Press, 1996.

Cixous, Helene, and Catherine Clement. *The Newly Born Woman*. Trans. Betsy Wing. Intro. Sandra M. Gilbert. Theory and History of Literature 24. Minneapolis: University of Minnesota Press. 1975.

Clark, Andy. *Natural Born Cyborgs: Minds, Technologies, and the Future of Human Intelligence*. New York: Oxford University Press, 2003.

—. *Supersizing the Mind*. New York: Oxford University Press, 2008.

Clark, Michael P., ed. *Revenge of the Aesthetic: The Place of Literature in Theory Today*. Berkeley, CA: University of California Press, 2000.

Cohen, Tom. *Ideology and Inscription: 'Cultural Studies' after Benjamin, de Man, and Bakhtin.* Cambridge, England: New York, NY: Cambridge University Press, 1998.

Conley, Tom. *The Graphic Unconscious in Early Modern French Writing*. New York: Cambridge University Press, 1992.

Critical Art Ensemble. *The Electronic Disturbance*. New York: Autonomedia, 1994.

Culler, Jonathan. *The Pursuit of Signs: Semiotics, Literature, Deconstruction*. Ithaca, NY: Cornell University Press, 2001.

Darroch-Lozowski, Vivian. *The Uncoded World: A Poetic Semiosis of the Wandered. Semiotics and the Human Sciences* 18. New York, NY: Peter Lang, 1999.

Davis, Diane. *Breaking Up (at) Totality: A Rhetoric of Laughter.* Carbondale, IL: Southern Illinois University Press, 2000.

—. *Inessential Solidarity: Rhetoric and Foreigner Relations.* Pittsburgh, PA: University of Pittsburgh Press, 2010.

Debord, Guy. *Society of the Spectacle and Other Films*. London: Rebel Press, 1992.

de Certeau, Michel. *Heterologies.* Minneapolis: University of Minnesota Press, 1986.

—. *The Practice of Everyday Life.* Berkeley: University of California Press, 1984.

DeLanda, Manuel. *Deleuze, History and Science*. New York: Atropos Press, 2010.

de Lauretis, Teresa. *Technologies of Gender.* Bloomington: Indiana University. Press., 1987.

Deleuze, Gilles, and Felix Guattari. *A Thousand Plateaus: Capitalism and Schizophrenia.* Minneapolis, MN: University of Minnesota Press, 1987.

—. *Anti-Oedipus: Capitalism and Schizophrenia.* Minneapolis: University of Minnesota Press, 1983.

—. *On the Line.* New York: Semiotext(e), 1983.

DeKoven, Marianne. *Utopia Limited: The Sixties and the Emergence of the Postmodern.* Durham, NC: Duke University Press, 2004.

de Man, Paul. Introduction, chs. 1, 4, 7-11, Appendix B. *Blindness and Insight: Essays in the Rhetoric of Contemporary Criticism.* Second ed. *Theory and History of Literature* 7. Minneapolis: University of Minnesota Press, 1983.

Derrida, Jacques. *Dissemination.* Trans. Barbara Johnson. Chicago: University of Chicago Press, 1981.

—. *Glas.* Lincoln: University of Nebraska Press, 1986.

—. *Of Grammatology.* Trans. Gayatri Spivak. 1st American ed. Baltimore: Johns Hopkins Press, 1976.

—. *Positions.* Chicago: University of Chicago Press, 1981.

—. *Spurs.* Chicago: University of Chicago Press, 1987.

—. *Writing and Difference.* Chicago: The University of Chicago Press, 1978.

Eagleton, Terry. *After Theory.* New York, NY: Basic, 2003.

Eliot, Valerie, ed. *The* Wasteland: *A Facsimile and Transcript of the Original Drafts including the Annotations of Ezra Pound.* San Diego: Harcort Brace, 1994.

Felman, Shoshana. Selections by Sibony, Felman, Spivak, Brooks, Sollers, Jameson, Johnson. *Literature and Psychoanalysis: The Question of Reading: Otherwise.* Baltimore: The Johns Hopkins Press, 1980.

Felski, Rita. *Literature after Feminism.* Chicago, IL: University of Chicago Press, 2003.

Feyerabend, Paul. *Against Method.* 3rd. ed. New York: Verso, 1993.

Fineman, Martha Albertson, and Nancy Sweet Thomadsen. *At the Boundaries of Law: Feminism and Legal Theory.* New York: Routledge, 1991.

Fish, Stanley. *Doing What Comes Naturally: Change, Rhetoric, and the Practice of Theory and Legal Studies.* Post-Contemporary Interventions. Durham, N.C.: Duke University Press, 1989.

—. *Is There a Text in This Class?* Cambridge: Harvard University Press, 1980.

Flax, Jane. *Thinking Fragments* [parts one & four]. Berkeley: University of California Press, 1990.

Foster, Hal. *The Anti-Aesthetic: Essays on Postmodern Culture* [essays by Jameson and Owens]. Port Townsend, Washington: Bay Press, 1983.

Foucault, Michel. *The Foucault Reader.* New York: Pantheon Books, 1984.

—. *The Order of Things: An Archaeology of the Human Sciences.* World of Man: A Library of Theory and Research in the Human Sciences. Gen. Ed. R. D. Laing. New York: Random House, 1970.

Freud, Sigmund. "A Note Upon 'The Mystic Writing-Pad'," "Fragment of an Analysis of a Case of Hysteria." *Collected Papers.* New York: Collier Books, 1963.

Gaskell, Philip. *From Writer to Reader: Studies in Editorial Method.* England: St. Paul's Bibliographies, 1984 [paperback edition].

—. "Night and Day: Development of a Play Text." McGann, *Textual Criticism*, 162-79.

Gefin, Laszlo. *Ideogram: History of a Poetic Method.* Austin: University of Texas Press, 1982.

Genette, Gérard; Newman, Channa; Doubinsky, Claude; Prince, Gerald. *Palimpsests: Literature in the Second Degree.* Stages. 8. Lincoln, NE: University of Nebraska Press, 1997.

Gordon, Deborah. "Writing Culture, Writing Feminism." *Inscriptions* 3/4 (1988): 7-44.

Greetham, D. C. *Theories of the Text.* Oxford, England: Oxford University Press, 1999.

Gribbin, John. *In Search of Schrodinger's Cat: Quantum Physics and Reality.* New York: Bantam, 1984.

—, and Martin Rees. *Cosmic Coincidences: Dark Matter, Mankind, and Anthropic Cosmology.* New York: Bantam, 1989.

Gruber, David. "Bodies Without Skin: Feeling a Way Out of a Ubiquitous Future." 9/20/2011. *CTheory.Net.* http://www.ctheory.net/articles.aspx?id=689. 10/25/2011.

Hayles, Katherine N. *The Cosmic Web: Scientific Field Models and Literary Strategies in the Twentieth Century.* Ithaca: Cornell University Press, 1984.

Hall, Donald E. *Queer Theories.* New York, NY: Palgrave, 2003.

Hansen, Mark; Hayles, N. Katherine. *Embodying Technesis: Technology beyond Writing.* Ann Arbor, MI: University of Michigan Press, 2000.

Harari, Josue, ed. *Textual Strategies.* selections by Harari, Barthes, Derrida, De Man, Foucault, Said, Serres, Deleuze, Riddel. Ithaca: Cornell University Press, 1979.

Hartman, Geoffrey. *Criticism in the Wilderness: The Study of Literature Today*. New Haven: Yale University Press, 1980.

—, and Sanford Budick, eds. "Introduction," "The Struggle for the Text," (Hartman), "Infinities of Torah in Kabbalah" (Moshe Idel), "Sacred Language and Open Text" (Betty Roitman), "The Plain Sense of Things" (Frank Kermode), "The Key" (Edmond Jabes), "Shibboleth" (Jacques Derrida). *Midrash and Literature*. New Haven: Yale University Press, 1986.

Hassan, Ihab. *The Dismemberment of Orpheus: Toward a Postmodern Literature*. New York: Oxford University Press, 1971.

—. *Paracriticisms*. Urbana: University of Illinois Press, 1975.

—. *The Postmodern Turn: Essays in Postmodern Theory and Culture*. Columbus: Ohio State University Press, 1987.

Kim, Hee-Jin. "The Reason of Words and Letters: Dogen and K an Language." LaFleur, 54-82.

Hendrix, Harold, et al, eds. *The Search for a New Alphabet: Literary Studies in a Changing World*. Amsterdam: Benjamins, 1996.

Hogan, Patrick Colm. *On Interpretation: Meaning and Inference in Law, Psychoanalysis, and Literature*. Athens, GA: University of Georgia Press, 1996.

Holquist, Michael. *Dialogism*. London, England: Routledge, 2002.

Houseman, A. E. "The Application of Thought to Textual Criticism" [first published in *Proceedings of the Classical Association* 28 (August 1921)] in *Selected Prose*, ed. J Carter. Cambridge: Cambridge University Press, 1961. 131-2.

Howe, Susan. *The Birth-Mark: Unsettling the Wilderness in American Literary History*. Hanover: University Press of New England, 1993.

—. *My Emily Dickinson*. Berkeley: North Atlantic Books, 1985.

Hoy, David Couzens. *Critical Resistance: From Poststructuralism to Post-Critique*. Cambridge, MA: MIT Press, 2004

Hutchinson, Allan C., ed. *Critical Legal Studies*. Totowa, NJ: Rowman and Littlefield Publishers, Inc., 1989.

Huyssen, Andreas. "High/Low in an Expanded Field." *Modernism/Modernity* 9.3 (2002 Sept), pp. 363-74.

—. *Twilight Memories: Marking Time in a Culture of Amnesia*. New York: Routledge, 1995.

Irigaray, Luce, and Stephen Pluhácek. *Between East and West: From Singularity to Community*. New York, NY: Columbia University Press, 2002.

Irigaray, Luce. *Speculum of the Other Woman*. Ithaca: Cornell University Press, 1985.

Iser, Wolfgang. *The Range of Interpretation*. New York, NY: Columbia University Press, 2000.

Jabes, Edmond. *The Book of Questions*. Trans. Rosmarie Waldrop. Connecticut: Wesleyan University Press, 1972.

Jackson, Stevi, and Jackie Jones, eds. *Contemporary Feminist Theories*. New York, NY: New York University Press, 1998.

James, William. *The Will to Believe and Other Essays in Popular Philosophy and Human Immortality*. New York: Dover, 1956

Jakobson, Roman. "Two Aspects of Language and Two Types of Aphasic Disturbances," "Linguistics and Poetics," "Shakespeare's Verbal Art in 'Th' Expense of Spirit'." *Language in Literature*. Cambridge: Belknap Press, 1987.

Joseph, Gerhard, and Jay Fellows. "Mixed Messages in Mr. Pecksniff's Grammar School: A Defense of that Celebrated though Much-Maligned Parasite's Architectural Principles, as Necessitated by a Universal Misunderstanding of Them, of Him, and of Chapter 35 of Martin Chuzzlewit, by Charles Dickins, the Dronken Architect of the House of Chuzzlewit or The Rift in Pater's Lute." *Perspectives on Perception: Philosophy, Art, and Literature*. *Reading Plus* 3. Gen. Ed. Mary Ann Caws. New York: Peter Lang, 1989.

Kasulis, T. P. *Zen Action Zen Person*. Honolulu: The University of Press of Hawaii, 1981.

Knoeller, Christian; Freedman, Sarah Warshauer. *Voicing Ourselves: Whose Words We Use When We Talk about Books*. Albany, NY: State University of New York Press, 1998.

Kostelanetz, Richard, comp. *A Critical (Ninth) Assembling (Precisely: 6789)*. New York: Assembling Press, 1979.

Kristeva, Julia. *Desire in Language: A Semiotic Approach to Literature and Art*. New York: Columbia University Press, 1980.

—. *Revolution in Poetic Language*. New York: Columbia Press, 1984.

—. *The Kristeva Reader*. Ed. Toril Moi. New York: Columbia University Press, 1986.

Lacan, Jacques. "The Agency of the Letter in the Unconscious or Reason since Freud," "The Signification of the Phallus," "The Function and Field of Speech and Language in Psychoanalysis," "The Mirror Stage as Formative of the Function of the I as Revealed in Psychoanalytic Experience." *Ecrits*. Trans. Alan Sheridan. New York: W.W. Norton, 1977.

—. "Intervention on Transference," The Phallic Phase and the Subjective Import of the Castration Complex," "Feminine Sexuality in Psychoanalytic Doctrine," "God and the *Jouissance* of The Woman," "A Love Letter," "Seminar of 21 January 1975," ["Introduction—II," by Jacqueline Rose]. *Feminine Sexuality*. Ed. Juliet Mitchell and Jacqueline Rose. New York: W. W. Norton, 1982.

LaFleur, William, ed. *Dogen Studies*. Honolulu: University of Hawaii Press, 1985.

Landow, George P. *Hypertext 2.0: The Convergence of Contemporary Critical Theory and Technology*. Baltimore, MD: Johns Hopkins University Press, 1997.

Latour, Bruno. *Aramis, or the Love of Technology*. Cambridge: Harvard University Press ,1996.

—. *We Have Never Been Modern*. Cambridge: Harvard University Press, 1993.

Latour, Bruno and Peter Weibel, eds. *Iconoclash*. Cambridge: ZKM, Centre for Art and Media, 2002.

Lavazzi, Tom. "Armand Schwerner's The Tablets." *Talisman* 19 (1998-'99): 90-94.

—. "Editing Schwerner: Versions of Armand Schwerner's 'design tablet'." *Text 8* (1995): 267-301.

—. "Fantasy.Com: Game One, ZIP—Through Žižek to Internet Pornography." *Rhizomes: Cultural Studies in Emerging Knowledge* 5 (2003). www.rhizomes.net. 10/24/2011.

—. "Punching the Line: Yippie, Fluxus, and the 1968 DNC." *Rhizomes: Cultural Studies in Emerging Knowledge* 9 (2004). http://www.rhizomes.net/issue9/index.html. 10/24/2011.

—. "Re(X)locating the Critical Self: The Global Subject in an Electronic Age." *Symploke: Journal of Comparative Literature and Theory* (spring 2002).

—. "Re programming the Rhythm Machine: Jayne Cortez's Earlier Poetry and W. E. B. DuBois' *Crisis* Writings." *Dialogism and Lyric Self Fashioning: The Voices of a Genre*. Pennsylvania: Susquehanna University Press, 2008.

Law, John, and John Hassard, eds. *Actor Network Theory and After*. Malden, MA: Blackwell, 1999.

—, and Kevin Hetherington. "Materialities, Spatialities, Globalities." Online paper. Department of Sociology and Centre for Science Studies, Lancaster University, UK. 12/7/2003. http://www.lancs.ac.uk/fass/sociology/papers/law-hetherington-materialities-spatialities-globalities.pdf. 10/25/2011.

Lee, Benjamin. *Talking Heads: Language, Metalanguage, and the Semiotics of Subjectivity*. Durham, NC: Duke University Press, 1997.

Lentricchia, Frank and Thomas Mc Laughlin, eds. *Critical Terms for Literary Study*. Chicago: University of Chicago Press, 1990.

Lionnet, Francoise. "The Politics and Aesthetics of Metissage." *Autobiographical Voices: Race, Gender, Self-Portraiture*. Ithaca: Cornell university Press, 1989.

Liu, Jian-Quin. "An evolvable proteomic computing method for robust artificial chemistry systems," *Artificial life and robotics* 6.3 (2002).

Leitch, Vincent B. *Theory Matters*. New York, NY: Routledge, 2003.

Lotman, Yuri M., Ann Shukman and Umberto Eco. *Universe of the Mind: A Semiotic Theory of Culture*. Bloomington, IN: Indiana University Press, 2000.

Loy, David. *Nonduality: A Study in Comparative Philosophy*. New Haven: Yale University Press, 1988.

Lyotard, Jean-Francois. *The Differend: Phrases in Dispute*. *Theory and History of Literature* 46. Minneapolis: University of Minnesota Press, 1988.

—. *The Postmodern Condition: A Report on Knowledge*. Minneapolis: University of Minnesota Press, 1984.

Magliola, Robert. *Derrida on the Mend*. West Lafayette, Indiana: Purdue University Press, 1984.

McCallum, E. L. *Object Lessons: How to Do Things with Fetishism*. Albany, NY: State University of New York Press, 1999.

McDonough, Tom, ed. *Guy Debord and the Situationist International: Texts and Documents*. Cambridge, MA: MIT Press, 2002.

McGann, Jerome. *Radiant Textuality: Literature After the World Wide Web*. New York: Palgrave, 2004.

—, ed. *Textual Criticism and Literary Interpretation*. Chicago: University of Chicago Press, 1985.

Mackenzie, Iain. *The Idea of Pure Critique*. New York, NY: Continuum, 2004.

Mann, Paul. *Masocriticism*. Albany, NY: State U of New York Press, 1999.

Marks, Elaine, and Isabelle de Courtivron. [selections by Dominique Poggi, Annie Leclerc, Claudine Herrmann, Catherine Clement,

Julia Kristeva, Xaviere Gauthier, Marguerite Duras, Chantal Chawaf, Francoise d'Eaubonne, Monique Wittig, Suzanne Horer/ Jeanne Socquet, Helene Cixous, Luce Irigaray, Simone de Beauvoir.] *New French Feminisms*. New York: Schocken Books, 1981.

Michaels, Walter Benn. *The Shape of the Signifier*. Princeton, NJ: Princeton University Press, 2004.

Miller, J. Hillis. *Speech Acts in Literature*. Stanford, CA: Stanford University Press, 2001.

Miller, Nancy. *Getting Personal: Feminist Occasions and Other Autobiographical Acts*. New York: Routledge, 1991.

—. "Arachnologies: The Woman, the Text, the Critic," "Changing the Subject: Authorship, Writing, and the Reader." *Subject to Change*. New York: Columbia University Press, 1988.

Moi, Toril. *Sexual/Textual Politics: Feminist Literary Theory*. New York: Methuen, 1985; London: Routledge, 2002.

Mulhern, Francis. *Culture/Metaculture*. New York, NY: Routledge, 2000.

Muller, John P. and William J. Richardson, eds., *The Purloined Poe: Lacan, Derrida, and Psychoanalytic Reading*. Baltimore: Johns Hopkins University Press, 1988.

Parisi, Luciana. *Abstract Sex: Philosophy, Bio-Technology and the Mutations of Desire*. London, England: Continuum, 2004.

Pell, Derek. *Assassination Rhapsody*. New York: Autonomedia, 1989.

Perloff, Marjorie. *Poetic License*. Evanston: Northwestern University Press, 1990.

Plottel, Jeanine Parisier. *Collage*. New York: New York Literary Forum 10-11, 1983.

Potter, Jonathan. *Representing Reality: Discourse, Rhetoric and Social Construction*. London: Sage, 1996.

—. *Wittgenstein's Ladder: Poetic Language and the Strangeness of the Ordinary*. Chicago, IL: University of Chicago Press, 1996.

Rabaté, Jean-Michel. *Jacques Lacan: Psychoanalysis and the Subject of Literature*. New York, NY: Palgrave, 2001.

Ray, Robert B. "The ABC of Visual Theory." *Visible Language* 22.2 (Autumn, 1988): 423-47.

Rojtman, Betty, *et al*. *Black Fire on White Fire: An Essay on Jewish Hermeneutics, from Midrash to Kabbalah*. Berkeley, CA: University of California Press, 1998.

Rabinowitz, Peter J. and James Phelan. *Before Reading: Narrative Conventions and the Politics of Interpretation.* Columbus, OH: Ohio State University Press, 1998.

Raqs Media Collective. 9/2/2005. *Sarai Reader.* www.sarai.net. 10/25/2011.

Reiman, Donald H. "'Versioning': The Presentation of Multiple Texts." *Romantic Texts and Contexts*. Columbia: University of Missouri Press, 1987: 167-80.

Ronell, Avital. *Crack Wars: Literature, Addiction, Mania*. Lincoln: University of Nebraska Press, 1992; Urbana: University of Illinois Press, 2004.

—. *The Telephone Book*. Lincoln: University of Nebraska Press, 1989.

Rutsky, R. L. "Popular/Theory." *Strategies: A Journal of Theory, Culture and Politics* 12:1 (1999 May).

Safran, Jeremy D. *Psychoanalysis and Buddhism: An Unfolding Dialogue*. Boston, MA: Wisdom, 2003.

San Juan, E., Jr. and Barbara Harlow. *Working through the Contradictions: From Cultural Theory to Critical Practice.* Lewisburg, PA: Bucknell University Press, 2004.

Saussure, Ferdinand.de. *Writings in General Linguistics*. Oxford, New York: Oxford University Press, 2006.

Sayre, Henry. *The Object of Performance: The American Avant-Garde Since 1970*. Chicago: The University of Chicago Press, 1989.

Schalkwyk, David. *Literature and the Touch of the Real*. Newark, DE: University of Delaware Press, 2004.

Sedgwick, Eve Kosofsky. *A Dialogue on Love*. Boston: Beacon Press, 1999.

—. *Fat Art, Thin Art*. Durham: Duke University Press, 1994.

—. *Touching Feeling: Affect, Pedagogy, Performativity*. Durham: Duke University Press, 2003.

Shaw-Miller, S. "'Concerts of everyday living': Cage, Fluxus and Barthes, interdisciplinarity and inter-media events." *Art History* 19 (March 1996), 1-25.

Shibayama, Zenkei. *Zen Comments on the Mumonkan.* New York: New American Library, 1974.

Shillingsburg, Peter L. *Resisting Texts: Authority and Submission in Constructions of Meaning.* Ann Arbor, MI: University of Michigan Press, 1997.

Showalter, Elaine, ed. "Towards a Feminist Poetics." *The New Feminist Criticism.* New York: Pantheon Books, 1985.

Sontag, Susan. "Against Interpretation," ["Notes on Camp," "Spiritual Style in the Films of Robert Bresson"], "On Style," "The Aesthetics of Silence." *A Susan Sontag Reader*. New York: Farrar / Straus / Giroux, 1982.

Souter, Kay Torney. "The Products of the Imagination: Psychoanalytic Theory and Postmodern Literary Criticism." *American Journal of Psychoanalysis* 60.4 (2000 Dec): 341-59.

Spariosu, Mihai I. *The Wreath of Wild Olive: Play, Liminality, and the Study of Literature*. Albany, NY: State University of New York Press, 1997.

Stefanovic, Darko. "Biomolecular computing: molecules that reason" *Nature Nanotechnology* 4 (2009).

Suzuki, Shunryu. *Zen Mind, Beginner's Mind*. New York: Weatherhill, 1970.

Talbot, Michael. *Beyond the Quantum*. New York: Bantam Books, 1988.

Tamen, Miguel. *The Matter of the Facts: On Invention and Interpretation*. Stanford, CA: Stanford University Press, 2000.

Tomas, David. *Beyond the Image Machine: A History of Visual Technologies*. London, England: Continuum, 2004.

Thomson, Clive and Hans Raj Dua, eds. *Dialogism and Cultural Criticism*. London: Mestengo, 1995.

Torgovnick, Marianna. "Experimental Critical Writing." *Profession 90*. 25-27.

Trungpa, Chogyam. *Meditation in Action*. Boston: Shambhala, 1985.

Tuathail, Gearoid. *Critical Geopolitics*. http://www.nvc.vt.edu/toalg/Website/CriticalGeopolitics.htm [this site includes links to several articles by Gearoid Tauthail]. 10/25/2011.

—. "Postmodern Geopolitics? The Modern Geopolitical Imagination and Beyond." Tuathail and Dalby, *ReThinking Geopolitics*, 16-38. PDF online. 1998. http://www.nvc.vt.edu/toalg/Website/Publish/Papers/ToalCh1PostmodernGeo.pdf. 10/25/2011.

—, and Simon Dalby, eds. *ReThinking Geopolitics*. New York: Routledge, 1998.

—, Simon Dalby, and Paul Routledge, eds. *The Geopolitics Reader* (2nd Ed.). London: Routledge, 2006.

Ulmer, Greg. *Applied Grammatology: Post(e)-Pedagogy from Jacques Derrida to Joseph Beuys*. Baltimore: Johns Hopkins Press, 1984.

Virilio, Paul. *The Aesthetics of Disappearance*. New York: Semiotext(e), 1991.

—. "Speed and Information: Cyberspace Alarm!" *Le Monde Diplomatique* (August 1995). Trans. Patrice Riemens. Rpt. in *CTheory*. 8/22/2005. www.ctheory.net. 10/24/2011.

—. *Strategy of Deception*. London: Verso, 2000.

—. *The Information Bomb*. London: Verso, 2000.

Victor Vitanza, Victor. "Two Gestures, While Waiting for a Third." In Mark Bousquet, *TechnoCapitalism.*

Volosinov, V. N. "Discourse in Life and Discourse in Art: Concerning Sociological Poetics." *Freudianism: A Marxist Critique*. New York: Academie Press, 1976. 93-116.

—. "Verbal Interaction." *Marxism and the Philosophy of Language*. New York: Seminar Press, 1973.

Wall, Anthony. "Levels of Discourse and Levels of Dialogue." In Thomson, Clive and Dua, Hans Raj, eds. *Dialogism and Cultural Criticism*. London: Mestengo, 1995.

Weber, Samuel. *Institution and Interpretation.* Stanford, CA: Stanford University Press, 2001.

Wheeler, Lesley. *Voicing American Poetry: Sound and Performance from the 1920s to the Present*. New York: Cornell University Press, 2008.

Widder, Nathan. "What's Lacking in the Lack: A Comment on the Virtual." *Angelaki* 5.3 (2000 Dec): 117-38.

Williams, Raymond. *Marxism and Literature.* Oxford: Oxford University Press, 1977.

Wolfreys, Julian. *Occasional Deconstructions*. Albany, NY: State University of New York Press, 2004.

Wood, Sarah. "Hotel Psychoanalysis: Pasolini, Libido, Sacher-Masoch, Humour, Freud, Women, Deleuze, Free Association, Adorno, Blindness, Cixous, Touch... and Other Distinguished Guests." *Angelaki* 9.1 (2004 Apr): 1-21.

Zukav, Gary. *The Dancing Wu Li Masters.* New York: Bantam, 1980.

Ziarek, Ewa Plonowska. *An Ethics of Dissensus: Postmodernity, Feminism, and the Politics of Radical Democracy*. Stanford, CA: Stanford University Press, 2001.

Žižek, Slavoj. *In Defense of Lost Causes*. New York: Verso, 2008.

—. *The Plague of Fantasies*. New York: Verso, 1997.

—. *The Spectre Is Still Roaming Around! An Introduction to the 150th Anniversary Edition of The Communist Manifesto*. Zagreb: Arkzin, 1998.

—. *Tarrying with the Negative: Kant, Hegel, and the Critique of Ideology*. Durham, NC: Duke University Press, 1995.

—. *The Ticklish Subject: The Absent Center of Political Ideology*. New York: Verso, 2000

***

Performance & Anthropological Theory/Criticism

Artaud, Antonin. "Theatre of Cruelty" [and other essays]. *Theatre and Its Double.* New York: Grove Press, Inc., 1958.

Attridge, Derek. "Singular Events: Literature, Invention, and Performance." Bissell, 48-65.

Barba, Eugenio. "Theatre Anthropology." *The Drama Review* 26.2 (1982): 5-33.

Battcock, Gregory and Robert Nickas. *The Art of Performance: A critical Anthology.* New York: E. P. Dutton, inc., 1984.

Benamou, Michel and Charles Caramello, eds. *Performance in Postmodern Culture.* Center for Twentieth Century Studies. Theories of Contemporary Culture, vol. 1. Madison, Wisconsin: Coda Press, Inc. 1977.

Benston, Kimberly W. "Being There: Performance as Mise-en-scene, Abscene, Obscene, and Other Scene." *PMLA* 107.3 (May, 1992): 434-49.

Blau, Herbert. *The Audience.* Baltimore: Johns Hopkins University Press, 1990.

—. *The Dubious Spectacle: Extremities of Theater, 1976-2000.* Minneapolis: University of Minnesota Press, 2002.

Boon, James A. *Other Tribes, Other Scribes: Symbolic Anthropology in the Comparative Study of Cultures, Histories, Religions, and Texts.* Cambridge: Cambridge University Press, 1982.

Boon, James A. *Verging on Extra-Vagance: Anthropology, History, Religion, Literature, Arts . . . Showbiz.* Princeton, NJ: Princeton University Press, 1999.

Brecht, Bertolt. *Brecht on Theatre.* Ed. John Willett. New York: Hill and Wang, 1964.

Broadhurst, Susan. *Liminal Acts: A Critical Overview of Contemporary Performance and Theory.* London, England: Cassell, 1999.

Butler, Judith. *Excitable Speech: A Politics of the Performative.* New York: Routledge, 1997.

Case, Sue-Ellen. (Introduction, chs. 1-4, 7.) *Feminism and Theatre.* New York: Nethuen, 1988.

Clifford, James. *The Predicament of Culture.* (Introduction, Part One, Part Two, Part Four.) Cambridge: Harvard University Press, 1988.

—, and George Marcus, eds. ""Introduction: Partial Truths" (Clifford), "Fieldwork in Common Places" (Mary Louise Pratt), "Hermes' Dilemma: The Masking of Subversion in Ethnographic Description" (Crapanzano), "On Ethnographic Allegory" (Clifford), "Post-Modern Ethnography: From Document of the Occult to Occult Document" (Stephen A. Tyler), "Contemporary Problems of Ethnography in the Modern World System" (George E. Marcus), "Ethnicity and the Post-Modern Arts of Memory" (Michael M. J. Fischer), "Representations Are Social Facts: Modernity and post-Modernity in Anthropology" (Paul Rabinow). *Writing Culture: The Poetics and Politics of Ethnography*. Berkeley: University of California Press, 1986.

Crapanzano, Vincent. *Hermes' Dilemma and Hamlet's Desire: On the Epistemology of Interpretation*. Cambridge: Harvard University Press, 1992.

—. *Imaginative Horizons: An Essay in Literary-Philosophical Anthropology*. Chicago, IL: University of Chicago Press, 2004.

—. "On Writing of Ethnography." *Dialectical Anthropology* 2 (1977): 69-73.

Culler, Jonathan. "The Fortunes of the Performative in Literary and Cultural Theory." *Literature and Psychology* 45.1-2 (1999): 7-28.

Daniel, E. Valentine and Jeffrey Peck. *Culture/Contexture: Explorations in Anthropology and Literary Studies*. Berkeley, CA: University of California Press, 1996.

Dolan, Jill. *The Feminist Spectator as Critic*. Ann Arbor: UMI Research Press, 1988.

Dwyer, Kevin. *Moroccan Dialogues: Anthropology in Question*. Baltimore: Johns Hopkins University Press, 1982.

Erickson, Jon. *The Fate of the Object: From Modern Object to Postmodern Sign in Performance, Art, and Poetry*. Ann Arbor, MI: University of Michigan Press, 1995.

Foreman, Richard. *Plays and Manifestos*. Ed. Kate Davy. New York: New York University Press, 1976.

Freedman, Barbara. *Staging the Gaze: Postmodernism, Psychoanalysis, and Shakespearean Comedy* [especially the introduction, chapter 1, and chapter 2]. Ithaca: Cornell University Press, 1991.

Gates, Henry Louis. *"Race" Writing, and Difference* [essays by JanMohamed, Pratt, Tompkins]. Chicago: University of Chicago Press, 1986.

Geertz, Clifford. "Blurred Genres: The Refiguration of Social Thought," "'From the Native's Point of View'": On the Nature of Anthropological Understanding," "The Way We Think Now: Toward an Ethnography of Modern Thought." *Local Knowledge: Further Essays in Interpretative Anthropology*. New York: Basic Books, 1983.

Goffman, Erving. *The Presentation of Self in Everyday Life*. Garden City, New York: Doubleday Anchor Books, 1959.

Goulish, Matthew. *30 Microlectures in Proximity of Performance*. London, England: Routledge, 2000.

Grover, Jan Zita: "The V-Girls in performance." *Women's Review of Books* 6.10 (fall 1989), Np.

Guerrilla Girls: Fighting Discrimination with Facts, Humor and Fake Fur Since 1985. www.guerrillagirls.com. 1/24/2011.

Hart, Lynda. *Between the Body and the Flesh: Performing Sadomasochism*. New York, NY: Columbia University Press, 1998.

Harvey, Penelope. "Feminism and Anthropology." Jackson and Jones, 73-85.

Iser, Wolfgang. "What Is Literary Anthropology? The Difference between Explanatory and Exploratory Fictions." Clark, 157-79.

Jarrett, Michael. *Drifting on a read: Jazz as a Model for Writing*. Albany, NY: State University of New York Press, 1999.

Kaprow, Allan. *Assemblage, Environments & Happenings*. New York: Harry N. Abrams, 1966.

—. *Essays on the Blurring of Art and Life*. Ed. Jeff Kelley. Berkeley: University of California Press, 1993.

Kondo, Dorinne. "Dissolution and Reconstitution of Self: Implications for Anthropological Epistemology." *Cultural Anthropology* 1.1 (1986): 74-88.

Kostelanetz, Richard, ed. *Scenarios: Scripts to Perform*. New York: Assembling Press, 1980.

Lecercle, Jean-Jacques. "The 'Turn' in Literary Studies: Anthropology, or Pragmatics, or Both." *REAL: The Yearbook of Research in English and American Literature*, 12 (1996): 1-15.

Lavazzi, Tom. "Avatars and Acting Bodies: Notes Toward an Aesthetics of Liminality, or Where Have All the Identities Gone?" *Women in Performance* 28 (2005).

—. " Catalected Pieces..." [on Armand Schwerner's poetry and methods of translation; textual performance] *Talisman* 21/22 (2001): 30-40

—. "Contents, One Other: Instructions Included [critical performance script]" *Utah Foreign Language Review* (1998):136-59.

—. "Eat, Drink, Be Merry, for the Food of the Performance Is Inedible" *Performance Practice* [UK] 3 (1997): 39-41.

—. "The Haircut: Notes Toward a Performance." *Hair*. Ed. Meredith Jones. Sydney, Australia: Trunk Books, 2009. 293-96.

—. "Strategies of Othering in Aphra Behn's Oroonoko [textual performance]" *Journal of Research* (3.1, 1998), 41-71.

McAloon, John J., ed. "Introduction: Cultural Performances, Cultural Theory" (John McAloon), "Liminality and the Performative Genres" (Victor Turner), "Borges's 'Immortal': Metaritual, Metaliterature, Metaperformance'" (Sophia S. Morgan), "Arrange Me into Disorder: Fragments and Reflections on Ritual Clowning" (Barbara A. Babcock), "A Death in Due Time: Construction of Self and Culture in Ritual Drama" (Barbara G. Myerhoff), "Carnival in Multiple Planes" (Roberto Da Matta). *Rite, Drama, Festival, Spectacle: Rehearsals Toward a Theory of Cultural Performance*. Philadelphia: Institute for the Study of Human Issues, 1983.

McDonald, Henry. "The Performative Basis of Modern Literary Theory." *Comparative Literature* 55:1 (2003 Winter): 57-77.

McKenzie, Jon. *Perform or Else*. London: Routledge, 2001.

Milman, Estera, ed. *Fluxus: A Conceptual Country, Visible Language* [Special Issue] 26.1-2. Providence: Rhode Island School of Design, 1992.

Minh Ha, Trinh. *Woman, Native, Other: Writing Postcoloniality and Feminism*. Bloomington, Indiana: Indiana University Press, 1989.

Phelan, Peggy. "Poststructuralism, Feminist Theory, and Performance." *TDR* (1988): 107-27.

—. *Unmarked: The Politics of Performance*. London; New York: Routledge, 1993.

Pizzato, Mark. *Edges of Loss: From Modern Drama to Postmodern Theory*. Ann Arbor, MI: University of Michigan Press, 1998.

Poirier, Richard. *The Performing Self: Compositions and Decompositions in the Languages of Contemporary Life*. New York: Oxford University Press, 1971.

Pontbriand, Chantal. *Performance Text(e)s and Documents*. Proceedings of the conference Multidisciplinary Aspects of Performance: Postmodernism. Montreal: Parachute, 1981.

Pratt, Mary Louise. "Scratches on the Face of the Country; or, What Mr. Barrow Saw in the Land of the Bushmen." *Critical Inquiry* 12.1 (1985). Rpt. in Gates, 138-62.

Rothenberg, Jerome, and Diane Rothenberg, eds. *Symposium of the Whole: A Range of Discourse Toward an Ethnopoetics* [essays by Lansing and others]. Berkeley: University of California Press, 1983.

Raqs Media Collective. *The Imposter in the Waiting Room* [text and installation catalogue, 11/11-12/23, 2004]. New York: Bose Pacia, 2004.

Saper, Craig. *Networked Art*. Minneapolis: University of Minnesota Press, 2001.

Schechner, Richard. *Between Theatre and Anthropology*. Philadelphia: University of Pennsylvania Press, 1985.

—, and Willa Appel, eds. *By Means of Performance: Intercultural Studies of Theatre and Ritual*. Cambridge: Cambridge University Press, 1990.

—. "Drama, Script, Theatre, and Performance," "From Ritual to Theatre and Back: The Efficacy-Entertainment Braid," "Toward a Poetics of Performance." *Performance Theory*. New York: Routledge, 1988.

Spivak, Gayatri Chakravorty. "French Feminism in an International Frame." *In Other Worlds: Essays in Cultural Politics*. New York: Methuen, 1987. 134-53.

Strauss, Claude Levi. "Bricolage." *The Savage Mind*. Chicago: University of Chicago Press, 1966. 16-33.

Slyomovics, Susan, and Judy Burns. "Preface," "Can There Be a Feminist Ethnography" (Lila Abu Lughod), "An Interview with Gayatri Spivak," "When I Was Grown Up" (Abla Farhoud), "Growing, Growing, Growing, Grown" (Jill MacDougall). *Feminist Ethnography and Performance. Women & Performance: A Journal of Feminist Theory* 5.1 (1990).

Toufic, Jalal. *Over-sensitivity*. Los Angeles: Sun & Moon, 1996.

Taussig, Michael. *Shamanism, Colonialism, and The Wild Man: A Study in Terror and Healing*. Chicago: University of Chicago Press, 1987.

Tompkins, Jane. "'Indians': Textualism, Morality, and the Problem of History." *Critical Inquiry* 13.1 (1986). Rpt. in Gates, 59-77.

Turner, Victor, and Edward Bruner, eds. "Performing Ethnography." *The Anthropology of Experience* [also essays by Myerhoff and others]. Chicago: University of Illinois Press, 1986.

—. "Dramatic Ritual/Ritual Drama," "Liminal to Liminoid in Play, Flow, and Ritual." *From Ritual to Theatre: The Human Seriousness of Play*. New York: Performing Arts Journal Publications, 1982.

—. "Anthropology of Performance." *On the Edge of the Bush: Anthropology as Experience*. Tucson: The University of Arizona Press, 1985.

van Oort, Richard. "Epistemology and Generative Theory: Derrida, Gans, and the Anthropological Subtext of Deconstruction." *Anthropoetics: The Electronic Journal of Generative Anthropology* 1.1 (1995 June).

—. "The Critic as Ethnographer." *New Literary History: A Journal of Theory and Interpretation* 35:4 (2005 Autumn): 621-61.
Williams, Emmett. *My Life in Flux and Vice Versa*. Stuttgart: Edition Hansjorg Mayer, 1991.
Zumthor, Paul. "The Impossible Closure of the Oral Text." *Yale French Studies* 67 (1984): 25-42.

"revoir!"? But "What have you got?"

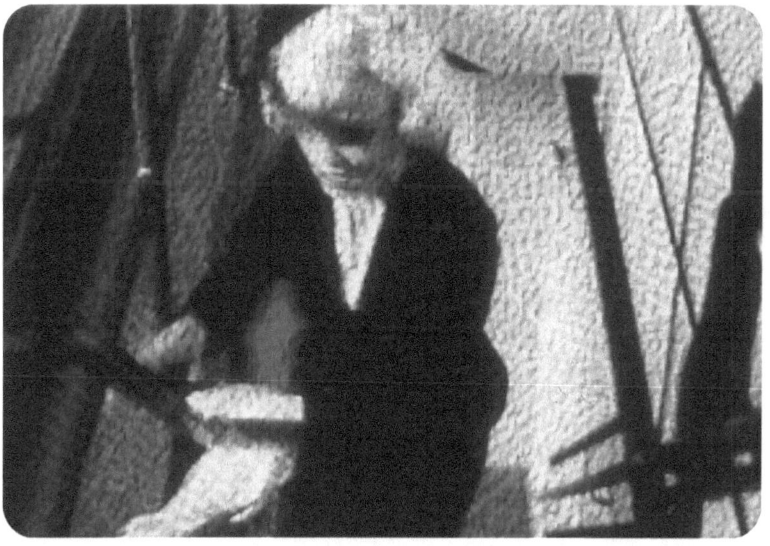

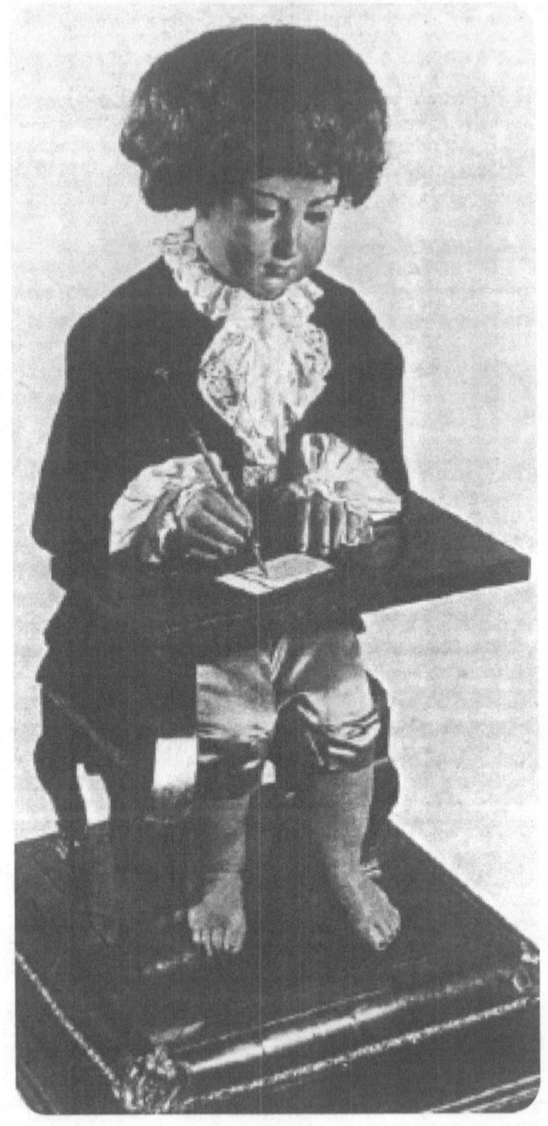

Fig. 14: *peu ecrivain:* New York Public Library. Public domain.

About the Author

Tom Lavazzi is Professor of English at CUNY-Kingsborough and directs the critical performance group TEZ. His poetry and criticism appear in such journals as *American Poetry Review*, *Postmodern Culture*, *Women in Performance*, *Symploke: Journal of Comparative Literature and Theory*, *Talisman*, *Sagetrieb*, *Midwest Quarterly*, *The Little Magazine*, *Mantis: Journal of Poetry, Criticism, Translation; Poetry in Performance*, *South Atlantic Review Genre*, *Post-Identity*, and *Rhizome: Cultural Studies in Emerging Knowledge*, among others. He has published three volumes of poetry: *Stirr'd Up Everywhere* (MOMA/Franklin Furnace, 1995), *Crossing Borders* (Mellen, 1996), and *LightsOut* (Bright Hill Press). His one-act play, *A Handful of Years* was published in *New Writing: The International Journal for the Practice and Theory of Creative Writing*.

www.ingramcontent.com/pod-product-compliance
Lightning Source LLC
LaVergne TN
LVHW041052080826
845145LV00007B/1543
* 9 7 8 1 6 0 2 3 5 2 4 6 9 *